Yale Historical Publications/Miscellany, 95

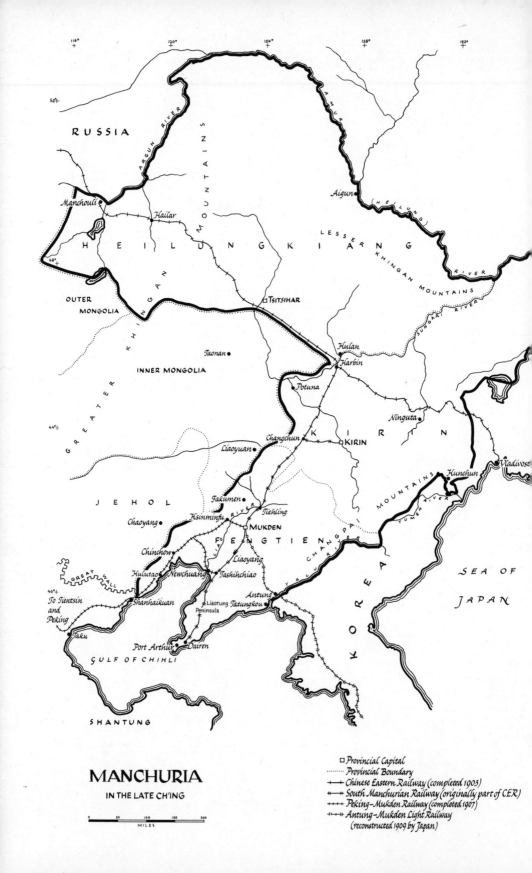

RUSSIA

ARGUN RIVER

AMUR

Manchouli

Hailar

HEILUNGKIANG

AIGUN

(HEILUNG)

RIVER

LESSER KHINGAN MOUNTAINS

OUTER MONGOLIA

Tsitsihar

SUNGARI RIVER

Taonan

INNER MONGOLIA

Hulan

Harbin

Potuna

Ninguta

Vladivostok

KIRIN

Changchun

KIRIN

Liaoyuan

Hunchun

Fakumen

JEHOL

Hsinminfu

Tiehling

TUMEN RIVER

Chaoyang

LIAO RIVER

MUKDEN

KOREA

Chinchow

FENGTIEN

MOUNTAINS

Liaoyang

CHANGPAI

Hulutao

Newchuang

Tashihchiao

YALU RIVER

SEA OF JAPAN

Shanhaikuan

Liaotung Peninsula

Antung

Tatungkou

GREAT WALL

To Tientsin and Peking

KOREA

Taku

Port Arthur

Dairen

GULF OF CHIHLI

SHANTUNG

MANCHURIA

IN THE LATE CH'ING

0   50   100   150   200
MILES

□ Provincial Capital
.... Provincial Boundary
+—+ Chinese Eastern Railway (completed 1903)
+—+ South Manchurian Railway (originally part of CER)
+++ Peking–Mukden Railway (completed 1907)
-+-+- Antung–Mukden Light Railway
        (reconstructed 1909 by Japan)

FRONTIER DEFENSE AND THE OPEN DOOR

MANCHURIA IN CHINESE–AMERICAN RELATIONS, 1895–1911

MICHAEL H. HUNT

NEW HAVEN AND LONDON, YALE UNIVERSITY PRESS, 1973

Published with assistance from the foundation
established in memory of Philip Hamilton McMillan
of the Class of 1894, Yale College.

Library of Congress catalog card number: 73–77152
International standard book number: 0–300–01616–6

Designed by Sally Sullivan
and set in Baskerville type.
Printed in the United States of America by
The Murray Printing Co., Forge Village, Mass.

Published in Great Britain, Europe, and Africa by
Yale University Press, Ltd., London.
Distributed in Latin America by Kaiman & Polon,
Inc., New York City; in Australasia and Southeast
Asia by John Wiley & Sons Australasia Pty. Ltd.,
Sydney; in India by UBS Publishers' Distributors Pvt.,
Ltd., Delhi; in Japan by John Weatherhill, Inc., Tokyo.

To my parents

CONTENTS

PREFACE

The prejudices every historian carries to the archives influence the kind of story he will tell and the significance he will see in it. Rather than veil my prejudices behind a plea of "neutral and objective inquiry," I prefer to clarify for the reader's benefit the assumptions and convictions that helped shape this work. I have tried to go beyond the historical simplicities which comfort and convince to explore complexity and ambiguity in relations between peoples. I believe that if we grasp a more authentic version of our past we can better cope with the present and dare to hope for a more humane future.

In addition to this article of faith, I have views on the nature of foreign relations and the role of the diplomatic historian which have found explicit expression in this study. First, I am convinced one country can effectively, consciously, and peacefully bring its influence to bear on another only within relatively narrow limits. The use of other means usually entails unforeseen consequences and unjustified costs. Our world may be shrinking, but it is still complex and difficult to manage. Second, a realistic definition of those limits of national influence presupposes an equally realistic understanding of the country to be affected. My impression is that, in the main, American diplomatic historians and American diplomats in contact with China have in common ignored the second principle and thus have never come to appreciate the first. Historians of our foreign policy and diplomacy have traditionally slighted the Chinese dimension in their work; too often a few clichés have sufficed. Policy-makers, it seems, have done no better; they, however, must live with the consequences of their misjudgments.

This fallibility of man in conducting his affairs is a theme in every country's history, but the diplomatic historian has no reason to ignore it because it is commonplace. On the contrary, he is uniquely equipped to provide the after-the-fact critique, the cautionary warning to our times and to our men of affairs. What by and large has stood in the way of such a critical evaluation in American–East Asian relations has been the lack of language and historical training to understand anything but half the story. The historian of foreign relations thus has tended to operate with the same background and disadvantages as the object of his study, the manager of foreign relations. To make the identification between the two even more complete, they have taken pleasure—one at first hand and the other vicariously—in the exercise of power. Little wonder the diplomatic historian has been more comfortable as a chronicler than as a critic.

I have approached this study with the conviction that the impact of the United States in world affairs has been increasingly deleterious in recent years and with the faith that it need not be so. The historian-as-critic can unearth new and, I hope, better possibilities for the present by exploring the past.

Accounts written on both sides of the Pacific concerning the relations between the United States and China have been particularly prone to facile judgments. Such rhetorical clichés as "American imperialism," "friend of China," and "helping hand" are now being scrutinized by American historians working from a better understanding of the Chinese perspective. Much work, however, remains. By plotting the trail we have covered in our relations with China, the historian can hope to smooth some of tomorrow's more dangerous rough spots. I, like others, am convinced that to gain this necessary understanding we must know two pasts, the American and the Chinese, as they have occasionally converged. My hope is that an awareness of the problems in our past relationship will prove a source of greater humility and caution in negotiating future pitfalls.

In my research I have worked with one eye open for the misconceptions and prejudices of American statesmen and diplomats and with the other following the Chinese side of the story. Occasionally this effort has caused eyestrain, but more generally it has been a historically fruitful and personally intriguing enterprise. Multiarchival history, I have discovered with satisfaction, is a matter of method with important interpretative implications. I have explored the problem of Manchuria from the Chinese and American perspectives with the hope not of just telling a good story but of contributing to some understanding of their shared past. I hasten to warn the reader that this story follows but one thread in the tangled skein of Manchuria's international relations.

I am indebted to many individuals and institutions for assistance. In particular I want to acknowledge the help of Gaddis Smith, Jonathan Spence, and the late Mary C. Wright, all of whom encouraged me in undertaking training for multiarchival research, supported this research project as a dissertation, and made many helpful suggestions along the way. John M. Blum, Akira Iriye, and Roger DesForges have given me the benefit of their critical readings. I am grateful to the Council on International Relations, Yale University, for making money available for language training and for travel; to the Fulbright-Hays program for support while I did research in Taiwan and Europe; to the Yale Graduate School for supplementary grants; and to both the Yale Graduate School and the Woodrow Wilson Foundation for predissertation fellowships. For making their research collections available and for assisting me in their use, I owe thanks to the Institute of Modern History at the Academia Sinica, Taiwan; to the United States National Archives; to the Manuscript Division of the Library of Congress; to the British Public Records Office; to the French Ministry of Foreign Affairs; to the Olin Library, Cornell University; to the Houghton and Baker libraries, Harvard University; and to the Myrin Library, Ursinus College. I was fortunate to have the editorial assistance of Edward Tripp and Judith Metro of Yale University Press in preparing this study for publication. Above all, for constant help and for the gift I cannot repay, I thank my wife. I alone am responsible for errors of fact and interpretation.

M. H. H.

New Haven, Connecticut
Autumn 1971

ABBREVIATIONS USED IN FOOTNOTES

CHINESE LANGUAGE SOURCES

CCS:HT   *Ch'ing Hsüan-t'ung ch'ao Chung-Jih chiao-she shih-liao* [Historical materials on Sino–Japanese negotiations during the Hsüan-t'ung reign] (Taipei reprint, 1963, originally published 1933), compiled by the National Palace Museum, Peking.

CCS:KH   *Ch'ing Kuang-hsü ch'ao Chung-Jih chiao-she shih-liao* [Historical materials on Sino–Japanese negotiations during the Kuang-hsü reign] (Taipei reprint, 1963, originally published 1932), compiled by the National Palace Museum, Peking.

CCST   *Ch'eng chiang-chün shou-chiang tsou-kao* [Memorials on Military Governor Ch'eng's defense of Heilungkiang] (Taipei reprint, 1968).

CWS:HT   *Ch'ing-chi wai-chiao shih-liao Hsüan-t'ung ch'ao* [Historical materials on late Ch'ing diplomacy: the Hsüan-t'ung reign] (Peking, 1935), compiled by Wang Liang.

CWS:KH   *Ch'ing-chi wai-chiao shih-liao Kuang-hsü ch'ao* [Historical materials on late Ch'ing diplomacy: the Kuang-hsü reign] (Peking, 1935), compiled by Wang Yen-wei and Wang Liang.

HLIK   *Hsi-liang i-kao tsou-kao* [Collected papers of Hsi-liang: memorials] (Peking, 1959), compiled by the Third Institute of History, Chinese Academy of Sciences, Peking.

HTCC   *Ta-Ch'ing Hsüan-t'ung cheng-chi* [Political records of the Hsüan-t'ung reign] (Manchuria, 1937).

LNCYJ   Wang Yün-sheng, *Liu-shih nien-lai Chung-kuo yü Jih-pen* [China and Japan in the last sixty years] (Tientsin, 1932–34).

SL:KH   *Ta-Ch'ing li-ch'ao shih-lu* [Veritable records of successive reigns of the Ch'ing dynasty] (Manchuria, 1937) for the Kuang-hsü reign.

THL:KH   *Kuang-hsü ch'ao Tung-hua hsü-lu* [Supplement to the Tung-hua records for the Kuang-hsü reign] (Taipei reprint, 1963, originally published 1909), compiled by Chu Shou-p'eng.

TKTCS   *T'ui-keng t'ang cheng-shu* [Collected official papers of Hsü Shih-ch'ang] (Taipei reprint, 1968; foreword, 1914).

TSSCL   *Tung-san-sheng cheng-lüeh* [Administration of the three eastern provinces] (Taipei reprint, 1965; foreword 1911), compiled by Ch'ien Neng-hsün and Wu T'ing-hsieh.

WWP   Records of the Wai-wu Pu, Diplomatic Archives, Institute of Modern History, Academia Sinica, Nankang, Taipei, Taiwan.

YCTK   *Yü-chai ts'un-kao* [Collected papers of Sheng Hsüan-huai] (Taipei reprint, 1968, originally published 1930)*.

WESTERN LANGUAGE SOURCES

DF   Decimal File, microfilm of the records of the Department of State, National Archives, Washington, D.C.

DIC   Diplomatic Instructions: China; microfilm of the records of the Department of State, National Archives, Washington, D.C.

FO   Records of the British Foreign Office, Public Records Office, London.

FRUS   *Papers Relating to the Foreign Relations of the United States* (Washington, D.C., yearly series), compiled by the Department of State.

MCD   Minister to China: Despatches; microfilm of the records of the Department of State, National Archives, Washington, D.C.

Min.   Archives of the French Ministry of Foreign Affairs, Paris.
Aff. Et.

NCR   Newchuang Consular Reports, microfilm of the records of the Department of State, National Archives, Washington, D.C.

NF   Numerical File, Record Group 59 (records of the Department of State), National Archives, Washington, D.C.

FRONTIER DEFENSE AND THE OPEN DOOR

INTRODUCTION

The newly rented temple had disadvantages. It lay outside Mukden's mud wall, and the monks still had access to the sanctuary. But their incense-heavy procession came only twice daily and in any case might prove a pleasant respite from routine. Nothing better was to be had in the city. The Japanese consul general had suggested the temple, and—joke or not—it pleased the new occupant, who was glad to settle in. The bleak winter stretched endlessly behind him. Now, standing before the temple, he could feel the bitter-cold wind over southern Manchuria gradually abate and see the rich earth shake off the snow.

Willard Straight had reached his post six months earlier, in October 1906, his commission from the president as consul general in hand. More important to him than his official credentials and the personal connections which had secured them were his hopes for the adventure a free spirit could find on this new frontier of American life. Here he sought "a life of energy and of endeavor." The long journey by rail across Siberia had exhilarated Straight and his friend and subordinate, Nelson Fairchild, but as winter closed in, narrowing their world to a small, isolated, and alien city on China's periphery, their spirits fell. Discomfort, boredom, and impatience had grated on nerves; emotions had turned from the enthusiasm for the adventure just begun to the charged tension of an uncertain relationship at close quarters. Straight would gladly forget if he could one particular December evening of morbid, careless conversation, a drink of port and a smoke after dinner, and his companion's sudden suicide.[1]

Warming weather revived his spirits and his dreams. His apprenticeship as a student in the Imperial Chinese Maritime Customs, as a correspondent during the Russo–Japanese War, and as a fledgling diplomat in Seoul and Havana had prepared him for his chosen role, man of affairs. Now, spring marked the beginning of his adventure and brought an end

---

1. Straight described the consulate in a dispatch of 25 March 1907, Straight Papers, Olin Library, Cornell University. The quote is from the Straight diary, 24 July 1903, Straight Papers. Reports on Fairchild's suicide are in NF 2876/6, 14.

to five years of training, watching, and waiting. Enthused by the prospects ahead of him, Straight immediately set to work. He improved and
repaired the modest temple and with accustomed flair erected a hundred-
foot flagpole to tower over the flat surrounding Manchurian countryside.
It was an unmistakable announcement of his own and his country's arrival on the scene.

Historians have been fascinated by the adventures of young Straight.
Charmed by his personality, attracted by the drama of his story, and
pleased by the detailed and colorful record he thoughtfully left behind,
all have acknowledged that he realized his ambition of becoming a man
of affairs. In their histories he bobs up time and again. His face is familiar
in nearly every important negotiation involving the United States and
China between 1907 and 1912. Indeed, in the history of Sino–American
relations in the early twentieth century, Straight and Manchuria have
been nearly synonymous.

Straight does deserve an important place in this history; however, the
long-accepted view of American relations with China makes more of him
than it should.[2] Long before Straight appeared on the scene, the fate of
Manchuria had preoccupied Washington and Peking. Consequently,
Straight worked within the context of two well-established policies. One
of them, the policy of promoting American investment in Manchuria, for
which he was to become famous as the formulator and chief practitioner,
was in large measure a Chinese creation. It was a facet of the larger
Chinese policy of frontier defense, as old as China but in the process of
adapting to new conditions.' As for the other policy, he followed in the
steps of those of his countrymen who advocated greater American involvement in Manchuria through the formal policy of the open door, hardly
older than Straight himself yet already well on its way toward becoming
dogma. Straight thus stuck his flagpole in Manchurian soil like a lightning
rod in a growing electrical storm. It quickly drew lightning only because
the storm clouds had long been gathering.

Straight, joined by others of similar persuasion, drew on these policies
and helped to build what had been under John Hay and Elihu Root a
minority view on China policy into the dominant one under Philander
C. Knox. However, to understand Manchuria and the relation of the
United States to it we must pick up the story well before Straight's appearance on the scene and examine both Chinese and American policies.

2. For a more detailed comment on Straight's place in the history of American relations with
China, see the appendix.

PART ONE

CHINA AND THE UNITED STATES

IN MANCHURIA, 1895–1900

1: FRONTIER DEFENSE

Manchuria was, through the nineteenth century and into the twentieth, a Chinese frontier. Culturally, Manchuria had been for more than two millennia at least in part Han. Chinese, particularly in the northern provinces of Shantung, Chihli, and Shansi, had in the wake of periodic famine, flood, and drought despaired of survival on densely populated ancestral grounds. Consequently, they had traveled by land and sea to the northeast, where they fought for a livelihood and attempted to re-create the familiar cultural patterns they had left behind. They at first concentrated in the Liao River valley and later slowly spread through the steppeland to the west and the forests and valleys to the north and east.

Manchuria at the end of the Manchu conquest of China in the late seventeenth century was still an attractive place for settlement. It was not the only major area of Chinese colonization during the Ch'ing. On the periphery of the empire, Szechwan, Sinkiang, Taiwan, and the region drained by the Han River as well as the interior provinces along the lower Yangtze attracted many migrants after the ravages of the Taiping rebellion. Nonetheless, Manchuria was uniquely rich in natural resources and untilled fertile land. Thirty years of conflict between loyal Ming troops and Manchu forces, followed by the shift of large numbers of Manchu banner troops and their dependents to garrison duty in the newly acquired empire, had lowered population levels. As population pressure increased within the Great Wall during the early years of the K'ang-hsi Emperor's reign (1662–1722), the northward migration increased. The trend frightened the Manchus in Peking, who regarded the growing flow of Han settlers as a threat to the livelihood and the distinctly martial culture of the Manchus still living in Manchuria. New settlers, in addition, made incursions on imperial prerogatives (and an important source of revenue) by smuggling ginseng and furs. Manchuria was also the home of the dynasty, "the place where the dragon rose," and thus the Manchu court was obliged to preserve sacred domain from Chinese settlement. As a result, the dynasty issued regulations limiting migration and, to contain new migrants within the Liao valley, strung a willow palisade in an arc across Manchuria from Shanhaikuan, where the Great Wall came down to the Gulf of Chihli, through Kaiyuan to the mouth of the Yalu River.[1]

Imperial regulations, repeatedly reissued during the Ch'ien-lung reign (1736–95), and a line of willow trees proved ineffective. At times, for example when disaster struck in northern China, this ban on migration to Manchuria was officially and temporarily lifted to clear the way for resettlement of refugees. Moreover, the ban never applied to many classes of people. Merchants and artisans—some genuine and some feigned— moved north freely at all times. Political prisoners and criminals were exiled to northern Manchuria, where living standards were low and life isolated and harsh. A small number of Manchu bannermen, whose impoverished and culturally threatened life in Chinese cities concerned the court, returned with their dependents to their Manchurian homeland under a largely unsuccessful program begun in the early years of the Ch'ien-lung period. By the mid-nineteenth century the official ban had become a dead letter. Meanwhile population pressure within the wall continued to mount; by the reign of Tao-kuang (1821–50), about 400 million lived there. In Shantung and Chihli, where land was particularly scarce and population dense, many lived on the economic margin. The devastating shift in the course of the Yellow River in 1852 and the rebellions of the Taiping and the Nien created a massive army of homeless and desperate people. Many settled permanently in Manchuria; others became seasonal laborers attracted by the higher wages in the under-populated region. Migrants from Korea, who before this time had only intermittently crossed the Yalu River to settle on the Chinese side, came in greater numbers.

Although statistics for this period are rough, they indicate that in the southern Manchurian province of Fengtien, which included the heavily Chinese Liao River valley, population grew from 800,000 to 2.5 million between 1787 and 1850. In Kirin province, in the eastern section of Manchuria, the population of 150,000 more than doubled during the same period. Heilungkiang province in the north remained sparsely

---

1. Robert H. G. Lee, *The Manchurian Frontier in Ch'ing History* (Cambridge, Mass., 1970), a study of settlement in Kirin and Heilungkiang. See especially chap. 5, "The Sinicization of the Manchurian Frontier." See also Kuo T'ing-yee, "Tung-pei ti k'ai-t'o" [The opening of the Northeast] in Ling Shun-sheng, ed., *Pien-chiang wen-hua lun-chi* [Collected essays on frontier culture] (Taipei, 1953), 1: 49–50; and Ho Ping-ti, *Studies on the Population of China, 1368–1953* (Cambridge, Mass., 1959), pp. 136–68. The most perceptive firsthand account by a Westerner of conditions in Manchuria during the late Ch'ing is given by a missionary doctor, Dugald Christie, in his *Thirty Years in Moukden 1883–1913* (New York, 1914). Owen Lattimore's *The Mongols of Manchuria* (New York, 1934) and his *Inner Asian Frontiers of China* (New York, 1951) contain provocative speculation on cultural interaction on the Manchurian frontier.

settled. In the late nineteenth century, migration gained even greater momentum. By 1897 Manchuria had a population of about 6 million. But despite this influx of settlers, it still remained for the most part under-populated and undeveloped.[2]

Manchuria was also a political frontier. Throughout its history it had lain on the periphery—sometimes within and sometimes outside—of the strongest unified empires of China. From its foundation, the Ch'ing dynasty had had a secure hold on the southern part of the region, which it used as a base to effect the conquest of China; however, it could not defend the sparsely populated and remote northern part of Manchuria, which lay across the path of Russian eastward advance. So after several years of conflict with Russia, the dynasty surrendered some of the peripheral territory north of the Amur River in the Treaty of Nerchinsk (1689) and thereby secured a century and a half of peace along the border. In mid-nineteenth century, Russia resumed the offensive against China, then too preoccupied with putting down the Taiping and Nien rebels and with fending off the British and French barbarians to resist. Thus, in the Treaty of Aigun in 1858, China surrendered more of the lands north of the Amur River. Two years later, China, her capital occupied by foreign troops, once again bowed to Russian demands and, in the Treaty of Peking, gave up the territory west of the Ussuri River.

China had lost a large part of northern Manchuria, strategically important buffer land, which in area was roughly equivalent to thirty-five Taiwans. The Tungus tribes inhabiting this region were either lost to Russian control or soon submerged by Chinese culture. In these territorial acquisitions, Russia had taken a giant step toward the Manchurian heartland.[3]

The growing Russian threat alarmed high officials in the central government. Prince Kung, the T'ung-chih Emperor's chief minister, judged the crisis in the northeast and elsewhere along China's inner Asian frontier of greater gravity than the threat posed along the coast by the sea-going barbarians and second in danger only to the rebellion at home.

Russia, with her territory adjoining ours, aiming to nibble away our

2. Kuo, "Tung-pei ti k'ai-t'o," pp. 50–53; Walter Young, "Chinese Immigration and Colonization in Manchuria," in *Pioneer Settlement: Cooperative Studies* (New York, 1932), pp. 330–59; Alexander Hosie, *Manchuria: Its People, Resources and Recent History* (London, 1904), pp. 155–56; and Li Kuang et al., *Chin-tai Tung-pei jen-min ko-ming yün-tung shih* [History of the people's revolutionary movement in modern Manchuria] (Changchun, 1960), p. 158.

3. Kuo, "Tung-pei ti k'ai-t'o," pp. 46–48; and Hsü Shuhsi, *China and Her Political Entity* (New York, 1926), pp. 44–56, 72.

territory like a silkworm, may be considered a threat to our bosom. . . .
Therefore we should suppress the Taipings and Nien bandits first, get
the Russians under control next, and attend to the British last. . . .[4]

The court's anxiety for Manchuria's future stemmed from its symbolic
significance and its strategic location. As the home of their ancestors,
Manchus regarded it as sacred land. As their base for the conquest of
China, they maintained a sentimental interest in it. In addition, Mukden
continued to function, at least nominally, as an auxiliary capital, and the
emperor's predecessors were buried nearby. "How," one eminent official
rhetorically asked, "could the present Emperor face his ancestors if it
were lost?"[5] The Manchu dynasty had reason to fear also that their
Chinese subjects would resent the loss of Manchuria as much as any
other part of the empire and regard such an event as a portent of their
rulers' loss of the mandate. Finally, the other barbarians might take the
Russian conquest of Manchuria as a sign of Ch'ing weakness and as an
invitation to acquire territory themselves.

Strategically Manchuria was also important. Poised just north of Peking,
Manchuria could not fall without directly endangering the capital and
providing a convenient base for the invasion of northern China along the
coast through Shanhaikuan. The memory of their own conquest of China
using this strategy could only sharpen Manchu anxiety.

Penetration of Manchuria by foreigners and Chinese had by mid-
nineteenth century created for the Ch'ing dynasty an acute double-edged
problem of control: how to govern the newly arrived Chinese and how to
block foreign encroachment. These two preoccupations merged in the
minds of responsible Ch'ing officials into the larger single problem of
converting this underpopulated area, rich in idle natural resources,
into an asset in resisting the foreigners. In short, their task was to turn
weakness into strength. But in attempting this transformation they neither
had effective ready-made solutions nor did they consistently work to
develop new ones. Shifts in policy and personnel, both in the capital and
in the region, affected the vigor and consistency of Manchurian frontier
defense. It developed by starts and jerks. Yet every official concerned with
Manchuria in the late Ch'ing had to acknowledge and grapple with the
interlocking problems of domestic control and foreign policy.

In coping with the Manchurian crisis, the dynasty first resorted to the

4. Prince Kung et al., joint memorial, 13 January 1861, translated in Ssu-yü Teng and John K.
Fairbank, *China's Response to the West: A Documentary Survey, 1839–1923* (Cambridge, Mass., 1954),
p. 48.
5. Liu K'un-i, memorial, 8 July 1895, CWS:KH, *chüan* (hereafter cited as ch.) 15.20.

traditional tools of frontier policy. It overturned the prohibitions on migration imposed during the K'ang-hsi reign and gave settlement official encouragement. Memorials suggesting migration as a means of coping with the Russian threat appeared in the early 1850s and provoked the serious discussion and consideration of the issue which in turn cleared the way for imperial approval of the idea a decade later. A policy of colonization, so one successful memorialist argued, would be useful in settling the homeless victims of rebellion and at the same time would increase government revenue. Most important, by filling up the frontier with Chinese settlers, colonization would place an obstacle in the path of the increasingly formidable Russians.[6]

While civilian and military settlement made Manchuria easier to defend against the external enemy, it created domestic problems. In remote areas the new migrants lacked government administration and were left to their own means of protection. In older areas of settlement, the swiftly growing population left the existing administrative machinery too understaffed and undeveloped to be effective. To make social control more difficult, a variety of outlaws and secret societies thrived in the remote and rugged Manchurian terrain. "Gold bandits," the *chin-fei*, furtively worked gold mines and smuggled ginseng. Mounted bandits, locally known as *hunghutzu* or redbeards, made their appearance in large numbers in mid-nineteenth century and remained through the rest of the Ch'ing a persistent and vexatious problem for local officials. The activities of the main secret societies—branches of the White Lotus Society *(pai-lien chiao)*—were important to many Manchurians for the political security they provided in the absence of government and clan organizations but often lay beyond official control. These social rebels found company after the wars of 1894–95, 1900, and 1904–05 in the disbanded soldiery and idle irregular forces that resorted to brigandage for their livelihood. Often well armed and determined in combat, these brigands frequently provided, for a price, the security which local communities, farmers, and merchants could not get from the government. They, like others beyond the pale of official respectability, acquired local influence by meeting the needs of Manchurian frontier life.

Ch'ing officials were always hard put to control or to eradicate these lawless elements. The remote mountains of Kirin and Heilungkiang were generally secure sanctuaries for both secret society members and brigands on the run. Officials often found, particularly in the case of bands of brigands, that the easier and even more successful course was to co-opt

6. Kuo, "Tung-pei ti k'ai-t'o," pp. 53–56.

and legitimize rather than to suppress these elements. The government frequently took brigand leaders into its pay, integrating their followers into the regular forces. Even so, the problem of internal order remained a disturbing one to Ch'ing officials in Manchuria, for this unruly population introduced an unpredictable element in the administration of the region. Between 1860 and 1866, coinciding with rebellions within the wall, Manchuria experienced scattered, sporadic anti-Ch'ing risings. A violent outburst, mainly antiforeign but also in part anti-Ch'ing, hit in late 1891 shortly after a similar explosion in the Yangtze valley. Antiforeign feeling again got out of hand in 1894 and 1895, stimulated by Japan's invasion and brief occupation of southern Manchuria. In each case the rebels of Manchurian frontier life—bandits, secret society members, Ming restorationists, and disgruntled soldiery—took a major part in challenging official control, and in each case the dynasty had to divert troops from other areas to subdue these rebels. Never sure how the population would behave, officials in Manchuria carried an extra burden in their efforts at frontier defense. In Manchuria, perhaps more than in any other region of China, the line between domestic and foreign policy was hard to trace.[7]

The Mongols of Manchuria were another uncertain element in the calculations of those charged with frontier defense. These inhabitants of the steppeland of western Kirin, northern Fengtien, and southern Heilungkiang posed a special problem of control for the Ch'ing. Like the Manchus, they found agricultural life unattractive and the Chinese eager to take up their land through rent or purchase. Thus, they were literally and figuratively losing ground to the Chinese newcomers. However, unlike the Manchus, the Mongols' ties to the ruling dynasty were not close. Their discontent, which grew as their position in Manchuria and in nearby cultivable areas of Inner Mongolia eroded, posed a threat to Chinese settlers and administration. This threat was compounded by another still greater: the Mongols of Manchuria, Jehol, and Mongolia could be for the Ch'ing dynasty either an enemy or an ally standing at China's northern frontier. Against the Russian threat the Mongols were of little positive use, but if in their disgruntlement they joined the Russians, China's position in the north would indeed be endangered. Encroaching Chinese settlement and the proximity and appeal of superior Russian force had already attenuated the Mongols' ties of loyalty to the dynasty. A Mongol insurrection in 1894, a precursor of later ones in the twilight

7. Li, *Chin-tai Tung-pei*, pp. 19–36, 58–67, 85–92; Daniel T. Robertson, *The Story of Our Mission in Manchuria* (Edinburgh, Scotland, 1913), pp. 20–22; and Hosie, *Manchuria*, pp. 169–71.

years of the dynasty and under the Chinese Republic, made clear to Ch'ing officials the seriousness of the problem and the opportunity which it offered Russia to fish in troubled waters. The Mongols of Manchuria were becoming a fifth column, a cause of domestic unrest beyond the ability of the military administration to cope with, and an uncertain element in China's relations with Russia. The disaffection of the Mongols took from the arsenal of frontier defense a traditional tool and left in its place another difficult and persistent problem of control.[8]

Aside from the Russian military threat to the frontier, other forces from abroad increasingly and in a variety of ways also threatened China's control over Manchuria. Missionaries had begun to make their influence felt by mid-nineteenth century. Their challenge to traditional cultural values, their interference in local affairs, and their dependence on foreign authority for protection created a potentially explosive antiforeign sentiment. Conventional foreign commercial penetration also proceeded beyond official control. The opening of a treaty port at Newchuang in 1860 and the resulting disruption of marketing patterns in southern and central Manchuria initiated a process of commercial change. The Russian railway, which appeared section by section across first northern and later southern Manchuria, accelerated this process. It left boatmen and wagoners unemployed; it outraged believers in geomancy; it facilitated Chinese migration to more remote areas; it stimulated exports of agricultural products; it broke the bandits' hold on commerce; and it gave birth to new and growing commercial settlements, Harbin and Dairen, for example, beyond official Chinese control. Nowhere else in China did the railway have as dramatic an impact as in Manchuria. Foreign armies further disrupted life in the region. In the three Manchurian conflicts between 1894 and 1905 they marched and countermarched across the landscape, supplementing in their destruction the normal quota of natural disasters.[9]

The crosscurrents of international and domestic pressures left Ch'ing officials in a difficult position, and, as Russian pressure increased through the 1890s, they struggled to make their position in Manchuria more tenable. It was clear that settlement alone might prove ineffective as an instrument of defense if the diverse and independent population were beyond social and political control. The only sure way of securing that control was to extend to newly settled and remote areas a well-staffed

8. "Kirin insurrection," *North China Daily News*, 5 June 1894; Li, *Chin-tai Tung-pei*, pp. 147–48; and Lattimore, *The Mongols of Manchuria*, pp. 86–87, 89–90, 114ff.

9. Lattimore, *Inner Asian Frontiers of China*, pp. 105, 144; and *Manchuria, Cradle of Conflict* (New York, 1932), pp. 264–75.

administration backed by sufficient troops. However, this program, begun under the impetus of the Russian threat, failed to keep pace with rapid settlement. The central government never provided funds, troops, or civil officials in numbers equal to the task at hand. The mid-nineteenth-century rebellions, followed by the exactions of the foreign powers, had thrown China's financial system into disarray. As a result, the Manchurian administration received only a fraction of the amount stipulated to supplement its own small revenue. This inability of the central government and the wealthier interior provinces to provide an ample subsidy for Manchuria particularly hobbled officials there. Moreover, the administration of Manchuria was essentially military in its orientation. The military governors controlling the three Manchurian provinces were bannermen appointed by Peking and were not generally equipped either by temperament or by experience to find a way of checking foreign penetration while at the same time securing domestic control.

Manchuria lacked both the human and financial resources as well as the reformed political administration necessary to meet the urgent tasks at hand. The disastrous war with Japan (1894–95) opened a Pandora's box of new complications. The resulting crisis hastened the search for a more effective strategy by supplementing old methods of frontier management with new means of defense.

During the 1890s Ch'ing officials began to introduce innovations into traditional border policy. The first of these innovations was a policy of railway building to which Ch'ing officials looked to consolidate their domestic hold and to preempt Russia's proposed Manchurian railway. The second was a policy of alliance with Russia to bolster their own weak and isolated international position. However, Chinese-built railways made no substantial progress, and the Russian alliance of 1896 proved disastrous for Manchuria. This double failure resulted in the abandonment of these two policies and the adoption of yet a third distinct and more radical policy, the resort to popular support to save Manchuria from foreign peril. The Boxer outbreak in northern China in 1900 provided the opportunity to test this desperate expedient. It too was to fail—with dire consequences for the region.[10]

10. Irwin J. Schulman's persuasive view of Ch'ing diplomacy in the latter half of the 1890s as a period of experimentation fits with some alteration the pattern of events in Manchuria during those same years. Schulman, "China's Response to Imperialism: 1895–1900" (Ph. D. diss., Columbia University, 1967). John Schrecker, "The Reform Movement, Nationalism, and China's Foreign Policy," *Journal of Asian Studies* 29 (November 1969): 43–53, deals with three major schools of thought on barbarian management which inspired the shifting strategies discussed by Schulman.

High Chinese officials first began to consider the railroad as an instrument for defending the northeast frontier in the early 1890s. It might serve as a means of extending political control, of promoting and controlling commerce, and above all of facilitating military operations against either Russia to the north or Japan to the east in Korea. The first formal proposal for a Manchurian railway appeared early in 1890 in a memorial by the Chinese foreign office, the Tsung-li Yamen, suggesting a program to protect China's position in Korea. The proposal was adopted by Li Hung-chang, the commissioner of northern ports and the most influential of provincial officials, and endorsed at court by Prince Ch'un and Tseng Chi-tse. Li's proposal, which he presented in two memorials in April 1890, was for a railway aimed primarily against the Russians. A ten-year project, it would begin within the Great Wall, proceed through Mukden to Kirin, and ultimately reach Hunchun, near China's border with Russia and Korea. Although the central government appropriated funds for the enterprise, Li soon realized they would not suffice and opened negotiations in Europe for a loan. But the talks in Europe collapsed. Thus, only limited government funds were available to finance work on the line, and by the time war with Japan broke out in 1894, the track extended only forty miles beyond the Great Wall into Manchuria. For several years thereafter, the dictates of the Russian alliance and financial stringency halted work on the railway altogether.[11]

The suspension of Manchurian railway construction did not go unchallenged. Chang Chih-tung, the commissioner of southern ports, made one unsuccessful attempt in 1895 to set it in motion again. He recognized that the Siberian railway which Russia was already building toward Manchuria would give her control of the flow of commerce there, and he warned that China herself must build and control any Manchurian line. Funds for construction could come from any country including Russia that wished to provide them. He even conceded that Chinese control could be adjusted to a possible alliance with Russia. Chang telegraphed his views to the Tsung-li Yamen, which, current rumor reported, had already agreed to an extension of the Russian railway into Manchuria. The yamen denied that it had made any concessions and suggested raising funds to continue Li's trans-Manchurian project to connect with Russia's Siberian

---

11. Li Kuo-ch'i, *Chung-kuo tsao-ch'i ti t'ieh-lu ching-ying* [Early railway enterprise in China] (Taipei, 1961), pp. 88–93; Percy H. Kent, *Railway Enterprise in China: An Account of Its Origin and Development* (London, 1907), pp. 38, 41–43, 46; and Albert Feuerwerker, *China's Early Industrialization: Sheng Hsüan-huai (1844–1916) and Mandarin Enterprise* (Cambridge, Mass., 1958), pp. 13–14; and Arthur L. Rosenbaum, "China's First Railway: The Imperial Railways of North China, 1880–1911" (Ph. D. diss., Yale University, 1971).

railway on the border at Hunchun. It agreed with Chang that if the rail concession were granted, "Russia would surely devour Manchuria, and the railway would never return to the control of China." The imperial decree on the memorial obliquely endorsed Chang's proposal to resume work on the Manchurian railway but in reality shunted it aside by referring it to the Chinese minister in St. Petersburg for discussion with the Russians.[12] A year later China entirely abandoned its own plans and sanctioned the construction of a Russian Manchurian railway as part of the price of alliance.

The Russian alliance, however, did not completely frustrate China's hopes to build her own railways in Manchuria. In the fall of 1897 the three military governors of Manchuria advanced a new railway proposal designed to block the Russians, who were showing interest in building a branch southward to the Liaotung Peninsula from their line along the south bank of the Amur River. The military governors envisaged the construction of a line from Potuna to Changchun and thence to Mukden to connect with the line going on to Shanhaikuan. Their proposal, although it immediately received imperial approval, died of neglect. At the same time, however, work was resumed on the line from Shanhaikuan begun by Li Hung-chang earlier in the decade. A new director was appointed, and he arranged a loan from the British Hong Kong and Shanghai Bank. By 1901 this railway had been completed through to Hsinminfu and a branch extended to Newchuang. Even so, the Chinese had in a decade made only a bare beginning in providing for themselves the rail network essential for control and defense of the frontier, whereas the Russians had penetrated even more deeply into Manchuria.[13]

China's defeat at the hands of Japan in 1895 revealed Manchuria's vulnerability to foreign invasion. The "dwarfs," as the Chinese contemptuously called the enemy, mauled China's fleet, routed her army, and occupied southern Manchuria. Chinese officials were first humiliated by their defeat and then outraged by Japan's peace terms. In late April 1895, less than a week after Li Hung-chang had signed the treaty of peace at Shimonoseki, rumors about its contents began to circulate in China. Relatives of the emperor, high provincial officials, censors, and obscure degree-holders joined in angrily protesting that Japan's terms did such

    12. Chang to the Tsung-li Yamen, telegram, 27 August 1895, CWS:KH, ch. 117.6–7; Hsü T'ung-hsin, *Chang Wen-hsiang-kung nien-p'u* [A chronological biography of Chang Chih-tung] (Taipei reprint, 1969), p. 93; Tsung-li Yamen, supplementary memorial, 19 October 1895, and imperial rescript of the same date, both in CWS:KH, ch. 118.2–3.
    13. Manchurian military governors, joint memorial, 15 October 1897, CWS:KH, ch. 127.14–15; and Kent, *Railway Enterprise in China,* pp. 51–55.

damage to the dynasty that the emperor must not approve them. One of the earliest protests came from Li Ping-heng, governor of Shantung and later famous for his support of the Boxers. He admonished the throne:

> The three eastern provinces are the places from which our dynasty issued. The frontier pass to this base and the capital are bound together. Moreover, the Imperial tombs are there; the comfort of the spirits of successive ancestors genuinely depends on them. Suddenly they are given over to a tribe of dogs and sheep. The Imperial spirits will certainly blush and not be at peace. Our Emperor is full of love and very filial. Hearing of these actions in defiance of right, one cannot approve of the treaty which would overthrow our ten thousand years [of rule]. . . .[14]

Critics resorting to other traditional arguments for the defense of Manchuria warned that cession of the Liaotung Peninsula might cost the Manchus the imperial mandate and encourage talk of partition. Protests continued for nearly three weeks. The agitation quieted only when Russia, France, and Germany forced Japan to return the Manchurian territory to China and when, nearly simultaneously, the emperor formally endorsed Li Hung-chang's fresh course of negotiations over the path of renewed resistance preferred by his critics.[15]

The future security of Manchuria remained a pending and urgent question. The intervention by Russia, France, and Germany to prevent Japan's annexation suggested Manchuria could for the moment be safeguarded only through an alliance with a strong power. Li Hung-chang, finding the commercial powers uninterested in protecting Manchuria for China, adopted the bold view that China should ally with Russia. She would thereby at once gain a powerful friend and neutralize a dangerous enemy. Li's proposal had support from Empress Dowager Tz'u-hsi as well as provincial officials such as Liu K'un-i and Chang Chih-tung.[16] A secret edict empowered Li to discuss the price with Russia. The bargain which he struck during a visit to St. Petersburg in 1896, ostensibly to attend the coronation of the czar, gave Russia the railway

---

14. Li, memorial, 23 April 1895, CCS:KH, 1:748.

15. The protests begin in CCS:KH, 1:744 and continue until the appearance of the imperial mandate of 1 May 1895 in CCS:KH, 1:857.

16. Wang Shu-hwai, *Wai-jen yü wu-hsü pien-fa* [Foreigners and the reform movement of 1898] (Taipei, 1965), p. 128; Hosea B. Morse, *The International Relations of the Chinese Empire*, vol. 3, *The Period of Subjection 1844–1911* (New York, 1918), p. 82. For memorials urging an alliance with Russia, see Chang, 19 July 1895, in Wang Shu-t'ung, comp., *Chang Wen-hsiang-kung ch'üan-chi* [Collected works of Chang Chih-tung] (Peking, 1928), ch. 37.36–38; Chang, 8 August 1895, CCS:KH, 1:902–03; and Liu, 8 July 1895, CWS:KH, ch. 115.20–21.

concession across Manchuria and the right to garrison it. A joint-stock company, the Russo–Chinese Bank, was to finance and operate the line, but in fact Sergei Witte, the Russian minister of finance and the father of the railway, held control in his own hands and made certain the line would serve Russian interests in Manchuria.

The policy of alliance worked out no more successfully than the plans for the construction of Chinese-controlled railroads. Two years later Russia raised the price of alliance to include a leasehold on the Liaotung Peninsula and a rail line to it. At the same time Russia provided no help to China in fending off Germany's demands in 1897 for a sphere of influence in Shantung. Once again rumors, fueled by reports in the Chinese press on the purported terms of Li's still-secret agreements, gave ammunition to his opponents. They charged that the loss to Russia of railway, harbor, mining, and garrison rights would give her a hold on Manchuria which China would not be able to loosen. Liu K'un-i regarded the concessions Li had made as excessive. Liu had originally opposed an alliance with Russia, only to reverse himself in July 1895 when he had thought China might purchase Russian support against Japan in Manchuria with a strip of territory in Sinkiang.[17] Chang Chih-tung, who had earlier dropped his proposal that China build and control all railroads in Manchuria in order to accommodate Russia's demand for a road to Dairen, now agreed with Liu's latest assessment.[18] The two joined in urging the court to abandon the alliance and to consider in its place an understanding with Japan and Britain. However, neither London nor Tokyo showed any interest in the scheme. Without their support, the Chinese government saw as pointless any attempt to shake off the Russian alliance.[19]

Again, as in 1895, one of the most trenchant, impassioned, and articulate attacks on the court's Manchurian policy came from the brush of Li Ping-heng. He considered Li Hung-chang's efforts to safeguard that region through an alliance with Russia ill-conceived He warned that China in her financial straits would later have difficulty repurchasing the Russian railroad, that as a troop transport it would give Russia a strategic advantage, and that the railway garrisons would endanger Chinese control. The court had given up a strategic harbor in the Gulf of Chihli, and the granting of mine concessions in the Changpai Mountains, the very home of the Manchus, was a blow to the prestige of the dynasty.

17. Liu, memorial, 8 July 1895, ch. 115.20–21.
18. Hsü, *Chang Wen-hsiang-kung nien-p'u*, p. 96.
19. Ibid.; Liu, memorial, 8 July 1895, CWS:KH, ch. 115.20–21; and Wang, *Wai-jen yü wu-hsü pien-fa*, pp. 147–51, 154–55, 162–64.

From his examination of the treaty, Li Ping-heng concluded that it was decidedly unequal.

> They [the Russians] cannot but enjoy the advantages and we incur the disadvantages. If a railway is built through our territory of Kirin and Heilungkiang to transport troops, Manchuria will not be ours. If they build docks at Kiaochow, Port Arthur and Dairen to anchor their fleet, the Yellow Sea to the north and the Liao Sea to the west will not be ours. We will have the territory and they will occupy it. We will have the mines and they will open them. Using our wealth and taking advantage of our troubles, they will shackle our authority and deceive our people. They will encircle and apply pressure on our frontier in order to control our fate. In this they not only coerce us and plot against us, but also despise us and treat us lightly.[20]

Russia had saved several districts from falling into Japan's hands. China in gratitude had virtually given her all of Manchuria and by so doing invited the other powers to make similar demands. Li urged revision of the treaty through negotiations in which China could barter away commercial concessions to get out from under the obligations of the alliance. International law and appeals to other powers, he warned, would be of no help if Russia remained unmoved. The time had come in any case for China to begin to strengthen herself in Manchuria with a view toward recourse—if all else failed—to war.[21]

In the Manchurian crisis of the 1890s the central government had played its alliance and railway strategies through to the bankrupt end. As a consequence, Manchuria was in more desperate straits than ever before: the Russians had secured the very territory they had saved for China in 1895; and their rail concessions, in the shape of a great *T* running across the north and through the center, dominated the region. As Li Ping-heng had suggested, China was left with no alternative but that of war. Reliance on popular antiforeign feeling was the only way Ch'ing officials could hope to pull Manchuria from the dangerous spot she was in. The outburst of Boxer activity in 1900 provided the opportunity to test this strategy.

The German advance into Shantung and the ensuing "scramble for concessions" heightened xenophobic feelings in Manchuria as elsewhere

---

20. Li, memorial, 12 January 1897, CWS:KH, ch. 124.14–20. See other protests in ch. 125.13–16 and 134.7–11.

21. Li, memorials, 12 January 1897, CWS:KH, ch. 124.14–20, and 17 October 1899, SL:KH, ch. 450.15.

in China. The Boxers first appeared in Fengtien in May, when they began holding meetings. Through June these meetings—as well as anti-foreign rumors, literature, and placards—became more commonplace. News of the attacks on foreigners in Shantung and Chihli ignited the unstable compound of antiforeignism in Manchuria in June 1900. In the last week of that month Boxers, occasionally joined by government troops and supported by some officials, launched their antiforeign campaign, which gradually spread northward into Kirin and Heilungkiang. The blast was directed against the Russian railway as well as the Christian missions. Although the Russians employed by the Chinese Eastern Railway escaped with their lives, the Boxers did extensive damage to railroad stations, tracks, and bridges. Like the Russians, the Protestant missionaries fled, but the Catholic missionaries and converts defended their cathedrals and villages and shared with the Chinese Protestants the brunt of the outburst. Terror reigned in the cities as well as in the countryside. It was not until early August that the outbreak began to subside.[22]

In the face of this popular explosion, the three military governors of Manchuria found themselves in a difficult position. The military governor in Fengtien bent with the blast and survived both the Boxer holocaust and the ensuing Russian occupation. This official, Tseng-ch'i, received on 21 June the empress dowager's directive to wage war against the foreigners. In the conference of high officials which he immediately called, he advocated maintaining order and thus avoiding giving offense to the Russians; however, his lieutenant governor, Chin-ch'ang, pressed for carrying out the directive by aiding the Boxers. In the following several days the situation in Mukden clearly got beyond the military governor's control. He gave way on 24 June and promulgated the empress dowager's edict, but only ofter having warned the missionaries of the coming storm. By 30 June destruction had begun on a large scale, and Chin-ch'ang's troops contributed to it. Not until early August, with the Russians moving through Manchuria and with the allied army advancing toward Peking, did Tseng-ch'i denounce the Boxers in public. On 11 August he began to employ troops against them. He offered no resistance to the Russian army of occupation and together with Chin-ch'ang fled Mukden in late September.[23]

22. Robertson, *The Story of Our Mission*, p. 49; Christie, *Thirty Years in Moukden*, pp. 131–61; John Ross, *Mission Methods in Manchuria* (London, 1908), pp. 254–68; and Li, *Chin-tai Tung-pei*, pp. 102, 108–10. Materials in Chester C. Tan's *The Boxer Catastrophe* (New York, 1955), pp. 157–69 were used in this and the following paragraphs on the Boxers in Manchuria.

23. On Tseng-ch'i, who held the Mukden post until 1905, see Li, *Chin-tai Tung-pei*, pp. 116–17, 124–25; Ross, *Mission Methods in Manchuria*, pp. 256–57; Christie, *Thirty Years in Moukden*, pp.

Chang-shun, the military governor of Kirin, also survived the turmoil of 1900 and remained in office until 1904. However, rather than being dominated by the Boxers as was Tseng-ch'i, Chang-shun managed to bring them under control by incorporating them into militia led by local officials loyal to him. He used the additional time it took Boxer influence to reach into Kirin from Fengtien to prepare against the outbreak by tightening social and political control. Later, Chang-shun, like Tseng-ch'i, offered no resistance to the Russian army of occupation.[24]

In Heilungkiang the military governor, Shou-shan, encountered a different set of circumstances, and his response was unlike either of his colleagues'. In Heilungkiang, as in Kirin, the Boxers made a delayed appearance, and thus Shou-shan did not have to cope immediately with the threat of a popular rising. He did, however, face a Russian army gathering strength across the Amur River. When it crossed into Manchuria in late July, he resisted. Despite later instructions from Li Hung-chang to avoid conflict with the Russian force, the battle in Heilungkiang continued for a month. On 29 August its administrative center Tsitsihar fell, and Shou-shan committed suicide.[25]

The occupation of all of Manchuria by Russian troops climaxed a decade of failure. From Peking and the yamens of the military governors, the view in 1901 after nearly four decades of steady losses was indeed gloomy. Russia had occupied Manchuria the previous year and showed no sign of leaving. No power had come forward to join China in contesting the occupation, and China, in disarray after the Boxer fiasco, was militarily impotent and for the moment closely watched by the foreign powers. The traditional rules of border defense had by themselves proved ineffective against the kind of threat the foreigners posed. And as the Rusian occupation evidenced, Ch'ing officials had also failed through the 1890s to find new ways to remove the pressure and to win for Manchuria at least a few years of respite. They had fared as badly as their predecessors in previous decades. Nonetheless, they were to continue their search for an effective policy of frontier defense to meet Manchuria's interlocking problems of foreign penetration and domestic unrest.

136–39, 149–50, 152, 161; Hsü, *China and Her Political Entity*, pp. 239, 244; and Henry J. Whigham, *Manchuria and Korea* (New York, 1904), pp. 123–24.

24. Li, *Chin-tai Tung-pei*, pp. 120–22, 124–25; and Hsü, *China and Her Political Entity*, pp. 239, 244.

25. Hsü, *China and Her Political Entity*, pp. 240–44.

2: THE OPEN DOOR

The Sino–Japanese War of 1894–95 forced a small but growing number of Americans to look at Manchuria more carefully. They were primarily bystanders in the dramatic developments of the late 1890s. Nonetheless, through that period they became increasingly alert to the process of foreign penetration in Manchuria, articulate about their nation's potential stake there, and concerned with developing a policy to defend American interests.

Commerce was the essential American concern in Manchuria. The United States possessed no other interest of substance there to protect. American missionaries, active elsewhere in China, stayed away from Manchuria during the late Ch'ing. French Catholics, there since the 1830s, and British, Irish, and Danish Protestants, there since the 1870s, had already come to dominate this field. The gold, silver, and coal mines of Manchuria, known in the 1890s for their richness, attracted only sporadic interest from American investors. During this and the following decade Americans never made a sustained attempt at securing uncontested ownership or at undertaking operation of these mines.[1]

America's trading stake in China was at this time concentrated in northern China and Manchuria. American exporters, principally the cotton textile industry and the Standard Oil Company of New York, had in Manchuria a small but promising market. By 1899 trade in American cotton piece goods, the major United States export to Manchuria, had grown to at least $4,380,000. Kerosene, flour, and lumber followed in order of importance. Russian railway enterprise in the region no less than Chinese consumers proved an important customer for American exports. Orders for American steel rails, locomotives, and other equipment kept furnaces in Baltimore and Philadelphia busy.

But in other respects American trade was unimportant. Few Americans

---

1. On these unsuccessful investment efforts, see B. A. Romanov, *Russia in Manchuria (1892–1906)*, trans. Susan W. Jones (Ann Arbor, Mich., 1952), pp. 376–77; and *K'uang-wu tang* [Records on mining affairs], comp. by the Institute of Modern History, Academia Sinica (Taipei, 1960), 6:3869–91, 3927–47, and 7:4131–46, 4158–59.

did business in Newchuang, Manchuria's only port open to foreigners, and virtually none penetrated the interior. Moreover, Americans gained relatively little carrying goods to Manchuria. American shipping into Newchuang in 1899 totaled only 2,100 tons (3 vessels), which, by comparison with Britain's 184,997 tons (185 vessels), was insignificant. Of goods exported from Manchuria, the United States took almost nothing, unless cheap contract labor in which Hawaiian plantation owners took a spasmodic interest be counted. Finally, in Manchuria as in the rest of China, a self-sufficient economy held back foreign trade. Overall United States trade with China, Manchuria included, during these years represented a mere 2 percent of the total American foreign trade.[2]

Essentially, America's involvement with Manchuria was future oriented. American exporters hoped to build their promising start in this virgin market into a booming trade. The preservation of a commercial open door was crucial to the realization of this dream. Manchuria's fall to foreign control would mean not only the closing of the door to commerce there and the demise of their hopes but also the general partition of China. Thus, some Americans viewed Manchuria from afar as a valuable but imperiled commercial prize and as a symbol of America's interest in the China market.

Manchuria also glittered in the eyes of some Americans as a new overseas frontier for pioneer spirits. It seemed to Americans in the 1890s that national energies had just exhausted the continental bounds. Americans had settled the West and practically exhausted their virgin land. The prospect of having their energies so confined now threatened the virility and ambition which had made the country great. Without challenge to meet and competition to overcome, ran the popular social Darwinist strains of the day, a nation, like an organism, ceased to evolve and progress. They began to look elsewhere for new frontiers equal to their abundant energy as well as to their burgeoning industrial production. For the

2. On general American trade in Manchuria, see Alexander Hosie, *Manchuria: Its People, Resources and Recent History* (London, 1904), pp. 252–56, 259–60; Henry B. Miller, "Russian Development of Manchuria" and "Notes on Manchuria," *National Geographic Magazine* 15 (1904): 122, 125, 261. On railway sales, see Thomas A. Bailey, *America Faces Russia* (Ithaca, N.Y., 1950), p. 172; Henry J. Whigham, *Manchuria and Korea* (New York, 1904), p. 50; and Hosie, *Manchuria*, p. 69. On the limitations of the China market, see Paul A. Varg, "The Myth of the China Market, 1890–1914," *American Historical Review* 73 (1968): 742–58. The American goods which reached Manchuria after being transshipped from major ports along the China coast (e.g., Hong Kong, Canton, Shanghai) or from Japan lost their national identity and thus were not recorded as "American imports" on Manchurian customs records. Since there is no *post facto* way of even crudely determining the extent of this category, all trade figures for American goods in Manchuria must be taken as a minimum which may grossly understate its magnitude both before and after 1900.

more adventuresome free spirits looking beyond the West to the lands across the Pacific, the great plains of Manchuria, its rugged mountains, and its abundant resources seemed a re-creation of the frontier the United States had just lost. One could recover the romance and challenge of that frontier in this new land, which, as one enthused American living there would later observe, "is really a new West, with cheaper labor and a soil almost equally fertile and rich in minerals."[3]

There was an ironic side to American preoccupation with the frontier which also shaped America's relations with China. As Americans, inspired by their own dreams, invaded China, Chinese crossing the Pacific in the opposite direction found that the door to settlement in the American West was closing on them. The fear in the western part of the United States that the era of the frontier—and with it domestic opportunity—was at an end contributed, together with nativism, to agitation for the exclusion of Chinese and to mob attacks against Chinese residents. Immigrants, drawn to the United States from their precarious life in southern coastal China by tales of wealth, gradually discovered that part of their Pacific frontier was no longer open to them. Denied the chance to live their dream, they stayed at home and watched with understandable and growing indignation as Americans nonchalantly made their sweeping claims for a place in China.

The railroad played a special role in stimulating American interest in Manchuria. While in historical perspective the advent of the railway marked the beginning of significant foreign political and economic penetration there, for Americans it was more important for the impetus it gave to dreams of the frontier and of a rich China market. The Russian railroad through Manchuria, the American minister to China rhapsodized in 1901,

> will open up to settlement and development the only great territory, still left on the globe, so favored with soil and climate as to promise great agricultural development and its concomitant of a strong people and resultant great trade progress. Its contiguity to the United States, and the possibility of connecting its great railroad system by direct lines of steamers across the Pacific with our own transcontinental routes . . . will make this trade route, which will practically encircle the globe, one of inexpressible potency and of mutual benefit.[4]

3. Willard Straight to E. H. Harriman, 15 November 1906, Straight Papers, Olin Library, Cornell University. A noteworthy study of the continental frontier is Henry Nash Smith, *Virgin Land: The American West As Symbol and Myth* (Cambridge, Mass., 1950).
4. Edwin H. Conger to John Hay, 7 September 1901, MCD.

What was more reminiscent of another, more familiar frontier than the drama of the railroad cutting through and conquering the wilderness? What was more likely to call to mind the American West than the Manchurian boom towns, which grew up along the tracks, with all their romantic lawlessness and opportunity?[5] And by confirming the parallel of Manchuria with the opening of the American West, the railway gave further impetus to awakening hopes of the expanding trade which such a railroad might promote.

American observers of the Manchurian scene had learned from their own national experience that the railway was important for its impact on commerce and settlement. They thus tended to stress the commercial opportunities which the Russian railway would open up and tended to minimize the railway as a tool of Russian foreign policy. The Americans were to learn less quickly than the Chinese the lessons of political and military penetration which the Chinese Eastern Railway had to teach.

The American ministers to China in the 1890s were the first to face the problem of Manchuria. The first of these was Charles Denby, a lawyer who through his labors in the vineyards of Democratic state politics had won the appointment to Peking in 1885. He arrived in his fifty-fifth year, a diplomatic innocent with little knowledge of China. Isolated and content in the closed community of foreign residents in China, supported by only the most rudimentary staff, and uninterested in the Chinese or their culture, he learned little during his fourteen years at his post.

Denby occupied his time bearing the white man's burden, which for him consisted essentially of protecting the activities of American missionaries from native attacks and official harassment and of urging the schemes of American businessmen on an uninterested Chinese government. Denby, who had convinced himself that the Chinese regarded only American enterprise as above suspicion, took up the role of civilizing agent representing the nation best suited to introduce progress to China.

> The statesman of China will understand that in our case foreign control does not mean territorial absorption nor governmental interference, while both these results are possible, or even probable, in dealing with European powers.[6]

His motivation was not completely altruistic. Like many of his countrymen, Denby feared the possibility of an industrial glut in the United

5. See, e.g., Willard Straight's description of Harbin and the Russian railroad in northern Manchuria in a report of 9 December 1907 in NF 2413/94.
6. Denby to John Sherman, 15 March 1897, MCD.

States. To avoid this catastrophe, overseas markets for surplus production had to be developed and protected. Of these potential markets the minister regarded China as the most promising. Thus, while trying to move his government toward a more active role in keeping the door to China open, Denby at the same time encouraged his nationals to enter it and, through their religious and business activities, to stake out America's future position. Self-interest and altruism proved in Denby's world opposite sides of the same coin.[7]

Denby's foggy ideas concerning civilizing China and his vague hope of promoting American commerce are reflected in his evaluations of the Manchurian crisis. The prospect in 1895 of Japanese domination of the Liaotung Peninsula as a result of her victory over China did not initially alarm him. At first he thought Japan a civilizing influence, entirely trustworthy because her conversion from barbarity had come at the hands of the United States. Both Denby and the Department of State expected the Japanese victory to result in the opening of Manchuria more fully to foreign trade.[8] Japan's peace demands, which he thought looked toward the domination of northern China, soon disillusioned him.

> Japan has been posing as the knight errant of civilization. She had intimated to the European powers that she intended to do many great things for foreign commerce, and under cover of these intimations she has securely pursued her own aggrandizement and the Western powers gain practically nothing.[9]

However, in this early stage of the developing Manchurian crisis, Denby still failed to identify any threat to American interests.

The retrocession of the Liaotung Peninsula by Japan to China on the insistence of Russia, France, and Germany did not restore affairs in Manchuria to the *status quo ante bellum*. It instead presented Denby with a new set of facts over which to exercise his wit, but he remained uncertain how to relate these developments to American interests. Now Russia was the power to watch, and a railroad across northern Manchuria was her

7. For biographical information on Denby see the sketch by the editor in his memoirs, *China and Her People* (Boston, 1906), 1:ix–xvi; and Herbert F. Wright's short study in *The Dictionary of American Biography*, 5:233–34. For Denby's views just after he left his post in Peking, see his "Shall We Keep the Philippines?" *The Forum* 26 (October 1898): 279–81. Denby's memoirs must be handled with care since many opinions he expressed in them do not correspond with those in his official reports to the State Department. *China and Her People* is useful for Denby's general views on missionary and commercial enterprises and on the Chinese. See especially 1:6–8, 34–45, 215–16, 218. For his fairyland view of China and Japan, see 2:237, 249.

8. Denby to Walter Gresham, 26 February 1895, MCD; and Edwin F. Uhl (acting secretary of state) to Denby, 8 June 1895, DIC.

9. Denby to Gresham, 29 April 1895, MCD.

first step. Initially Denby, like most of his contemporaries, ignored the political significance of the move. In September 1896 he reported back to the State Department that "I have never seen any reason why the United States should object to this scheme, and I have not the least desire or intention to intervene in any manner to thwart it."[10] However, by April of the following year he had revised his opinion to the extent of warning Washington that Russia would tighten her grip on Manchuria to the detriment of the interests of the United States and Britain.[11]

Denby began in 1897 to apply himself to the question of how to protect his country's Manchurian trade against Russia. In the resulting reflections and recommendations, the minister oscillated between a passive and cautious policy of maintaining the traditional open door and a more activist policy which required greater risk, involvement, and effort for the United States. Like most Americans in contact with China, he remained ambivalent on the course to pursue.

Denby's inconsistencies mirrored two major and divergent China policies. The traditional open door policy, as it was practiced in Denby's China, was above all a British creation. Great Britain had opened China to the foreign trade of all nations on a basis of commercial equality. By incorporating the most-favored-nation clause in treaties with China, the United States in turn gained for its citizens the same trading rights enjoyed by others without any significant military or diplomatic effort. In this convenient arrangement it was the real powers in the Far East who first wrested from the Chinese, and then defended, the commercial advantages of which American businessmen so easily availed themselves.

The Chinese were a necessary accessory in this traditional open door system. Their policy of benevolently allowing the barbarian-merchants of all the foreign tribes, including the United States, to participate under the restrictions of the Canton scheme (c. 1760–1834) in China's trade substantially fitted the needs and limits of American interests in China. Even after the militarily superior Westerners (without significant American support) destroyed the Canton arrangement, China tried in the ensuing period of unequal treaties to save the old principle of showing imperial benevolence to all those who came from afar, on which the Canton scheme had in the Chinese view rested. The idea of granting favors equally to all was a way of maintaining the attitude of Chinese superiority over foreigners, who meekly and gratefully received the emperor's generosity. It was also, more realistically, a way of balancing the

10. Denby to Richard Olney, 2 September 1896, MCD.
11. Denby to Sherman 2 April 1987, MCD.

powers and preventing any one from dominating the field. But the cost
China paid for maintaining her attitude of superior benevolence and for
attempting to manage the barbarians in this way was the guarantee that
any privilege granted to one would be granted to all. The result was a
ratchet effect; an advance by one meant an advance by all. And, of course,
no one surrendered acquired privileges.[12]

In 1860 the Treaty of Peking opened the port of Newchuang to foreign
trade and residence, thus extending this arrangement to Manchuria.
During the next forty-five years American goods found their way into the
Manchurian market through that port. However, the impending breakup
of China threatened to overturn this arrangement for commercial equality
cherished by Americans, while the prospect of Russian control of Manchuria raised the specter of a closing door to commerce at Newchuang.
American policy makers became troubled over the future of Manchuria
but initially avoided aggressive counteraction. They were content trying
to accommodate old open door principles to new conditions.

Minister Charles Denby hoped during the unsettled period following
the Sino–Japanese War that the passive open door would continue to
protect American trade interests and that Britain, anxious to safeguard
her large share of the China trade, would continue her role as the protector
and promoter of free trade.[13] But Denby, who ignored Britain's diplomatically isolated position, was leaning on a weak reed. Britain's later
uncertain response to the battle for concessions in 1897 and 1898 doomed
his hopes that the open door policy under the lead of the foremost commercial power would function in the late 1890s as it had in the past.
If Britain would not defend free trade in Manchuria, the United States
would have the alternative, Denby suggested, of updating the traditional
open door by arriving at a working arrangement with Russia. Denby
argued that careful cultivation of her friendship, including recognition
of her dominant position in Manchuria, was price enough to secure in
return a guarantee of participation in the commercial development of
Manchuria. The bargain would cost the United States nothing and would
preserve the open door in Manchuria.

In fact Denby himself sponsored an attempt by the American China
Development Company in 1896 and 1897 to accommodate American
interests to the Russian sphere of influence. The company had been
organized immediately after the Sino–Japanese War by American

---

12. John K. Fairbank, "The Early Treaty System in the Chinese World Order," *The Chinese World Order: Traditional China's Foreign Relations* (Cambridge, Mass., 1968), pp. 260–63.
13. Denby to Sherman, 2 April 1897, MCD.

capitalists to exploit the opportunities for railway construction in China. Its agents had tried to secure from China a Manchurian railway concession including exclusive rights to exploit natural resources and a thirty-year monopoly on railway construction there. Since the route was to connect with the Russian Siberian railway and to cross territory in which Russia had taken a keen interest, the company needed Russian as well as Chinese approval for its scheme. The company's agents tried to win the Russians with the argument that their group had no political or territorial ambitions and thus posed no threat to Russian plans. They offered a "secret understanding," which included full recognition of Russia's sphere of influence in Manchuria. Although the Russian government turned down the scheme, Denby still hoped to reach an agreement which would accommodate Russian and American interests in the area.[14]

In contrast to the idea of updating the open door, there existed an activist strain in American China policy. The activists viewed the emerging spheres of influence as a greater danger to American interests than did those who favored updating the open door; hence the activists were willing to go farther in combating the spheres. They recognized that those spheres were becoming a fact of international life and represented commercial and financial interests of other nations which would narrow, if not exclude, American activities. The United States could protect her stake either by neutralizing the spheres or by staking out a distinct area of activity for Americans. The activists were emphatic in their conclusion that the country would have to abandon passive measures, such as the open door, for bolder measures if it wished to safeguard its interests in China. The activist argument appealed to a wide variety of people. Speculators desired to preserve their opportunity to make a quick killing on the China market. Those concerned with the prospect of financial and industrial surplus at home were also alarmed and insisted on vigorous action. The consular chauvinists in the treaty ports, described by one seasoned diplomat as "those young diplomatic hopefuls who are always ready to recommend to their Government 'forward policies' in the hopes of thereby acquiring credit for activity and patriotism," were certain to voice not only their own fears for national prestige and interest but also those of the other alarmists as well.[15] In short, the activist strain represented most fully the search for new frontiers, financial and personal, for Americans. Traces

14. Denby to Olney, 2 September 1896, and Denby to Sherman, 2 April 1897, both in MCD; *Amerika v. Bor'be za Kitai* (Moscow, 1935), pp. 99, 101; Romanov, *Russia in Manchuria*, pp. 63, 76–77, 152.

15. The phrase is Baron Roman Rosen's from *Forty Years of Diplomacy* (London, 1922), p. 142.

of it could be found in the thinking of nearly every prominent American concerned with the Far East, Denby and Secretary of State John Hay included.

Activism was not a new phenomenon in the 1890s. There was the interest in annexing Taiwan dating back to the 1850s, the missionary imperialism of Peter Parker and W. A. P. Martin, and the fantastic plot in 1894 to overthrow the Manchus.[16] But this activism became, from the late 1890s onward, a more pronounced aspect of China policy. It fore-shadowed for the following decade first the chauvinism of American consuls in Manchuria and ultimately dollar diplomacy there. In Man-churia, more than anywhere else in China, the United States faced most acutely the problem of coping with spheres of influence, and there the activist voice was heard most loudly.

Denby, who explored the possibilities for American action in the framework of the passive open door, simultaneously experimented with the activist prescription. His freedom from a systematic view allowed him to conclude that the American government would have to abandon some of its traditional cautiousness and promote more actively the interests of its private citizens abroad. In short, to compete effectively against im-perialists, one had to adopt some of their methods. Otherwise there was no hope of equal opportunity for Americans.[17]

Denby's primary concern was that as minister he could not act as vigorously on behalf of American interests as he thought necessary. In 1896 his complaints finally drew from Secretary of State Olney permis-sion to use "all proper methods" to promote American commerce through official dealings with the Chinese government. The vagueness of Olney's phrase liberated the minister from the more restrictive guidelines laid down by Olney in 1895, which stipulated that American citizens could only be "introduced and vouched for" by Denby.[18] Unsatisfied, Denby urged more. The next step was to move away from open door orthodoxy. The partition of China, contemporary observers repeatedly warned, spelled disaster to commerce; support for the Ch'ing dynasty was the means to prevent it. This generalization had been an essential piece of

16. On the Taiwan annexation scheme, see Huang Chia-mu, *Mei-kuo yü T'ai-wan* [The United States and Taiwan] (Taipei, 1966). On the dreams of empire nursed by Parker and Martin, see Jonathan Spence, *To Change China: Western Advisers in China 1620–1960* (Boston, 1969), pp. 55, 158–59. On the scheme to overthrow the Manchus, see Marilyn B. Young, *The Rhetoric of Empire: American China Policy 1895–1901* (Cambridge, Mass., 1968), pp. 27–30.

17. Denby to Sherman, 24 May 1897 and 31 January 1898, MCD.

18. Olney to Denby, 22 June 1895, DIC; Denby to Olney, 5 November 1896, MCD; and Olney to Denby, 19 December 1896, FRUS, 1897, p. 56. Hay confirmed for Denby's successor the general tenor of Olney's instructions of 1896 in Hay to Conger, 12 July 1899, DIC.

intellectual baggage for those who had espoused the venerable doctrine of the passive open door. Now, the ambitions of the powers had put in doubt the survival of that dynasty. Denby wished to save it from its own ineffectual government and European demands by instituting a period of Anglo-American tutelage under which "the principle of extra-territoriality should be pushed to its utmost limit in its application to great schemes of improvement."[19] Denby had naïvely concluded that the Chinese, secure in their trust of America's good will and disinterested desire to help, would prefer to become a protectorate of the United States and Britain than be swept from the board altogether. Denby failed to convince his own government—not to mention the Chinese—of the wisdom of this proposal, but simply by raising it he had revealed the trend of his own thought toward a new policy of full American participation not just in commerce but in the imperialist policy of informal and extensive control in Chinese life.

Denby's successor, Edwin H. Conger, who reached Peking in July 1898, shared Denby's lack of qualifications for his post and inherited Denby's uncertainties about the path which United States China policy should follow. Like Denby, Conger was a lawyer from middle America who came to his job with a mind uncluttered by detailed information about China; he had earned his way into diplomacy through loyal service to the Republican party in local politics and in the House of Representatives.[20] Perceptive neither by nature nor by training, Conger wrote reports on developments in China which could easily have come from the pen of any careful reader of the American daily press. Indeed, with no contacts in the Chinese official community, which the legation disdainfully neglected to cultivate, and with no consulates in Manchuria to keep him informed of local developments, Conger, like Denby, was thrown on the rumor mill and the press for his information. His vague, speculative reports to Washington accurately reflected the nature of his sources of intelligence.

Conger contributed to the development of the activist strain in China policy by advocating America's need for a coaling station on China's coast. He urged the retention of Manila after its capture during the Spanish–American War but warned it was only second best "to controlling a desirable port and commodious harbor in China," which might serve as a base for American "commercial conquests" there.[21] Embolden-

19. Denby to Gresham, 5 March 1895, and Denby to Sherman, 15 March 1897, MCD. The quote is from the latter.
20. A sketch of Conger by John E. Briggs is in *The Dictionary of American Biography*, 4:344–45.
21. Conger to William R. Day, 26 August 1898, MCD.

ed by McKinley's acquisition of the Philippine harbor several months later, he raised the issue again for Washington's consideration.

> We ought to be ready, either by negotiation or by actual possession, to own and control at least one good port from which we can potently assert our own rights and effectively wield our influence.[22]

Earlier, Taiwan had been the favored site of American coaling station enthusiasts. Japan's acquisition of the island in 1895 deflected their interest to other parts of China. As the possibility of partition emerged more distinctly, Conger decided that Chihli, the only province unclaimed by any of the powers, would be the best choice. He admitted in a prize understatement that the other powers might object to the United States's controlling that province, which, he failed to note in his suggestion to Hay, contained the Chinese capital.[23] Although Washington proved for the moment cool to his suggestion, Conger, undaunted by difficulties, continued through 1902 to apply himself to the problem of locating a satisfactory naval station.[24]

Along with Denby and Conger, Secretary of State John Hay was looking for a Manchurian policy more assertive than the passive open door but without the burdens of active and steady involvement in Far Eastern diplomacy. Hay's diplomacy at the turn of the century also reflected the perplexity which developments in China had created in the minds of interested Americans.

Hay's first important step in defining his China policy was the attempt in September 1899 to breathe new life into the open door through an exchange of notes committing the powers "to insure to the commerce of the world in China equality of treatment," specifically in regard to harbor dues, railway rates, and customs tariffs.[25] The easiest way to see the ambiguities in the position Hay took at that time is to look at his open

22. Conger to Hay, 3 November 1898, MCD.

23. Conger to Hay, 1 March 1899, MCD.

24. Conger to Hay, 23 November 1900, 13 September 1901, and 22 September 1902, all in MCD.

25. FRUS, 1899, pp. 128–43. I have neglected the well-known steps in the formulation of the open door notes of 1899; however, those interested should see A. Whitney Griswold, *The Far Eastern Policy of the United States* (New York, 1938), and Charles S. Campbell, Jr., *Anglo-American Understanding, 1898–1903* (Baltimore, 1957), pp. 12–21, 162–69, 201–04, on the open door in Anglo-American relations; Campbell, *Special Business Interests and the Open Door* (New Haven, Conn., 1951), on the influence of commerical pressure groups; and Griswold, *The Far Eastern Policy of the United States*, Paul A. Varg, *Open Door Diplomat: The Life of W. W. Rockhill* (Urbana, Ill., 1952), and Harvey Pressman, "Hay, Rockhill, and China's Integrity: A Reappraisal," *Papers on China* 13 (1959): 61–79, on the contributions of Hay, Rockhill, and Hippisley.

door note through the eyes of the Russians, whose actions in Manchuria had in part provoked his initiative. The Russian minister of foreign affairs, Muraviëv, was puzzled and defensive after studying Hay's proposal.

> In this note the editing of which is so unclear, the confusion of treaty ports, spheres of influence and leased territories is such that it is hard for us to understand the intentions of the American Government. . . . We have long considered that it would be advantageous for us by means of an exchange of opinions with the Washington Government on this question to induce the latter to recognize our privileged position in this part of China [i.e., Manchuria]. But above all we must be convinced that the claims of the United States do not spread to the Kwantung [Liaotung] Russian leased territory. . . .[26]

Muraviëv was personally opposed to opening the door to Manchuria too wide. Earlier, he had instructed the Russian ambassador to the United States to "take energetic action" against any American enterprises planned for Manchuria which might impinge on Russian interests there.[27] To Muraviëv the question of recognizing Russia's Manchurian sphere was the crucial one in American–Russian relations in China, and he clearly would have preferred an explicit statement of recognition from the Americans. He had just reached an agreement with Britain delimiting the railway spheres of interest in China. Recognition from the United States would have further strengthened the Russian position and been worth a guarantee of trade opportunity.

But Hay in his note had hardly come halfway toward meeting Muraviëv. He demanded only equality of commercial opportunity and omitted any reference to equal investment opportunity, implying toleration of the Russian sphere. However, while the ambiguity of the note on this point made it generally palatable to the Russians, it also rendered Hay's recognition—if that is indeed what he intended—diplomatically valueless

---

26. Minister of Foreign Affairs Muraviëv to Ambassador to the United States Cassini, telegram, 19 November 1899, quoted *in extenso* in Edward H. Zabriskie, *American–Russian Rivalry in the Far East: A Study in Diplomacy and Power Politics, 1895–1914* (Philadelphia, Pa., 1946), p. 55. The Russians were not alone in their confusion. In London Secretary for Foreign Affairs Lord Salisbury found the American note proposing a guarantee of the open door "obscurely drafted." Faced with a proposal liberally laced with such undefined terms as "spheres," "spheres of influence," "spheres of interest," and "free ports," Salisbury resolved his perplexity by setting Hong Kong and the adjoining leased territory outside the scope of the agreement. Joseph Choate to Salisbury, 22 September 1899; Salisbury, minutes of 30 September 1899; and Salisbury to Choate, 30 November 1899, all in FO 17/2408.

27. Muraviëv to Cassini, 10 February 1898, quoted in Zabriskie, *American–Russian Rivalry in the Far East*, p. 200.

to them. Thus, the open door note, instead of leading to a bilateral exchange of trade rights for recognition of Russia's dominant position in
Manchuria, had merely fogged the issue. To further complicate things,
Hay made his proposal not bilaterally but multilaterally, thereby drawing in Japan and the European powers. Hay may have feared that an
explicit bilateral deal with Russia, while perhaps guaranteeing American
trade, would provoke the partition he and his contemporaries feared and
lead to the exclusion of American trade from other sections of the Chinese
empire if not from Manchuria. Such a deal in realpolitik was not in the
American style, nor had the State Department yet come to such a clear
view of American needs in the Far East.

Elsewhere within the Russian government, the minister of finance took
a different reading of Hay's intentions. Sergei Witte, whose program of
railway construction was the spearhead for Russian penetration into
Manchuria, interpreted Hay's note as nothing more than a simple call
for equal commercial opportunity. Witte suggested to the minister of
foreign affairs a positive reply to the American proposal, and the Russian
response which ultimately made its way to Hay's desk followed Witte's
draft almost verbatim. Witte was prepared to guarantee the equality of
commercial opportunity which Hay desired but pointedly excluded the
Russian Liaotung leasehold from the guarantee. This was an important
reservation since it left Russia free to discriminate in trade at Dairen,
which was to become Manchuria's most important port. Witte's reply
also conditioned Russia's acceptance of the open door obligations on the
full agreement of the other powers to the same obligations. Here was
another important reservation, an easily implemented escape clause.
Witte's reply equaled Hay's proposal in ambiguity, and the minister of
foreign affairs adopted it as the easiest way out of a tangled situation.[28]

In July 1900 Hay added to the confusion with a second open door note,
this one in response to the talk of partition provoked by the Boxer rebellion. He followed a line favored by his adviser, W. W. Rockhill, and suggested to all of the powers a guarantee of China's integrity and independence, which the year before he had included only and incidentally in the
open door note to Britain. This was a treasured part of the passive open
door that had become increasingly hollow with foreign penetration. The
integrity principle conflicted, of course, with the hopes of reformers like
Denby or imperialists like Conger, all of whom desired for the United
States greater influence in China's administration, or even territorial

28. Witte to Muraviëv, 14 December 1899, excerpted in Romanov, *Russia in Manchuria*, pp.
175–76.

control. In addition, this insistence on maintaining China's integrity was largely incompatible with the tacit recognition of the Russian sphere of influence the year before. This new element of policy could be and was taken as an attack on this kind of sphere, for by creating exceptional economic, political, and military conditions beyond the control of the Chinese government, any enclave of foreign influence could not but violate this principle. Thus, Hay's integrity principle could serve as a handy bludgeon with which to beat the other powers for the privileges they had accumulated.

While Hay was in the midst of piloting his open door policy through the shoals created by the reservations of the powers, he briefly turned off on a new and totally divergent tack. The Chinese minister in Washington, Wu T'ing-fang, came to see Hay in November 1899, after Hay had sent out his open door notes to Russia, Britain, and Germany. Wu, who was not privy to their contents, was troubled by rumors that the United States might seize a piece of Chinese territory for itself, and he wanted a denial from Hay. Hay's disturbing reply was

that if at any future time, which I did not now anticipate, we should desire any conveniences or accommodations on the coast of China we should approach the Chinese Government directly upon the subject.[29]

Wu's government was then in the midst of a major crisis with Italy over a concession on the China coast and obviously wanted Wu to find out where the United States stood. But it could not have been measurably reassured by Hay's qualified denial of current interest in what he euphemistically called "conveniences or accommodations" on Chinese territory.

A year later Hay took another step toward a forward policy. Conger and the secretary of the navy had apparently convinced him of the need for an American naval station on the China coast. In November 1900 Hay cabled to Conger an order to try to secure Samsah Bay in Fukien province. The Japanese had an interest in this area and protested the intrusion in terms—"to preserve the territorial entity of that Empire"—which the secretary of state must have recognized as his own. Embarrassed by the protest, Hay withdrew his instructions to Conger.[30] His attempt had shown though that, while promoting the traditional policy of the open door, Hay could at the same time get caught red-handed implementing,

29. Hay to Choate, 13 November 1899, Hay Papers, Manuscript Division, Library of Congress. See also Hay to Wu, 11 November 1899, Hay Papers.
30. Hay to Conger, telegram, 19 November 1900, DIC; and Japanese minister to the United States to the secretary of state, 11 December 1900, FRUS, 1915, pp. 114–15.

perhaps unknowingly, bold innovations. For a moment Hay seemed to hesitate, undecided whether the open door policy was a viable alternative to imperialism.

With his notes of 1899 and 1900 Hay had formalized the concept of the passive open door. Nonetheless, his notes, together with his heretical attempt at securing a naval base, indicate he had neither a consistent nor a coherent view of the problem which the spheres of influence, particularly Russia's Manchurian sphere, posed for American policy. Americans, like Chinese, were having a difficult time adjusting their vision and their inherited principles to new conditions in Manchuria. They were still torn between the beautiful simplicity and effortless effectiveness for the United States of the old passive open door, on the one hand, and, on the other, the need for a more energetic and aggressive policy to preserve from loss the perceived interests, present and future, of the United States in China. They hung back, unsure whether to attack or to accept the "new conditions" in China. Hay's open door notes, almost studied in their ambiguities, accurately reflected his own and his subordinates' policy gropings. The eventual acceptance at home of Hay's position by traditionalists and activists alike indicated how much of both views Hay had embodied.

At the turn of the century there flowed from the pens of a handful of American publicists a series of works which in sum argued forcefully and explicitly for a more active and adventuresome China policy. The publicists were no more aware than any other group of Americans of the problems China faced in defending her northeast frontier, but they were unique—and far ahead of their contemporaries—because they astutely recognized the developing spheres of influence as a potential threat to the future of American trade and investment and offered a coherent program to cope with them. They saw that if American trade should run into political obstacles abroad, the repercussions would reach back to the United States. Overproduction would then overwhelm the domestic market, creating social and political as well as economic chaos. Since they regarded a flourishing foreign trade as essential to the future prosperity of the United States, they logically concluded that their government would have to devote greater energy and foresight to defending both investment and commercial markets overseas. China, which lay conveniently at the other end of America's Pacific trade route, had not yet been formally staked out by the other world powers and thus seemed the most promising site to implement this new imperative national economic program. Since

United States trade interests were more intensely threatened in Manchuria than anywhere else in that empire, it was essentially to that region that the publicists wished their government to direct its efforts. The evolving relations between China and the powers required this change in policy; at the same time America's newly won place on the stage of international politics finally conferred the prestige and self-confidence to attempt it.

Of these advocates of an activist policy Brooks Adams took the most serious view of the danger to the United States in the situation in the Far East. Adams's literary shot in the dark, *America's Economic Supremacy,* was in great measure precipitated by the Manchurian crisis. In Adams's view, that region was unquestionably already Russian; if the forces of central European civilization continued to move across northern China toward domination of the entire subcontinent, they would block America's westward movement. The resulting altered world balance "might shake American society to its foundation, and would probably make the scale of life to which our people are habituated impossible."[31] Adams drew his conclusion starkly and boldly. "To-day the nation has to elect whether to continue to expand, cost what it may, or to resign itself to the approach of a relatively stationary period."[32] The China problem would continue to plague Americans, Adams warned. Whether they chose to run or to fight, they could not escape. The best course, thus, was for the country to follow an energetic and assertive policy in China which would guarantee for the United States a more secure future. Adams challenged his countrymen to prepare mentally and militarily for the long grind of protecting their commerce.

Brooks Adams enjoyed the company of Josiah Strong, Alfred Thayer Mahan, and Charles A. Conant in his concern for the China market.[33] The latter three authors also published in 1900 works which collectively warned of the impending glut in the home market and of the exhaustion of the continental frontier. They, like Adams, directed their countrymen to begin seriously looking abroad to the markets of East Asia. The American government, they warned, would have to abandon the old principles of isolation and nonentanglement and adopt new expedients in order to guarantee Americans an equal opportunity in the increasingly stiff commercial rivalry among the great powers.

---

31. *America's Economic Supremacy* (New York, 1900), p. 43.
32. Ibid., p. 49.
33. Strong, *Expansion under New World Conditions* (New York, 1900); Mahan, "Effects of Asiatic Conditions upon International Policies," *North American Review* 171 (November 1900): 609–26; and Conant, *The United States in the Orient: The Nature of the Economic Problem* (New York, 1900).

> The United States cannot afford to adhere to a policy of isolation
> while other nations are reaching out for the command of these new
> markets. . . .
>
>   . . . Whether the United States shall actually acquire territorial
> possessions, shall set up captain-generalships and garrisons, whether
> they shall adopt the middle ground of protecting sovereignties nominal-
> ly independent, or whether they shall content themselves with naval
> stations and diplomatic representatives as the basis for asserting their
> rights to the free commerce of the East, is a matter of detail.[34]

The general course advocated by Adams, Strong, Conant, and Mahan
found specific application to the Manchurian crisis in Albert J. Beveridge's
The Russian Advance. He daringly and brilliantly drew together a prescription for an activist policy of dollar diplomacy long before Philander C.
Knox came on the foreign policy scene. Beveridge, like the other publicists,
believed in the promise of a booming China maket for Americans and the
certainty of disruption in American life if the market were closed to
American products.[35]

During a visit to Russian-occupied Manchuria in 1901 Beveridge had
been impressed with its commercial and strategic potential.

> Here, then, is an empire capable of sustaining fifty millions of people,
> and with scarcely more than fifteen million inhabitants at present; an
> empire with two of the best ports in the world for commercial and
> military purposes; . . . an empire which, in its strategic situation on the
> Pacific and in all Oriental affairs is second only to the commanding
> position of Japan itself.[36]

He had become convinced that Russia was firmly fastening her grip on
the region; however, her policy disturbed him not as an immediate threat
but as a potential one to the future development of United States interests
there. Beveridge realistically recognized that along with the railway
necessarily went "concrete and tangible power."[37] The problem was to
balance Russian railway penetration and the sphere of influence it had
created in Manchuria with an equally active American commercial
policy.

Beveridge's policy prescription boiled down to a call for a more energetic
government role in protecting the national stake in China. The means had

---

34. Conant, *The United States in the Orient*, p. 29.
35. *The Russian Advance* (New York, 1904), pp. 171, 179–80.
36. Ibid., p. 9.
37. Ibid., p. 170.

to fit the ends—keeping the door open or else prying it open where it seemed closed, as in Manchuria.

> Here are markets. . . . Let us occupy them. But be it remembered that they are not to be occupied by polite notes or banquet speeches. They have got to be occupied by ships, commercial agents, modern methods, the expenditure of money, and the resourceful vigilance of a firm and comprehensive business policy.[38]

The government first had to secure for itself a voice in the councils of the powers commensurate with the American stake in China's future.[39] Only with that accomplished would the government be in a position to aggressively promote trade and the internal reforms essential to smoothing the way for American goods.

Beveridge regarded the construction of railways by Americans as the key to promoting trade and guarding the position of the United States in the China market. Railway development would facilitate the distribution of American goods and open up new markets in the interior. "Wherever a line of railroad goes, trade goes, and where a line of railroad goes the trade of the nation which built it is chiefly carried."[40] The railroad could serve the United States as it had Russia in laying down and exploiting a sphere of influence.

> Two or three lines of road, built by our citizens and backed by our government with its indorsement (not necessarily financial, of course) and diplomatic aid, could be built in China, and a firm foothold could thus be secured, from which the future of American commerce in the Orient might be safeguarded and satisfactorily and practically increased.[41]

According to Beveridge, other essential goals in the government's program should include the expansion of the merchant marine; reform of the consular service; and creation of a single, effective financial instrument of national policy to avoid self-defeating competition among American interests. The navy should have a base on the China coast to facilitate defense of American interests as well as to impress the easily awed "Oriental." Businessmen should avail themselves of their own and their government's resources to promote their products and to adapt methods

38. Ibid., pp. 206–07.
39. Ibid., p. 178.
40. Ibid., p. 189. Beveridge's program of reforms is outlined on pp. 180–202.
41. Ibid., p. 190.

and goods to Chinese practices and tastes. In sum, Beveridge's program for the creation and defense of an informal commercial empire pointed to the conclusion that new opportunities and necessities, not outdated principles, must guide American policy.

It is said "self-government" and "non-interference" and many other excellent things are American characteristics; and so they are. But *the* American characteristic is adaptability. We ought to adapt ourselves, and will, to the world's geography, and to our trade as influenced by that.[42]

Traditional principles of policy had failed in the Far East. The United States, to protect itself from its own dynamic growth, would have to act forcefully to keep China open as the new frontier of finance and commerce. Beveridge's prescription for an active Manchurian policy was to find increasing numbers of influential supporters in the years ahead.

42. Ibid., pp. 206–07.

3: INITIAL POSSIBILITIES AND PROBLEMS OF COOPERATION

What were the chances of American–Chinese cooperation in Manchuria? Each had an interest in keeping it out of Russian hands. And, in the abstract, the concept of the open door was elastic enough to encompass the interests of each. Significantly, some Chinese officials gave thought to the possibilities of cooperation. There are good reasons for the infamously culture-bound Chinese having seen through their prejudices to a path of cooperation. In part it was the desperation of China's diplomatic situation between 1895 and 1901 which drove them to make the first tentative efforts toward enlisting the United States in their cause.

Equally important was the existence of officials who had learned to move with facility through the cultural maze of the West. The likes of Wu T'ing-fang, for example, fluent in two cultures, were not to be found in the stable of American diplomatic talent. He was born in Singapore in 1842, returned to his ancestral land in Kwangtung four years later and was educated in Hong Kong. At thirty-three he left for London, where he took up legal studies at Lincoln's Inn. After graduation he returned to Hong Kong to practice law and advise the colonial administration on matters concerning the Chinese community. The skills and experience acquired abroad brought Wu invitations to serve the Ch'ing. In 1882 he finally accepted, perhaps for financial reasons. Wu moved up the bureaucratic ladder under the patronage of the late Ch'ing statesmen, Li Hung-chang and, later, Chang Chih-tung and Yüan Shih-k'ai. The knotty problems of railway affairs initially occupied Wu. Then in 1895 he assisted Li and Chang Yin-huan with peace negotiations with Japan at Shimonoseki and in 1897 again joined Chang in coping with the German intrusion in Shantung. As a diplomat, Wu practiced what one acquaintance vividly described as

> an *enfant terrible* style of conversation, of impertinent questions and cryptic answers, most novel and effective. His perfectly natural simplicity and bonhomie passed for the subtlest form of Oriental diplomacy.[1]

1. J. O. P. Bland, *Recent Events and Present Policies in China* (Philadelphia, 1912), pp. 212–13.

Wu brought to his official duties strong convictions on the urgency of recovering economic rights and political control from foreign hands and on the wisdom of cooperating with the commercial powers in a broadly applied policy of the open door.

Wu was well acquainted with the United States. Nearly every year from 1896 to 1909 he was diplomatically in close contact with China's United States policy. He served as minister to the United States between 1896 and 1902 and then again between 1907 and 1909. He helped negotiate the commercial treaty of 1903 and held a post in the Chinese foreign office, the Wai-wu Pu, between 1903 and 1907, contentious years in Sino–American relations. As early as 1895 Wu had suggested that the United States was a nation whose help might be useful in one of the succession of crises confronting China.[2] In again recommending the United States to the court in 1898, Wu noted that the United States had shown itself to be "most respectful and submissive," traditional attributes of a good tribute state.[3]

Some officials more influential than Wu shared his optimistic view on the possibility of making the United States a partner in defense. The victory over Spain in 1898 and the acquisition of Pacific holdings, which together announced America's arrival as a world power, made the role more credible. Nearly invariably in the late 1890s and during the period of Russian occupation of Manchuria, Chinese officials grouped the United States with Japan and Britain as the mainstays of the open door and China's independence.[4]

The first official to test the possibilities of cooperation with the United States was Chang Chih-tung, the governor general of Hunan and Hupeh and an advocate of using the commercial powers to check the ambitions of

---

See also Wu's diverting but lightweight memoir, *America Through the Spectacles of an Oriental Diplomat* (New York, 1914); Shen Yün-lung, *Chin-tai wai-chiao jen-wu lun-p'ing* [Discussions on personalities in modern diplomacy] (Taipei, 1968), pp. 122–28; and Howard L. Boorman, ed., *Biographical Dictionary of Republican China* (New York, 1967–1971), 3:453–55. Wu T'ing-kuang, *Wu T'ing-fang li-shih* [A history of Wu T'ing-fang] (Shanghai, 1922), essentially an anecdotal account, has little to say about Wu's activities and views during his years as a Ch'ing official. A recent attempt to piece together from limited source material a picture of Wu's life is Linda P. Shin, "China in Transition: The Role of Wu T'ing-fang (1842–1922)" (Ph. D. diss., University of California at Los Angeles, 1970).

2. Wu, address to the central government, 1895, in Yü Pao-hsüan, comp., *Huang-ch'ao hsü-ai wen-pien* [A collection of literature written under the ruling dynasty] (1902 preface; Taipei reprint, 1965), ch. 3.7.

3. Wu, supplementary memorial, 10 February 1898, CWS:KH, ch. 129.16–17. In addition, see Wu's telegraphic supplementary memorial, 26 July 1900, in Shen Tsu-hsien, comp., *Yang-shou-yüan tsou-i chi-yao* [Selected memorials of Yüan Shih-k'ai] (Taipei reprint, 1966), pp. 178–79.

4. For examples from the late 1890s, see Liu Shu-t'ang (governor of Honan), memorial, 4 April 1896, CWS:KH, ch. 125.13–16; and Sheng Hsüan-huai to Chang Chih-tung, telegram, 7 May 1898, YCTK, ch. 32.2.

France, Russia, and Germany. Chang, who needed someone to finance and build railways in central China, looked to Americans. However, the contract which the agents of an American enterprise, the American China Development Company, proposed in 1897 for the Hankow–Peking railway got relations off on a bad start. Chang found that their terms gave "all the rights and privileges to the American merchants. I consider the intention behind their coming deceitful in the extreme."[5] Despite the initial bad impression, hardly more than a year later Chang gave the same company the prized contract for a different line, this one between Hankow and Canton through a heavily populated and commercially important region.[6]

Both Chang and the central government had supported the construction of the Hankow–Canton line as an important self-strengthening measure and had given it priority over other projected lines. At first Chang had hoped to construct it with Chinese funds, but when this had proved impossible he had begun to look abroad for money. Soon he was besieged by European commercial and banking agents, all backed by their governments. Chang circumvented the politically suspect claims of the Europeans by giving the contract to the Americans in 1898.[7] Chang apparently based his decision on his estimate that the United States had neither political ambitions in China nor, in any case, the military power to enforce such ambitions and that, therefore, he could safely deal with the American company. "The United States is a most distant country from us and still

5. Chang to Sheng, telegram, 12 March 1897, YCTK, ch. 26.9. Sheng, Chang's assistant in charge of railway affairs, agreed. "The evils of it [the proposed contract] are very great. The English are more compromising." Sheng to Jung-lu, telegram, 10 May 1897, YCTK, ch. 27.2.

6. Percy H. Kent, *Railway Enterprise in China* (London, 1907), pp. 109–21, remains the best general account in English of this railway contract. William R. Braisted, "The United States and the American China Development Company," *Far Eastern Quarterly* 11 (1952): 147–65, adds material from the State Department archives but fails to improve appreciably on the story told in Kent. An account, based essentially on printed Chinese primary sources and highly critical of American railway imperialism in the late 1890s, is Sun Yü-t'ang, "Chung-Jih chia-wu chancheng hou Mei-ti-kuo chu-i chüeh-to Lu-Han, Ching-Chen, yü Yüeh-Han chu t'ieh-lu ti yinmou" [American imperialist plots to seize the Peking–Hankow, Tientsin–Chinkiang, and Hankow–Canton railways after the Sino–Japanese War of 1894], in *Mei-ti-kuo chu-i ching-chi ch'in-Hua shih lun-ts'ung* [Collected articles on the history of American imperialist economic aggression against China] (Peking, 1953), pp. 16–43. Li En-han's "Chung-Mei shou-hui Yüeh-Han lu-ch'üan chiao-she" [Sino–American negotiations over the recovery of rights over the Hankow–Canton railroad], in *Chi-k'an* [Bulletin of the Institute of Modern History, Academia Sinica], no. 1 (1969): 149–215, is the most comprehensive account, drawn both from English language and Chinese primary sources, of the much disputed railway concession and its ultimate repurchase by the Chinese government.

7. Chang et al., memorial, December 1897 or January 1898, YCTK, ch. 2.10; Chang, telegraphic memorial, 28 March 1898, YCTK, ch. 21.11; and Hsü T'ung-hsin, *Chang Wen-hsiangkung nien-p'u* [A chronological biography of Chang Chih-tung] (Taipei reprint, 1969), pp. 110–12, 124, 130.

has no intention of taking advantage of our territory," he observed.[8] In addition, Chang counted on the American-built railway to create an equipoise to railway concessions already secured by other powers, leaving no single power dominant in any region.

For several years after concluding the contract Chang remained hopeful that the project would work out as he had planned. Even though the American company made new demands, Wu T'ing-fang, who was handling the negotiations, urged acceptance with the hope of getting in return some American diplomatic support for China, then in the midst of the Boxer troubles. Sheng Hsüan-huai, Chang's assistant in charge of railway affairs, endorsed this view. Chang accepted their advice. He still hoped the urgently needed rail line would soon be completed without loss of political rights.[9]

This railway contract briefly buoyed hopes on both sides of the Pacific. In the United States it fed dreams of great financial gain and hopes for constructing an American railway empire. In China, American efforts promised to provide an important trunk line railway speedily, on financial terms no worse than others demanded, and without political entanglements.

Despite the auspicious beginning, the Hankow–Canton railway contract was ultimately to prove a major obstacle to cooperation between the two nations. It contained the seeds of diplomatic controversy. By 1903 the Belgians had secured real control of the American China Development Company and had occupied key company posts in China and in New York. The control by the Belgians, whose finances often went in tandem with Russian diplomacy, stirred Chinese suspicions. The company's lack of progress—it had built only an insignificant section of the line by 1903—and charges that its chief engineer and agent in China was both corrupt and antagonistic toward Chinese officials further blemished the relationship. It now appeared that Chang, by granting the concessions to Americans, had managed neither to keep it outside the

8. Chang et al., memorial, June or July 1902, YCTK, ch. 7.17. See also his memorial of 8 August 1895, CWS:KH, ch. 116.35–37, discounting the United States as a power in the Far East.

9. Hsü, *Chang Wen-hsiang-kung nien-p'u*, p. 135. Wu's telegram is summarized in a memorial in YCTK, ch. 7.18. Indeed, Chinese acceptance of the American company's revised terms may have been considered by Chang and Wu as clearing the way for appeals to the United States government for sympathy during the Boxer crisis. These appeals, however, fell on deaf ears. See the message sent in the name of the emperor to the American president, reproduced in Conger to the Tsung-li Yamen, 20 July 1900, WWP: Mei-kuo chao-hui [Communications from the United States]; and appeals to the State Department from Chang and Wu on 21 June and 11 November 1900, noted in Hsü, *Chang Wen-hsiang-kung nien-p'u*, pp. 133, 140.

pressures of international diplomacy, to gain the sympathy of the United States government, nor to get the line speedily constructed. The company's mismanagement gave the Chinese government cause to reconsider its dealings with the American businessmen and with the American government, which had fully endorsed the company's integrity and ability. In addition, the acquisition by the United States of a Pacific empire in the intervening years and her participation in both the Boxer expedition and the subsequent occupation of Peking cast doubt on Chang's earlier estimate of her limited role in Far Eastern affairs. As a result, the stage was set for canceling the contract and writing off as a failure this attempt at limited Sino–American cooperation.

The company had been compromised not only by Chinese misgivings but also by the American financial market, too weak to underwrite railway construction in China. Indeed, it had taken Wu T'ing-fang nearly a year to find any American ready to invest in the Hankow-Canton railway. He had discovered that interest was practically nonexistent. "They invariably said that their money could be just as easily, and just as profitably, invested in their own country, and with better security than was obtainable in China."[10] The American China Development Company had been organized as a speculative venture, inadequately capitalized. The death in December 1898 of Senator Calvin Brice, a New York railway lawyer on whose financial, entrepreneurial, and political connections the project depended, had further undercut the company's domestic position. The company's sad performance in the years thereafter proved that the United States still had no need to export capital—China market rhetoric to the contrary.

Ministers Denby and Conger bemoaned the lack of capital and interested entrepreneurs necessary to keep the door open in China for late-coming American merchants and financiers. Denby complained that Americans would not "touch" large Chinese loans and that they lacked interest in making the China market a commercial reality.[11] Conger too found American investors and industrialists frustratingly uninterested. In 1898, on the subject of the China market, he warned, "If our capitalists really desire a share they must have brains and money here."[12] When neither appeared on the scene, activists were confronted with the contradiction between the dream of Americans leading in the economic

10. Wu, *America Through the Spectacles of an Oriental Diplomat,* pp. 71–72.
11. Denby to Olney, 25 January 1896, and Denby to Sherman, 24 May 1897 and 20 October 1897, all in MCD.
12. Conger to William R. Day, 31 July 1898, MCD.

development of China and their apparent preoccupation with developing their own country.

The failure of the Hankow–Canton railway project was ominous. A combination of the most financially powerful men in the United States—including J. P. Morgan, E. H. Harriman, Jacob H. Schiff, and the presidents of the National City Bank and of the Chase National Bank—had failed to get the brains and money to China to complete a straightforward job of railway building. The shadow of this failure should have hung heavily over subsequent attempts by the same financial moguls to penetrate the Manchurian market.

Obstacles of another sort, deriving in large measure from cultural differences between Americans and Chinese, also stood in the way of close cooperation at the turn of the century. The dispute over the treatment which the natives of one country received in the other country was the basic stumbling block. Here both displayed, despite their cultural differences, strikingly similar strains of xenophobia. Separated from each other by the broad Pacific, Americans and Chinese could talk of "friendly relations." At close quarters, contact between them tended to arouse mutual antipathy.

To Americans in China the occasional antiforeign riot and the sporadic popular antimissionary outburst were the best proof of the barbarity and reactionary character of the Chinese and the impotence of their government. That foreigners, as the agents of progress, should be safe in China was for Americans in the 1890s a self-evident proposition. They hotly resented any Chinese expression to the contrary.

In parallel, many Americans at home proved as inhospitable as the Chinese to strangers from the opposite side of the Pacific. They regarded the "celestials" with contempt and treated them to large doses of violence. Such outbursts were officially condoned or winked at, just as was often the case in China. To Americans like Denby there was no contradiction in the view that Chinese in the United States should be closely restricted while foreigners in China should enjoy full protection and privileges. "That all countries have the inherent right to exclude all foreigners from their borders, either as temporary or permanent residents, admits of no kind of doubt."[13] Denby defended the American exclusion policy with arguments which could have as easily come from a Chinese xenophobe.

13. The quote is from Charles Denby, *China and Her People* (Boston, 1906), 2:100. Denby repeats this view in 2:104. For his comments on the place of the foreigner in China, see 2:70–72, 89–90.

We cannot safely amalgamate into our political system people in great numbers who cannot in a generation be made to understand the principles on which our government is based. . . .

. . . The "yellow peril" [read for Chinese "foreign peril"] would attack our institutions, our customs, and habits, and overwhelm them.[14]

Just as massacres of missionaries in China had been for some time an explosive issue in the United States, so also was the treatment of Chinese by Americans becoming a controversial issue in China. Federal legal restrictions, official harassment, and outbursts of popular violence usually condoned by local officials added up, particularly in the western states, to an antiforeignism the virulence of which the Chinese only in the northern provinces, and then only in 1900, were able to meet and surpass.

The ministers to the United States and other Ch'ing officials had long been sensitive to this nativism. The minister, invariably a native of Kwang-tung like most of the Chinese emigrants to the United States, was bound for both personal and official reasons to resent and to attempt to ameliorate the abusive treatment about which his fellow provincials complained. In a recurrent refrain, minister after minister protested the abuse heaped on Chinese visitors and residents. Why should the American government, they asked rhetorically, countenance the oppression of Chinese and fail to redress wrongs when such an attitude and actions by the Chinese government would be cause not just for diplomatic protest but for a display of force as well?[15] One Chinese minister, speaking before an American audience, bluntly drew the damaging comparison.

More Chinese subjects have been murdered by mobs in the United States during the last twenty-five years than all the Americans who have been murdered in China in similar riots. . . . In every instance where Americans have suffered from mobs, the authorities have made reparation for the losses, and rarely has the punishment of death failed to be inflicted upon the guilty offenders. On the other hand, I am sorry to say that I cannot recall a single instance where the penalty of death has been visited on any member of the mobs in the United States

14. Ibid., 2:110–11.
15. Jung Hung to the State Department, 9 March 1880, in Chu Shih-chia, *Mei-kuo p'o-hai Hua-kung shih-liao* [Historical materials on American oppression of Chinese laborers] (Peking, 1959), pp. 60–61; Chang Yin-huan, *San-chou jih-chi* [A diary of three continents], reproduced in part in A Ying (Ch'ien Hsing-ts'un), *Fan-Mei Hua-kung chin-yüeh wen-hsüeh chi* [Collected literature on opposition to the American treaty excluding Chinese laborers] (Peking, 1960), pp. 581–82; Yang Ju, memorial, 5[?] May 1894, in Chu, *Mei-kuo p'o-hai Hua-kung shih-liao*, p. 141; and Wu T'ing-fang to Hay, 19 May 1902, FRUS, 1902, p. 216.

guilty of the death of Chinese, and in only two instances out of many has indemnity been paid for the losses sustained by the Chinese.[16]

Appeals to fairness, equity, and treaty rights as well as international law all proved unavailing. In a remarkable imitation of the procedures for which Americans castigated the Chinese government, these appeals by Chinese ministers to the State Department were passed on time and again to local governments, to the Treasury Department, or to the Department of the Interior and finally lost in the bureaucracy of an unsympathetic government backed by the most vocal of the citizenry.[17] Aside from provoking Chinese nationalists, the American policy of discrimination alienated such rising Chinese officials from Kwangtung as Wu T'ing-fang, T'ang Shao-i, and Liang Tun-yen, all of whom had been educated abroad, were viewed by the State Department as "advanced" and "progressive," and were otherwise friendly to the United States. American lack of hospitality toward the Chinese thus created a potentially strong anti-American sentiment in China, consequently rendering cooperation on issues of common concern more difficult.

Another obstacle in the path of cooperation was the attitude of many Americans, who, like other Westerners, carried a stereotype of the Chinese as passive, cowardly, unpatriotic, conservative people. Symptomatic of this set of attitudes was Arthur H. Smith's *Chinese Characteristics* (first published in Shanghai in 1890), a kind of bible for Americans on the "care and feeding" of Chinese. This and subsequent editions occupied an honored place in the home of every old China hand and stood prominently on the bookshelf in the American legation in Peking. Smith's peculiar interpretation of the Chinese as reflected in such chapter titles as "The Absence of Nerves," "Intellectual Turbidity," "The Disregard of Time," "The Absence of Altruism," and "The Disregard of Accuracy" perpetuated a long-popular view of this people. As one student of the period has neatly put it,

> Old China Hands built up a sort of cracker-barrel philosophy of the Treaty Ports on the proper way to handle "Orientals" and "Oriental authorities." The latter were never to be trusted and would squirm out of international commitments as soon as pressure was removed: ergo,

16. Liang Ch'eng, minister to the United States, 1902–1907, quoted in Arthur H. Smith, *China and America To-day: A Study of Conditions and Relations* (New York, 1907), p. 165.

17. See Notes from the Chinese legation in the United States to the Department of State as well as Notes to foreign legations in the United States (both microfilms of records of the Department of State, National Archives) for examples of this system of obfuscation and delay.

never remove the pressure. It was only under the tutelage of the white man . . . that they might serve in commercial and fiscal administration. It was, moreover, the mandarins and not the people that wanted to exclude foreigners. It was an integral part of the folklore that the Chinese, a trading and business people, would participate in foreign trade on a vast scale . . . once mandarin squeezes and obstructions were removed.[18]

The philosophy of the treaty ports tended to dominate thinking on China. Even newcomers to China, subjected to informal indoctrination within the closed foreign community, quickly fell into step. The views of an American engineer, formulated during a brief sojourn in the country, are typical. He found the Chinese "a great mass without cohesion," "a huge jelly-fish" with a "natural tendency to deal with the strongest." His conclusion that China "is a nation which died centuries ago, but which has never been buried, and continues to remain above ground as a sort of vivified mummy" was commonplace.[19] These views also prevailed in the United States, propagated above all by articulate American missionary-educators during the latter part of the nineteenth century.

The Peking legation under Ministers Denby and Conger also subscribed to this generally unanimous opinion on China and the Chinese. The implications it carried for relations between the United States and China were of the first importance, for it limited the perspective of those Americans who reported on developments in China and those who made China policy. In particular, American diplomats were deeply impressed by the submissiveness of the Chinese and frequently commented on it. Lacking patriotic courage, Chinese leaders easily fell under the influence of the most intimidating, aggressive, and selfish of the powers (like Russia) while ignoring the reasonable advice and requests of the pacific and friendly powers (like the United States). Charles Denby's observation in 1897 that "Li Hung-chang is the obedient servant of Russia" is a typical

18. Nathan A. Pelcovits, *Old China Hands and the Foreign Office* (New York, 1948), pp. 6–7. Donald F. Lach, *China in the Eyes of Europe: The Sixteenth Century* (Chicago, 1968), and Jonathan Spence, *To Change China: Western Advisers in China 1620–1960* (Boston, 1969), offer numerous examples of the fundamentally similar feeling of superiority and of an equally basic misunderstanding of China which gripped other foreigners in other ages. Harold Isaacs, *Scratches on Our Minds* (New York, 1958), is an admirable attempt at tracing the shifting stereotypes which Americans have applied to China down to our day. Isaacs's observations are borne out by Robert McClellan, *Heathen Chinee: A Study of American Attitudes toward China, 1890–1905* (Columbus, Ohio, 1970).

19. William B. Parsons, *An American Engineer in China* (New York, 1900), pp. 135, 142–43, 172. Denby commented in a similar vein: "The Chinese are without courage or spirit and have a horror of war." Denby to Sherman, 19 November 1897, MCD.

example of the simplistic conclusions which Americans repeatedly drew from their generalizations on Chinese national character.[20] This view provided a catchall interpretation for events beyond the understanding of the legation or its patience to explain. Its pithiness and apparent clarity depended on the popular assumption that the Chinese were to be dominated and not treated as equals. The ring of conviction it carried in the midst of the rumor-plagued and politically uncertain atmosphere of Peking made it a stock phrase in official dispatches.

From this observation of Chinese lack of backbone, American diplomats concluded that only the commercial powers stood between China and partition. "The people of China would make no opposition to the partition of the Empire," Denby wrote back to his superiors. "They would rather welcome it, and would gladly transfer their allegiance to a European power."[21] Clearly China's defense was not to be entrusted to the Chinese. Even their cooperation would be a hindrance. One defended the Chinese with the distant hope that time would be gained for the forces of progress to wear down their blind conservatism and finally enable them to defend themselves.

In this assessment enthusiasts of a more forward China policy differed hardly a whit from the more cautious advocates of the traditional open door policy. Both groups looked askance at the Chinese. The activist Beveridge, in a variation on an old theme, observed that

> the two elements at the bottom of Chinese national incapacity are, on the one hand, individual selfishness, so profound that we cannot fathom it; and, on the other hand, a singular respect for power and force, which is the common characteristic of all Oriental peoples.[22]

John Hay, who favored a more conservative policy than did Beveridge, was equally intent on ignoring the Chinese. In 1899 Hay had not even bothered to inform the Chinese of his open door proposition.[23] The defense of American interests in Manchuria was a task too important to share with the Chinese.

Americans were convinced that China's difficulties in defending Manchuria were rooted in conservative attitudes and an outmoded cultural tradition and had basically nothing to do with foreign relations or internal politics. Even Americans on the scene, who could have learned the most,

20. Denby to Sherman, 2 April 1897, MCD.
21. Denby to Sherman, 11 December 1897, MCD.
22. Albert J. Beveridge, *The Russian Advance* (New York, 1904), p. 175.
23. Hay to Choate, 13 November 1899, Hay Papers, Manuscript Division, Library of Congress. See also Hay to Wu, 11 November 1899, Hay Papers.

tended to isolate themselves in the islands of Western influence in Peking and the treaty ports, safely away from the natives and their affairs. There thus was no motive or opportunity for Americans to search out China's reasons—cultural, strategic, and symbolic—for defending Manchuria or to appreciate her continuing effort to devise an effective defense. Americans substituted the folklore of the old China hands for knowledge and contact. They looked on China as a strange land where everything seemed perversely different, if not exactly contrary, to civilized Western norms. They fell back on a body of stereotypes and clichés on the Chinese character. It provided a secure refuge from uncertainty and from the labor of finding a new basis of knowledge and understanding which might reveal among other things China's problems in Manchuria and the variety of her responses to them. This picture of the kinks in the Chinese character carried over with minor variations from the 1890s into the following decade. It weighed like a dead hand on policy.

PART TWO

FIRST CONTACTS, 1901–1907

4: THE RUSSIAN OCCUPATION OF MANCHURIA

It was in the aftermath of the Boxer rebellion that Chinese and American leaders first established contact over the Manchurian crisis. From 1901 to 1903 the American government showed increasing concern about the Russian threat to United States interests in Manchuria. However, tangible American stakes remained small and the government's commitment to defend them consequently limited. In addition, the Peking legation, poorly informed and working on dubious assumptions, never gave serious thought to the possibility of cooperation with China in defense of Manchuria. The State Department, in turn, was no more inclined than the legation staff to give China's Manchurian problems a close, sympathetic look. Yet Manchuria continued to preoccupy Americans, principally as a symbol of their China dreams; events there were for them an omen for the future of all China.

Chinese leaders, in the wake of the Boxer fiasco and the Russian occupation of Manchuria, finally realized that the Manchurian question had entered a new phase and that their policy would have to reflect this change. The prime problem was no longer that of preventing foreign penetration. In the late 1890s the Russians had gained a secure foothold which, as they had demonstrated in 1900, they were prepared to defend. Under these new conditions the aim of Ch'ing diplomacy in Manchuria through the remaining years of the dynasty was to limit, balance, and, ultimately, diminish foreign influence while augmenting its own control. Ch'ing officials thus resumed the search for a better approach to the problem of defending the Manchurian frontier.

The reports sent to the central government by Manchurian officials after the Russian occupation painted an alarming picture. Although Chinese officials, many of whom had fled either the Boxers or the Russians, returned one by one to their posts to take up the reins of the administration, the Russian military retained a virtual veto over their decisions. For example, Russia had so limited Chinese troops that Chinese officials could not even quell banditry. They were left with the appearance of authority

without the reality—"a helpless dignified aloofness," as one knowledgeable eyewitness described it.[1] Their provinces disrupted by the popular
turmoil and foreign invasion of the previous year, the three military
governors were quick to admit that the situation, particularly in regard to
suppressing banditry and negotiating with the Russians, was completely
beyond them and that they were without a plan. Their only hope was for
the Wai-wu Pu, the recently reorganized Chinese foreign office, to negotiate
a Russian withdrawal.[2] In addition, they asked the central government for
funds to begin reconstruction, to encourage colonization in order to block
Russian seizures of territory, and to develop natural resources so that
Russia would not gather them in her own hand and to her own profit.
Without financial strength, one military governor warned the court,
Manchuria could not hope to recover from the devastating blow she had
suffered, let alone to resume her own defense. Manchuria desperately
needed troops, money, and diplomatic support.[3] With hands tied, Chinese
anthorities there waited impatiently for the central government to act.

These disturbing reports from China's northeast frontier increased
anxiety in a court already fearful for its own immediate future. Nominally
on an inspection tour of the provinces, the court was in reality in flight
from the allied army which had lifted the Boxer siege of the legations
and occupied Peking. The central government could do little more than
sympathize with the plight of the region since, for the moment, it was
immobilized by the cruel policy dilemma the occupation posed. To
acquiesce in Russian conditions for evacuating its army meant regaining
Manchuria in name but in reality losing control over it. At the same time
it would stimulate the other powers to imitate Russian methods elsewhere
in China. The obvious alternative, to oppose Russian demands, risked the
loss of even nominal control of Manchuria.

Empress Dowager Tz'u-hsi, who had resumed governing in 1898 after
relegating the youthful Kuang-hsü Emperor to the role of figurehead,
realized the gravity of the Manchurian situation. A politically astute

1. The quote is from Dugald Christie, *Thirty Years in Moukden 1883–1913* (New York, 1914)
p. 196.
2. See, e.g., Chang-shun (military governor of Kirin) to the Wai-wu Pu, 2 November 1901 and
4 January 1902, and memorials by Sa-pao (acting military governor of Heilungkiang) and by
Chang-shun, received by the Wai-wu Pu on 5 December 1901 and 23 December 1901 respectively, all in WWP: Tung-san-sheng chiao-she an [File on Manchurian negotiations (1901)]. Also,
Tseng-ch'i (military governor of Fengtien), memorial, sent by the Grand Council to the Wai-wu
Pu on 4 June 1902, WWP: O-ping ch'e-t'ui Tung-sheng shan-hou an [File on reconstruction
after Russian troop evacuation from Manchuria].
3. Sa-pao, memorial, 6 January 1902, *Hsi-hsün ta-shih chi* [Journal of the western inspection
trip] (n.p., foreword dated 1933), comp. by Wang Liang and published as a supplement to *CWS*
ch. 11.37–40.

woman whose dignity, age (sixty-seven years in 1900), and talents commanded the loyalty of her officials, she was to oversee in the few years after the Boxer outbreak a consistent and cautious Manchurian policy, a contrast to the shifting and finally desperate efforts of previous years.

Tz'u-hsi determined on a course which balanced Russian expansionism against the interests of the commercial powers. China could not now appeal to arms in dealing with Russia's Manchurian ambitions and thus had to resort to a careful diplomatic game of neither grievously offending nor completely satisfying that power. At the same time, Chinese officials surreptitiously kept the commercial powers informed of Russia's demands. They hoped that by provoking the anxiety of these powers over Manchuria's safety they might create a counterweight to Russia without involving China in an unequal test of strength. If China could create this balance of power, she would be in a position to restore her authority in Manchuria and thus to reestablish the basis for the continued struggle to defend the frontier. But for now the only weapon in the arsenal of frontier defense was foreign policy. With it alone China hoped to recover her grip on Manchuria.

In pursuing this strategy of balancing foreign antagonisms, the court found it necessary also to balance off the divergent views of high officials. One point of view was expressed by Li Hung-chang, whose diplomatic ventures in the previous decade had resulted in his political eclipse. The empress dowager had recalled him to high office in 1900 to help extricate China from her post-Boxer difficulties. Once again Li wished to compromise with Russia, this time in order to regain Manchuria. The occupation was a *fait accompli* beyond China's power to reverse; resistance to Russian demands, he feared, would constitute an excuse for further encroachment. The other point of view was that of the Yangtze governor generals, who as in the late 1890s opposed Li's "pro-Russian" policy. They argued that China should instead engage the commercial powers against Russia. Britain, Japan, and the United States, in their eagerness to prevent Russia from seizing Manchiura, would safeguard the region for China. The court listened attentively and drew on both sets of recommendations with the hope of conciliating all the powers, keeping peace within officialdom, and, in the bargain, regaining Manchuria as well.

Li took the lead in trying to reach the accommodation in which he believed. In September 1900 he began secret discussions with an agent of the Russian minister of finance. By January 1901 the Russians had decided on thirteen points on which they conditioned their evacuation of Manchuria. The points included a Russian veto over the appointment of the

Manchurian military governors; a promise that China would not give to any third party concessions in Manchuria, Mongolia, or the provinces of northern China; and a provision for Russian administration of Manchurian customhouses. When Li objected, the Russian government, taking a conciliatory attitude, withdrew the thirteen points and further agreed to cancel a provisional agreement between the Fengtien military governor, Tseng-ch'i, and the govenor general of Liaotung, Alexieff, which the Chinese government had already repudiated. Soon, however, Russia resubmitted the old demands, somewhat modified in substance and phrasing, as a package of twelve demands. The only major change was the addition of certain economic concessions for Russia and the elimination of her claim to administer the Manchurian customs. On 25 February 1901 Minister of Finance Witte told Li to accept these demands or face the end of the talks.[4] When Li received this ultimatum, he advised the court to accept the Russian terms for the restoration of Manchuria to China.

> All compromise has been exhausted and it is appropriate to conclude the matter as soon as possible. . . . They [the commercial powers] will not stand up against the Russian government but can only wag their tongues at us.[5]

March 1901, the deadline for the ultimatum, was a crisis-filled month in the Chinese capital. The court, fearful that Li's policy might result in the loss of China's northeast territory beyond the Great Wall, hesitated to either accept or reject the ultimatum. At the same time, Chang Chih-tung and Liu K'un-i, the most influential of the Yangtze governor generals, set the weight of their opinion against the Russian demands. To accept them would be not only to lose Manchuria but, worse, to invite partition of China. They argued that the central government must instead instruct its ministers in Britain, Japan, Germany, and the United States to inform those countries of the issues at stake and to enlist their support against Russia, promising in return equal commercial privileges in all of Manchuria. While diplomatic representations by the commercial powers in St. Petersburg would keep pressure off China, their commerce would prevent Russia from swallowing Manchuria. "What could be better,"

---

4. Masataka Kosaka, "Ch'ing Policy over Manchuria (1900–1903)," *Papers on China* 16 (1962): 128–29. This detailed account of China's Manchurian policy draws on an admirably broad range of diplomatic sources.
5. Li to the court, telegram, 27 February 1901, LNCYJ, 4:112–13.

Chang and Liu asked, "than a policy in which we involve them through commerce?"[6]

The court was unsure how to respond to that question. At first it improvised asking Russia to modify the terms for ending the occupation while simultaneously requesting the commercial powers to intervene on China's behalf. But finally, after agonizing over the decision until late March, the central government courageously decided to reject the Russian demands. On 4 April Russia abandoned her ultimatum and demands.[7]

The Manchurian crisis thus cooled, but the issue of how to cope with the Russian occupation remained. When Li resumed negotiations in July, Chang returned to the attack, criticizing Li's cautious diplomacy of compromise.

> The [proposed] treaty with Russia leaves us to administer Manchuria while entirely snatching away our political and military authority. It makes us no more than servants to control the Chinese there in behalf of the Russians. The advantages thus go to Russia; ours are the disadvantages. In name it is a treaty returning Manchuria to us while in fact it is a treaty ceding Manchuria to Russia.[8]

He again warned that approval of Russian demands would be an invitation for others to make similar demands and might lead to the final calamity —partition of China. "Those who in the slightest are loyal to their sovereign and love their country are pained."[9] Chang continued his criticism of Li's diplomacy well into the fall, when he again suggested that China use the commercial powers to break the Russian plot by promising an open door for commerce in Manchuria.

> Now, if we allow men from every country into the interior of that area, to live where they wish (but not to establish concessions), to make no differentiation between Chinese and foreigners in labor, commerce, mining and railroad interests, we then allow all countries to promote

6. Chang, Liu, and Sheng Hsüan-huai, joint telegram to the Wai-wu Pu, 21 March 1901, *Hsi-hsün ta-shih chi,* ch. 6.9–10. The activities of Chang and other opponents of the policy of accommodation during the crisis of February–March 1901 are summarized in Hsü T'ung-hsin, *Chang Wen-hisang-kung nien-p'u* [A chronological biography of Chang Chih-tung] (Taipei reprint, 1969), pp. 145–46. The Governor of Anhwei, Wang Chih-ch'un, supported his neighbors with much the same argument. The prospect of profits from railroads, mining, trade, and industry would be enough to lure the United States, Great Britain, and Japan into opposition to Russia. The plan had its dangers but none greater than Russian domination. Time, he warned, was too short for delay. Telegram to the Grand Council, 23 March 1901, *Hsi-hsün ta-shih chi,* ch. 6.17–19.
7. The court's hesitations during this time are chronicled in LNCYJ, 4:134–42.
8. Chang to the Wai-wu Pu, telegram, 27 July 1901, *Hsi-hsün ta-shih chi,* ch. 9.6–8.
9. Ibid.

their interest and each country shares in it. The authority to govern will still be ours to exercise. We will reap all the advantages. We will exercise customs, legal and police powers. Officials will be appointed by us and troops will be stationed by us. Our sovereignty will not in the slightest be lost.[10]

How was Secretary of State John Hay to react in early 1901 to the Russian occupation of Manchuria and to China's appeals for support? In shaping his response to the crisis, he relied in part on the reports from his diplomats in China. Hay no doubt counted himself fortunate to have W. W. Rockhill on the scene in Peking to keep him informed of developments. Rockhill brought to his diplomacy a knowledge of China rare among his countrymen. He had gone to China in 1884 to begin his apprenticeship as a diplomat under Denby. There he hoped to find the horizons and the opportunities for experience lacking in the United States. "Rather a cycle of Cathay or Korea than fifty years of America for me."[11] During those early years in China he continued to develop his expertise— more sinological than diplomatic—in China's inner Asian frontiers. After several years out of the diplomatic service, Rockhill rejoined it and served in the Balkans. Then in 1899 he became Hay's adviser on Chinese affairs.[12] The next year as commissioner to the Peking conference which followed the Boxer uprising, Rockhill returned to what he half jokingly called the "tedious and ill-paid exile" of the American diplomat in China.[13]

Rockhill was prepared better than any other important official in the service of the State Department to understand the Chinese on their own terms. Yet even he shared some of the attitudes common among his countrymen. For example, Rockhill, like Denby, had at first viewed with pleasure the extension of Japan's civilizing influence to China after 1895, then had become alarmed by the battle among the powers to obtain new privileges in China and by the danger it posed for American interests there. And he, like others, was at first uncertain how to cope with this problem. But gradually Rockhill had come to the conclusion that the best way to ensure an unhampered flow of trade and at the same time internal order in China was to strengthen the central government. He

10. Chang, memorial, 6 October 1901, in Wang Shu-t'ung, comp., *Chang Wen-hsiang-kung ch'üan-chi* [Collected works of Chang Chih-tung] (Peking, 1928), ch. 55.2–3.

11. Rockhill to Hippisley, 17 December 1889, Rockhill Papers, Houghton Library, Harvard University.

12. Rockhill's early years are summarized in chaps. 1–3 of Paul A. Varg, *Open Door Diplomat: The Life of W. W. Rockhill* (Urbana, Ill., 1952). See also Esson M. Gale's sketch of Rockhill in *The Dictionary of American Biography*, 16:66–67.

13. The phrase comes from a memo, Rockhill to Adee, 29 March 1904, MCD.

sought to achieve this goal on the one hand by committing the powers to respect China's integrity and on the other by encouraging the Chinese to undertake reform. Thus, he urged Hay in 1899 and again in 1900 to send notes to the powers on the principle of China's integrity. And in subsequent years he would urge the Chinese to put their house in order, particularly through fundamental financial and educational reform. "If she does not," he wrote in 1900, "partition and subjection to foreign rule are but questions of a little time."[14]

Rockhill would have been the first to admit that his hopes for China were not well founded, for he was profoundly skeptical of the ability of the Ch'ing dynasty to carry out the program of national reform essential to its own and China's survival.

> I greatly fear that under the present Chinese rule things will not improve; reforms will not be seriously undertaken, . . . for there is no life, energy or patriotism throughout the whole governing class. It looks to me very dark ahead for China.[15]

Rockhill's suspicions of the Chinese government were so profound and his devotion to his own conception of reform was so strong that, despite his familiarity with China, they tended to narrow his vision and betray his judgment.

From his Peking vantage point Rockhill reported back to Hay in 1901 on the situation in Manchuria. He thought the outlook for China unfavorable. He shared the fear of the Yangtze governor generals and many foreigners that the loss of Manchuria to Russia might be the first step in the partition of China. He noted that Japan was looking for support but that, with Great Britain too involved elsewhere to be of assistance, she hesitated to advance alone in opposition to Russia. Rockhill concluded pessimistically that regardless of how China's talks with Russia progressed she "will only retain nominal control over Manchurian provinces which seem to be irretrievably lost to her."[16] Even so, Rockhill saw no cause for merchants in the United States to become alarmed, for Russia would not be able for some years to compete commercially with them in East Asia.[17]

14. Rockhill, "The United States and the Future of China," *The Forum* 29 (May 1900): 330. See also Rockhill, memo, 27 August 1899, Rockhill Papers; and Marilyn B. Young, *The Rhetoric of Empire: American China Policy 1895–1901* (Cambridge, Mass., 1968), chap. 7.
15. Rockhill to Hay, 16 June 1901, Hay Papers, Manuscript Division, Library of Congress.
16. Rockhill to Hay, 19 January 1901 and 28 March 1901, MCD. The quote comes from the latter report.
17. Rockhill to Hay, 29 January 1901, Hay Papers.

Rockhill returned to Washington in October 1901 to resume his duties as director of the International Bureau of American Republics and to continue to "meddle in Chinese matters" as Hay's informal adviser.[18] Minister Conger, to whom the duties of Manchuria-watching fell upon Rockhill's departure, took a view as dim as Rockhill's on the region's future. He had no doubt that Russia was intent on securing that prize and that she already had at hand the tools for the job.

> Russia's railroad and other interests in Manchuria are enormous, and it is to be presumed that she will negotiate to adequately and permanently conserve them, and that in doing so she will undoubtedly finally acquire sovereign control thereof. It is not a pleasant prospect for us to contemplate, for, judging by the past, she will probably so discriminate against foreign products at the ports or differentiate against them during their movement to the interior as to seriously hamper, if not destroy, foreign trade.[19]

Repeatedly between 1901 and 1903, Conger, like Denby earlier, urged on Hay a policy of accommodation with Russia as the only way to guarantee American trade in Manchuria. He assumed that China could not stem the Russian advance and that consequently the United States would have to join with the other powers who had an important stake in Manchuria in an attempt to elicit from Russia a guarantee of "the *status quo ante* as to trade."[20] He felt Russia would respond favorably since she would surely prefer to share the Manchurian treasure rather than to become locked in a conflict over it.

Whether Secretary of State John Hay in Washington accepted Rockhill's and Conger's pessimistic on-the-spot appraisals of Manchuria's future is difficult to know. However, he clearly did not share Conger's faith in the efficacy of an agreement with Russia. During the first phase of the Sino–Russian negotiations over Manchuria, Hay simply contented himself with keeping an eye on developments through his observers in China. He still hoped that China together with Great Britain and Japan would manage to keep Russia's ambitions in check and that the United States would only have to contribute an occasional "amen" to their joint

18. The quotes are from Rockhill to Hippisley, 16 April 1902, Rockhill Papers.

19. Conger to Hay, 7 September 1901, MCD. Also see Conger to Hay, 5 February 1901, MCD.

20. Conger to Hay, 7 September 1901, MCD. Conger's policy recommendations also appear in dispatches to Hay of 9 November 1901 and 4 May 1903, both in MCD. Townley, the British chargé in Peking, informed the Foreign Office (telegram, 2 May 1903, FO 17/1603) that his American colleague "does not think that his Government would much mind if Russia did have Manchuria so long as written assurances were secured that it would be kept open to foreign trade and treaty ports established."

effort. As the talks on Manchuria reached their first climax, Hay on 16 February 1901 issued a circular to China and the powers which lent support to the cause of Governor Generals Chang and Liu. He warned China not to agree to Russian demands without first consulting the other powers; for China to do otherwise would be improper, inexpedient, and extremely dangerous.[21] When finally Russia withdrew her demands in April 1901, thus tempering the Manchurian crisis, the State Department and the Peking legation gained a temporary respite from their anxious vigil.

The Chinese and Russian negotiators entered the second major phase of their talks on Manchuria in late 1901. As earlier, Chinese officials tried to follow the negotiations and continued to debate the best course to pursue in dealing with the Russians. The United States too watched developments. Through the summer and into the fall of 1901, Li Hung-chang had discussed with Russian representatives the terms of a troop evacuation agreement. At the same time, he negotiated several "private" contracts to be concluded between the Chinese government and the Russo–Chinese Bank. Russia had made the conclusion of these agreements, which among other things prohibited China from granting railway and other concessions in Manchuria to any third party, a precondition for troop withdrawal. Li died in November before any of these agreements were concluded, and the following month Prince Ch'ing took up the reins of the negotiations and immediately secured some concessions. Russia agreed to reduce the period of evacuation from three to two years, eliminated the clauses in the evacuation agreement restricting Chinese forces in Manchuria, and revised the private agreements, which, however, still gave Russia an even more privileged position in Manchuria.[22]

Through these months of talks, the court's anxiety about the implications of prolonged occupation of Manchuria came more and more to dominate its calculations. "Every day the agreement is not concluded . . . is yet another day the three eastern provinces cannot be returned. Our homeland has long been occupied by the Russians, who have established their operations, sparing no effort."[23] An agreement with Russia

---

21. The circular is quoted in Hay to Rockhill, telegram, 1 March 1901, DIC. On 19 February 1901 a copy of the circular went to the Chinese minister, Wu T'ing-fang.

22. Kosaka, "Ch'ing Policy over Manchuria," pp. 139–41. A sketch of Prince Ch'ing appears in Arthur W. Hummel, ed., *Eminent Chinese of the Ch'ing Period* (Washington, D.C., 1944), 2:964–65.

23. Wai-wu Pu to Chang Chih-tung and Liu K'un-i, 5 February 1902, WWP: Ni-i chiao-shou Tung-san-sheng t'iao-yüeh t'iao-k'uan an [File on determining the provisions for the treaty restoring Manchuria].

now seemed the only way to avoid diminution of China's sovereignty in Manchuria. Acknowledging persistent protests from provincial officials,[24] the central government admitted the disadvantages of such an agreement, but it saw no better way to regain the region. The proposal that China promote a commercial open door there would avail nothing since the commercial powers were not prepared to drive the Russians out. In addition, no one could know what ambitions these powers might harbor. For China to resist the Russians without assistance would be foolhardy, and to incur new debts to the commercial powers might prove dangerous. Acceptance of the proffered Russian terms was, the court reasoned, the lesser of two evils.[25] Consequently, Prince Ch'ing, convinced he had made the best bargain possible, prepared to conclude an agreement with Russia.

Through this second attempt to negotiate an end to the Russian occupation, Hay watched and waited until he feared that the Chinese were ready to come to terms with the Russians. Finally, in early December Hay, following Japan and Britain, sent a warning to the Wai-wu Pu couched in language general enough to cover the undisclosed terms of the Sino–Russian agreement.

> The President trusts and expects that no arrangement will be made with any single Power which will permanently impair the territorial integrity of China or injure the legitimate interests of the United States or impair the ability of China to meet her international obligations.[26]

When Conger delivered Hay's warning, Prince Ch'ing assured him that the United States need not worry since the final Sino–Russian agreement would preserve China's sovereignty and respect all treaties and international obligations.[27]

Conger was not reassured and found particularly objectionable the monopolistic provisions of one of the contracts between the Chinese government and the Russo–Chinese Bank. Hay agreed. He decided to follow once again the lead of Japan and Britain. He had Rockhill draft

---

24. Liu and Chang to the Wai-wu Pu, telegrams, 17 February 1902, WWP: Ni-i chiao-shou Tung-san-sheng t'iao-yüeh t'iao-k'uan an; and 14 March 1902, WWP: Ting-li yüeh-chang an [File on drawing up treaty terms].

25. Wai-wu Pu to Chang and Liu, 5 February 1902, WWP: Ni-i chiao-shou Tung-san-sheng t'iao-yüeh t'iao-k'uan an; and imperial edict in reply to a memorial of 6 October 1901 by Chang and Liu, in Wang, *Chang Wen-shiang-kung ch'üan-chi*, ch. 55.15.

26. Hay to Conger, telegram, 6 December 1901, DIC. Conger's warning is in MCD, telegram, 3 December 1901, and full report, 4 December 1901.

27. Conger to Hay, 12 December 1901, MCD.

a protest which stated American objections in terms even more sweeping than before:

> An agreement by which China concedes to a corporation *the exclusive right to open mines, construct railways or other industrial privilege* can only be viewed with concern by the Government of the United States. Such monopoly would distinctly contravene treaties of China with foreign powers, affect rights of citizens of [the] United States by restricting rightful trade, and tend to impair sovereign rights of China, and diminish her ability to meet international obligations.[28]

Hay thus argued that Russia could not acquire additional exclusive privileges in Manchuria without violating her endorsement of the open door.

The opposition of the commercial powers, increasingly adamant and underlined by the conclusion of the Anglo–Japanese alliance in February 1902, stiffened Prince Ch'ing's resistance and intimidated Russia.[29] On 8 April he secured Russia's promise to withdraw her troops on terms far better than those to which he had been prepared to acquiesce several months earlier. Russian troops were to leave Fengtien province within six months, and all of Manchuria was to be free within two years. From the Chinese perspective the negotiations had been brought to a successful conclusion.

Conger, however, remained predictably pessimistic about Manchuria's future. The recently concluded Anglo–Japanese alliance, he warned, meant that war between Japan and Russia was in the offing.[30] Throughout the year, moreover, his conviction grew that even after the departure of Russian troops from Manchuria Russia would maintain considerable influence there.

> In fact, with practical ownership of the main seaport and all railroads, the possession and control of the Customs and Postal service, and with the necessary armed garrisons and requisite military and civil officials all Russian, there will be but a small equity of power or influence left to China. . . .[31]

28. Hay to Conger, telegram (italics added), 2 February 1902, MCD. See also Rockhill to Hay, memos, 31 January 1902 and 1 February 1902, Hay Papers.

29. On the relationship between the Manchurian crisis and the conclusion of the first Anglo–Japanese alliance, see Ian H. Nish, *The Anglo–Japanese Alliance: The Diplomacy of Two Island Empires, 1894–1907* (London, 1966), chaps. 5, 6, 11, 12.

30. Conger to Hay, 13 February 1902, MCD.

31. Conger to Hay, 17 December 1902, MCD.

In Conger's view the agreement did nothing but delay the Manchurian question for future resolution.

Conger's dire predictions failed to move Hay, who was satisfied in mid-1902 with the course he had chosen.[32] Without exposing the United States to appreciable risk, he had apparently protected—as much as diplomacy alone could—the American stake, real and symbolic, in Manchuria. The diplomatic maneuvering which had strengthened the Chinese and finally alarmed the Russians had also reconstituted the elements of the old open door system. The United States had taken its stand behind the other commercial powers, who were in turn prepared to put military force behind their diplomacy. The alliance between Japan and Britain promised that the new combination of commercial powers would be neither transitory nor timid.

The stand Hay had taken during the Manchurian imbroglio in 1901 and 1902 had resulted in an apparent diplomatic success but had done little to clarify the meaning of the "open door" on which Hay based his China policy. Obviously, he was intent on defending American claims to equal commercial treatment in Manchuria. However, in pursuing this goal, he had significantly broadened his earlier definition of the conditions necessary for such equality of commercial opportunity. In his open door note of 1899, Hay had indicated he felt American exporters would enjoy equal commercial opportunity as long as they were not subjected to discriminatory railway and harbor rates or customs duties. But by 1902 he had come to regard as unacceptable not only the specific forms of discrimination listed in 1899 but any regional monopoly of investment, mining, or industrial opportunity as well. In this manner Hay himself had launched the open door on its evolution from narrow expedient to broad doctrine involving the United States more deeply in Chinese affairs.

The concept of the open door, ambiguous to begin with, had evolved amidst confusion. In particular, Hay and his ministers in China were unclear about what a sphere of influence was, what impact it would have on American interests, and how in consequence the United States should react to it. As Hay's successors were to learn, the sphere by definition involved predominant influence on the part of one power within a region of the Chinese empire. In such a situation discrimination of some sort was unavoidable. Inevitably, American commercial opportunities would be affected. The same was true for the opportunity to invest in mines and

32. Hay to Roosevelt, 1 May 1902, Hay Papers.

railways, which were the imperialists' favorite means of staking out a sphere. Russia's Manchurian sphere—the Chinese Eastern Railway, mining concessions, and the Port Arthur leasehold—was a perfect example. Hay, despite his growing uneasiness over some of the specifics of Russian policy (for example, the Russo–Chinese Bank contract), showed no recognition that equality of commercial or investment opportunity was incompatible with the Russian sphere of influence itself and that American policy would have to aim at the neutralization of the latter to preserve the former. Instead, Hay embraced the dubious view that he could recognize Russia's "exceptional position" on the one hand, while on the other be sure

> that, no matter what happens eventually in northern China and Manchuria, the United States shall not be placed in any worse position than while the country was under the unquestioned domination of China.[33]

Hay increased the already ample confusion surrounding his concept of the open door by associating it with Rockhill's idea of maintaining China's integrity. In the first open door circular, the idea of defending China's integrity had been subordinate to the task of maintaining commercial opportunity. In the second circular, that of 1900, it took on a life of its own. Hay's protest in February 1902 further elevated the "sovereign rights of China" to a general principle of policy. Here again confusion reigned. Clearly the spheres of influence diminished China's authority, and, as these spheres were more distinctly marked out (as Russia had done in Manchuria), China's sovereignty (again, as in Manchuria) accordingly suffered. Nonetheless, Hay refused to recognize the contradiction between the existing spheres, which he generally tolerated, and his policy of protecting China's sovereign rights.[34] The concept of China's integrity, used simply as a means to protect American trade against the interference of other powers, further muddled the meaning of his open door policy.

There were alternatives to the tortuous course Hay took. He could have struck a realpolitik bargain and recognized the spheres in exchange for a guarantee of commercial opportunity and thus updated the traditional

33. Ibid.
34. For example when Conger noted the dangers of Russian control of customs and telegraph services in Manchuria, Hay accepted Rockhill's judgment that the situation was not a serious threat to American commerce or to China's integrity. Rockhill to Hay, memo, 26 December 1902, MCD. Rockhill's suggestion provided the basis for Hay's reply to Conger, 3 January 1903, DIC.

open door. He could have determined to battle not only for commercial and investment opportunity but also for Chinese sovereignty by allying with China against the other powers. He could have abandoned all efforts and left the China trade and the dreams associated with it to fate. Hay declined these clear alternatives and depended instead on ambiguous general principles, note writing, and good luck to see him through. The Anglo–Japanese alliance, above all else, saved Hay's illusions. He thus failed to see that Chinese sovereignty was already seriously compromised by the powers' pursuit of investment and trade advantages and that the United States could secure such advantages for herself only by resorting to the same methods of coercion in dealing with China and by taking the same risks of high diplomacy in dealing with other powers.

The imprecision in Hay's open door eventually allowed other Americans to shape it to their own ends. The unfolding facts of international life in the Far East served as a primer for the eager students in the camp of the activists who were in the years ahead to take Hay's protests in behalf of the open door and bend them into a basis for demanding access to the Manchurian sphere. They were to use his principle of Chinese sovereignty as an obstacle to encroachment by other powers. At the same time they would cite the open door policy as evidence of America's benevolence toward China and as justification for new privileges for the United States there. Thus, those in favor of a more active policy found the open door a double-purpose tool, a shoehorn for wedging the United States more deeply into China's affairs and a bludgeon to use against the similarly expansionist policies of others.

Hay is not entirely to blame for the ambiguities and contradictions of the open door policy. Americans, while old hands in the China trade, were new to power politics in the Far East and disliked involvement in the European rivalries which reached to China. The Department of State excelled at handling legal questions involving treaties and the protection of missionary and commercial clients but lacked a knowledgeable staff to advise Hay on Far Eastern affairs. Hay was further hindered by the inadequacies of the legation in Peking. Conger, like Denby, knew little more about China when he left in 1905 than when he arrived in 1898. His reports were filled with the popular generalizations and anxieties of the time, but they contained pitifully little detail to guide policymakers in Washington.

Conger's legation staff gave him little assistance. Understaffed, underpaid, and untrained, the legation operated only at the most rudimentary level.[35] "Our Legation is *not* in close touch with the Chinese, Conger and everyone in it knows this as well as I do," Rockhill advised Hay on his own return from China. "It has never been in close touch with the Chinese Government—this is notorious."[36] Despite growing American concern during the post-Boxer Manchurian crisis, the time-consuming press of diplomatic routine hobbled the legation in gathering information on major developments for Washington's guidance. All the while, the work load was increasing. The volume of correspondence with the Chinese foreign office, only a fraction of the legation's duties, quadrupled between 1898 and 1902, and the burden of conducting diplomatic business promised to increase when the court returned to Peking. Within Conger's legation only E. T. Williams was familiar with the Chinese language.[37] Alone, he could not keep up with the growing pile of press clippings and official correspondence to be translated and the ever more numerous meetings to be attended. In contrast, Britain had six Chinese-speaking staff members in its legation, Germany four, France six, Japan three or four, and even Belgium two. Clearly the American legation could not hope to match the others in the quality of its information.[38] And without accurate, timely, detailed information which had been intelligently screened and presented, policy-makers could only work in the dark. One perspicacious contemporary who observed that Americans possessed " 'a vast and varied ignorance' of anything and everything at a distance" came very near to describing Hay's diplomats in China.[39]

The single American consulate in Manchuria, located at Newchuang, gave the legation little assistance in keeping up with the events in that region. The acting consul between 1886 and 1901 was J. J. Fred Bandinel, an English businessman who devoted his spare time to the job. His reports, prosaic and perfunctory, reflected his view of the job as a sinecure.[40] However, even in the hands of an able man the Newchuang consulate, located on the edge of Manchuria looking in, was too isolated to provide

35. This unsatisfactory situation was nothing new. For example, when the war between Japan and China caught the American minister home on leave, the legation was under the charge of his son aided only by an American interpreter and a few Chinese translators. Charles Denby to Gresham, 3 October 1894, MCD.

36. Rockhill to Hay, 31 December 1901, Hay Papers.

37. Williams was one of a long line of missionary–linguists going back to S. Wells Williams and Peter Parker on whom American diplomats depended throughout much of the nineteenth century. He had joined the foreign service in 1896 and served as adviser on Chinese affairs until 1922. Esson M. Gale, "Edward Thomas Williams, 1854–1944," *Far Eastern Quarterly* 3 (1943–44): 381–83.

38. E. T. Williams to Conger, 24 July 1903, enclosed in Conger to Hay, 23 July 1903, MCD.

39. The quote is from Arthur H. Smith, *China and America To-day: A Study of Conditions and Relations* (New York, 1907), p. 109.

40. See NCR for those years.

anything resembling a full picture of affairs there. Newchuang, while a
port of considerable commercial importance, had no political significance
and was distant from the Chinese Eastern Railway (the main commercial
artery) and from the centers of Chinese and Russian political administration. To put the legation under further disability, there were not in Manchuria, as there were in other regions of China, American missionaries
whose many years of residence and intimate relations with the people
and officials often gave them an unsurpassed knowledge of the locale on
which the legation could draw.

Americans were aware of these shortcomings, and in fact some tentative
remedial steps were taken in the years before the outbreak of the Russo–
Japanese War. A training program for student interpreters was begun in
1903. Under the tutelage of E. T. Williams, whose idea the program was,
students were introduced to Chinese language and culture. The program,
however, was much inferior to those of the legations of the other powers
in China. The students—poorly selected, poorly paid, and frequently
loaned out by the legation to its short-handed consulates—progressed
slowly.[41]

The State Department had more success in upgrading and extending the
legation's eyes and ears in Manchuria. As early as February 1899 Conger
had requested the department to provide a full time "active patriotic"
consul at Newchuang. "It seems necessary that the growing American
interests should have much more particular care and watchful supervision
than can be expected from an Englishman."[42] Hay finally secured money
from Congress, and in the spring of 1902 the new, full-time consul reached
Newchuang.[43]

The next logical step to take in watching over American interests in
Manchuria would have been for the State Department to extend consular
posts into the interior. However, Hay showed no desire to open it further
either to American diplomats or to American businessmen. The Sino–
American commercial treaty, which China had in the Boxer Protocol
committed herself to revise, would have been the most suitable instrument
for opening the interior, but Hay omitted from his instructions to Rockhill
in 1901 and then to Conger in 1902 any reference to the opening of new
ports or to the establishment of new consulates.[44] Instead, he recom-

41. Williams to Conger, 24 July 1903, enclosed in Conger to Hay, 23 July 1903, MCD; and
Rockhill to Root, 3 May 1906, MCD.
42. Conger to Hay, 8 February 1899, MCD.
43. Hay to Conger, 1 April 1899, DIC.
44. Hay to Rockhill, 11 April 1901, and Hay to Conger, 25 January 1902, both in DIC.

mended as a model for Conger the British draft commercial treaty, which entirely ignored Manchuria. "We may safely let her take the lead, and . . . safeguard all our interests."[45] Conger was equally unconcerned and indeed rebuffed a suggestion from the consul in Newchuang that the United States pressure China into opening all Manchuria to trade in order to prevent Russia from gaining exclusive control there.[46]

In April 1903 Russia revived the Manchurian crisis. She announced delay of the latter stages of her troop evacuation, reoccupied Mukden, and presented China with seven demands, including the exclusion of all non-Russian foreigners from public service in northern China and a ban on China's opening new treaty ports in Manchuria.[47] The new Russian policy caused Hay abruptly to change his mind. He now called for the opening of new ports in Manchuria, and Conger, revising his earlier view, agreed with him that such a demand would be "a good test of the sincerity of Russia's declarations as to the integrity of the Chinese Empire, the acquisition of territory, the open door, etc."[48]

The American demand was obviously a reaction to the Russian announcement. In fact, if Hay had valued the new ports in themselves, he would have acted sooner, in the tranquil months between April 1902 and April 1903, to secure Chinese agreement and to prepare to open consulates at strategic points in the interior. Hay would thus have provided businessmen a court of appeals against alleged Russian discrimination. He would also have given the State Department diplomatic listening posts at the center of the storm. Commercial interest and diplomatic foresight had dictated such a move, but Hay had let the opportunity pass.

Now, in April 1903, Hay turned to the Chinese with the hope that they would quickly approve the demand aimed at putting Russia on the diplomatic defensive; however, he found them unexpectedly uncooperative. Earlier, the Yangtze governor generals had urged a similar scheme of opening Manchuria. But now the Chinese could not approve the American request without provoking the Russians, whose new demands specifically excluded the creation of new treaty ports or consulates in Manchuria. At the same time they did not want to refuse the Americans and jeopardize even the limited support the United States might give China

45. Hay to Conger, 19 March 1902, DIC.
46. Conger to Henry B. Miller (consul general, Newchuang), 10 March 1903, enclosed in Conger to Hay, 10 March 1903, MCD.
47. Kosaka, "Ch'ing Policy over Manchuria," p. 142.
48. Conger to Hay, 29 April 1903, MCD. The American note to the Wai-wu Pu on opening the ports made the motive behind the demand clear. Conger to Prince Ch'ing, 27 April 1903, WWP: Mei-kuo chao-hui [Communications from the United States].

in the crisis. Hay's badly timed demand put Chinese officials in a familiar quandary. The solution to this as to many other crises in Chinese foreign policy was to delay, playing for time and better luck.

The Chinese negotiating team for the commercial treaty was headed by Lü Hai-huan, an experienced diplomat serving in the Wai-wu Pu. Wu T'ing-fang, recalled from the United States to participate in the talks at the suggestion of Chang Chih-tung, brought to the Chinese side some knowledge of the Americans. The third member of the team, Sheng Hsüan-huai, left after only a brief time at the negotiations to observe the obligatory period of mourning after his mother's death. In setting out on the negotiations, both sides agreed that the recently concluded Anglo–Chinese commercial treaty was a good model to follow; however, the Chinese negotiators soon found their opposites inexplicably resentful at having to imitate the British.

> They say when MacKay [the British negotiator] came to China he was not aware of conditions, and so one cannot compare them with Mac-Kay. As soon as we bring forward the English treaty, the American representatives reject it, saying the United States is a great country and cannot in every respect follow the example of Britain. It is an affront to their honor.[49]

The talks were made even more difficult by the belatedly introduced open port issue and by the failure of the State Department and the Peking legation to do their homework before raising the question. The suddenness of Hay's decision had caught the legation unprepared and ill-informed.

The first list of desired ports presented to the Chinese specified Mukden and Tatungkou in Manchuria together with Peking. In response, Chang Chih-tung advised the Wai-wu Pu that it was unthinkable to open the capital as a port. The foreign office agreed. As a result, Conger in turn revised his suggestion, replacing Peking with Harbin. Why the United States demanded Peking opened in the first place is a mystery. Diplomatically it had been open for about forty years, and commercially it was of no importance. Minister Conger, who had been participating in the ordered life of the Peking legation quarter for several years, was presumably aware of these facts. The substitution of Harbin for Peking proved equally ill-advised; the United States was forced to withdraw it too, admitting that since it was administered by Russia, China could not after all open it. Inexplicably, the United States compounded this latest error by

49. Lü and Wu to the Wai-wu Pu, 7 May 1903, WWP: Chung-Mei i-ting shang-yüeh [China and the United States settle the commercial treaty].

ignoring the opportunity to establish in the Chinese town adjoining Harbin a consulate to keep an eye on political and commercial developments in that mid-Manchurian center of Russian influence. Now the Americans seemed satisfied to settle for the two ports left on their list, Tatungkou and Mukden. With the treaty all but signed, however, the British attaché wickedly informed Conger that the former site was not suitable as a port; American naval reconnaissance confirmed the error. The persistent American minister selected as a substitute Antung, a business and shipping center of importance about twenty miles up the Yalu River from Tatungkou. The State Department searched in vain on its maps for Antung and finally had to accept this change on faith. Conger then formally applied, no doubt to the amusement of many in the Chinese capital, to make yet another alteration. The Wai-wu Pu obligingly approved the application, thus drawing the curtain on the farce of the Americans in search of a treaty port.[50]

But for the Chinese the American comedy of errors was black humor indeed. The precipitate American demand per se contained no point of advantage for China, nor was it redeemed by any attractive *quid pro quo*. It only made Peking a pawn in Washington's contest of wills with St. Petersburg. Moreover, the unfocused and improvised attempt by the American negotiators in Shanghai to carry out their instructions most likely left a bad impression of American diplomatic methods.

The Chinese sought safe ground on which to defend their interests. High-ranking officials who participated in shaping Manchurian policy agreed that to include the ports in the treaty with the United States would be a provocation to Russia that China should not risk. Yüan Shih-k'ai, the commissioner of northern ports and the first to react to the American demands, saw nothing but disadvantages for China in granting the American request. It would only complicate already tense relations with Russia and provide a precedent for all the other powers to demand the opening of ports elsewhere in China. China's interest was to be served by refusing the request and instead promising that as soon as Manchuria fully reverted to China's control she would open the ports herself. Yüan argued that this tactic would take China off a collision course with Russia and would give the United States reason to spur the Russian evacuation. In addition, Yüan recommended the substitution of self-opened ports (which China

50. On the selection of the ports: Lü and Wu to the Wai-wu Pu, telegrams, 29 April and 10 May 1903, CWS:KH, ch. 170.17 and 171.9; Chang to the Wai-wu Pu, telegram, 8 May 1903, CWS:KH, ch. 171.6–8; Conger to Hay, 23 July 1903 and 9 and 12 September 1903, MCD; and Adee to Hay, 9 September 1903, Hay Papers.

could open selectively and on her own terms) for treaty ports (which inevitably in the past had entailed loss of control to foreigners).[51] The Wai-wu Pu, responding to continued Russian pressure and Yüan's advice, telegraphed its negotiators in Shanghai that it was inadvisable to agree to the American demand.[52]

Chang Chih-tung concurred on the need for caution. In the previous crises with Russia, he had urged China to join the commercial powers in an open door policy precisely similar to the one on which the United States was now intent. His present lack of support for the American demand did not indicate he had abandoned his old views. He had made the shift, largely a tactical one, because Japan and Britain had already given signs of not tolerating the Russian policy and no longer seemed to need encouragement in their defense of Manchuria. By contrast, the United States had not impressed Chang as having either the power or the will to defend Manchuria. In addition, Chang was an old opponent of the traditional treaty port arrangement through which foreigners were able to exercise disproportionate political and commercial influence. He thus favored Yüan's proposal that China herself open Manchuria.[53]

Hay and Conger would not take kindly to these conclusions. First, they obviously needed China's cooperation in their attempt to probe Russia's intentions. China could stymie their maneuver by refusing to incorporate the port provision into the commercial treaty; without the sanction of treaty rights behind him, Hay could not try the door to commerce in the Manchurian interior. Thus, Hay was faced with a test of wills with the Chinese which he had no intention of losing.

> We have done the Chinks a great service, which they don't seem inclined to recognize. It will never do to let them imagine they can treat us as they please, and that the only power they need fear is Russia.[54]

Moreover, Hay and Conger were opposed to the Chinese idea of self-opened ports. It was precisely because Chang and Yüan wished to promote

51. Yüan to the Wai-wu Pu, telegrams, 30 and 14 April 1903 and 8 July 1903, all in CWS:KH, ch. 170.19, 171.9–10, 173.4.
52. Wai-wu Pu to Lü and Wu, telegram, 1 May 1903, and Wai-wu Pu to the commissioner of southern ports, Wei Kuang-tao, 2 July 1903, WWP: Chiao-shou Tung-san-sheng an [File on the restoration of Manchuria], *ts'e* 4 and 5.
53. Chang to the Wai-wu Pu, telegram, 8 May 1903, CWS:KH, ch. 171.6–8. For Chang's opposition to the old style treaty ports, see his memorial of 26 February 1897, CWS:KH, ch. 125.9–12; and Hsü, *Chang Wen-hsiang-kung nien-p'u*, pp. 112, 125. Hsü also deals with Chang's perspective on the 1903 commercial treaty negotiations on pp. 151, 158, 172–73, 178.
54. Hay to Rockhill, 24 July 1903, Rockhill Papers.

Chinese authority and to limit foreign influence in the newly opened areas of Manchuria that they favored this procedure.

> The regulations and limits [of the new ports] should be determined by us. Police should be established by us. We absolutely cannot follow the example of the ports already opened, which resulted in the loss of our sovereignty.[55]

On the contrary, Hay and Conger were unwilling to subject foreigners living and working in Manchuria to what they saw as the evils of Chinese administration. Accordingly, the American negotiators flatly stated that the designated places would have to be opened by treaty and could not be self-opened, while the determination of the regulations governing the ports could be delayed for settlement at a later date.[56]

Through mid-1903 the open port issue alone held up conclusion of the commercial treaty. Prince Ch'ing stalled negotiations by succumbing to a diplomatic illness brought on by Russian and American cross-pressures. Meanwhile, Conger was growing more and more frustrated by the impasse and impatient with both the Chinese and the Russians. To begin with, the American minister could not get his Russian colleague to clearly state his government's position on the American demand. Furthermore, while the Russians "trifled" with him, Conger was sure that the Chinese government was using the alleged Russian opposition to opening new ports as an excuse to play its old antiforeign game of obstruction. "It is not a long step from this to the belief that upon this question, at least, a friendly understanding exists between the two countries."[57]

The American and Chinese negotiators slowly worked toward a compromise. Earlier, in mid-May, Lien-fang, vice-president of the Wai-wu Pu, had informed Conger that the Russians were still exercising pressure to keep Manchuria closed and had suggested delaying completion of the treaty until 8 October, the date assigned for the restoration of Manchuria to China. In the meantime, the Wai-wu Pu instructed its Shanghai negotiators to maintain the position that they could not include the port provision in the treaty but that China would later open the ports herself.[58]

55. Chang to Yüan as well as to Lü, Wu, and Sheng, telegrams, 7 July 1903, WWP:Chung-Mei i-ting shang-yüeh.

56. Lü and Wu to the Wai-wu Pu, telegram, 10 May 1903, CWS:KH, ch. 171.9.

57. Conger to Hay, 18 June 1903, MCD.

58. Conger to Hay, 14 May 1903, MCD; Wai-wu Pu to Lü and Wu telegram, 15 May 1903, WWP: Chiao-shou Tung-san-sheng an, *ts'e* 5; and Wai-wu Pu to Conger, 27 May 1903, WWP: T'ung-shang shui-wu tsa-hsiang an [File on miscellaneous matters concerning customs on foreign trade], *ts'e* 1. At this point in the impasse the Wai-wu Pu received but discarded a suggestion for a compromise from its negotiators in Shanghai, Lü Hai-huan and Wu T'ing-fang. They urged joining the United States in testing the Russians, who in public had declared that they

In response, Washington suggested to the Wai-wu Pu that China, instead of entering the provision into the treaty at once, could instead simply commit herself in writing to include such a provision after the 8 October evacuation deadline and then to approve the treaty and open the ports.[59] At the same time Washington marshaled the opinion of the other commercial powers behind its position; both the British and the Japanese foreign offices informed the Wai-wu Pu of their support for opening new Manchurian ports.[60]

Prince Ch'ing recovered enough from his "illness" to reject Washington's compromise. He responded with the already familiar plan to conclude the treaty immediately without any mention of the ports, which he would promise to open upon Russian evacuation.[61] Prince Ch'ing stood his ground against American pressure and public Russian denials— contrary to fact—that they blocked the opening of Manchuria.[62] In mid-August, Conger again presented Washington's plan, revised now so that China need not open the ports at once but could open them as she reestablished her authority. Prince Ch'ing at last reluctantly agreed, promising Conger he would sign the treaty on 8 October whether or not the Russians met that deadline.[63]

Conger and Prince Ch'ing still had to settle the status of the ports and the details of their opening. They left these seemingly minor matters to their negotiators in Shanghai, who, however, quickly discovered they had received from their superiors mutually irreconcilable instructions. Without any objection from the Americans, the Chinese had all along referred to the ports as *tzu-k'ai* (self-opened). The Chinese meant by this phrase that they themselves would, as Yüan and Chang had earlier

---

would not block the opening of Manchuria. All the while, of course, they stood in the way. The two negotiators suggested that all the Wai-wu Pu had to do was to ask the Russian minister if his country objected. If he did, then the Wai-wu Pu could send Conger to see him. The United States as a result could deal with Russia directly, and China would free herself of pressure. If the Russian minister did not object, then China could seize the opportunity to proclaim the ports self-opened, presenting the United States with a *fait accompli*. The United States would then have no basis for continuing her demands to include the port provision in the treaty. Wu and Lü to the Wai-wu Pu, 10 May 1903, CWS:KH, ch. 171.9.

59. Conger to the Wai-wu Pu, 1 June 1903, WWP:T'ung-shang shui-wu tsa-hsiang an, *ts'e* 1; and Liang Ch'eng to the Wai-wu Pu, 1 August 1903, WWP:Feng-t'ien-sheng k'ai-pu an [File on open ports in Fengtien], *ts'e* 2.

60. Townley to the Foreign Office, 14 June 1903, FO 17/1603, and to the Wai-wu Pu, 13 June 1903, WWP: T'ung-shang shui-wu tsa-hsiang an, *ts'e* 2.

61. Conger to Hay, 1 July 1903, MCD.

62. Conger to the Wai-wu Pu and Wai-wu Pu to Conger, 20 July 1903, and Wai-wu Pu to the commissioners for the commercial treaty negotiations, 28 July 1903, WWP: T'ung-shang shui-wu tsa-hsiang an, *ts'e* 1 and 2.

63. Conger to Hay, 14 August 1903, and Hay to Conger, 16 August 1903, MCD; and Conger to Prince Ch'ing, 12 September 1903, WWP: Chung-Mei i-ting shang-yüeh.

suggested, open the ports and settle the details of administration. Although Hay and Conger objected to this procedure, the Peking legation and the American negotiators in Shanghai had overlooked the significance of the Chinese term. The Americans wished to extend to Manchuria the old-style, nineteenth-century treaty port, where foreigners controlled the police and the administration of their enclave. The appropriate term for this arrangement was *yüeh-k'ai* (treaty-opened). To add to the confusion, Conger's instructions were self-contradicting. The first half provided for self-opened ports, just as the Wai-wu Pu had all along insisted; however, the second part spelled out the port regulations, which followed the treaty port model detested by the Chinese. Conger apparently had accepted China's claim to open the ports on her own initiative but assumed at the same time that she would surrender control over foreigners there. The Chinese negotiators and the Wai-wu Pu were justifiably puzzled by the American position.[64] In the end, the Chinese and Americans agreed that the ports would be designated in the treaty as self-opened but delayed the thornier question of port regulations for later settlement.[65]

Even with the treaty concluded, friction over the ports continued. Conger was still suspicious of Chinese intentions and impatient to have the ports opened. Chinese officials, not wishing to provoke the occupying Russians, refused to be hurried. When in November the American and Japanese consuls at Newchuang traveled to Mukden to investigate commercial conditions, Yüan Shih-k'ai protested that, in going where they were not entitled, they might create for China new problems with Russia. He suggested that the Wai-wu Pu delay memorializing for imperial approval to open the ports.[66] Prince Ch'ing and his associates in the foreign office agreed. When Conger asked for an imperial edict to announce opening of the ports, the Wai-wu Pu declined with the excuse that such a procedure was unprecedented. The irrepressible American minister, still wanting to ostentatiously publicize what the Wai-wu Pu wished, on the contrary, to minimize, then asked that the military governor of Fengtien make such a proclamation to the local populace. That official, Tseng-ch'i, worried by the Russian troops still in his area, responded that the proclamation might cause trouble and was, in any case, premature.[67]

64. Lü, Wu, and Sheng to the Wai-wu Pu, 21 September 1903, CWS:KH, ch. 175.1–3; and the Wai-wu Pu to Chang, 3 October 1903, WWP: T'ung-shang shui-wu tsa-hsiang an, *ts'e* 3.
65. Yüan, Chang, Sheng, Wu, and Lü, joint memorial, 3 January 1904, CWS:KH, ch. 179.13. The treaty text is in John V. A. MacMurray, ed., *Treaties and Agreements with and Concerning China, 1894–1919*, vol. 1: *Manchu Period (1894–1911)* (New York, 1921), pp. 423–32.
66. Yüan to the Wai-wu Pu, telegram, 16 November 1903, CWS:KH, ch. 177.20.
67. Conger to Hay, 10 February 1904, MCD; and Wai-wu Pu to Tseng-ch'i, 19 January 1904,

On the outbreak of the Russo–Japanese War in 1904, the two governments finally put aside the issue of the open ports in Manchuria. Hay had gained his treaty but had failed to put Russian intentions to a test. The Chinese had secured the right to call the new ports self-opened but had yet to make sure China's authority would prevail in them.

and Tseng-ch'i to the Wai-wu Pu, 10 February 1904, WWP: T'ung-shang shui-wu tsa-hsiang an, *ts'e* 7.

5: AGREEMENTS AND DISAGREEMENTS

Between 1901 and 1903 the United States and China had come into contact over the problems posed by the Russian occupation of Manchuria. Unfortunately, they had failed to find a basis for working together toward the mutually desirable goal of limiting Russia's influence there. By late 1903 their Manchurian policies were roughly similar. American leaders were growing increasingly sensitive to the threat posed by Russian policy to their Manchurian interests and irritated by Russia's crude diplomacy. Hay and Roosevelt, restrained by public apathy on Far Eastern affairs, could not themselves respond forcefully, but they could take consolation in the knowledge that Japan would defend her own—and incidentally America's—interests against Russia in Manchuria. The Chinese, hobbled by military weakness, decided after a futile appeal for American intervention that they too could afford to suffer Russian troops a while longer; Japan's army and navy might soon cut the Manchurian knot that China's diplomats had not been able to untie. Thus, both the American and Chinese governments agreed on the widsom of depending on Japan to pull their chestnuts from the Manchurian fire. When war broke out between Russia and Japan, the two governments again agreed that they, particularly China, should avoid involvement in the conflict even though their sympathies and interests rode with Japan. But while this agreement on policy immediately before and during the war seemed a favorable sign for postwar cooperation, disagreements over peacemaking and other issues served as a reminder that misunderstanding and antagonism would continue to trouble Sino–American relations and make more difficult any attempt to cooperate in Manchuria.

Increasingly through the summer of 1903 President Theodore Roosevelt took over from John Hay, who was debilitated by illness, the handling of the Manchurian crisis. Roosevelt was ready to accept Russia's sphere of influence provided she did not violate American treaty rights.

We have always recognized the exceptional position of Russia in relation to Manchuria. We have done nothing to interfere with her progress and her legitimate aspirations. We have only insisted upon that freedom of access and of opportunity for commerce which has been guaranteed to us. . . . [1]

The president allowed little place for China in the scheme of things in Manchuria. Roosevelt, who like Hay had a conventional view of China, regarded her leaders with disdain and would not consider working through them to protect American and Chinese rights in Manchuria. As he saw it, their policy was one of inertia. They respected strength, not justice. They lacked patriotism and the martial virtues—serious deficiencies in Roosevelt's scale of values. Indecisive, face-saving behavior was typical of them. The very term "Chinese" meant for him an inability to see things clearly, to face facts and act accordingly. Roosevelt saw the Chinese as an uncivilized people, a prey to the vigorous countries of the West.[2] Those of Conger's dispatches from Peking which reached the president's desk served only to confirm this view.[3]

Although Roosevelt did not himself wish to carry the white man's burden in China, he had not at first minded Russia's doing it. He had initially greeted the Russian occupation of Manchuria as a "task for the immeasurable benefit of civilization, and above all, for the benefit of the provinces taken."[4] Although his attitude toward the Russian occupation later changed, he still remained indifferent to China's claim to Manchuria. By 1903 Roosevelt cared little whether the region slipped from China's grasp. "In this Manchurian matter we are not striving . . . to prevent Russia from acquiring any political control of the territory in question."[5] The president was clearly not an enthusiastic defender of China's integrity. The fate of Manchuria was important to him only insofar as it affected American commercial rights. In his opinion the United States had its hands more than full protecting its own interests and had no business taking on the added responsibility of protecting the hapless Chinese. Thus Roosevelt differed from Hay because he had a clear,

1. Roosevelt to Albert Shaw, 22 June 1903, in Elting E. Morison et al., eds., *The Letters of Theodore Roosevelt* (Cambridge, Mass., 1951–54) [hereafter referred to as Morison], 3:497–98.
    2. Roosevelt to Rockhill, 22 August 1905, in Morison, 4:1310; to Arthur H. Smith, 3 April 1906, Morison, 5:206; to George Ferdinand Becker, 8 July 1901, Morison, 3:112; to George V. L. Meyer, 19 June 1905, Morison, 4:1242; and to Henry White, 23 August 1905, Morison, 4: 1313.
    3. For examples, see Conger to Hay, 18 April 1903 and 4 May 1903, MCD.
    4. Roosevelt to Frederic René Coudert, 3 July 1901, and to George Ferdinand Becker, 8 July 1901, Morison, 3:105–06 and 112 respectively. The quote is from the former.
    5. Roosevelt to Lyman Abbott, 22 June 1903, in Morison, 3:500–01.

vain hopes about defending China's integrity. The conditions which he asked others to observe in dealing with American interests in Manchuria were both more limited and more explicit than Hay's.

Despite these differences, as the president became involved in the Manchurian question, he hewed closely to the path already marked out by his secretary of state. Hay's response to the renewed crisis created by Russia's postponement of her evacuation from Manchuria in April 1903 had been much the same as during the crisis of 1901 and 1902. He had resorted to a cautious policy of note writing in defense of American interests. He had pressed Russian diplomats in St. Petersburg and Washington for information about the demands and warnings from Russia concerning the opening of Manchurian ports, which the Chinese kept insisting were real. And he had demanded that a clause opening the Manchurian ports be included in the commercial treaty in order to force China to call Russia's bluff. Roosevelt agreed with Hay that the Russian attempt at sealing off Manchuria to Americans violated American rights and should be resisted. The prolongation of the Russian occupation itself, however, did not disturb either of them because they felt it did not substantially affect American trade in Manchuria or violate treaty rights.

The president fumed over Russian diplomatic maneuvering and "mendacity," but he could do little more than maintain the pressure on Peking and St. Petersburg that Hay had begun to apply.[6] Public apathy and a lack of information narrowed his policy alternatives.

> I do not have to tell you . . . that while something can be done by public men in leading the people, they cannot lead them much further than public opinion has prepared the way. . . . Now, as yet our public opinion is dull on the question of China, and moreover, we all are somewhat in the dark as to the exact facts.[7]

Indeed, although resentment against Russian highhandedness had grown between 1901 and 1903, the American public still regarded crises in China as distant and minor compared to those closer to home. When Roosevelt in midsummer began to imagine that the public might eventually come around to supporting a war against Russia, his view principally reflected his hatred for "being in the position of seeming to bluster without consistent view of the sphere of influence and because he entertained no

6. Ibid.; as well as Hay to Henry White, 22 May 1903, in William R. Thayer, *The Life and Letters of John Hay* (London, 1915), 1:369; and Hay to Roosevelt, 12 May 1903, Hay Papers, Manuscript Division, Library of Congress.
7. Roosevelt to Alfred Thayer Mahan, 18 March 1901, Morison, 3:23.

backing it up."[8] It was his way of indulging his frustrations over the limitations an uninterested American public imposed on his actions in the Far East.

In the fall of 1903 the Chinese tested the limits of Roosevelt's Manchurian policy. In August they had given way to the United States on including the port provision in the treaty, and the following month they had compromised on some of the details of opening the ports. During these same months Hay in interviews with the Chinese minister in Washington had tried to reassure "those poor trembling rabbits" that no harm would come from Russia.[9] The Chinese government now sought support from Washington against the Russian occupation. In the manner Chang Chihtung had so often suggested, the Chinese government had given a commercial power a stake in Manchuria. What would the United States do to protect it?

In September the Wai-wu Pu formally raised the question. On the twenty-second, Prince Ch'ing asked the American minister to help him end the Russian occupation. Conger replied there was little chance. The following day Prince Ch'ing again discussed with him the situation in Manchuria and on the twenty-fourth sent him a formal request that the United States intercede with Russia to solve the Manchurian dispute. Conger described in his usual pessimistic tone the Chinese government's plight. "They are in a pitiable condition, for if they yield to Russia's demands, they practically give away their territory, and if they do not agree Russia keeps it."[10] Conger thought the occupation ruinous for American trade, a violation of American treaty rights, and an incitement to the partition of China. Nonetheless, he had nothing to say in favor of the Chinese request.

The Wai-wu Pu briefly set aside the plea for help and then revived it in late October through its minister in Washington, Liang Ch'eng. At first the Chinese saw a glimmer of hope. On 26 October Liang asked Hay to see if the president would mediate between his country and Russia. The next day an interview with Rockhill encouraged Liang with the prospect of success. And indeed, Roosevelt was seriously considering the request, which Hay had relayed to him. But news from St. Petersburg that Russia would fight to defend her position alarmed Roosevelt. In a meeting with his cabinet, he concluded that the public would not, after all, be in sym-

8. Roosevelt to Hay, 22 May 1903 as well as 18 and 29 July 1903, all in Morison, 3:478, 520, and 532 respectively. The quote is from Roosevelt's letter of 22 May.

9. Hay to Roosevelt, 2 August 1903 and 3 September 1903, Hay Papers.

10. Conger to Hay, 24 September 1903 and 29 October 1903, MCD. The quote is from the latter dispatch.

pathy with a war over Manchuria and that he had best not get involved in the dispute. Roosevelt instructed Hay to write a negative reply to the Chinese minister. The note composed by Hay blandly explained that, although the president was inclined to help, he lacked sufficient information on Russia's demands and China's concessions to know what to do.[11] Roosevelt and Hay still had no intention of letting the pleas of the "poor devils of Chinese" draw them beyond the limits they had already set to their involvement in the Manchurian crisis.

Liang Ch'eng pressed Hay for an explanation of the disappointing reply. Hay frankly told Liang that the American public had a strong distaste for overseas conflicts and that consequently the president could not decide within a month's time to fight for thirty years of growing trade between the United States and China without running into embarrassing political opposition. Liang explained this to his superiors and reported that he had tried to stir public opinion by interesting the powerful press, but for the moment it too remained unconcerned. He recommended as the best long-range approach the appropriation of funds for his legation to use in influencing the fourth estate.[12]

Although the United States would not and the Chinese could not resist Russia with arms, Roosevelt as well as Hay thought Japan would save the situation.[13] In protecting her own security from the Russian threat Japan would also protect the lesser American interest. The conclusion of the Anglo–Japanese alliance gave substance to this hope. Particularly for Roosevelt, Japan was a worthy friend on which to depend. She seemed well along on the road of progress. Compared to the Russians, the Japanese were the paragons of civilization. Roosevelt more and more regarded Russian intentions in Manchuria with suspicion; her untrustworthy leaders and reactionary institutions stirred his distaste. His comparison of Japan with China was again flattering to Japan. "What nonsense to speak of the Chinese and Japanese as of the same race! They are of the same race in the same sense that a Levantine Greek is of the same race

11. Hay to Liang Ch'eng, 28 October 1903, Notes to foreign legations in the United States, microfilm records of the Department of State, National Archives.
12. Liang to the Wai-wu Pu, telegram, received 4 November 1903, WWP: Chiao-shou Tung-an-sheng an [File on the restoration of Manchuria]; dispatch, received 26 November 1903, WWP:O-ping ch'e-t'ui Tung-sheng shan-hou an [File on reconstruction after Russian troop evacuation from Manchuria]; and dispatches, 23 December 1903, WWP: O-jen ch'in-chan Tung-san-sheng i Mei-kuo tiao-t'ing an [File on discussions concerning American mediation of the Russian occupation of Manchuria].
13. Hay to Roosevelt, 28 April 1903 and 12 May 1903, Hay Papers; and Roosevelt to Hay, 26 July 1904, Roosevelt Papers, Manuscript Division, Library of Congress.

with Lord Milner."[14] Japan's concern for Manchuria meant that Roosevel
could pursue, as Hay had before, a low-keyed diplomatic campaign ir
defense of the Manchurian open door.

The president's cautious policy did not go unchallenged in the foreigr
affairs bureaucracy. The loudest dissenting voice belonged to the Ameri
can consul in Newchuang, Henry Miller. After thirty years of Oregor
business life, Miller had tired and gone off in search of new horizons. Ir
1900 he had joined the consular service, and he served in Manchuria be
tween 1901 and 1904. Miller was inexperienced in diplomacy and un
familiar with the part of the world into which his new career thrust him
Eager to demonstrate his energy and determination, he was through anc
through a consular chauvinist, the first in a line of activist Americar
consuls in Manchuria. During his years in Newchuang he became in
creasingly obsessed with local problems. Miller was isolated within th
Newchuang community of Western businessmen and soon came to shar
their hopes for a flourishing American trade in Manchuria, their fear fo
its demise under Russia's grip, and their contempt for the Chinese. Losin,
his perspective, he exaggerated minor incidents into major crises.

No sooner did Miller arrive than he came to the unshakable convictior
that Russia did not intend to loosen in any way her hold on Manchuri.
and that the United States would, as a consequence, eventually be ex
cluded from an area of phenomenal trade potential. With his wonderfu
facility for generalizations, he grandiloquently concluded, hardly a mont'
after his arrival, that

> the United States has now reached a position in production and com
> merce where its prosperity is dependent upon its export trade along th
> lines consumed by the trade of Manchuria. . . .
>
> . . . [Russia] will annihilate American trade here, and with he
> political methods will make industrial slaves of the Chinese race an
> soon become a serious obsticle [*sic*] to the extention [*sic*] of our trad
> in all the Orient, and eventually a menace to our higher Civilization.[1]

Miller looked to Washington to direct a full-fledged attack on the Russia
sphere. Backed by a powerful navy, the State Department would have t
launch an energetic diplomatic campaign to preserve access for Amer:

14. Roosevelt to Hay, 2 September 1904, Morison, 4:917.
15. Miller to H. G. Squeirs (chargé, Peking), 27 June 1901, NCR. The British consul i
Newchuang reported more prosaically but accurately that he saw no evidence for Russia
discrimination against the trade of others and that there was little reason for discriminatic
since "Russian goods are not imported to any appreciable extent, and exports to Russia are st
less numerous." Fulford to Jordan, 27 May 1903, FO 228/1501 (Newchuang consulate).

cans to this promising market. At the same time the government would have to encourage American bankers and merchants to exploit it.[16] Miller clung to these conclusions until he left his post in December 1904.[17]

Miller did not confine his attacks on the Russians to paper. He convinced the State Department to station a gunboat in Newchuang for the winter of 1901–02 as a warning to Russia of American concern for Manchuria. The result was a long, contentious season of friction in the ice-bound port among Miller, local Russian authorities, and American sailors. Miller's pugnacious defense of American prestige and his representations in behalf of the local agent of the Standard Oil Company produced diplomatic repercussions reaching to Peking and finally to Washington. The Russian government protested to the State Department against the tactless conduct of the American consul. Soon Miller received polite but firm advice from his superiors to moderate his antagonisms and practice more restraint.[18]

At first these superiors were not sympathetic to Miller's views. They failed to share his sense of crisis. Minister Conger in Peking, whose hopes of seeing an "active patriotic" consul in Newchuang were more than fulfilled, was embarrassed by Miller's enthusiasm. In Washington, Rockhill warned Hay that Miller was "too much of an alarmist" and that he should discount the consul's reports. Both Conger and Rockhill advised setting aside Miller's unfounded allegations of trade discrimination.[19] However, the renewed crisis in 1903 over the Russian occupation of Manchuria prepared for Miller a more receptive audience. Rockhill, who had earlier dealt with Miller so summarily, began reading his reports with more interest. He even made the consul's "strong and vivid" warnings recommended reading for Secretary Hay.[20] Rockhill concluded that Russia

16. Miller to Conger, 30 April 1902; Miller to Hill, 24 September 1901 and 24 March 1903; and Miller to the State Department, 2 July 1904, all in NCR.

17. For repetitions of these views, see Miller to Conger, 30 April 1902 as well as 5 March 1903 and 7 August 1903; and his reports to the State Department, 19 March 1903, 5 May 1903 and 8 December 1903, all in NCR. Miller also tried to get across his view on commercial opportunity in Manchuria in "Russian Development of Manchuria" and "Notes on Manchuria," *National Geographic Magazine* 15 (1904): 113–27 and 261–62 respectively.

18. Miller to Squeirs, 19 July 1901, and Miller to Conger, 21 September 1901, NCR; Hill to Conger, 19 November 1901, DIC; and Miller to Hill, 19 February 1902, NCR. The details of the winter incidents come from reports in NCR, December 1901–May 1902.

19. Miller to Conger, 27 December 1901, NCR; Conger to Miller, 7 January 1902, MCD; Rockhill to Hay, memo, 31 October 1901, NCR; Rockhill to Adee, memo, 20 February 1902, MCD; and Hay to Conger, 25 February 1902, DIC.

20. Rockhill to Carr, memo, 5 January 1904, endorsing Miller's report to the State Department of 20 November 1903, both in NCR. Miller, whose next consular post was Yokohama, Japan, would shift his attention after the Russo–Japanese War from Russia's to Japan's plot to dominate the Manchurian market.

had perhaps succeeded more than he had imagined in discriminating against trade, and he urged on Hay a more active defense of national interests.

> It seems to me high time to bring the matter to the attention of the Russian Government. I don't think we can secure what Consul Miller suggests in this despatch—"the same liberty and rights that Russian subjects enjoy in our country"—but I certainly think it may be possible, by tactful representations at St. Petersburg, to secure serious consideration of the perfectly arbitrary and unjustifiable efforts of the Russian authorities in Manchuria to exclude us from the markets there.[21]

Hay agreed and left instructions for the drafting of a protest.[22]

Undeniably, Russian intransigence through the latter half of 1903 strained tempers in Washington, the president's included. Henry Cabot Lodge, an intimate of both Roosevelt and Hay, reflected the new balance of opinion.

> Our trade and industry in the East are large and growing, and certain sections of the country are getting very sensitive about it, and I find an unusual feeling of hostility to Russia here. . . . That we must take strong grounds there against exclusion from China by Russian intrigue I consider inevitable, but I do not think we shall be drawn into any war.[23]

The change in attitude at the State Department and at the White House was not yet great enough either to arrive at the kind of activist views Miller espoused or to surpass the limits Hay and Roosevelt had set for themselves in United States Manchurian policy. Still, American fascination with the Manchurian market was dragging her willy-nilly toward greater involvement.

Upon the long-anticipated outbreak of war between Japan and Russia in 1904, the governments of the United States and China were in rare agreement on what China's role should be during the conflict. Manchuria, the center of contention, promised to become the main battleground, but the war could overflow into adjoining areas of China. From Washington's perspective, the disturbance to commerce the war would cause in Manchuria was regrettable but unavoidable; Hay did hope,

21. Rockhill to Hay, memo, 24 December 1903, NCR.
22. Hay, memo, 24 December 1903, NCR.
23. Lodge to Henry Lee Higginson, 7 January 1904, Higginson Papers, Baker Library, Harvard University.

however, to keep the combatants out of the rest of China, where their presence would intensify political as well as commercial confusion and uncertainty. Conger had already warned him that China might stumble into the war. The minister thought that anti-Russian sentiment among "the over-ridden and oppressed inhabitants of Manchuria" ran high and understood that some important officials were in favor of making common cause with Japan against Russia.[24] Hay decided to act to safeguard American interests and to protect the Chinese from their own folly. In February 1904 he asked Tokyo and St. Petersburg to keep the hostilities localized and to respect China's neutrality and independence. Hay's stand reaffirmed pro forma a year later by Roosevelt, further committed the United States to the defense of China's integrity and more closely linked this idea to the open door concept.[25]

The Chinese government came to substantially the same conclusion on the desirability of neutrality. Earlier, in November 1903, Yüan Shih-k'ai together with Chang Chih-tung had been hurriedly called into audience to discuss the Manchurian crisis, undoubtedly in anticipation of war between Japan and Russia. During the following two months, Yüan responded to queries from the court by urging neutrality as the best response to the impending conflict. The court at first hesitated to act on his advice, but finally, impelled to decide by the outbreak of war, it agreed. On 12 February 1904 an imperial edict proclaimed China neutral.[26]

Yüan had not decided in favor of neutrality without considering the alternatives. In the frenzy of diplomatic calculations and consultations in Peking in the few months before the war began, he had considered aiding Japan with transport and supplies against Russia in case of war, but his distrust of Japan's intentions in Manchuria, the magnitude of the gamble, and the opposition of Britain, Japan, and the United States to Chinese involvement had turned him toward the conservative course of neutrality.[27]

24. Conger to Hay, 26 December 1903, MCD.

25. Hay, circular, 10 February 1904, DIC; Hay to Henry White, 12 February 1904, and Hay to Joseph Choate, 27 February 1904, Hay Papers; and American circular to the powers, 13 January 1905, FRUS, 1905, p. 1.

26. The details of this major conference on Manchuria of 2 November 1903 between the throne and Yüan and Chang are not known. Hsü T'ung-hsin, *Chang Wen-hsiang-kung nien-p'u* [A chronological biography of Chang Chih-tung] (Taipei reprint, 1969), p. 176; and imperial edict, 1 November 1903, SL:KH, ch. 521.6. See also Yüan to the Wai-wu Pu, telegram, 27 December 1903, CWS:KH, ch. 179.4–6; Yüan, memorial, 22 January 1904, CWS:KH, ch. 181. 3–5; Yüan to the Wai-wu Pu, telegram, 11 February 1904, CWS:KH, ch. 181.18; and imperial edict proclaiming neutrality and edict on neutrality regulations, 12 February 1904, CWS:KH, ch. 181.19–23.

27. Sir Ernest Satow (British minister to China) to Lord Lansdowne (secretary for foreign affairs), 5 November 1903 and 29 December 1903, and 14 and 27 January 1904, FO 800/120.

As Conger had reported, some high officials were not happy with the kind of advice Yüan and the commercial powers were giving the central government. The opponents of neutrality wished above all to safeguard China's Manchurian territory from the ravages of war. Yüan's critics suggested that if China could induce Russia to withdraw her troops from Manchuria, she might both forestall the conflict and at the same time recover China's territory. If Russia refused to budge, then China's interest lay in preparing to aid Japan in the war. They saw neutrality as an empty gesture exposing Manchuria to destruction and the ambitions of the victor.[28]

Although overruled by the court, the critics continued through the war to snipe at the policy of strict neutrality. In the spring and again in the winter of 1904, the commissioner of southern ports, Wei Kuang-tao, led attempts to have the central government both reexamine the wisdom of its policy and take steps to end the costly war. The undercurrent of official discontent again surfaced in that same year when the throne requested advice on postwar Manchurian policy. Rather than speak to the subject, most respondents reverted to the themes of the critics. Already the war had devastated Fengtien, and the Manchurian military governors warned that, if not soon ended, it would do the same to Kirin and Heilungkiang as the Russian army retreated northward. The war might mean the restoration of Manchuria, but it also might make the region a place of desolation. As it was, the number of homeless was mounting into the hundreds of thousands. Several memorialists suggested that the Wai-wu Pu should enlist one of the powers—the United States was mentioned prominently—to mediate an end to the war.[29]

Yüan Shih-k'ai resisted these efforts from within to undermine China's declared neutrality. He warned that Japan and Russia, who were already

Satow's dispatch of 5 November 1903 contains details of an interview with T'ang Shao-i, whom Yüan had sent to the British legation to discuss China's response to the outbreak of war. See also George A. Lensen, ed., *Korea and Manchuria between Russia and Japan, 1895–1904* (Tallahassee, Fla., 1966), pp. 254, 258–62.

28. Imperial edict, 1 November 1903 (in response to Ts'en Ch'un-hsüan), SL:KH, ch. 521.7 Ting Chen-to (governor general of Yunnan) and Lin Shao-nien(governor of Yunnan)to the Grand Council, telegram, 20 January 1904, CWS:KH, ch. 181.2; Ts'en Ch'un-hsüan (governor general of Kwangtung and Kwangsi) to the Wai-wu Pu, telegram, 10 February 1904, CWS:KH, ch. 181.16–17; Ch'eng-hsün (governor of Anhwei), 23 January 1904, CWS:KH, ch. 181.5–8.

29. For the views of the critics of neutrality, see Hsü, *Chang Wen-hsiang-kung nien-p'u*, pp. 186–87 (on the initiatives by the commissioner of southern ports); Tseng-ch'i, memorial, 30 January 1905, SL:KH, ch. 540.9–10; Tseng-ch'i et al., supplementary memorial, 2 May 1905, CWS:KH, ch. 189.23; Ch'eng Te-ch'üan (military governor of Heilungkiang), memorial, 2 December 1904, CCST, ch. 2.49–51; and Hsü Chüeh (minister to Italy), 2 December 1904, CWS:KH, ch. 186.11–14. The imperial edict of 2 August 1904 inviting opinions on postwar policy is in SL:KH, ch. 532.15.

closely scrutinizing this policy, might not tolerate an attempt at mediation and would likely regard it as partisan interference in the conflict.
If compromised, China might risk spreading the war from the Manchurian war zone to other areas of China, adding new misfortunes to old.
In defending neutrality, Yüan received yeoman support from Chang
Chih-tung. From the time the war had loomed on the horizon, Chang
had favored a strictly neutral course even though he sympathized with
Japan and hoped for close Sino–Japanese cooperation against Russia
after the war. Through the war he worked to protect this policy from its
critics.[30] The throne by consistently setting aside the protests from dissi-
dent officials confirmed its original decision in Yüan's favor.

As the conflict between Russia and Japan drew to a close, the points of
agreement on wartime policy shared by the United States and China
began to dissolve, giving way to a variety of diplomatic disagreements.
The Chinese government was concerned above all with the terms, presumably to be spelled out in the peace treaty, on which China would
resume her control of Manchuria. She was no longer willing to trust her
interests to Japan, nor did she desire any longer to stay aloof from the
contacts between the belligerents. In order to guard her interests in the
peace settlement, then, the Chinese government wished to secure full
participation in the upcoming peace talks, scheduled to begin in Portsmouth, New Hampshire, in August 1905. To this end, it looked hopefully
for the assistance of the United States, which had supported China in
maintaining her neutrality during the war and which was now sponsoring
the peace conference.
The American response was frosty. The new American minister in
Peking, W. W. Rockhill, warned Yüan Shih-k'ai and Prince Ch'ing in
veiled terms against sending a delegate. His advice reflected his low estimate of the Chinese government's ability to fend for itself.

> The lack of any settled policy among the high officers of the Chinese
> Government, I refrain from using the word statemen as I fear there is
> not one to be found in China at the present day, is terribly evident.
> Indecision and a determination to drift with any current is shown on
> every side. . . . China is quite unable to manage her international
> affairs without strong support and constant pressure from without.[31]

30. Chang, memorial, 24 October 1904, in Wang Shu-t'ung *Chang Wen-hsiang-kung ch'üan-chi*
[Collected works of Chang Chih-tung] (Peking, 1928), ch. 64.4–8; and Hsü, *Chang Wen-hsiang-
kung nien-p'u,* p. 187.
31. Rockhill to Hay, 1 July 1905, MCD.

Since so inept a government would find "the vast and intricate questions which must inevitably come up for settlement on the conclusion of the war" entirely beyond its limited ability, Rockhill concluded that China should trust the United States to watch over her interests at the conference. The minister, informing Prince Ch'ing of this conclusion, assured him, however, that the conference would not touch on matters concerning China's sovereignty in Manchuria.[32]

Russian officials urged China to represent herself at the peace table, hoping thereby to embarrass Japan's attempt to gather up the prizes of war. But Japan, Britain, and France all echoed the American view.[33] This common stand by the commercial powers settled the question. The emperor, who reportedly had favored sending a representative—Wu T'ing-fang was the rumored choice—abandoned his decision. Instead, he put on the best possible face by asking the American president to use his influence to protect China's interests.[34] Things had apparently worked out as Rockhill wished. China, the neutral whose territory had served as the battleground, was now to be absent when the powers readjusted their position there.

Rockhill's euphoria over China's acceptance of his advice lasted only twenty-four hours—until the other half of China's policy toward the peace conference became clear. The Wai-wu Pu bluntly informed the ministers of the United States, Russia, and Japan that if China were not to be represented, then she would reserve judgment on the issues of concern to her which were to be decided without her participation.[35] It was now clear that she had no intention of leaving her vital interests in the hands of the American president.

The Chinese, as Rockhill had correctly guessed in his reports back to Washington, were most concerned with the disposition of Russia's privileged position in southern Manchuria. The key decisions for China, memorialists repeatedly pointed out, concerned the Liaotung leasehold, including Port Arthur, and above all the Russian railway, which com-

32. Ibid.
33. Wai-wu Pu to Hu Wei-te (minister to Russia), 20 July 1905, CWS:KH, ch. 190.11–12; and Rockhill to the secretary of state, 6 July 1905, MCD.
34. The Kuang-hsü Emperor to Roosevelt, 5 July 1905, FRUS, 1905, p. 816. Another version of the story appears in an article by Liang Ch'i-ch'ao in *Hsin-min ts'ung-pao* [New people's miscellany, no. 20 (1905), pp. 81–85.
35. The Wai-wu Pu to Hu Wei-te, 6 July 1905, CWS:KH, ch. 190.5–6; Rockhill to the secretary of state, 8 July 1905, MCD; and Prince Ch'ing to Rockhill, 6 July 1905, FRUS, 1905, p. 818. Chang Chih-tung in a telegram to the Grand Council, 24 July 1905, welcomed the Wai-wu Pu's decision not to send a delegate to the talks. He trusted to a degree Japan's fairness but felt that the foreign office was wise to reserve judgment on the peace terms. See CWS:KH, ch. 190.12–15.

mercially and strategically dominated the region it traversed between the leasehold and Harbin.[36] However, China's hopes for regaining these foreign-held concessions or neutralizing foreign privileges were not to be realized under Theodore Roosevelt's auspices. He was too busy peace-making and ratifying a balance of power in the Far East favorable to the United States to bother with the views of China, a cipher in power politics. Early in the war, for example, he had toyed with the idea of returning Manchuria to China, but only on the condition that Germany appoint the Chinese governor of the region.[37] Now from the Chinese he only wished good behavior and ready acquiescence in the decisions of the powers.

Roosevelt's main aim was to create a balance of power in Manchuria, and that required a stake in the region for Japan equal to Russia's. For the same reason, he did not want Russia, whatever her sins against free trade and civilization, driven from Manchuria. "It is best that she should be left face to face with Japan so that each may have a moderative action on the other."[38] Roosevelt had decided that Japan's dominance in East Asia, won through her military success, justified her claim to the Russian concessions in southern Manchuria and that American interests lay in helping her get them. Specifically, he wanted Manchuria to revert to China's control, while Korea, Russian rights in the Liaotung Peninsula, and most of the southern branch of the Chinese Eastern Railway were to go to Japan.[39] Thus, he swiftly recognized Japan's control of Korea by withdrawing the American consulate from Seoul and acknowledged Japan's

> paramount interest in what surrounds the Yellow Sea, just as the United States has a paramount interest in what surrounds the Caribbean; but with . . . no more desire for conquest of the weak than we had shown ourselves to have in the case of Cuba. . . .[40]

It was not an encouraging prospect for the Chinese to be placed on the same level as Cuba or given the same chances of emerging unscathed from big power politics as Korea.

China's cautious wait-and-see attitude toward the terms of peace struck Roosevelt as obstructive misbehavior. He would not tolerate it.

36. Rockhill to the secretary of state, 8 July 1905, FRUS, 1905, p. 818.

37. A. L. P. Dennis, *Adventures in American Diplomacy, 1896–1906* (New York, 1928), p. 390. Roosevelt commented to the Australian correspondent George Morrison in September 1905 that he doubted that China would ever again govern Manchuria. Cyril Pearl, *Morrison of Peking* (Sydney, Australia, 1967), p. 156.

38. Roosevelt to Lodge, 16 June 1905, Morison, 4:1230. See also Roosevelt to George V. L. Meyer, 6 February 1905, Morison, 4:1116.

39. Morison, 4:1116.

40. Roosevelt to Cecil Spring-Rice, 13 June 1904, Morison, 4:830–32.

On completion of the Portsmouth treaty, he telegraphed to Rockhill that "if China makes any trouble" on the transfer of the Manchurian concessions, he should simply inform her officials that they "cannot with propriety question the efficacy" of this arrangement.[41] The president wished China to be independent, but he also wished her docile. Above all, he did not want Chinese scruples to stand in the way of the new East Asian power arrangements.

Chinese leaders could not fully appreciate Roosevelt's peacemaking efforts. Admittedly, he had helped end the war and the suffering in Manchuria. But another six months of conflict would have so exhausted the spirit and treasury of both Russia and Japan that they might have had no taste for further adventures in the region. Manchuria thus might have had a respite from power politics. Instead, Roosevelt's peace had introduced yet another foreign power into Manchuria against whose designs China would have to guard.[42]

Roosevelt's indifference and Japan's determination had doomed China's hopes at the conference. Although the Treaty of Portsmouth spelled the end of the Russian occupation of Manchuria, it also transferred to Japan the Russian concessions from Changchun south.[43] China did not accept this transfer with alacrity. She announced her objections to the decisions reached at Portsmouth on the timing of troop withdrawals, the size of foreign railway garrisons, Japan's protectorate over Korea, and above all the transfer of the Russian concessions without her approval.[44] However, China's earlier reservation over the outcome of the peace conference and her eventual protest turned out to be mere verbal expressions of independence and dissatisfaction; she altogether lacked the means to overturn the decrees of the powers. Before the year was out she had recognized in talks with Japan that she would not soon regain full control of Manchuria.[45]

In addition to the divergence of views during the peace settlement, other issues touching more intimately on relations between the two coun-

41. Roosevelt to Rockhill, telegram, 10 September 1905, Morison, 5:18.

42. Roosevelt is so indicted by Sun Yü-t'ang, "Jih-O chan-cheng hou Mei-ti-kuo chu-i ch'in-lüeh Chung-kuo Tung-pei ti yin-mou" [American imperialist plots to invade China's northeast after the Russo–Japanese War], in *Mei-ti-kuo chu-i ching-chi ch'in-Hua shih lun-ts'ung* [Collected articles on the history of American imperialist economic aggression against China] (Peking, 1953), p. 44.

43. The treaty, signed 5 September 1905, appears in John V. A. MacMurray, ed., *Treaties and Agreements with and Concerning China, 1894–1919*, vol. 1: *Manchu Period (1894–1911)* (New York, 1921), pp. 521–26.

44. Wai-wu Pu to Hu Wei-te and to Yang Shu (minister to Japan), 20 September 1905, CWS:KH, ch. 191.22–23.

45. The official minutes of the Sino–Japanese Peking conference, which ran from 7 November

tries also created animosity. Between 1904 and 1906 the obstacles which earlier had blocked the way to a better understanding on Manchuria loomed larger than ever.

The most important of these obstacles was the continued discontent felt by Chinese and Americans over the treatment accorded each in the country of the other. Opinion in the United States, particularly in the West, ran strongly in favor of stringent measures to limit the entry not just of Chinese laborers but of all classes of Chinese. The Chinese Bureau of the Immigration Service, laced through and through with anti-Chinese prejudice, had gradually stretched the meaning of Congress's immigration laws—passed in violation of treaty provisions in the first place—and applied the process of exclusion, harassment, and humiliation to Chinese businessmen, students, high officials, and even relatives of the emperor.[46] Two well-publicized events heightened Chinese dissatisfaction over this treatment. The first, the application of insulting regulations to Chinese businessmen-exhibitors and officials invited to the St. Louis Exhibition of 1903, stirred a small furor among their countrymen.[47] Feelings became even more roused when in January 1904 Congress extended for an unlimited time the diverse restrictions on Chinese living in or trying to enter the United States.

As a result of this growing public resentment, the Chinese government announced its refusal to automatically renew for ten years the treaty governing immigration into the United States, and Prince Ch'ing, the head of the foreign office, stoutly resisted pressure from Conger and Hay to do so. With the stage set for an official confrontation on the issue of discrimination, a popular anti-American commercial boycott developed along the China coast in the spring of 1905. It was spearheaded by students and supported by businessmen, by some local officials, and (at least tacitly) by the central government. It centered in Shanghai and Canton but reached as far north as Newchuang.[48]

1905 to 22 December 1905, as well as the final agreement appear in CWS:KH, ch. 193.1–194.37 and ch. 195.8–12. A translation of the latter document is in MacMurray, *Treaties and Agreements with and Concerning China*, 1:549–50.

46. Mary R. Coolidge, *Chinese Immigration* (New York, 1909), is a valuable contemporary indictment of the treatment accorded Chinese in the United States. Two more recent accounts of worth are Gunther Barth, *Bitter Strength* (Cambridge, Mass., 1964), and Elmer C. Sandmeyer, *The Anti-Chinese Movement in California* (Urbana, Ill., 1939).

47. See for example the comments of the official newspaper *Pei-yang kuan-pao* [Pei-yang official gazette], translated in Conger to Hay, 3 July 1903, MCD. See also WWP:Ko-kuo yao-ch'ing ts'an-yü yu-kuan ch'ing-tien chi-nien sai-hui nien-hui [Invitations from various nations to participate in ceremonies of congratulations, memorials, exhibitions, and anniversaries], *ts'e* 4–6.

48. The contemporary official American perspective is contained in FRUS, 1905, pp. 204–304.

In these same years leaders of public opinion in China launched an attack on American interests at another point. The American China Development Company, which had bungled its Hankow–Canton railway concession, became the target of attack by the gentry of Hupeh, Hunan, and Kwangtung, the provinces through which the line was to run.[49] They demanded cancellation of the contract. Chang Chih-tung surrendered all hopes for the completion of the line under American auspices and acted to take the concession back into China's hands. In view of the company's violation of its contract, Chang would have been justified in simply voiding it. Instead, he took the more conciliatory path of buying back the concession with funds borrowed from the British Shanghai and Hong Kong Bank.[50]

For American leaders the boycott and railway agitation burst on the scene unexpectedly. When news of the effectiveness of the boycott reached Washington, President Roosevelt was at first puzzled,[51] then angered. Drawing a lesson from the text of the China hands, he instructed Rockhill to apply pressure on the Chinese government to end the boycott.

It is absolutely necessary for you to take a stiff tone with the Chinese where they are clearly doing wrong. Unless I misread them entirely they despise weakness even more than they prize justice, and we must make it evident both that we intend to do what is right and that we do not intend for a moment to suffer what is wrong.[52]

At the same time the War Department supported the president's diplomacy by preparing plans to send an expeditionary force to Canton.[53] However, Roosevelt could not entirely deny the justice of the Chinese

---

Chinese language sources and recent scholarly studies on this topic are: *Fan-Mei Hua-kung chin-yüeh wen-hsüeh chi* [Collected literature on opposition to the American treaty excluding Chinese laborers], comp. by A Ying (Ch'ien Hsing-ts'un) (Peking, 1960); *Mei-kuo p'o-hai Hua-kung shih-liao* [Historical materials on American oppression of Chinese laborers], comp. by Chu Shih-chia (Peking, 1959); articles in *Chin-tai shih tzu-liao* [Sources on modern history], including those by Ting Yu and Su Shao-ping; A Ying, "Fan Hua-kung chin-yüeh yün-tung" [Movement against the treaty excluding Chinese laborers], in his *Wan-Ch'ing hsiao-shuo shih* [A history of novels in the late Ch'ing] (Shanghai, 1937); Chang Ts'un-wu, *Kuang-hsü sa-i-nien Chung-Mei kung-yüeh feng-ch'ao* [Public upheaval in 1905 over the Sino–American labor treaty] (Taipei, 1966); Edward J. M. Rhoads, "Nationalism and Xenophobia in Kwangtung (1905–1906): The Canton Anti-American Boycott and the Lienchow Anti-Missionary Uprising," *Papers on China* 16 (1962): 154–97.

49. For official correspondence dealing with the abuses by the American company of its concession, see CWS:KH, ch. 171.14; 182.14; 186.4; 190.1,16.

50. These events of 1904–06 are described in Percy H. Kent, *Railway Enterprise in China: An Account of Its Origin and Development* (London, 1907), pp. 117–21.

51. Adee to the Peking legation, telegram, 16 August 1905, DIC.

52. Roosevelt to Rockhill, 22 August 1905, Morison, 4:1310.

53. Roosevelt to Taft, 11 January 1906, Morison, 5:132–33.

complaints which lay behind the boycott. Despite his earlier conviction that the immigration laws were fairly applied to the Chinese, he now sternly ordered immigration officials to moderate their prejudices.[54]

Roosevelt did not consider the Chinese desire to redeem the Hankow–Canton railway as serious an injustice to American interests as the boycott, but it still disturbed him. "I think it would be a real misfortune to let go this great line of railway—a blow to our prestige and to our commerce in China."[55] He once again instructed Rockhill to stand up for American rights and urged J. P. Morgan, who in 1905 had recovered control of the company from Belgian stockholders, to try to hold on to it. Roosevelt's displeasure was heightened by a third irritant in an already strained relationship between the two countries: the massacre of American missionaries at Lienchow in Kwangtung, which provoked the usual horrified outcry in the United States.

In Washington's opinion, conditions in China began at last to improve in the latter months of 1905. The Chinese government's swift and satisfactory action against its offending subjects in the aftermath of the missionary massacre assured Americans it did not condone the attack. In August, Morgan accepted the Chinese offer for reclaiming the railway contract, thereby ending that dispute. And the boycott, against which the central government had finally set itself, began to lose steam.

The events of 1905 gave the first sign of the birth of a new nationalistic China, a development subversive of the premises of American policy. An articulate public opinion, intolerant of the unfavorable status quo which the United States helped perpetuate through the system of unequal treaties, began to take form. Students joined gentry, merchants, and officials in giving vent to popular sentiment. Cultural superiority found new expression in nationalism, and the old xenophobia reemerged as civilized antiforeignism. The deep changes in Chinese life which would finally leave the Manchu dynasty outmoded and exhausted surfaced for the first time on a wide scale in 1905.[56]

The year 1905 thus gave the first obvious hint that China was becoming a nation, but Americans hardly recognized the change. American China

54. Roosevelt to Herbert H. D. Pierce (acting secretary of state), 24 June 1905, and Roosevelt to Victor H. Metcalf, 16 June 1905, Morison, 4:1251–52 and 1235–36 respectively. The president's earlier view of the system is expressed in a letter to Henry Cabot Lodge, 23 May 1904, Morison, 4:803.
55. Roosevelt to J. P. Morgan, 18 July 1905, Morison, 4:1278–79.
56. "The Rising Tide of Change" is a lengthy introduction to *China in Revolution: The First Phase, 1900–1913* (New Haven, Conn., 1968) by its editor Mary C. Wright. She convincingly argues the importance of the ferment in Chinese life in the decade preceding the 1911 revolution.

policy, along with its rationalizations and public rhetoric, flowed on un-
disturbed by the issues which directly challenged popular American views
about the Chinese and the "harmonious" relations between the two
countries. By contrast, Americans would greet the revolution of 1911—
long considered one of the crucial gauges by which to measure their
country's accommodation to a changing China—with an emotional out-
pouring over the birth of a sister republic and the entrance of a progressive
and Christian China into the family of nations. Americans would be
able to afford enthusiasm precisely because the events of that year would
do nothing to challenge the verities of American China policy. In fact,
the revolution would leave in its wake precious little substantial change.
An empire would become a republic overnight, but the faces and problems
familiar in the late Ch'ing would still be abundantly in view in 1912.

It was their stereotyped view of the Chinese which blinded American
leaders to the significance of the outburst of patriotic activity in 1905. They
retained their view that the Chinese were passive and unpatriotic, unconcerned with their country or countrymen. The number two man in the
State Department spoke for his colleagues when, after the events of 1905,
he observed, "The inertia of China is disheartening, but what can you
expect of a jellyfish."[57] They continued to build policy on the premise that
the "celestials" only respected force. In addition, American leaders, badly
informed about China, cast about for domestic analogues to Chinese
phenomena, often with ludicrous results. The condemnation by Elihu
Root, the new secretary of state, of the boycott activity as "combinations
in restraint of lawful trade" mixed domestic commercial regulation with
nascent Chinese nationalism and illustrated how parochial American
policy-makers remained.[58]

American leaders, at first resentful of Chinese injustice to foreigners and
ingratitude to Americans, finally discounted anti-American activity as the
inexplicable pique of a few malcontents. Although Chinese "agitators"
had succeeded in recovering their railway and in forcing the president to
improve treatment of Chinese, they had failed to break the confining
mold in which Americans formed their thoughts about China and the
Chinese. Old views maintained their hold on the imagination of men in
Washington. Nothing had happened, so they thought, to discredit deeply
carved impressions of Chinese inferiority and passivity.

Nothing illustrates the problems of understanding across cultural divides

---

57. Adee to Denby, memo, 30 August 1906, NF 143/11.
58. Root to Rockhill, 26 February 1906 (quoted in Rockhill to Root, 5 March 1906, MCD).

so well as the quandary of W. W. Rockhill as minister to China. According to one intimate,

> he spent most of the day closeted in his library bent over Chinese manuscripts or drafting despatches to the State Department. He was proficient in the spoken and written Chinese language, and once had successfully travelled in Tibet. . . . Rockhill was essentially a Chinese scholar, who cared deeply for the country and was naturally highly respected by the Chinese officials with whom he came into contact.[59]

Rockhill applied to the duties of this post he had long desired a trained mind and a reasonably sound understanding of China. His arrival had coincided with the height of the immigration and railway disputes. His efforts to elucidate for Washington these issues and the changes in China they reflected earned for Rockhill, a considered and sometimes harsh critic of the Ch'ing bureaucracy, a reputation as a sinophile. His views cost him Roosevelt's trust, and those within the State Department who favored a more aggressive China policy and who carried a more conventional view of China became suspicious of his judgments.

Rockhill had returned to China in mid-1905 to discover that the government he had the year before called "weak and corrupt" was interested in reform and that its subjects, far from confirming his old view of them as "devoted to their individual interests and devoid of public spirit," were showing traces of nationalism.[60] For the next two years Rockhill tried to alert Root and Roosevelt to this important change.

> There is now coming into existence in China a public opinion and a native press; both crude and usually misinformed, but nevertheless there is *a* public opinion, and the Government knows it and recognizes that it must be counted with. This public opinion and press are at least developing a national spirit in China and exciting the various elements in the provinces; they are both opposed to the acceptance of Japanese leadership and advocate on every subject "China for the Chinese."[61]

In 1906 and 1907, with fears high in the United States that the Chinese were about to let loose on an orgy of antiforeign riots, Rockhill continued to urge his views and at the same time tried to calm the jitters at home.

---

59. William Phillips, *Ventures in Diplomacy* (Portland, Me., 1952), pp. 17–18.
60. The quotes are from Rockhill, "The United States and the Chinese Question," lecture delivered at the United States Naval War College, 5 August 1904, Rockhill Papers, Houghton Library, Harvard University.
61. Rockhill to Roosevelt, 7 July 1905, Rockhill Papers. See also Rockhill to Root, 14 November 1905, MCD.

In an articulate and remarkably perceptive report to Root, he explained that developments, far from dangerous, were a cause for optimism.

> The Chinese Government is now irrevocably committed to a vast scheme of national progressive reform. . . . In the success of the innovations it is now introducing it sees the only possibility of strengthening its rule and of resisting the incessant encroachments of foreigners, while giving a greater degree of material prosperity to the people, who think that all the wealth of China is passing into the hands of foreigners through the railways and the few mines which have been opened, and who long for the fabulous millions which they imagine are being taken out of and away from the country. To carry out its plans it is essential to the Government that it should be on terms of amity with all foreign nations; any semblance of hostility toward them which might precipitate new interference by foreign powers . . . would be disastrous to its policy.[62]

Rockhill was not arguing for anything as daring as an alliance with China nor for anything as shocking as tolerance of the massacre of foreigners. His point was that his government should support and encourage the government in Peking, whose continued existence was best calculated to maintain the order and peace essential to the interests of Americans in China. He wrote in May 1907,

> China's efforts to put her house in order deserve our sympathetic support and I sincerely hope and believe that she will get it and that we will not believe in the reported dangers of the rights recovery policy and anti-foreignism.[63]

Rockhill harkened back to his long-held opinion that the maintenance of China's integrity and not an unthinking insistence on every iota of treaty right was the key to a successful China policy. Within this framework American interests could be protected and progress introduced to China without disruption.

Aside from these "heretical" opinions, which might incur official sus-

62. Rockhill to Root, 26 February 1906, MCD.
63. Rockhill to Root, 31 May 1907, NF 7608/-3. Like Rockhill during the same period, British Minister to China Satow urged his supperiors to take a more patient and conciliatory attitude toward an awakening China and deprecated fears of an anti-foreign outbreak. Satow to Grey, 14 December 1905 and 11 January 1906 and 31 March 1906 (all in FO 800/44), and 22 February 1906 (in FO 371/25). However, unlike the State Department, the more knowledgeable and less excitable Foreign Office attentively read Satow's dispatches and quickly incorporated his views into the guidelines of British policy. Grey, minutes of 2 June 1906; and Grey to Jordan, 2 June 1906, 7 and 31 August 1906, and 6 September 1906, all in FO 371/35.

picion, Rockhill's views on policy were generally in line with his superiors'. He agreed for the most part with Root's defense of American treaty rights in China and shared the president's even-tempered acceptance of Japan's leading role in the Far East.[64] His reporting on Chinese internal affairs, even though reflecting his careful judgment and knowledge of China, was nonetheless in many respects conventional. As before, he still pinned his hopes for China's future on financial and educational reforms. Rockhill felt that the United States was best suited to lead China in these changes but acknowledged with disappointment that China seemed not to appreciate his country's disinterested concern.

It is a great pity that the Chinese Govt does not more openly recognize that we are the one power which seeks to act justly in its dealings with her, and seek and follow more frequently our advice.[65]

The waywardness of his Chinese wards drove Rockhill at times to despair and to deal caustically with the lethargic, cumbersome, and benighted Chinese officialdom.

The present blindness of the Government in all economic matters is only equalled by its obstinacy and its determination, for the time being, to disregard every lesson of experience, every dictate of prudence, let alone every rule of political economy.[66]

Although he appreciated the importance of the new developments in China's public life, he still had second thoughts about them. At times Rockhill could not control his impatience with the Chinese government for not guiding its reform program as he himself preferred and for pursuing a rights recovery policy to the neglect of essential reforms. Nor could he hide his exasperation with the "malcontents and agitators for political reform" who exploited the newly roused popular patriotism.[67]

Rockhill mixed prescriptions for policy change into his largely reassuring dispatches but made precious little headway in altering his superiors' views on relations with China. He finally ran into trouble when, having

64. Rockhill, "The United States and the Chinese Question," 5 August 1904; and Rockhill to Roosevelt, 7 July 1905, both in Rockhill Papers.

65. The quote is from an undated fragment written between 1902 and 1905, Rockhill Papers. Rockhill's views on reform, fairly consistent over the years, emerge from Rockhill to Hippisley, 30 October 1894, and a memo, 27 August 1899, both in Rockhill Papers; Rockhill to Hay, 28 March 1901, MCD; and Rockhill to Root, 24 January 1907 and 31 October 1908, NF 1518/27 and NF 788/193 respectively.

66. Rockhill to Root, 6 October 1906, NF 2321/-. See also, by way of example, his unflattering appraisal of leading government figures in a dispatch to Root, 29 August 1906, NF 1518/-1.

67. Rockhill to Root, 4 September 1906, NF 1518/2.

failed in his attempt to educate Roosevelt and the State Department, he actively resisted their hostile response to Chinese nationalism. The president had appointed him to the Peking post, "in the center of the storm," confident in his ability, but he was soon disappointed by the minister's halfhearted defense of national interests.[68] Rockhill described the boycott as a "dangerous force if not directed to lawful ends, but a hopeful one for China if properly guided and developed" and concluded that the Chinese government "is all right, but cannot reach this agitation and stop it." He argued against making any protest so tough that it might undermine its authority with the people.[69] But Roosevelt rejected Rockhill's conciliatory approach and insisted on administering a stern rebuke to the Chinese for their gross misbehavior. A second collision in 1905 came over the cancellation of the Hankow–Canton railway contract. Rockhill had long felt that the American China Development Company was guilty of bad faith in taking on the concession and that the American government had misled the Chinese government by endorsing the company's questionable claim to integrity.

> The promoters have no earthly intention of attempting to develop [the concession], and . . . they simply use [it] as an asset on the stock markets of Europe and America for purposes of speculation.[70]

But the president brushed aside Rockhill's views, accusing him of "a complete misapprehension of the facts."[71]

Roosevelt also found fault with Rockhill for his inattention to the minor obligations of his post. Complaints of the minister's sins of omission and commission reached back to the president. One of the first to complain was the powerful E. H. Harriman, who during a visit to Peking had asked Rockhill to open the imperial palace for him. Rockhill refused this request, which he knew to be offensive to the Chinese; Harriman and others traveling with him faulted the minister for discourtesy. Rockhill similarly irritated another influential tourist in Peking—Alice Roosevelt, the president's

68. Roosevelt to Rockhill, 6 August 1906, Morison, 5:344–45; and Roosevelt to Meyer, 26 December 1904, Morison, 4:1079.

69. The quotes are from Rockhill to the secretary of state, 26 August 1905, MCD; and Rockhill to Hippisley, 29 March 1906, Rockhill Papers. See also Rockhill to Roosevelt, 30 October 1905, Rockhill Papers. The British minister also doubted the wisdom of a strong American protest. "It appears . . . that the American Government intend to employ strong language to the Central Government, as though it had the power of enforcing its will in opposition to that of the provinces; this course will, I consider, more probably result in uniting it with the provinces against foreigners. The effect produced on the popular mind by this warning . . . will be that the foreign Powers are bullying her." Satow to Grey, 2 March 1906, FO 371/25.

70. Rockhill to Hay, 19 January 1901, MCD.

71. Adee (acting secretary of state) to Rockhill, 15 August 1905, DIC.

daughter. In addition, missionaries complained that Rockhill had insulted them by scheduling conferences with them on Sunday. The head of the Associated Press accused Rockhill of favoring the correspondent for the London *Times* over an American newsman in Peking. In the two latter cases the president rebuked the minister, whose failure to cultivate his countrymen left him even more isolated.[72]

Rockhill's new perspectives on a changing China and his insensitivity to the lesser duties of his post cost him friends and support in the bureaucracy. This scholar–diplomat, who loved exotic Central Asia more than he did legation routine, had greeted his assignment to China as a chance to resume his academic studies at first hand. Rockhill's understanding of China's culture, notably in advance of anyone else of rank in the State Department, and his interpretive reporting on contemporary China aroused suspicions among his fellow officials that his esoteric studies had drawn him to strange ideas and that his contact with the natives had clouded his judgment.[73] Their reaction was to conclude that the minister was a sinophile whose views ought to be discounted and whose lack of devotion to duty ought to be condemned. He was out of step with his influential and sometimes zealous contemporaries.

By 1907 the man in the diplomatic service with the best claim to expertise in Chinese affairs and with the best chance of making his voice heard had largely lost his influence with the president, and the personnel in the State Department tended to greet his views with misgiving and occasional hostility. Under the Taft administration Rockhill's prestige would continue to decline.

72. Roosevelt to Rockhill, 18 May 1905 and 6 August 1906, Morison, 4:1184 and 5:344–45; Rockhill to Root, 28 November 1905, MCD; and Phillips, *Ventures in Diplomacy*, pp. 25–26.

73. Bacon to Root, memo, 16 January 1906, MCD. Speck von Sternburg, the German minister to the United States, wrote back to Berlin that Root and Roosevelt felt Rockhill was looking too much from the Chinese point of view. Dispatch noted in Alfred Vagts, *Deutschland und die Vereinigten Staaten in der Weltpolitik* (New York, 1935), 2:1250.

6: POSTWAR MANCHURIAN POLICY

The outcome of the Russo–Japanese War justified China's refusal to impale herself on either horn of the Manchurian policy dilemma posed by the Russian occupation. By allowing international rivalry to accomplish what alone they could not do, the Chinese secured Russian evacuation from Manchuria and regained much of their authority there. Now China could resume her efforts at containing and controlling the foreign threat. At the same time, she had to deal with a host of domestic problems which had perforce lain neglected since mid-1900. China had in her hands a new opportunity, and with growing concern she attempted to make the most of it in developing and executing a better method of frontier defense.

Even while the war was still in progress, the prospect of a Japanese victory over Russia had stimulated the government in Peking to look closely to its postwar policy for Manchuria. As one of its goals, the Chinese government had sought a Russo–Japanese settlement favorable to China. Moreover, it had begun shape to a long-term policy for managing the Manchurian frontier.

While China had failed to reduce foreign rights in Manchuria during the period of peacemaking in the latter half of 1905, the outcome of the war did allow her to once again assert her authority there. Discussions of the problems of frontier defense which had continued during the occupation, had become more urgent as Manchuria's return to China became imminent. Already during the war the throne had issued two edicts inviting opinions from high officials and had held audiences with them on the subject.[1] On this question of bringing the machinery of frontier defense back into operation after the earlier failures, the government found plentiful advice.

The most thoughtful and comprehensive suggestions for updating traditional methods of frontier defense came from Ch'eng Te-ch'üan.

1. The first edict, dated 2 August 1904, inviting opinions is in SL:KH, ch. 532.15. The respondents concentrated more on the damage being done to Manchuria by the war than on postwar planning. A second summons was issued on 23 and 25 June 1905, SL:KH, ch. 545.7,9. With peace in sight high officials in the provinces and abroad finally shifted their attention to the kind of peace settlement they wished to see in Manchuria.

100

A native of Szechwan and a holder of the *hsiu-ts'ai*, the first degree in the Chinese examination system, he had served in Manchuria almost steadily since 1891. His experience there had been in Heilungkiang, where he had occupied a variety of official posts—diplomatic, financial, and military—befitting the ideal omnicompetent official. In 1906 his adroit handling of his responsibilities and his long experience in the northeast earned him the honor of becoming the first nonbannerman Chinese to act as a military governor in Manchuria.[2]

As early as 1903 Ch'eng had called for thoroughgoing reform in Manchuria. During the Russian occupation he had spoken out against the incompetence and the venality of administrative personnel in Heilungkiang and had deplored the shortage of civil officials to attend to the needs of a growing Chinese population. He had attacked the ethnic prejudices and official prerogatives of the banner population, which dominated the local government and harassed Chinese settlers. Ch'eng had also expressed his mistrust of Russia and Japan and recommended a coherent program of development to assure China's control over Manchuria.[3] During the war years and after, Ch'eng continued to develop his views, presenting detailed plans to the government for the renovation of the tradition-bound military administration of Heilungkiang. His farsighted suggestions anticipated most of the programs which the court was to sanction in the future and revealed the growing sophistication of Chinese thinking on frontier defense.

The program Ch'eng formulated during his years as military governor of Heilungkiang was meant to meet the interrelated foreign and domestic difficulties of his area. Russia was still a formidable problem. Although weakened by the war with Japan and by internal dissent, her overall influence in northern Manchuria was undiminished, and her troops remained in temporary occupation. Ch'eng warned that Russia's combined military, political, and economic strength would gradually reduce Chinese sovereignty in Heilungkiang to an empty shell unless the native administration took immediate and vigorous countermeasures. The domestic side of this two-sided problem was the continuing lack of effective Chinese authority in this frontier area. The Boxer uprising, the Russian occupation, and the Russo–Japanese War had aggravated this problem of control. In addition, the frontier was still short of such basic amenities as schools, police, and competent civil officials. These administrative shortcomings put in question China's claim to sovereignty in Manchuria.

2. Robert H. G. Lee, *The Manchurian Frontier in Ch'ing History* (Cambridge, Mass., 1970), pp. 140–41.
3. Ch'eng expressed these views in an audience in 1903. Ibid., pp. 141–42.

Since the problem was complex, the solution which Ch'eng advanced was by necessity many faceted. The greatest need was for a sufficient number of well-trained and well-equipped troops to deal with rebellion or foreign aggression. To consolidate internal control, he suggested extending the political administration to newly settled areas, about one-third of the territory of Heilungkiang. Moreover, in previously settled areas the administration had to be upgraded to meet the communities' needs. Everywhere more officials were needed, particularly to provide security, handle taxation, and promote education. Ch'eng urged the central government to encourage colonization. Settlers drawn by free transportation as well as by starting grants of supplies and money would gradually but inexorably tighten China's hold on Heilungkiang.

Heilungkiang—even though guarded, settled, pacified, and well governed—would still be a vulnerable object of foreign ambition and a drain on China's financial resources. Ch'eng saw that the promotion of commerce and industry under official auspices was the means to make it an asset to China and resistant to foreign encroachment. Thus the government could transform weakness into strength. Heilungkiang was rich in minerals and timber. A government bureau was needed to encourage their exploitation by Chinese and to supervise foreign enterprise. Ch'eng also recommended the extension of a Chinese-controlled transport system throughout the province to promote commerce and facilitate colonization. Steamship lines along the Sungari and Amur rivers as well as railways through the interior were the chief steps in that direction. Through these diverse projects Ch'eng hoped to limit foreign influence and to bring to Heilungkiang a prosperity which would fill the local treasury and allow the government to take even more vigorous action.

The crucial missing link in Ch'eng's ambitious plans, as in those of other active officials with reform on their minds, was money. Heilungkiang was too poor to provide the requisite funds. Only from the coffers of the central government and the more prosperous provinces to the south could Ch'eng obtain them.

> Russia has built the Chinese Eastern Railway and Japan has seized economic interests in the Liaotung Peninsula. These two neighbors are drawing on the financial strength of their whole country and are channeling it to the East. How can we, still shrinking from using our own national wealth to manage our own nation's affairs, do nothing?[4]

4. Ch'eng, memorial, 4 April 1907, CCST, ch. 16.30–35. He deals most comprehensively with the problems of Heilungkiang and their solution in this memorial and another dated 10 January 1906, in CWS:KH, ch. 195.19–21. On neither of these did the throne take definitive action. See

Ch'eng warned that without outside financial support the local projects were doomed and that, as a result, Heilungkiang would never become strong, prosperous, and financially self-sufficient.

An equally ambitious blueprint for reform took shape in Fengtien. This province was longer and more densely settled, especially in the Liao River valley, than the rest of Manchuria. The long-neglected needs of its fast-growing population urgently required attention. Questions of foreign relations in Fengtien were even more difficult than in Heilungkiang, where the status quo generally prevailed. Chinese officials in the south were confronted with Japan's awakening ambitions. She had secured through expenditure of blood and bullion a commercial and strategic position of advantage in southern Manchuria, and she now began to strengthen and extend her influence there.

The official to whom the difficult Fengtien post fell was Chao Erh-sun, a Chinese bannerman from an eminent family of Tiehling, in that province.[5] A product of traditional education, he had gained his *chin-shih*, the third and highest degree in the Chinese examination system, at thirty-eight. In 1904 the central government had ordered Chao, then at the honored age of sixty, to surrender the governorship of Hunan and proceed to Fengtien. Delayed by the war, he served briefly in Peking as acting president of the Board of Revenue, deliberated on plans for Manchuria, and then finally took up his post in 1905. Chao saw the need for administrative reform and troop reorganization as well as for the promotion of commerce, education, and colonization. He would lay the foundation for the more ambitious efforts of his successors although financial dearth made full realization of his program impossible during his own two-year tenure.[6]

In Fengtien, coping with the complex and treacherous foreign threat was at the top of the official agenda. Chao, like many Chinese officials, resented the influence which the Japanese had won in southern Manchuria

---

also Ch'eng's memorial of 2 December 1904 and his draft memorial (which he never dispatched) of 7 October 1906, both in CCST, ch. 2.49–51 and 13.21–25. His memorial of 3 December 1905 on rehabilitation and reform and his letter sent to the Grand Council in the autumn of 1904 are both summarized in Lee, *The Manchurian Frontier in Ch'ing History*, pp. 142–45.

5. See the entry on Chao in Howard L. Boorman, ed., *Biographical Dictionary of Republican China* (New York, 1967–71), 1:141–42; report by E. T. Williams, enclosed in J. G. Coolidge (chargé, Peking) to Hay, 26 May 1905, MCD; and Dugald Christie, *Thirty Years in Moukden 1883–1913* (New York, 1914), p. 197.

6. On Chao's policy, see his memorial, 16 January 1906, SL:KH, ch. 553.6; and his telegram to the Grand Council, 16 March 1907, CWS:KH, ch. 201.5–7. Foreigners living in Mukden recorded with admiration the vigor of his reform program. See, for example, Christie, *Thirty Years in Moukden*, pp. 197–203; J. W. Inglis, "Moukden in 1911," *Chinese Recorder and Missionary Journal* 42 (July 1911): 394–97; Sammons to Rockhill, 10 March 1906, NCR; and a report by Straight, 18 November 1906, NF 914/9.

and suspected their intentions, but he did not have—nor was he likely to acquire in the near future—the military force to resist their demands. In addition, Chao was preoccupied with Russia's activities in Mongolia, which lay at Fengtien's flank, as well as with her still secure grip on northern Manchuria. "These two powers contend for Manchuria; the whole world eyes it. Indeed, if we do not wholeheartedly devote ourselves to planning, we will fail in our life and death struggle."[7] His principal recommendation was the construction of a railway from Fengtien through Mongolia. It would serve both to pull Mongolia more securely into China's orbit and to recover from Japan some of the influence her railway exercised over Manchurian commerce. Chao also suggested constructing a new ice-free port near Chinchow, on the Gulf of Chihli. This port, Hulutao, would supplement Newchuang, which was frozen in during the winter months and losing trade to the nearby Japanese port of Dairen. To further hold back Japanese penetration, China must reserve exploitation of Fengtien's rich mines for Chinese alone. To allow either Europeans or Americans to invest in or operate them would give the Japanese an excuse to make their own claims. In these ways Chao planned to diminish Japan's financial and commercial influence and to increase China's.

Although Chao obviously agreed in general with Ch'eng Te-ch'üan on Manchurian policy, Chao's attitude toward the other military governors of Manchuria, together with factional rivalry, unfortunately made a concerted policy for the whole region impossible. In the first place, Chao, responsive to the feelings of fellow bannermen, resented Ch'eng's sharp criticisms of that group in Heilungkiang. Consequently he ostentatiously avoided consulting Ch'eng as well as the less energetic military governor of Kirin, Ta-kuei. Moreover, Chao kept his distance from Ch'eng because the latter was not, as Chao was, an intimate of Yüan Shih-k'ai. Yüan had earlier begun extending his influence into Manchuria; indeed, Chao's appointment had already brought southern Manchuria under his sway. Yüan's next logical step was to place his own lieutenants in Heilungkiang and Kirin. Ch'eng, already charged by his local opposition with corruption and mismanagement and undoubtedly aware of Yüan's

---

7. Chao to the Grand Council, telegram, 16 March 1907, CWS:KH, ch. 201.5–7. See also Chao to the Wai-wu Pu, received 20 July 1906, *K'uang-wu tang* [Records on mining affairs] (Taipei, 1960), comp. by the Institute of Modern History, Academia Sinica, 6:3811; and a report by Straight to the State Department, 18 November 1906, NF 914/9. Suggestions on Manchurian policy, generally similar to Ch'eng's and Chao's were made by Chang Chih-tung, telegraphic memorial, 24 July 1905, CWS:KH, ch. 190.12–15; and by Lu Pao-chung (president of the censorate), memorial, 23 April 1906, WWP: Kuang-hsü sa-erh-nien fang-wu an shang [File on defense measures for 1906—first half], *ts'e* 2. Chang's proposals were unique for the degree of cooperation with Japan on which they were predicated.

intentions, finally offered to resign. And Hsü Shih-ch'ang, another of Yüan's allies, who was assigned to investigate the complaints of the bannermen, not surprisingly recommended that the court accept the resignation even though he found no evidence for the charges.[8]

Despite their personal and political differences, Chao and Ch'eng agreed that the railway lay at the heart of any effective plan for managing Manchuria. They each adopted a two-pronged railway policy. One was to restrict the influence of foreign-controlled railways by interpreting foreign rights narrowly. The other was to construct competing lines under Chinese control. In sparsely settled areas of Heilungkiang and Kirin and along the long Russian border, they valued the railway primarily for facilitating colonization and defense. In Fengtien, where problems of foreign penetration were more complicated and population greater, the railway figured more prominently as an instrument for recovering economic interests and stimulating native commerce.

Ch'eng Te-ch'üan and Ta-kuei together proposed the creation of a central office at Harbin, a counterpart to the long existing Russian office there, to oversee the activities of the foreign-controlled railways of Manchuria and to coordinate negotiations with them. The existing decentralized management of railway affairs, which left each of the three provinces to manage for itself, made for divergent policies and often contradictory decisions. The military governors also suggested that the central government take advantage of the original railway agreement with Russia to send a Chinese official to act as codirector of the Chinese Eastern Railway, a right unexercised since 1900. The throne welcomed both these suggestions, referring them to the Peking bureaucracy for execution.[9]

In southern Manchuria, Chao Erh-sun was at loggerheads with Japan over conflicting interpretations of the conditions governing Japan's operation of the former Russian railway. The central issue was the status of the South Manchurian Railway Company, which Japan had organized in 1906 in such a way as to exclude China from meaningful participation in its operations. The Chinese regarded this as a violation of a Japanese agreement in the Peking talks of 1905 to stick to the terms of the original

---

8. Lee, *The Manchurian Frontier in Ch'ing History*, pp. 145–46.
9. Ch'eng and Ta-kuei, memorial and supplementary memorial, 5 October 1905, WWP: Tung-san-sheng chung-tung t'ieh-lu an [File on the Chinese Eastern Railway in Manchuria], *ts'e* 1. The rescript, dated 31 October 1905, is appended to the above document. Ch'eng first broached the proposal for a central railway office to oversee the Chinese Eastern Railway in a memorial, 5 April 1905, CWS:KH, ch. 188.1–4. The throne turned aside a more comprehensive and restrictive program for regulation of foreign railways in Manchuria, presented by Ch'eng in a memorial of 16 December 1905, CWS:KH, ch. 195.1–5.

Russo–Chinese railway agreement, but they could only lodge diplomatic protests and withhold Chinese money from the enterprise.[10]

Aside from restraining foreign railways, the other major goal of China's Manchurian railway policy was the construction of Chinese railways deep into the Manchurian interior. The impetus came, as in other Manchurian policy initiatives, principally from Ch'eng Te-ch'üan. He proposed the construction of a railway from Hsinminfu, the northernmost point on the Peking–Mukden line, through Potuna and Hulan to Tsitsihar to serve as the axis for a new Manchurian railway system under Chinese control. Later, Ch'eng foresaw that its proximity to the South Manchurian Railway might provoke Japan's opposition and result in delay. Accordingly he suggested shifting the proposed line toward the west, so that it would run from Hsinminfu to Taonan and thence across the Chinese Eastern Railway to Tsitsihar, with an extension to Aigun on the Russian border. He wished to exclude foreign investors in order to protect China's control of the line; however, his intention to obtain construction funds exclusively from Chinese merchants was unrealistic in the light of earlier failures at building Chinese railways with native capital.[11]

In March 1906 Ch'eng secured a rescript sending his railway proposal on for consideration by the Board of Posts, the Board of Revenue, and the Board of Agriculture, Industry, and Commerce. In early 1907 Chao Erh-sun endorsed the idea of a new Manchurian railway from Hsinminfu to Heilungkiang and, despite Japanese displeasure, went as far as to survey a route through Fakumen and Liaoyuan to Tsitsihar. Sharing Ch'eng's misplaced confidence, Chao too invited Chinese merchants to invest their money in the project.[12] Soon thereafter the boards, after nearly a year of discussion and delay, jointly presented a favorable reply, and in April 1907 the throne concurred on the desirability of Ch'eng's project. The reorganization of the Manchurian government that year, however, brought discussions to a halt. The fate of the project would rest largely in the hands of newly appointed officials.[13]

After the conclusion of the Portsmouth peace treaty, American China

10. Yüan Shih-k'ai to the Wai-wu Pu, 12 October 1906, and Chao Erh-sun to the Wai-wu Pu, both in WWP: Nan-man-chou t'ieh-lu an [File on the South Manchurian Railway].

11. See Ch'eng's memorials, 10 January 1906, CWS:KH, ch. 195.19–21; 19 February 1906, CCST, ch. 10.13–15; 8 March 1906, SL:KH, ch. 155.12; 14 January 1907, CWS:KH, ch. 200.1–2; and 4 April 1907, CCST, ch. 16.30–35.

12. Chao, memorial, 16 March 1907, CWS:KH, ch. 201.7.

13. The Board of Posts, the Board of Finance, and the Board of Agriculture, Industry, and Commerce, joint memorial, n.d. [30 April 1907], *Yu-ch'uan Pu tsou-i lei-pien* [A classified collection of memorials by the Board of Posts] (Taipei reprint, 1967), comp. by the Board of Posts and the Ministry of Communications, 2:485–90. The edict of approval is appended to this document.

policy followed along in the well-established line of protecting limited interests in Manchuria with the limited means immediately at hand. While the Chinese attended to defense of their frontier territories, Americans stuck to defense of their trade there. The general framework for the conduct of American Manchurian policy was Theodore Roosevelt's policy of balanced antagonisms. Limited by public opinion and insignificant naval strength in the Pacific, he could only marginally influence the situation in Manchuria. Nonetheless, he hoped to protect tangible American commercial interests by depending on the mutual suspicions between Japan and Russia and the desire of each to keep American goodwill. Roosevelt was unwilling to imperil his country's interests in Manchuria by antagonizing either of these powers over lesser issues. His policy of balanced antagonisms represented no more than a realistic acceptance of power relations in the Far East and an acknowledgement of the limited American stake in Manchuria. It was a cautious plan of inaction.

In July 1905 the president had brought Elihu Root, a close friend and trusted adviser, back into his cabinet to fill the post left vacant by John Hay's death. Root, who was guided by his own conservative legal instincts and his loyalty to the president, would bear the burden of applying the president's cautious guidelines to developments in Manchuria. The game Root played there was a four-sided contest for advantage. The peace had left the two former combatants suspiciously eyeing each other across an imaginary east-west line through Changchun. Each was in his sphere careful not to leave unclaimed any advantage gained by the other in his. Both were at the same time preoccupied with resisting the restrictive claims of the Chinese; neither would give up to China more than the other. Although caught between these two powers, China was intent on asserting her control in the area and on securing favorable settlement of a multitude of minor diplomatic issues which in sum had major implications for Manchuria's future. Root's goal in this postwar game was to guard American commerce from the interference of the other three players.

Root was soon faced with complaints by American businessmen against Japanese discrimination in the Manchurian market and with settling the regulations for the new open ports there, held over from 1903. In dealing with these problems he relied on international contracts. He tried to hold Peking, Tokyo, and St. Petersburg to his understanding of existing agreements. Where existing contracts were not enough, he sought new ones to guarantee the open door. His dependence on treaty rights, long the centerpiece of China policy, was calculated to secure his objectives with a minimum of controversy at home or risk abroad.

This legalistic approach to China policy also appealed to Root and his aides for good personal reasons. Root had been trained as a lawyer and had practiced before the bar. Furthermore, the State Department was dominated by men such as Robert Bacon and James B. Scott with similar backgrounds and instincts. Their legal training and habits led them to view the problems of international relations in a legal framework. They were at their best drafting, negotiating, and interpreting treaties. They found the subtleties of international law far more absorbing than the subtleties of international power and influence.

Soon after taking over the State Department, Root began to hear allegations of Japanese discrimination against American trade in Manchuria. The business complaints reached their peak in the first half of 1906. The British–American Tobacco Company, a British firm substantially owned by Americans and a major purchaser of American tobacco, officially complained that its Japanese competitors were getting goods into Manchuria customs-free through Japanese-controlled Dairen, where customs had not yet been established. Meanwhile, the company continued to enter its goods through Newchuang, where customs had long existed. It also complained that, like other foreign companies, its personnel were not allowed to enter the extensive zone of Japanese occupation to do business. Swift and Company lodged a similar complaint. The American Association of China, a Shanghai business organization, expressed its doubts that trade opportunity was equitably arranged in Manchuria and petitioned the secretary of state for relief.[14]

The charges of discrimination against American trade in Manchuria were in part an expression of frustrated hopes. The Manchurian market for American goods was not living up to the glowingly prosperous picture painted by its enthusiasts. In fact, after a period of slow but appreciable growth, this trade now plunged into a sharp decline. During the Russian occupation American trade, contrary to the fears of many, had grown handsomely. The value of American exports—as earlier, principally cotton, kerosene, and flour—to the region had grown to $16,560,000 in 1903 and then to $19,260,000 in 1904. The appetite of the Russian and Japanese war machines had sent the figure for 1905 zooming to $56,060,000. Goods from the United States, which in 1900 had made up no more than one-tenth of the value of Newchuang imports, had reached one-half

14. Root to the Tokyo embassy, telegram, 21 February 1906, and Robert Bacon (acting secretary of state) to Rockhill, 20 April 1906, in FRUS, 1906, pp. 17–71 and 186 respectively; Bacon to Rockhill, 31 July 1906, DIC; and the American Association of China to Rockhill, 2 July 1906, FRUS, 1906, pp. 209–13.

by 1905. Figures for American cotton goods to China, the bulk of which ultimately reached the markets of Manchuria and northern China, reflected the upswing. Sales between 1900 and 1904 had averaged 212 million yards annually, an increase over previous years. When the sales in 1905 hit 563 million yards, earlier predictions of a booming commercial market in Manchuria seemed to be coming true. Statistics for other export items, showing similar performances, tended to confirm that boom times had come.

Then the bottom dropped out. In 1906 cotton exports to China from the United States fell by over one-half, and in 1907 they would fall again, to less than one-tenth of the 1905 volume. The depression equally affected other American exports to Manchuria. Sales were on the decline and showed little indication of reviving.[15]

Disgruntled American businessmen in Shanghai and Newchuang attributed the decline in their trade to unfair Japanese competition, particulárly in cotton goods and cigarettes. They specifically charged that the Japanese army was impeding the travel of foreigners in southern Manchuria. Further, they argued that the failure to establish customs offices at Dairen gave Japanese trade, which entered Manchuria mainly through that port, a price advantage over American goods, which tended to go through Newchuang customs. Their third, more sweeping accusation was that Japanese authorities were intentionally using the means at hand, particularly their control over the South Manchurian Railway, to promote Japanese trade at the expense of others.

Root received from his agents in the Far East a steady flow of information on the trade' situation. Thomas Sammons, the consul general at Newchuang, reported after a tour through southern Manchuria in early 1906 that "as a general proposition the Japanese military and civil administration in Manchuria have, apparently, avoided commercial interference."[16] Sammons's successor in the Newchuang post was also skeptical of the charges circulating among businessmen. "They have nothing to offer in the shape of proof."[17] Even the suspicious business community

15. On Manchurian trade, 1901–07: article from *Japan Mail*, 4 July 1906, NF 551/7; Thomas Sammons (consul general, Newchuang) to Rockhill, 28 September 1906, NF 914/3; O. P. Austin (chief, Bureau of Statistics) to Oscar S. Straus (secretary of commerce and labor), 13 March 1908, NF 12471/-1; Miller to Squeirs, 27 June 1901 and 19 March 1903, NCR; Sammons to Rockhill, 21 February 1906, NCR; and trade statistics in *Journal of Commerce*, 12 November 1910.

16. The quote is from Sammons to Rockhill, 10 March 1906, NCR. See also Sammons's reports to the State Department, 27 July 1905, and to Rockhill, 24 October 1905, 1 November 1905, and 12 March 1906, all in NCR.

17. Albert W. Pontius to Rockhill, 18 January 1907, NF 4360/9.

was hard pressed to substantiate its feeling. A committee of interested Americans from Shanghai concluded after a tour of Manchuria that the decline of trade was due to natural conditions rather than to a Japanese conspiracy.[18] The minister in Peking, W. W. Rockhill, reported to the State Department that the Japanese bore no blame for the fall in American trade. He knew that the American business community in China was discontent, but he was also aware that bad business conditions were affecting British and Japanese firms as well. Moreover, since American businessmen had not formally brought specific charges of discrimination to his attention, the question remained for him officially a moot one.[19] Luke E. Wright, the American ambassador in Tokyo, made inquiries in official and commercial circles but—like Rockhill, the Shanghai committee, and the consuls in Manchuria—found no reason to suspect Japan's intentions.[20]

Indeed, the Japanese government seemed intent on avoiding suspicion and repeatedly pledged its support for equal trade opportunity. It argued that its restrictions on travel in Manchuria were a legitimate exercise of the powers of occupation and would terminate as the occupation ended. True to its word, the government opened its railway in southern Manchuria to general commercial use in Noverber 1905. As the evacuation proceeded on schedule, travel in the interior became easier. In addition, the Japanese could claim that preferential railway rates, which had disturbed American businessmen, formed no basis for official complaint since they applied to all goods, regardless of ownership or origin. In fact, the same kinds of rate structures were common in the British empire.[21] Finally, the Japanese government announced its agreement on the need to establish customs offices in newly opened Manchurian ports; however, this action hinged on the concurrence of China and Russia.

In reality, the Manchurian trade depression can be explained primarily by the elementary economic laws of supply and demand. The Russo–Japanese War had greatly increased the demand for goods, American goods included, in late 1904 and 1905, and consequently trade had prospered. When the guns fell silent, commerce declined. To worsen the crisis, the civilian population, impoverished by the war and uncertain about Japan's withdrawal and the resumption of China's control, failed

18. Report by Rudy, Seaman, and Thomas to Gilbert Reid, 25 June 1906, and "Notes of a Visit to Enquire into Trade Conditions of Manchuria," 9 June 1906, both in NF 551/3.

19. Rockhill to Root, 15 and 29 June 1906, MCD, and 11 October 1906, NF 551/13.

20. Wright to Root, 11 August 1906, NF 551/9.

21. Sammons to Rockhill, 17 November 1905, NCR; and the British Board of Trade to the Foreign Office, 18 April 1910, FO 371/857.

to purchase enough foreign goods to take up the military slack or even to reach prewar levels of consumption. This drastic fall in demand caught business firms, optimistic about future sales, painfully overstocked. Trade was also affected by the disruption of finance and transportation caused by the war. The monetary system, thrown into confusion by the multiplicity of currencies, was unstable. The coastal trade had in a measure shifted from Newchuang to Dairen, and land and riverine transport in the interior was still unsettled. Finally, the appearance of Japanese competition on a major scale increased the pinch for American traders, especially in cotton goods. Japanese exporters enjoyed a marked competitive advantage because of government subsidies and other forms of economic support, cheap labor, familiarity with the Manchurian market, and their proximity to it.

Even if some inequities did exist in the Manchurian market, they still did little to hinder American trade specifically. For one, most American goods lost their national identity on their way to Manchuria. The bulk, especially cotton and flour, was obtained in the United States or from American firms in Shanghai and then carried into Manchuria and marketed there not by American firms but by Chinese, Japanese, British, and German agencies. Furthermore, Dairen, as a customs-free port in the years immediately after the war, did not exclude trade in American goods. One contemporary conservatively estimated that one-third of all foreign imports through that duty-free port were American.[22]

There were few American businessmen working actively in Manchuria. In 1906 they totaled only six—four in Newchuang, the center of American business activity, and two in the interior of Fengtien. (Ironically, at least an equal number were in the area working in the Manchurian consulates to protect trade or in the customs service to tax it.[23]) Generally, American firms established their headquarters in Shanghai, and few bothered to branch off into the Manchurian market despite its alleged importance. The only exceptions were the Standard Oil Company of New York and, if its American ties be counted, the British–American Tobacco Company. "This apparent lack of interest . . . discriminates more against us than any other cause, be it Japanese or Chinese," Rock-

22. Heintzleman (vice-consul in charge, Dairen), report to the State Department, 23 March 1907, NF 143/45.

23. Pontius (consul, Newchuang), report to the State Department, 29 December 1906, NF Minor File, Newchuang; and Straight, "Protection of American Interests," December 1906, Post Records, Mukden, To, Consular (Records of the Foreign Service Posts of the Department of State, National Archives).

hill wrote back to Washington.[24] This lack of visible American enterprise —in contrast with Japanese energy—revealed how illusory were the hopes of seeing Manchuria develop as a major American market.

Reports to the British Foreign Office, both from Peking and from Manchuria, gave no support to the charges made against the Japanese. Criticism, particularly from the China Association and the British–American Tobacco Company, reached British officials just as it did their American counterparts. Sir Edward Grey, the secretary for foreign affairs, repeatedly had the charges of Japanese discrimination thoroughly investigated by his diplomatic service, better staffed and trained than Root's. Particularly impressive are the reports by the experienced British commercial attaché, Sir Alexander Hosie, who, despite his suspicion that Japan intended to dominate Manchuria, honestly admitted that several detailed inspections in 1906 and 1907 failed to unearth any basis for the charges of commercial discrimination. As a result, the British Foreign Office dismissed reports to the contrary by some of the more activist American consuls in Manchuria. "Our experience is that American Consuls are not very reliable reporters," observed William Langley, head of the Far East Division of the Foreign Office. Although the British did not hesitate to pressure Tokyo to help restore commercial conditions to normal by hastening the evacuation of her troops from Manchuria and by establishing customs in the new ports, they at the same time saw no grounds for complaining of intentional commercial discrimination.[25]

The allegations of Japanese discrimination failed in the end to worry Root. In March 1906 he asked the Japanese government to hasten the return of normal trading conditions in Manchuria and received a reassuring response.[26] By the spring the Japanese military evacuation was well under way and per se posed no further hindrance to trade in the interior. Moreover, the charges of discrimination, lodged chiefly against the Japanese railway, seemed to Root unfounded and not deserving of diplomatic action.

By contrast the absence of customhouses at Dairen and Antung—discrimination or no—had a disturbing effect on general commerce.

24. Rockhill to Root, 11 October 1906, NF 551/13. In addition to this report, the most valuable sources on trade conditions in Manchuria and the American stake in the immediate postwar period are reports by Shanghai businessmen to Gilbert Reid, 9 June 1906, NF 551/3; reports by Sammons in NCR; Charles F. Remer, *The Foreign Trade of China* (Shanghai, 1926), pp. 121, 153–54; and O. P. Austin to Oscar S. Straus, 13 March 1908, NF 12471/-1.

25. The quote is found in minutes of 9 February 1907, FO 371/384. The reports on Manchurian trade are bound together in FO 371/180 and 384. Hosie's full reports are dated 14 March 1906 and 14 November 1907.

26. Raymond A. Esthus, *Theodore Roosevelt and Japan* (Seattle, Wash., 1966), pp. 118–19.

Here was the single complaint from the business community that justified action. Moreover, the solution was clear: treaties said customs were to be established, and Japan had already voiced her support. Root took the advice of Rockhill and Consul General Sammons and gave priority to getting these customhouses established.[27]

But a settlement was not immediately forthcoming. The Chinese insisted that the customs could be established only after complete Japanese evacuation. Meanwhile, Russia and Japan displayed no hurry to be the first to establish customs in their respective spheres. Each delayed, fearful that the other might later refuse and thereby gain an economic advantage and a diplomatic edge. Under American prodding, directed mostly at the Chinese, agreements for opening customs in Manchuria were finally concluded in July 1907.[28] Root could now be satisfied that he had done the most within his power to restore trade conditions in Manchuria to normal. Here Root's legal instincts had led him to a successful course of action; the desired goal was reached with a minimum of fuss.

Root's legal instincts did not serve him as well in his attempts to settle with the Chinese the regulations for opening the ports provided for in the Sino–American commercial treaty of 1903.[29] During those negotiations the issue involving the terms under which the ports of Mukden and Antung were to be opened had proved intractable. Both sides had agreed to call the ports "self-opened," but they had postponed a precise definition of the term. Later, after the Russo–Japanese War, Chinese policy in southern Manchuria still aimed at narrowing as much as possible the rights and privileges of foreigners in these ports and at simultaneously increasing China's own jurisdiction. Primarily, Yüan Shih-k'ai and

27. Sammons to Rockhill, 12 June 1906, NCR, and 28 September 1906, NF 914/3; Rockhill to the secretary of state, 26 June 1906, FRUS, 1906, pp. 198–202; and Adee (acting secretary of state) to Rockhill, 29 August 1906, FRUS, 1906, pp. 219–20.
28. Rockhill to Root, 15 August 1906, NF 551/10. Paul A. Varg, *The Making of a Myth: The United States and China 1897–1912* (East Lansing, Mich., 1968), pp. 144–46, deals with the details of these negotiations. His account relies heavily on Rockhill's interpretation of the respective aims of China, Japan, and Russia.
29. This second attempt to settle the port dispute, in which the Chinese tried to limit foreign residence to a special settlement under Chinese control and to tax goods leaving it, is recounted from the American perspective in Varg, *The Making of a Myth*, pp. 142–44. The key documents are in FRUS, 1905, p. 164; FRUS, 1906, pp. 293–94; FRUS, 1907, pp. 219,221; NF 788; MCD particularly Rockhill to Root, 26 June 1906); NCR (particularly Sammons to Rockhill, 13 March 1906); WWP: Feng-t'ien-sheng k'ai-pu an [File on open ports in Fengtien]; WWP: Mei-shih ch'ing shang-ting Feng-t'ien-fu An-tung-hsien liang-ch'u shang-pu chieh-chih chi kuan-i chang-ch'eng [The United States minister requests settlement of the regulations concerning boundaries and management of the commercial ports at Mukden and Antung]; and CWS:KH, ch. 198.9 and 200.1.

Chao Erh-sun wished to restrict the Japanese throughout the region many in areas still officially closed to foreigners. These Japanese were source of friction with the local Chinese, and minor incidents between the two peoples frequently resulted in intervention by Japanese consular and military officials. The Chinese resented both their interference in purely domestic affairs and the muscle-flexing for which these incidents were the occasion. Chinese officials looked for American understanding and co operation. Chinese-imposed restrictions against the Japanese would be unavailing unless the United States were willing to accept the same re strictions for the handful of its private citizens in Manchuria.

Unfortunately, they looked for understanding in vain. Root counted the symbolic defense of previously secured treaty rights more important than the substantial impact of his decision on Chinese plans to restrict the Japanese. He, like Hay before him, was chiefly concerned with pre venting the Chinese from either overturning or narrowing the precedent which the traditional treaty ports had set in determining the status of foreign residents in China. As any lawyer knew, a precedent had to be consistently and tenaciously defended in order to be preserved. If this were true in civilized countries, how much truer it was in relations with wayward China. However, the flaw of this staid traditional position was that it ignored the realities and opportunities of the Manchurian situation and stood to benefit only the few Americans living in Manchuria.

Although Root's subordinates in China loyally supported his legalistic approach to the problem, they were not altogether taken by his logic, and from time to time they cautiously and obliquely argued the advantage of conciliating the Chinese on this issue. Rockhill, for one, cautiously weighed the Chinese proposals concerning the Manchurian port regula tions against the existing body of American rights which he did not wish to see diminished.

> One cannot but sympathize with the Chinese desire to be masters in
> their own country, but the measures they are seeking to enforce should
> be most carefully scrutinized by us before acceptance, and many of
> them strenuously resisted.[30]

Rockhill concluded that the Chinese regulations would do no damage to American trade and would in any case affect only a few Americans. But in the final analysis he sided with the secretary of state.[31]

30. The quote is from Rockhill to Root, 18 December 1906, NF 4277/-. See also Rockhill to Straight, 4 April 1907, and Rockhill to Root, 16 July 1906, both in NF 143/5.
31. Rockhill to Root, 31 July 1906, NF 143/14. Rockhill expressed the same view to the British minister. Jordan to Grey, 4 October 1906, FO 371/180.

The consuls in Manchuria repeatedly heard Chinese officials there express hope for American assistance in solving China's tangled relation with Japan. Chao Erh-sun told Consul General Sammons that

> he considered the United States China's best friend and added that when he left Peking to assume his office Viceroy Yüan Shih-kai had impressed upon him a statement to that effect. He hoped the United States would have sympathy for China. . . .[32]

The consul general in Mukden, Willard Straight, who reached his post in late 1906, reported Chao's continued requests for support and his complaints against the senseless obstruction of China's plans.

> You Americans, what do you do this for? Your business is a wholesale business, you don't do a pettifogging trade. The Japanese retailers are going into the city, they pay no taxes and are competing with our own merchants. How can we expect to withstand them?[33]

Straight, whose anti-Japanese feeling grew as his stay in Mukden lengthened, was susceptible to Chao's argument. Straight too wished to see the Japanese—particularly those who lived and worked in the interior, a low type in his opinion—restricted by the Chinese as much as possible. Tentatively, he suggested that the State Department, while standing by American treaty rights, should at the same time be prepared "to welcome and to encourage the consolidation of Chinese authority as constituting the strongest guarantee of the equality of opportunity in Manchuria."[34] Straight's attempt to reconcile Washington's insistence on the extension of previously secured treaty rights with China's policy of exercising her sovereign rights proved futile. In the end he, like Rockhill, ignored his misgivings and fell into step with the department's policy.

The Chinese were not so agreeable. They could not carry out their views on opening the Manchurian ports in the face of opposition, but neither would they back down. By mutual consent, the United States and China left the issue in abeyance. As a result, the United States in effect won an empty victory in defense of its position, and the Chinese lost the substance of control over foreigners which they had sought.[35]

32. Sammons to Rockhill, 8 August 1906, NF 914/2. See also Sammons to Rockhill, 10 March 1906, NCR.
33. Straight, "Interview with the Viceroy on December 31, 1906," NF 788/42. See also Chao's views on the dispute, recorded in Straight to Rockhill, 31 December 1906, NF 788/23; Chao to Straight, 28 December 1906, NF 788/24; and Straight to Rockhill, 1 April 1907, Rockhill Papers, Houghton Library, Harvard University.
34. Straight, report to the State Department, 19 June 1907, NF 2321/12. See also his reports of 4 and 27 December 1906, NF 788/10–11 and 19–21.
35. On the temporary solution of the problem, see the documents in NF 788/56–59 and 63;

Root's uncomprehending response to China's call for understanding on the issue of port regulations was nothing new. Roosevelt had similarly ignored China during the Portsmouth conference, just as Hay had earlier done during the Russian occupation. The policy and attitudes prevailing in Washington made it difficult for Americans to detect the ferment in China's Manchurian policy in the postwar years. Even Rockhill in Peking, unusually perceptive for an American diplomat, on this occasion suffered the same failure of vision. Despairing over China's lethargy, he often failed to understand her Manchurian policy, particularly her hostility to Japan.[36] The view from Washington, if dimmer because of the distance, was substantially the same: the incompetent Chinese had predictably mishandled the postwar settlement. Deeply founded pessimism over China's ability to manage her own affairs and heavy reliance on a narrow "treaty rights" policy in dealing with her blinded American leaders to a creditable effort at defending Manchuria and to the opportunity for providing assistance.

NF 143/5; NF 4277/1–8, 14–18 and 23–31; and Sammons to Rockhill, 21 March 1906, NCR.
    36. Rockhill to Root, 28 December 1905 and 29 June 1906, both in MCD, and 6 October 1906, NF 2321/-.

PART THREE
FIRST ATTEMPT
AT COOPERATION, 1907–1908

While American policy remained in the rut of legalism, changes in China in 1907 and 1908 created circumstances favorable to cooperation with the United States in defense of Manchuria. In those years Yüan Shih-k'ai oversaw the first sustained effort to turn American interest in Manchuria to China's advantage.

Yüan first came into intimate contact with the Manchurian problem during the Russian occupation, when he was serving as the commissioner of northern ports. The responsibilities of this post also involved him in the talks with the United States over opening new ports in Manchuria. Before the outbreak of the Russo–Japanese War, Yüan convinced the court of the risks of involvement and the advantages of neutrality. The court gave him the responsibility of enforcing the neutrality within the war zone and of overseeing Chinese military preparedness in case neutrality should fail and the capital be endangered.[1]

After the war Yüan's views on Manchuria commanded respect as none other's could. His position at court was for the moment secure, particularly with the empress dowager, who was obliged to Yüan for timely assistance in crushing the reform movement initiated with the approval of the young emperor in 1898. Her favor as well as his own ability and caution had hastened his rise within officialdom.[2] Another factor pushing Yüan to the fore was age, which was taking its toll among senior advisers on Manchurian policy. Li Hung-chang had died in 1901, Liu K'un-i in 1902, and Jung-lu, a favorite of the empress dowager, in 1903. The influence of the remaining elder statesmen, Chang Chih-tung and Prince Ch'ing, was still great, but they had to ration their energy carefully. In 1905 Chang, at age sixty-eight, delivered his last formal statement on Manchuria, thereafter deferring to Yüan and concentrating on questions closer to his tastes and responsibilities. Prince Ch'ing, as old as Chang, had

1. Imperial edict, 17 January 1904, SL:KH, ch. 584.1; and Yüan, memorial and supplementary memorial, 19 January 1904, in Shen Tsu-hsien, comp., *Yang-shou-yüan tsou-i chi-yao* [Selected memorials of Yüan Shih-k'ai] (Taipei reprint, 1966), pp. 503–09.

2. Jerome Ch'en, *Yuan Shih-k'ai, 1859–1916: Brutus Assumes the Purple* (London, 1961). Chap. 5 deals summarily with Yüan's years spent in Tientsin and Peking between 1901 and the death of the empress dowager in 1908.

his time taken up with the matters of high policy which came before him as chairman of the Grand Council. On Manchurian questions he leaned on Yüan for advice.

After the Russo–Japanese War, he coordinated China's postwar policy, orchestrating from the governor general's office in Tientsin the actions of the military governor of Mukden and the central government in Peking. In late 1905 Prince Ch'ing left him, acting jointly with Grand Councillor Ch'ü Hung-ch'i, to negotiate a settlement with Japan of the questions left unanswered by the Treaty of Portsmouth. And in 1906 and 1907 he oversaw the evacuation of the Japanese forces and the opening of Manchurian ports and customs. In these years Yüan began to build up his influence in the area. He had appointed Chao Erh-sun military governor of Fengtien in 1905. Chao, an old colleague, took along as a private secretary Yüan's twenty-eight-year-old son, K'o-ting. In the years through 1908 Yüan continued to consolidate his influence in the region—and at the same time to improve the quality of government—by sending there personally selected, young, foreign-educated officials.[3] A notable number, prominently Liang Ju-hao (M. T. Liang, Newchuang *tao-t'ai* [intendant]), Shih Chao-chi (Alfred Sze, Harbin *tao-t'ai*), T'ang Shao-i (Fengtien governor), Tsai Shao-chi (Newchuang *tao-t'ai*), and Chou Ch'ang-ling (Newchuang *tao-t'ai*), were American educated. Yüan hoped to apply to Manchuria the policy he had initiated against Germany as governor of Shantung from 1899 to 1901—namely, that of asserting Chinese sovereignty at the expense of foreign control.[4]

In 1907 Yüan was ordered from his provincial post to the capital to become president of the Wai-wu Pu. Initially both his political position in Peking and his control over the foreign office were uncertain. Part of his difficulty stemmed from the anomalous relation of the Wai-wu Pu to the rest of the bureaucracy and from the shifting, undefined decision-making process in Chinese foreign affairs.

China's first formal foreign office, the Tsung-li Yamen, had been one of the major creations of the midcentury reign of the T'ung-chih Emperor.[5]

3. Sammons to Rockhill, 10 March 1906 and 12 and 13 June 1906, NCR.

4. John E. Schrecker, *Imperialism and Chinese Nationalism: Germany in Shantung* (Cambridge, Mass., 1971), chaps. 4 and 5.

5. On the Tsung-li Yamen and China's midcentury plunge into international relations, see Masataka Banno, *China and the West, 1858–1861: The Origins of the Tsung-li Yamen* (Cambridge, Mass., 1964); Immanuel C. Y. Hsü, *China's Entrance into the Family of Nations: The Diplomatic Phase, 1858–1880* (Cambridge, Mass., 1960); and Meng Ssu-ming, *The Tsungli Yamen: Its Organization and Functions* (Cambridge, Mass., 1962). Mary C. Wright, *The Last Stand of Chinese Conservatism: The T'ung-chih Restoration, 1862–1874* (Stanford, Calif., 1957), is the classic study on the period.

Nominally its purview had encompassed all aspects of relations with foreigners, including the cultural and technological as well as the diplomatic, but in practice it had functioned best as a bureaucratic buffer against Western demands. The reform of the Tsung-li Yamen demanded by the powers as part of the Boxer settlement had effected changes in name and form but still left much to the initiative of various individuals whom the throne selected depending on the time and the nature and gravity of the issue. The change of name of the foreign office to Wai-wu Pu and its elevation to the status of a full ministry—indeed the most senior of them— had in fact done little to stabilize court politics, which raised and toppled a succession of leaders in foreign affairs. The reforms also had failed to alter the Confucian inclination to entrust responsibility to virtuous men rather than to morally neutral institutions. Essentially the foreign office, still chiefly occupied with diplomatic routine, remained an appendage of the Grand Council, whose decisions were to guide its activities. The relationship between the two institutions was still defined by making the chairman of the Grand Council the superintendent of the less important body. The Wai-wu Pu's dependence on the Grand Council was further ensured by diffusing authority at the top through creation of the post of concurrent manager, an intermediate position between the president and the superintendent.

His new post put Yüan in charge of the daily affairs of the Wai-wu Pu, but he lacked the independence and freedom of action that presidents of the other ministries enjoyed. Yüan was outranked, nominally at least, by Prince Ch'ing, who had been the head of the Tsung-li Yamen from 1884 to 1894 and again from 1898 to 1900 and who had held the post of superintendent since the reorganization of the foreign office in 1901. Yüan was also outranked by Na-t'ung, the concurrent manager. Prince Ch'ing had little time to spare from his other responsibilities to give to the Wai-wu Pu, and Na-t'ung, younger but also occupied with other duties, only gave it intermittent attention. Still, the policies Yüan could pursue were restricted to those which his absentee superiors would not veto. Yüan had also to take into account the views of the throne, whose approval he needed on major points of foreign policy. In practice his suggestions to the throne on policy, presented either orally in audience or in a written memorial, went to the empress dowager. If she disapproved because she regarded the suggestion either untimely or categorically unacceptable, she could set it aside without consulting the Grand Council. However, she would usually submit the matter to that body, where most foreign policy decisions were made under her guidance. The Grand Council also possessed the right to deal with a proposal in a similar fashion, either accepting it in full or in a modified form or rejecting it altogether.

Yüan had to contend with the views of still others. Censors, officials charged with speaking out against the abuses and errors of their fellows, often expressed their views on foreign policy as well as on the rectitude of policy-makers. Their criticisms were at least a potential source of annoyance and embarrassment to Yüan and at worst a threat to his position. High provincial officials, too, could contribute to the making of foreign policy. Like the censors, they could appeal directly to the throne through memorials. Moreover, where policy issues fell under their jurisdiction, the central government usually solicited their advice and often left the details and the execution of policy in their hands. Others, outside the official system, such as the gentry in the provinces and an increasingly vocal press, would scrutinize Yüan's actions, ready to criticize any misstep.

The Chinese bureaucracy, prizing caution and stability over ill-considered action, hedged every post with counterbalances. That Yüan's new post was more hedged about than most was an indication of the importance of foreign affairs in the late Ch'ing. Foreign penetration had worked so deeply into the fabric of Chinese life that the threads of foreign policy often mixed with those of domestic policy. The disadvantageous position of the central government relative to the foreigners after 1900 made it necessary that it reach its decisions carefully and execute them cautiously. Tradition and the needs of the times called for prudence and rule by committee.

The ministry to which Yüan fell heir in 1907 was not well suited to play even its limited role in China's foreign affairs. The 1901 reforms demanded by the powers had effected some improvements. For example, under the old system each major office had been given a variety of unrelated tasks, many of which overlapped with those of other offices. This unwieldy maze of checks had given way to a more efficient organization under the Wai-wu Pu, which was divided into five sections, each with a unique function. In addition, in the years after 1901 some of the responsibilities of the Wai-wu Pu had been transferred to other parts of the central bureaucracy. The Board of Posts had assumed primary responsibility for railway and postal affairs; the Board of Commerce for industrial and mining enterprises; the Revenue Council for customs affairs; and the Board of Finance for negotiating foreign loans. As a consequence, the Wai-wu Pu had more time to devote to more conventional diplomatic affairs.

But the most serious internal flaw in the institution, the lack of specialized and experienced personnel, had remained. Its chief officials, two vice-presidents to assist the president, and some thirty-five junior officials and clerks, had still been for the most part traditionally educated and generally isolated from foreign contacts. A scattering of younger officials educated overseas had begun to appear before 1907, but the methods and attitudes of the Wai-wu Pu, reflecting the style of the majority, had continued in a traditional mold.[6]

Yüan's major contribution to increasing the efficiency of his ministry was the transfusion of new talent to supply this lack of expertise in diplomatic affairs. He had alway sought the services of young men returning from study abroad with new and useful skills. He now brought them into the Wai-wu Pu.[7] The American-educated Liang Tun-yen was the most highly placed of the new men.[8] A native of Kwangtung, he had first studied in the United States with the Yung Wing mission in the early 1870s and then begun his career under the patronage of Chang Chih-tung. Liang later had become associated with Yüan, who brought him from Tientsin to Peking. There Liang occupied the post of junior vice-president, previously held by two fellow provincials, T'ang Shao-i and Wu T'ing-fang.

This new breed of foreign-educated officials provoked the suspicions of older, more conservative officials for a variety of reasons. For one, Yüan's protegés owed their swift rise in officialdom to particular skills acquired abroad. While they might be forced to pose as omnicompetent officials, which was the bureaucratic ideal, their detractors naturally guessed they were not. Indeed, some did lack the classical education and official experience necessary to work effectively in a Confucian system of government. For example, Shih Chao-chi, an American-educated official, depended on an aide familiar with bureaucratic forms and practices to guide him through his work.[9] In addition, these new men had acquired their experience through long contact with foreigners, first as students

---

6. Some information on the Wai-wu Pu can be gleaned from Ts'ao Ju-lin's "I-sheng chih hui-i" [Recollections of a life], serialized in *Ch'un-ch'iu tsa-chih* [Spring and autumn magazine]. See particularly no. 160 (1964): 14. The memoirs by Ts'ao, who began his diplomatic career in 1905, must be used cautiously. Also of value is Esther Morrison, "The Modernization of the Confucian Bureaucracy: An Historical Study of Public Administration" (Ph. D. diss., Radcliffe, 1959), pp. 456–83, 735–36, and 1041.

7. These new talents included Chou Tzu-ch'i and Kao Erh-lien (who served respectively as senior and junior councillors of the Wai-wu Pu); Chang Yin-t'ang and Shih Chao-chi (both later appointed minister to the United States); Chu Tzu-wen; Wei Ch'en-tsu; and Hu Wei-te (a Russian specialist brought into the Wai-wu Pu and later posted to Japan).

8. For a sketch of Liang, see Thomas E. LaFargue, *China's First Hundred* (Pullman, Wash., 1942), pp. 124–32.

9. Sao-ke Alfred Sze (Shih Chao-chi), *Reminiscences of His Early Years*, trans. Amy C. Wu (Washington, D.C., 1962), pp. 47–50 and 52.

abroad and later as diplomats. Who knew what unconventional ideas had rubbed off? Here too a kernel of truth lay in the suspicion, for although most of these new officials were careerists and were to eschew open revolutionary activity against the dynasty, they in general held views considered "advanced" in the last decade of the Ch'ing. They were generally associated with the "Young China Party" and the "rights recovery policy." The suspicions which followed these modern "barbarian managers" no doubt hindered to a degree their effectiveness in officialdom.

In the midst of these changes Yüan needed to maintain some institutional continuity. This he did through Tsou Chia-lai, an old bureaucrat known by his co-workers as "the walking dictionary of the Wai-wu Pu." Already Yüan had purged some of the older, more traditional officials, appointing some to minor posts overseas, to make way for the newcomers. However, Tsou, in many ways comparable to Alvey Adee, the senior workhorse in the United States State Department at that time, remained. Tsou, during his years of service in the Tsung-li Yamen and the Wai-wu Pu, had mastered in detail the procedures of foreign affairs, treaty obligations, and other matters of routine and substance. Although he had only a traditional education, knew no foreign languages, and held conservative views, he nonetheless performed an essential task under the new regime by giving a helping hand with what were to the newcomers unfamiliar problems in an unfamiliar institution.[10]

Yüan had to neutralize his political enemies before he could count himself secure in the capital. Early in 1907 they launched a strong attack against him and his policies. The reasons for their animosity dated back to the 1898 reform movement, which Yüan had helped crush. His chief opponent in 1907 was Ts'en Ch'un-hsüan, the governor general of Kwangtung and Kwangsi, who early in the year had been promoted to the presidency of the Board of Posts. Ts'en had supported the reformers in 1898 and still remained sympathetic to K'ang Yu-wei. More progressive in his domestic policy and more aggressively nationalistic in foreign affairs than Yüan, he had since then repeatedly come into conflict with him. They had disagreed over China's response to the outbreak of the Russo-Japanese War. While Yüan had strongly, repeatedly, and finally successfully recommended neutrality, Ts'en had favored fighting alongside Japan and driving Russia from Manchuria.[11] They had also differed over

10. An appreciative sketch of Tsou appears in Ts'ao, "I-sheng chih hui-i," no. 158 (1964): 10–11.

11. See chap. 5, pp. 86–87 on this debate.

the 1905 anti-American boycott. From his post in the south Ts'en had expressed strong sympathy for the outrage his fellow provincials felt against discriminatory treatment and refused to move against the boycott.[12] Yüan too was sensitive to the mistreatment of Chinese by the United States, which his official paper, the *Pei-yang kuan-pao*, had on more than one occasion criticized. But for reasons of larger policy he opposed the boycott. Yüan moved against it within his own province in late June 1905. Later in the month he joined Rockhill in having the throne issue an edict proscribing the movement nationwide.[13] On both these occasions Yüan had succeeded in convincing the court of the wisdom of conservative policies which, in the eyes of his critics, cost China an opportunity in one instance to fully reclaim Manchuria and in the other to defend the dignity of Chinese abroad.

The attack on Yüan in 1907 began indirectly. Censors in accord with Ts'en's views charged Yüan's political clients—T'ang Shao-i, Liang Tun-yen, Shih Chao-chi, Chang Po-hsi, and Chu Pao-k'uei—with misconduct.[14] Soon, however, the principals themselves began to exchange accusations and to draw in their major political allies. Yüan was defended by Prince Ch'ing, Hsü Shih-ch'ang, and Shih-hsü, a grand councillor. Ts'en got yeoman support from the censor Chao Ch'i-lin and from Ch'ü Hung-ch'i, a grand councillor from Hunan who, like Ts'en, could trace his resentment of Yüan back to 1898. With Prince Ch'ing now drawn into the fray, Yüan's enemies also attacked him and his associates, prominently Tuan Chih-kuei, the military governor of Heilungkiang.[15] The empress dowager, aiming to prevent the feud in Peking from getting out of hand, appointed Tsai-t'ao and Sun Chia-nai to investigate the charges against Prince Ch'ing. Still, neither this action nor the reappointment of Ts'en in early spring to his former post in Kwangtung, a move engineered by Yüan and Prince Ch'ing, ended the quarrel. The empress dowager finally took sides when Yüan and Prince Ch'ing insinuated that their

12. Ts'en to the United States consul, 21 August 1905, reproduced in Chu Shih-chia, comp., *Mei-kuo p'o-hai Hua-kung shih-liao* [Historical materials on American oppression of Chinese laborers] (Peking, 1959), pp. 163–64.

13. Chang Ts'un-wu, *Kuang-hsü sa-i-nien Chung-Mei kung-yüeh feng-ch'ao* [Public upheaval in 1905 over the Sino–American labor treaty] (Taipei, 1966), pp. 67–68 and 153–54.

14. Jordan to the British Foreign Office, 21 January 1907 and 5 February 1907, FO 371/217; Howard L. Boorman, ed., *Biographical Dictionary of Republican China* (New York, 1967–71), 3:306–07; J. O. P. Bland, *Recent Events and Present Policies in China* (Philadelphia, 1912), pp. 208 and 214; Ts'en Hsüeh-lü, *San-shui Liang Yen-sun hsien-sheng nien-p'u* [A chronological biography of Mr. Liang Yen-sun (Shih-i) of San-shui] (Taipei reprint, 1962), pp. 57–58; Sze, *Reminiscences of His Early Years*, pp. 38–39; and Ts'en Ch'un-hsüan, *Lo-chai man-pi* [Random notes from the studio of Lo] (Taipei reprint, 1962), pp. 14–17.

15. Tuan was forced to give up his post, and Ch'eng Te-ch'üan was again put in charge in Heliungkiang. SL:KH, ch. 571.14.

enemies, implicated in the reform effort of 1898, were attempting to revive that old dispute and that in fact they were still on good terms with the reformers. She thereafter removed Ch'ü from the Grand Council, relieved Ts'en of his post, and transferred Lin Shao-nien, an ally of Ch'ü's, from the presidency of the Board of Posts.[16]

By the end of the year Prince Ch'ing and Yüan had markedly strengthened their political position in the capital. In the Grand Council two opponents, first Ch'ü and then two months later Lin, had been replaced by Lu Ch'uan-lin, an old ally of Prince Ch'ing, and by Yüan himself. As a balance Chang Chih-tung, who had not taken sides in the struggle, and Prince Ch'un, the future regent, brother of the emperor and no friend of Yüan, also joined the body. In sum, by late summer of that year four of the six members of that highest policy-making body could be counted friendly to Yüan and Prince Ch'ing, and Yüan could now be sure of a sympathetic hearing in the Grand Council and of his effective control over the Wai-wu Pu. He was finally in a position to speak with more authority and security than when he had entered Peking nine months earlier.

The foreign policy for which Yüan's domestic political successes had by the fall of 1907 cleared the way aimed for limited cooperation with the United States against the Japanese menace to Manchuria. One diplomat in Peking observed:

> Nothing brings men and people together as much as having the same enemy. The aggressive policy which Japan follows in the Far East does not injure China alone; at the same time it touches the United States. Their interests menaced by the same adversary, can the United States and China agree to resist her?[17]

Yüan had first revealed his interest in cooperation with the United States when he struck against the boycotters in 1905. In a local decree he stressed that at the end of the Russo–Japanese War China would be dependent on

---

16. Ts'en, *Lo-chai man-pi*, pp. 14–17; Boorman, *Biographical Dictionary of Republican China*, 3:306–07; Wang I-nien, *Wang Jang-ch'ing hsien-sheng chuan-chi* [A biography of Mr. Wang Jang-ch'ing (K'ang-nien)] (n.p., 1938), ch. 4.6–14; Hsü T'ung-hsin, *Chang Wen-hsiang-kung nien-p'u* [A chronological biography of Chang Chih-tung] (Taipei reprint, 1969), p. 207; and Shen Yün-lung, *Hsien-tai cheng-chih jen-wu shu-p'ing* [Collected articles on leading political figures of contemporary China] (Taipei, 1966), pp. 60–65. Shen, who bases his account essentially on Wang I-nien's, reproduces an interesting letter from Yüan to Tuan-fang, dated 28 May 1907, describing some of the political in-fighting. Also of value are the reports sent by British Minister Jordan to the Foreign Office on 3, 14, 28, and 29 May 1907, 18 and 21 June 1907, and 4, 18, and 30 September 1907, all in FO 371/226.

17. Edward Bapst (French minister to China) to Pichon, 5 March 1905, Min. Aff. Et., Chine, NS 178.

American support in Manchuria. The boycott, he warned, would alienate the Americans and reduce their willingness to help in Manchuria. Yüan used the same argument in a telegram to the Wai-wu Pu at the same time. 'China is in a very weak position," he wrote. "We must trust the American government to maintain justice and rely on her assistance."[18] Later, immediately after the war, Chao Erh-sun and Yüan's son, K'o-ting, encouraged the American consul in Newchuang to consider adopting a more cooperative attitude toward Chinese policy in Manchuria and invoked Yüan's support for their views on Sino–American cooperation in Manchuria.[19]

Yüan had little choice in 1907 but to continue to look to the United States. An alliance system was being woven about Manchuria as the old coalition of commercial powers, led successively by Britain and Japan, dissolved. First, both Japan's and Russia's opposition to a vigorous Chinese policy in Manchuria created an increasingly explicit mutual understanding between them. In July 1907 they set aside former antagonisms and together marked off exclusive spheres of influence and pledged to defend the status quo against China. Britain, her hands tied by her second alliance with Japan in 1905 and by her treaty with Russia of August 1907, could exert herself only marginally in defense of Manchuria. France was bound to Russia by alliance and to Japan by the entente of June 1907 and could not act in China's behalf.[20] Only the United States along with Germany lay outside the charmed circle, free of international commitments which might make cooperation with China in defense of Manchuria impossible.

Yüan had reason to feel that Americans might respond favorably to Chinese overtures. During the Russian occupation of Manchuria, American leaders had agonized over their impotence and in 1903 had briefly considered taking a more militant stand. Now some Americans were complaining against Japan's unyielding stand in the immigration controversy with the United States and against Japan's trade discrimination in Manchuria. In the United States, war talk made headlines. Yüan could also be encouraged by the favorable estimate of Theodore Roosevelt which the Chinese minister in Washington sent back to Peking. The

18. Telegram quoted in Chang, *Kuang-hsü sa-i-nien Chung-Mei kung-yüeh feng-ch'ao*, pp. 67–68, found in the Wai-wu Pu archives, telegraph books.

19. Sammons to Rockhill, 10 March 1906, NCR.

20. E. W. Edwards, "The Far Eastern Agreements of 1907," *The Journal of Modern History* 26 (1954): 340–55, shows the way tensions in Europe set Britain, France, and Russia on a search for security at home and how in compensation they acted to safeguard their interests in East and Southeast Asia through the round of accords with Japan. See also David J. Dallin, *The Rise of Russia in Asia* (New Haven, Conn., 1949), pp. 87–98.

American president emerges from Liang Ch'eng's dispatches as a man of good character ("upright and principled"), well informed on world affairs. Roosevelt had expressed himself as sympathetic to China's complaints against American immigration policy and to China's desire to redefine her relations with the powers on more equitable terms. He had advised Liang that a sound army and modern education were the key to a better future for China.[21] To Yüan, Roosevelt must have seemed an altogether agreeable partner.

Yüan had to develop his strategy carefully, avoiding an unequal, dependent relationship with the United States while at the same time not settling into inaction. An open alliance was clearly out of the question, for Yüan must have been aware of the American aversion to foreign entanglements. He also knew that few in his government would accept the idea of a full alliance. The memory of the disastrous outcome of the unequal Russian alliance was still in mind and inhibited Yüan from moving in a similar direction, even if on better terms. Yüan realized that a one-sided agreement in which China could contribute nothing to the bargain but the promise of special privileges for her partner ran contrary to the rights recovery spirit of the day. It was hard to imagine a diplomatically isolated and militarily weak China forming an alliance on a basis of equality.

The other pole of foreign policy, the passive maintenance of an open door in Manchuria, was also unsatisfactory. If China promised only equal commercial advantage to the United States, as Chang Chih-tung had before and after the Boxer uprising, the United States might not move aggressively enough to establish and defend its interests. China would be reduced to the unnecessarily passive role of sitting and waiting for the Americans to act. Yüan would have to work toward some cooperative arrangement which positively served China's interests in Manchuria and at the same time provided an incentive sufficiently attractive to involve the United States.

Yüan was left with one crucial question to ponder: Were the methods of frontier defense and defense of the open door compatible means of checking Japan and to a lesser degree Russia? Logically and in the abstract, the interests of the United States and China in Manchuria seemed compatible, indeed complementary. Americans guided by the open door policy desired at minimum free access to the Manchurian market and an equal opportunity to sell their goods. A maximum open door program

21. Liang Ch'eng to the Wai-wu Pu, received 6 July 1905, WWP: Chin-kung-yüeh chi ko-k'ou ti-chih Mei-huo [The labor exclusion treaty and the boycott of American goods at various ports]; and 16 August 1907, WWP: P'ei-k'uan an pu-tsu [Supplementary (Boxer) indemnity file].

included unhindered investment opportunity. China, although pre-occupied with defending this frontier, was ready to keep the door open and to encourage American goods and dollars to pass through it. An American stake in trade and investment would serve as a balance to the influence of Japan and Russia and would help China develop and defend Manchuria.

While Yüan gave thought to enlisting the United States in defense of Manchuria, two associates worked in the context of frontier defense to put cooperation with the United States on a concrete basis. These two officials, who depended on Yüan for advice and for mustering support in the capital, were the governor general of Manchuria, Hsü Shih-ch'ang, and the governor of Fengtien, T'ang Shao-i.

Hsü, born in 1855, came from a poor Honan family distinguished only by several minor official posts. At thirty-one he had won his *chin-shih* and thereafter had entered the service of the Ch'ing dynasty. Hsü owed his rise to prominence to his own abilities and to Yüan, a long-time personal friend who had employed him in his new army. Hsü was open-minded, relatively advanced in his views on reform, and pliant enough to move with remarkable ease through the thickets of Peking politics. Rockhill, perennially critical of Chinese officials, gave an indication of Hsü's stature when he described him at age fifty as "strong of body and of purpose, ready and anxious to learn and a very fine type of Chinese."[22]

Hsü's first on-the-scene exposure to the problems of Manchuria came in 1906. He had been appointed to conduct with Tsai-chen, the son of Prince Ch'ing, an inspection of the region and then to make policy suggestions. The likely reason for Hsü's appointment was Yüan's desire to have an able and respected associate to propose and carry out the changes in Manchuria which Yüan's experience had convinced him were needed. Yüan could thus avoid having to take the risk of personally putting forward the proposals himself. In late November and through most of December of 1906 Hsü toured the three Manchurian provinces. He recognized, as others had before him, the threat from Russia and Japan and the economic and political backwardness of Manchuria, which made it a difficult region for China to defend but an easy one for these powers to penetrate.

22. The quote is from Rockhill to Root, 29 August 1906, NF 1518/-1. On Hsü's background, see Boorman, *Biographical Dictionary of Republican China*, 2:136; Ching-min [pseud.], *Hsü Shih-ch'ang* [Biography of Hsü Shih-ch'ang] (Canton and Hong Kong, 1922), p. 8; and E-tu Zen Sun, "The Chinese Constitutional Missions of 1905–1906," *The Journal of Modern History* 24 (1952): 266.

Hsü returned to the capital in January 1907 and prepared his observa
tions. He recommended to the throne construction of a Chinese-controlle
system of transport, encouragement of colonization, development c
natural resources, reform and extension of the local political administra
tion and, finally, involvement of other powers in China's behalf. In hi
initial report Hsü in large measure drew on the program of reform pre
viously blocked out by others, chiefly Ch'eng Te-ch'üan and Chao Erh
sun, both of whom he had consulted during his inspection tour. Eve
Hsü's proposal to reorganize and centralize the Manchurian administra
tion, which Chao and Ch'eng had neglected to make, had been suggeste
as early as 1902.[23] In April 1907 the central government appointed Hs
the first governor general of Manchuria and charged him with consolidat
ing Chinese control by carrying out these changes, including the replace
ment of the military administration with the kind of civil administratio
prevailing in China's provinces within the Great Wall.[24] Civil governor
were to take the place of the military governors. From the newly create
post of governor general, Hsü was to supervise their activities and se
policy in consultation with Peking. For the first time Manchuria woul
have a centralized civilian administration and a unified policy.

The changes announced for Manchuria in the spring of 1907 were no
isolated events. The central government itself was in the midst of change
The empress dowager had tentatively decided on a policy of nationa
reform in January 1901, and in September 1906 she had announce
detailed plans. A complementary program of provincial reform, whic
envisaged making Manchuria a testing ground for political innovations
appeared in July of the following year.[25] In embarking on these reform
the government was not responding just to official recommendations
Popular feeling was beginning to affect decisions on Manchurian polic
just as it was beginning to influence policy in other areas. Popular intere
had first focused on Manchuria in 1903 when the announced delay in th
Russian evacuation had stirred up an outburst of patriotic indignation
Through May of that year anti-Russian protests from Shanghai gentr

23. Lu Shu-fan, aide memoire, 7 February 1902, WWP: Tung-san-sheng kai-she hsing-shen,
[On converting Manchuria into provinces]; and Robert H. G. Lee, *The Manchurian Frontier i*
Ch'ing History (Cambridge, Mass., 1970), pp. 151–52.

24. See THL:KH, p. 5556, for the decree of 19 October 1906 sending Hsü and Tsai-chen o
the Manchurian inspection; see TKTCS, 1:213–382, for Hsü's reports to the throne containin
impressions of conditions in Manchuria and proposed remedies for its problems; and see SL
KH, ch. 571.4, for the edict of 20 April 1907 appointing Hsü and authorizing reorganization
Hsü's recommendations in TKTCS, 1:363–76 are particularly noteworthy. Lee, *The Manchuria*
Frontier in Ch'ing History, pp. 146–55, deals in detail with Hsü's tour, his report, and the ensuin
institutional reforms.

25. Prince Ch'ing, memorial, 7 July 1907, THL:KH, p. 5669.

and merchants and obscure degree holders, together with those from high officials and the commercial powers, had rained in on the Wai-wu Pu.[26] Thereafter Manchuria's fate was the byword of nationalists for the peril in which foreign ambitions had placed China.

Consciousness of the crisis was growing even in Manchuria itself. Its inhabitants were not as awakened to China's problems and opportunities as their countrymen in the provinces along the coast or along the Yangtze River. Manchuria generally lacked well-developed guild traditions or a body of well-educated, wealthy, and influential families or clans ready to mold local opinion. Nonetheless, during the years just prior to Hsü's appointment, there had been evidence of growing nationalism. The guild merchants of Newchuang, the most influential in the region, had briefly flexed their muscle in 1905 by joining in the boycott of American goods until pressure from the Japanese occupation forces and their own government stopped it.[27] Moreover, patriotic students had begun in 1905 to make their influence felt in the area and continued in the following years to voice their anxieties about their region's future.

> Alas! I cry for my China and I cry for my East Asia. Europeans announcing the Yellow Peril, dare I not to tell you [truthfully] and really about the White Peril? If you do not believe that, please look at this land.[28]

In 1907 Manchurian students in Tokyo would sharply criticize Japanese policy toward Manchuria as well as the acquiescent attitude of their own government.[29] In 1908 merchants in Manchuria would stage a boycott of Japanese goods.[30]

For Hsü this awakening regional and national sentiment was a two-edged sword. It would work to his advantage, particularly in stirring the central government to support him, if he took a resolute stand against foreign aggression. However, if he bowed to foreign demands, this sentiment could help to undermine him as well as the dynasty.

---

26. Mary Backus Rankin, "The Manchurian Crisis and Radical Student Nationalism, 1903," *Ch'ing-shih Wen-t'i* 2 (October 1969): 87–106; and Akira Iriye, "Public Opinion and Foreign Policy: The Case of Late Ch'ing China," in Albert Feuerwerker et al., eds., *Approaches to Modern Chinese History* (Berkeley, Calif., 1967), pp. 216–38. Some of the protests of 1903 are preserved in WWP: Chiao-shou Tung-san-sheng an [File on the restoration of Manchuria]. On the Shen Chin affair, see the report by E. T. Williams, enclosed in Conger to Hay, 7 August 1903, MCD.

27. Reports from Sammons (Newchuang) in June, July, August, and September 1905, NCR.

28. Translated in a report dealing with student activism in Liaoyang. Sammons to Rockhill, 21 March 1906, NCR.

29. Petitions from Manchurian students to the Wai-wu Pu, received 28 August 1907 and 11 September 1907, collection of documents on Sino–Japanese relations to be published by Li Yü-shu of the Institute of Modern History.

30. HTCC, ch. 44.14; 45.15,18; 46.22. See also the reports from the American consuls in Newchuang and Mukden in NF 12705.

Hsü selected his subordinates to take along to Manchuria from three different groups: traditionally educated generalists, military men from Yüan's Peiyang Army, and young foreign-educated specialists of the type Yüan was employing in the Wai-wu Pu.[31] Of the last group T'ang Shao-i was the most important. He was the nephew of a wealthy merchant from Kwangtung and an alumnus of the Yung Wing educational mission to the United States in the 1870s. A man of energy and ability, he had served under Yüan in Korea before the Sino–Japanese War and later as customs *tao-t'ai* in Tientsin. He had also negotiated with the British over Tibet and helped finalize the postwar Manchurian settlements with Japan in 1905 and with Russia in 1906. T'ang's experience had exposed him to the frustrations of bargaining with the foreigners from weakness and convinced him that "wealth and power" were the prerequisites for administrative autonomy and territorial security as well as for successful diplomacy. His political views, which were advanced by the standards of Ch'ing official-dom, caused foreigners to label him a "progressive" and to associate him and other Cantonese with the "Young China Party" and its program of rights recovery.[32] Although he had been driven from office early in 1907 by Yüan's political enemies, his appointment as governor of Fengtien placed him at the age of forty-seven back in office and away from his opponents in the capital. In his new post T'ang could draw on his long experience in the art of dealing with foreigners to advise Hsü on the best foreign policy for Manchuria and to help him deal with the heavy agenda of pending diplomatic controversies.

Chao Erh-sun's traditional education, long service in provincial government, and familiarity with financial matters had provided a fund of wisdom for renovating the Manchurian administration, but the former military governor had not been able to resolve a host of diplomatic

31. Of Hsü's traditional generalists, the most outstanding were his senior councillor, Ch'ien Neng-hsün, and the governor of Heilungkiang, Chou Shu-mo, who replaced Ch'eng Te-ch'üan in March 1908. Both had, like Hsü, obtained their *chin-shih* and were tied to him by student bonds. Of the Pei-yang officers, Ts'ao K'un, Meng En-yüan, Ni Ssu-chung, and Chang Hsün were the most important. Of the foreign-educated specialists, the best known, aside from T'ang Shao-i, were Liang Ju-hao (M. T. Liang; United States), Hsü's junior councillor and a linguist, Hsü Shih-ying (Japan), a legal expert; Ch'en Chen-hsin (United States), an agricultural expert; Huang K'ai-wen, an expert in industry and languages; and Lu Tsung-hsing (Japan), an economist. See Ching-min, *Hsü Shih-ch'ang*, pp. 49–61; Boorman, *Biographical Dictionary of Republican China*, 2:137; Ts'ao, "I-sheng chih hui-i," no. 159 (1964): 16; and Liu Feng-han, *Hsien-chien lu-chün* [The new army] (Taipei, 1967), p. 112.

32. Bland, *Recent Events and Present Policies*, pp. 159–60 and 215–16, gives a sharp sketch of T'ang's personality. See the entry for T'ang in Boorman, *Biographical Dictionary of Republican China*, 3:232–36, as well as the treatment in LaFargue, *China's First Hundred*, pp. 117–19.

difficulties stemming from the Portsmouth treaty and the end of the Japanese occupation. Now a wide variety of diplomatic questions, principally with regard to Japan, faced Hsü and T'ang upon their arrival in Mukden.

Japan had already fastened a protectorate over Korea and then gone on to strengthen her hand in southern Manchuria through agreements with France and Russia recognizing her influence there. Within the region she bolstered her influence by commercial penetration; by making new claims over railway, mines, timber, and fishing rights; by broadening existing rights concerning residence, commerce, and the administration of land owned by the South Manchurian Railway Company; and by retaining property seized during the war. Japan's Manchurian railways, to be linked to Korea by a proposed bridge across the Yalu River, would allow her to bring an army onto the scene quickly. All the while Russia watched, ready to claim for herself in northern Manchuria any right or privilege gained by Japan in the south.[33]

To contain foreign penetration, Hsü and T'ang elaborated and began to execute a program of general reform and commercial development, the major themes stressed in earlier policy recommendations to the throne. Their detailed plans—discussed, formulated, and submitted for approval throughout the summer of 1907—looked forward to strengthening domestic control and improving Manchuria's international position. They intended to pursue the former goal through colonization under official auspices as well as by upgrading local military forces; exerting tighter control over the restive Mongols; reforming educational, financial, and judicial affairs; and promoting native commerce and industry.[34] In their foreign policy

---

33. Hsü and T'ang gave an idea of the complexity and number of the disputes they faced from the time they arrived in Mukden in a telegram to the Grand Council, 5 August 1907, CWS:KH, ch. 203.18–19. The best sources on the issues plaguing Sino–Japanese and Sino–Russian relations in the latter half of 1907 and throughout 1908 are the collection of documents (nos. 4419–4638) from the Wai-wu Pu archives soon to be published by Li Yü-shu of the Institute of Modern History; CWS:KH; CCS:KH; and LNCYJ, 5, which contains some important documents not available in other printed or archival collections. Hsü Shuhsi, *China and Her Political Entity* (New York, 1926), pp. 284–90 and 299–326, treats many of the Manchurian diplomatic disputes.

34. For evidence of the vigor of the new administration's reform and modernizing efforts, see the testimony of the medical missionary, Dugald Christie, a long-time resident of Mukden. *Thirty Years in Moukden 1883–1913* (New York, 1914), pp. 226–32. Consular reports (e.g., the British consul in Mukden Willis to Minister Jordan, 2 February 1909, FO 371/612) confirm his favorable impressions. On efforts by the Hsü administration to promote colonization, see memorials by the Board of Posts, 1 January 1908 and 16 July 1908, *Yu-ch'uan Pu tsou-i lei-pien* [A classified collection of memorials by the Board of Posts] (Taipei reprint, 1967), comp. by the Board of Posts and the Ministry of Communications, 2:685–87 and 1:403–13 respectively; and by Chou Shu-mo, 9 October 1908 and 15 January 1909, *Chou chung-ch'eng fu-chiang tsou-kao* [Memorials of Governor Chou of Heilungkiang] (Taipei reprint, 1968), ch. 1.35–36 and 1.57–59.

Hsü and T'ang sought the support of other powers to check Japan and Russia.

Hsü had recognized during his inspection trip to Manchuria in 1906 that the success of any frontier defense policy depended on controlling railways and on securing broad financial support to carry out the program of reform and development. The existing railways and the territory adjoining them were the foundation of Japanese and Russian influence.

> Now all the open ports adjoin the railway. The Russians have increased their railway land and begun lumbering. Along the Japanese section in "adjoining land" they carry on commerce, colonize, establish police and self-governing bodies, struggle to control taxation, etc. All of this has a very intimate relation with our local political authority and economic rights. The struggle is never-ending.[35]

Hsü's goal was to neutralize the importance of these concessions. One approach was to restrict the foreign lines by rigid enforcement of treaty provisions. Hsü renewed the recommendation made earlier by Ch'eng Te-ch'üan that China avail herself of the right, specified in an 1896 railway agreement with Russia, to appoint an official to oversee the operations of the Chinese Eastern Railway and the South Manchurian Railway. An official with experience in railway affairs and a knowledge of foreign languages could act to protect China's interests and to coordinate the Chinese position on railway affairs in Manchuria. This recommendation went unheeded in Peking.[36]

Because the prospect of repurchasing Russian and Japanese concessions in Manchuria seemed distant, the most practical policy was to construct competing railways under Chinese control. Additions in Manchuria to the already existing Peking–Mukden railway network would extend China's control over commerce, bolster defense, and promote colonization. When he took office Hsü put high on his agenda the proposal for a railway between Hsinminfu and Aigun which Ch'eng Te-ch'üan had made in 1906, Chao Erh-sun had subsequently endorsed, and the Board of Posts had tentatively approved. Hsü envisaged building the road in stages, each requiring relatively small outlays of funds. The first, the southernmost section from Hsinminfu (on the Peking–Mukden line) to Fakumen, would tap the rich agricultural market west of the Liao River and divert trade

35. Hsü to the Wai-wu Pu, 28 January 1909, CWS:HT, ch. 1.4.
36. Hsü first made the suggestion to the Wai-wu Pu on 18 October 1907, WWP: Chung-tung t'ieh-lu p'ai-i tu-pan an [File on assigning a commissioner to the Chinese Eastern Railway], and repeated it on 28 January 1909, CWS:HT, ch. 1.4.

from the South Manchurian Railway.[37] The longer and less profitable sections between Fakumen and Taonan and between Taonan and Tsitsihar would follow. Hsü gave Ch'eng's proposal for an extension from Tsitsihar to Aigun such low priority that it was of no practical significance for the moment.[38]

Hsü knew China would have to borrow abroad to secure the funds necessary for his ambitious program. Shortly after his return to Peking from his inspection tour of Manchuria, he had suggested a foreign loan and the creation of a bank under official control to oversee the use of the loan funds.[39] Hsü's proposal drew in part on the bank plans advanced some years before by two other officials, Ma Hsiang-po (a private secretary of Li Hung-chang's) and Sheng Hsüan-huai.[40] Hsü also drew upon a recent suggestion by Yüan Shih-k'ai himself for borrowing money abroad. In May of 1905 the Wai-wu Pu had informed Yüan, who was then serving as the commissioner of northern ports, that the United States was prepared to return the unclaimed portion of its share of the Boxer indemnity. Like other high provincial officials, he was perennially short of funds to meet the financial needs of his administration and welcomed the prospect of uncommitted money becoming available. He suggested that the funds be devoted to mining and railway affairs, items high on the agenda of his government.[41] In all probability, a substantial portion of these funds would have under Yüan's guidance found their way to Manchuria, a crisis area in which he was already involved. The Wai-wu Pu, under pressure from the United States to devote the funds to education, had shunted Yüan's self-strengthening proposal aside.[42] For the moment he had done nothing else to influence the decision on how to use the money.

In 1907 Hsü took up Yüan's earlier proposal (it seems likely at the suggestion of Yüan himself) in a modified and more detailed form and looked to Yüan for support in the capital for getting approval of the plan.

37. Board of Posts to the Wai-wu Pu, received 16 September 1907, WWP: Hsin-Fa t'ieh-lu an [Hsin-Fa railway file], *ts'e* 1.

38. Hsü and T'ang to the Wai-wu Pu, 20 November 1907, CWS:KH, ch. 207.9–10; and TSSCL, pp. 6699–6702 and 1925–26.

39. TKTCS, 1:363–76, for Hsü's memorial on Manchurian policy, and 3:1755–76, for his memo suggesting the creation of a bank.

40. Ma's unsuccessful trip to Wall Street in 1886 to find the capital for an official bank is recounted in Chang Jo-ku, *Ma Hsiang-po hsien-sheng nien-p'u* [A chronological biography of Mr. Ma Hsiang-po] (Changsha, 1939), pp. 162–78. Sheng's attempts are mentioned in Hsü, *Chang Wen-hsiang-kung nien-p'u,* and in YCTK.

41. Yüan to the Wai-wu Pu, received 23 May 1905, WWP: Mei-kuo mieh-shou p'ei-k'uan [The United States remits the (Boxer) indemnity]. The American Boxer indemnity is treated in detail in my "The American Remission of the Boxer Indemnity: A Reappraisal," *Journal of Asian Studies* 31 (May 1972): 539–59.

42. The Wai-wu Pu to Yüan, 1 June 1905, WWP: Mei-kuo mieh-shou p'ei-k'uan.

Although at this early stage Hsü had not yet specifically linked the bank loan to the Boxer remission, he watched for an opportunity, to come later in the year, to do so. In June 1907 Hsü formally presented to the throne the idea of organizing a Manchurian bank under official control to allocate funds borrowed from abroad, to oversee their use, and to collect the profits. At the same time he appealed to Prince Ch'ing and Lu Ch'uanlin for their support when the proposal came before the Grand Council for consideration. The following month he received permission to begin his search for the 20 to 30 million taels (in 1907 worth about $16 to $24 million) necessary to organize the bank.[43]

This decision to look abroad for money was another important forward step in the evolution of frontier defense in Manchuria. Chao and Ch'eng had formulated imaginative programs and had to a degree set them in motion. But neither had found a way to fill their coffers with the requisite funds. Their hopes of building railroads with capital obtained from local merchants had been illusory. Chang Chih-tung and others had attempted in vain the same feat in provinces where merchants were both richer and more numerous. Nevertheless, both Chao and Ch'eng had refused to consider a foreign loan because they feared that foreign investors would wrest control of any enterprise from China. Chao had been particularly fearful that the introduction of foreign capital from any source would pave the way for the entry of more Japanese capital and thereby strengthen Japan's already substantial hold on Manchuria's economic life.

Hsü agreed with Yüan that his administration would need the help of a friendly foreign power. He frankly recognized that he could not obtain the money he needed from either the central government or local sources and that he would have to borrow foreign funds if he were to realize his railway and bank projects. Hsü also knew he would need foreign diplomatic support to clear his way against Russian or Japanese interference in the execution of these plans. Despite the growing rights recovery movement, Hsü was moved by the desperateness of the situation and the absence of any other source of financing. The lack of an influential gentry in Manchuria, compared to other regions where local elites tended to be vocal on the subject of foreign economic control, made this course easier to take.

Through railway construction and the organization of a bank, Hsü hoped to turn the technology and institutions used by the foreigners in penetrating Manchuria against them. He hoped that China could now

43. TKTCS, 1: 471–75, for Hsü's memorial. His letter to Prince Ch'ing and Lu are in 4:1830–34. The edict of approval of 22 July 1907 is in SL:KH, ch. 575.9.

Prince Ch'ing

Yüan Shih-k'ai

Wu T'ing-fang

T'ang Shao-i

Hsü Shih-ch'ang

Hsi-liang

Prince Ch'un with the Hsüan-t'ung
Emperor (standing)

Na-t'ung and Tsai-tse (foreground)

John Hay

W. W. Rockhill

Willard Straight

Huntington Wilson

Theodore Roosevelt

Peter A. Juley

Elihu Root

William Howard Taft

Philander C. Knox

Kaystone View Co.

imitate the successes achieved by the foreign-run railways (the Chinese Eastern and the South Manchurian) and the foreign banks (the Russo–Chinese Bank and the Yokohama Specie Bank). In turning the tables, Hsü carried the concept of frontier defense a step farther in sophistication with the hope of altering the balance of power in Manchuria in China's favor.

The open door policy, ambiguous at birth in 1899, was even less precise by 1907. It had become a conveniently elastic principle capable of accommodating the differences of opinion over American Far Eastern policy. Roosevelt and Root followed a policy which reflected a narrow, traditional definition of the open door. They retreated from the view John Hay had taken during the Russian occupation of Manchuria of the open door as a guarantee of investment as well as trade opportunity. In addition, the president and his new secretary of state were not inclined to accept the notion that the open door policy obliged the United States to defend China's integrity.

Within Root's State Department a circle of young officials took a different view of the open door. They made of Hay's policy a battle cry for their attack on the Manchurian spheres of influence, particularly Japan's, which, they argued, threatened the future of American interests. The activists put a broad construction on the meaning of the open door, as Hay had tended to do, by including investment along with trade as part of the American interest to be defended. Moreover they too were inclined to accept the obligation to defend China's integrity.

The activists' commitment to defending China's integrity offered a sound basis for cooperation with China. Indeed, the logic of their anti-Japanese stance inclined them in that direction. Moreover, patronage of the Chinese might be the way to establish an informal American empire in East Asia. The price they would have extracted from China for neutralizing Japan's sphere of influence was a sphere of influence for the United States. The renewed Chinese initiative in Manchuria, an open invitation to join in defense of common interests against common foes, gave them an unprecedented opportunity. However, the activists thought of China in conventional stereotypes and lacked a coherent and detailed body of knowledge about either China or Japan to guide them. Although they were the most enthusiastic advocates of cooperation, they simply would not take seriously Chinese efforts in defense of Manchuria.

One north China newspaper in 1908 described Japan as a predatory feline stalking about East Asia and asked, "Who Will Bell the Cat?" Its answer, that "President Roosevelt is at least one of the sager mice, and . . . it is no part of the American policy to attempt risky work," was substantially accurate.[1] In 1908 no less than in 1905 Theodore Roosevelt based his Far Eastern policy on the necessity of deferring to Japan in certain areas of East Asia. He accepted Japan's sphere of influence in southern Manchuria. In return he expected Japan to continue to respect the rights of American commerce there, a minimal demand which Japan could easily meet. The immigration question, which had come to the fore in 1906, had roused passions on both sides and forced Roosevelt in the spring of 1907 to embark on a campaign for naval armament, insurance against the possibility of some future rift with Japan.[2] But this development did not call into question his Manchuria policy. On the contrary, it gave him the opportunity to effect a trade: American forbearance in Manchuria in exchange for Japanese patience and cooperation in stemming the flow of immigrants to the United States and solving the related questions of discrimination against Japanese in the United States. The gentlemen's agreement of February 1908 satisfied American demands on the immigration question; Roosevelt reciprocated in November of the same year with the Root–Takahira agreement. Roosevelt was indeed not going to bell the cat.

Elihu Root's diplomacy reflected his full agreement with the president.[3] As before, Root kept his eye open for violations of American commercial rights in Manchuria, but he did so with a skeptical and accommodating attitude which deterred him from making the precipitate protests recommended by some of his subordinates. Root would object to mistreatment only when he had evidence at hand and could quote chapter and verse from treaty texts.

Early in 1908 Root became embroiled in just such a dispute over commercial rights in Manchuria, and it preoccupied him until he resigned in

1. *Peking and Tientsin Times*, 3 March 1908.
2. On Roosevelt's policy in the Pacific during these years, see Charles E. Neu, *An Uncertain Friendship: Theodore Roosevelt and Japan, 1906–1909* (Cambridge, Mass., 1967), and Raymond A. Esthus, *Theodore Roosevelt and Japan* (Seattle, Wash., 1966). The report by Roosevelt's special agent in Japan, John C. O'Laughlin, summarized on pp. 279–80 of Neu, is of particular interest.
3. Root to Whitelaw Reid (American ambassador to Britain), 3 September 1908, Reid Papers, Manuscript Division, Library of Congress.

January 1909. Although the dispute involved only Russian claims to administer railway land in Harbin, the outcome of the issue would be significant for all of Manchuria. If the powers, the United States included, acquiesced in this violation of treaty rights, Russia would apply the precedent elsewhere in northern Manchuria, and Japan would follow suit in the south in an effort to retain a position of parity. Root responded by following a moderate Manchurian policy of preserving treaty rights but at the same time of avoiding any major diplomatic schism with either Japan or Russia. China's rights and interests in Manchuria entered into Root's calculations only marginally.

The dispute between China and Russia began in November 1907 after the Chinese Eastern Railway announced its intention of establishing its own local administrations in Harbin and other cities located on its land. The dispute turned essentially on which version of an 1896 agreement between the Russian railway company and the Chinese government was authoritative. Russia justified the action by a clause in the French text which gave the company the right to "govern" its land. The Chinese government countered that the Chinese text gave the company simply the power of "management" of railway affairs and then only within the land purchased by the company. The Chinese government reasoned that to give way to the Russian claims would be to abandon its sovereignty over the land.[4]

Through the early months of 1908 Root's representatives in China reported on the issue posed by the Russian demarche. The American consul in Harbin, Fred Fisher, protested the creation of the local governments.[5] The consul general in Mukden, Willard Straight, and the third assistant secretary of state in Washington, William Phillips, recommended that the secretary of state endorse Fisher's protest as a necessary measure to protect China's sovereignty.[6] In April 1908 Root decided on the basis of these recommendations to support the protest of his consul.[7] But he refused to take the part of the Chinese by making the issue one of sovereignty. He agreed with Russia that a government was needed in Harbin "to bring about conditions of order and good government."[8] Root objected only to Russian means. To the American ambassador in London, he wrote,

4. TSSCL, pp. 1973–81.
5. Fisher to Fletcher (chargé, Peking), 20 December 1907, and report to the State Department, 24 February 1908 and 15 April 1908, NF 4002/4, 35, 92.
6. Straight, report to the State Department, 2 January 1908, and William Phillips, memo, 6 March 1908, NF 4002/11, 26.
7. Root to the Russian ambassador to the United States, 9 April 1908, NF 4002/2.
8. Root to Reid, 11 April 1908, Reid Papers.

We do not wish any controversy on the subject, but all the treaty powers would seem to be equally interested in having the municipal government to be established at Harbin and at other points along the line of the railroad, both in Russian and Japanese control, based upon extraterritorial rights under the treaties rather than upon an erroneous construction of the railroad grant.[9]

Moreover, a municipal government similar to that in the treaty ports enjoying extraterritorial jurisdiction would satisfy all the powers by representing their citizens proportionately to their numbers and interests.[10]

The key to success for Root's solution was the endorsement of the other interested powers not yet involved in the dispute. He worked through his ambassadors in London and Berlin to marshal support there. At the same time, he tried to keep Japan from openly joining the fray on Russia's side by explaining the American position to the Japanese ambassador in Washington and also by inviting the British government to intercede with the Japanese government.[11] However, a Russian diplomatic counteroffensive in Europe undercut his efforts. Although the pressure he had applied directly and indirectly might have contributed to Japan's maintaining a wait-and-see attitude, it did not bring the expected support from either Britain or Germany. As a result, Root failed to maneuver Russia into an agreement. Nevertheless, during the stalemate both sides showed a genial tolerance, neither willing to seriously antagonize the other.[12]

Root's search for British support had proved fruitless for a number of reasons. As yet no British subjects had lodged protests, so the Foreign Office saw little reason to offend Russia in Manchuria to the detriment of the peaceful settlement of other issues, particularly in South Asia and the Middle East, where British interests were greater. By April 1908 Grey had already concluded, "We must not be pulled into the position of fighting other people's battles when our interest is so slight."[13] In addition, the British had already acknowledged northern Manchuria as a Russian sphere. Sir John Jordan, the minister to China, was particularly pessimistic about China's hold there. He felt that Russia and Japan would increasingly determine the fate of the region. He found Chinese plans to

---

9. Ibid.
10. Root to the Russian ambassador, 9 April 1908, NF 4002/2.
11. Root to Reid, 22 May 1908 and 31 July 1908, both in Reid Papers, and 20 May 1908, in NF 4002/80; as well as William Phillips to Rockhill, 3 June 1908, Rockhill Papers, Houghton Library, Harvard University.
12. The stalemate is reflected in the dispatches and memos, particularly numbers 110 and 113, n NF 4002.
13. Grey, minutes, 4 April 1908, FO 371/426.

defend it extravagantly impractical and unlikely to succeed.[14] Finally, the British view that American policy was unsteady and often unsound and that her diplomatic apparatus was unreliable influenced the Foreign Office's response.[15] Consequently, Sir Edward Grey, secretary of state for foreign affairs, assured Root of British agreement in principle, but in fact he did little beyond dispatching a consul to Harbin.[16] Britain was "not going to pull American chestnuts from the Manchurian fire."[17]

The German response, equally encouraging in tone, proved as insubstantial. The president and Kaiser Wilhelm II had repeatedly exchanged assurances during the Russian occupation of Manchuria and the Russo–Japanese War that each supported the integrity of China.[18] Roosevelt knew that after the war the kaiser had remained preoccupied by the possibility that a coalition, which had grown to include not only France and Britain but Russia and Japan as well, would attempt to exclude Germany from China. Roosevelt also had intimations that the kaiser wished to promote a German–American alliance to protect China. Although the American president privately discounted the fear of a coalition as "mere lunacy" and denigrated the alliance as a "pipe dream," he did nothing to discourage these ideas, for German reliance on American support in the Far East might prove useful.[19] When Root tried to involve the Germans in the Harbin question, the response from Berlin proved disappointing. The German government, like the British, accepted the American view in principle but never found the right occasion to support it with a diplomatic protest. By March 1909 the German minister in Peking had still not received instructions from his government regarding the matter, and only in April did a German consul proceed to Harbin.[20]

14. Jordan to Campbell, 15 March 1908, 13 May 1908, and 11 June 1908, FO 800/244; and Fletcher to Root (on an interview with Jordan), 14 February 1908, NF 4002/36.

15. See, e.g., Francis A. Campbell, minutes, 14 December 1908, FO 371/435. The reasoning of the Foreign Office in the dispute can be followed in the minutes contained in FO 371/426, particularly those for 9 March, 4 April 1908, 2 May 1908, and 9 June 1908.

16. Reid to Root, telegrams, 12 and 18 June 1908, NF 4002/111, 112.

17. Jordan to Campbell, 11 June 1908, FO 800/244; and Campbell, minutes, 9 June 1908, FO 371/426.

18. Selections from the correspondence between 1901 and 1905 appear in Morison, 3:172–73 and 239–40; 4:731, 1099, 1100, 1166, and 1288–89.

19. The phrases appear in Roosevelt to Reid, 28 April 1906 and 6 January 1909, and in Roosevelt to Root, 17 February 1908, all in Morison, 5:230, and 6:1466–67 and 946. See also Roosevelt to Charlemagne Tower (American ambassador to Germany), 19 November 1907, Roosevelt to Wilhelm II, 4 April 1908, and Roosevelt to Root, 8 August 1908, Morison, 5:853, and 6:993 and 1163–64. Luella Hall, "The Abortive German–American–Chinese Entente of 1907–08," *The Journal of Modern History* 1 (1929): 219–35, documents this episode from the German perspective.

20. Telegrams to the secretary of state from David J. Hill (ambassador to Germany), 1 July 1908 and 2 March 1909, and from Rockhill, 2 March 1909, NF 4002/119, 153, 152 respectively.

While Root strove to win support in Europe, the Chinese continued
their own separate campaign against the Russian initiative.[21] But they
could not take a common stand with the United States against Russia
because Root, as in the Manchurian port question, once again had put
himself squarely in opposition to one of the main goals of Chinese policy—
the defense of her sovereignty. The creation of a foreign municipal government on Manchurian soil, whether justified by extraterritorial rights as
Root wished or by the terms of a private agreement as the Russian contended, would either way encroach on China's sovereign control and set a
precedent for Japan in the south.[22] When T'ang Shao-i in December
1908 made his government's view explicit,[23] Root, rather than reconsider
his position, continued to push the idea on the Chinese as well as the Russian governments.[24] From the Chinese perspective, Root seemed to be
trying to defend treaty rights at the expense of China's sovereign rights,
a bad omen for the success of Chinese overtures to the United States.

Changes were brewing in Elihu Root's State Department that would
eventually influence Washington's reception of Chinese initiatives toward
cooperation. The new, forceful personalities who had a broad conception
of the role of the United States in the Pacific and a strong anti-Japanese
bias made their appearance in the foreign affairs bureaucracy beginning
in 1905. Willard Straight is the best known of this group of activists;
however, Huntington Wilson, who shared many of Straight's views, was
ultimately more influential in shaping American policy toward China.
Others impatient with a cautious Far Eastern policy were William Phillips,
Henry Fletcher, Frederick Cloud, Charles Arnell, and Charles Denby, Jr.
They had been schooled in the imperatives of economic expansion. As
youths they had watched their country establish itself as a power in world
affairs and acquire a Pacific empire. As adults they became preoccupied
with Manchuria either at first hand or from a distance. During their early
years abroad they developed a contempt for "Orientals," confirmed their
taste for power and the diplomatic game, and nursed their ambitions.

For Willard Straight wanderlust was the legacy of an unsettled childhood. His father had died of tuberculosis in Willard's sixth year, and his

21. Negotiations between China and Russia in 1908 and early 1909 are covered in TSSCL,
p. 2011–33 and 2035–38.
22. The Chinese view is expressed in communications between the Wai-wu Pu and the Hsü
administration found in TSSCL, pp. 1983–87, 1989–94, and 2003–2009.
23. See memos of conversations with T'ang by Willard Straight, 11 December 1908, and by
Huntington Wilson, n.d. and 14 December 1908, in NF 4002/110.
24. Root to the Russian ambassador, 29 December 1908, NF 4002/110; and Rockhill to Root,
February 1909 and 3 March 1909, NF 4002/177–79.

mother four years later of the same cause. Without roots at home, he resolved during his college years at Cornell to set off for China, a new frontier, to find and prove himself. His unfocused interest led him to try after 1900 a variety of jobs which introduced him to north China, Korea, and Japan. None of these jobs satisfied his desire to lead "a life of energy and of endeavour," but all reflected his Kiplingesque desire to play the man of action in a strange land.[25] "The world is passing through an interesting phase. Times are not in the least hum-drum, it is the great game in earnest."[26] Repeatedly through his career Straight drew on this phrase, "the great game," to express the romantic, elusive goal he pursued. It served as a motto for his love of the strenuous life and for his unprofessed creed, social Darwinism.

Early during his stay in China, Straight acquired the contemptuous attitude toward the natives common in foreign communities and assimilated the popular stereotype that the Chinese were supremely self-interested and entirely unpatriotic, or, in his own words, preoccupied with "buy and sell." "The China man doe'snt [sic] care a damn who is running the Government as long as business is brisk."[27] Straight was interested in China only as a backdrop for his own personal drama. Aside from learning some spoken Chinese and observing the picturesque aspects of the life about him, he paid scant attention to the culture. He regarded the sinologue—"brains and no body"—with distaste.[28]

Straight did not come into close contact with the Japanese until he served as a correspondent during the Russo–Japanese War. He reacted to their proud assertiveness and repeated successes with racial hatred.

I now find myself hating the Japanese more than anything in the World. It is due I presume to the constant strain of having to be polite and to seek favors from a yellow people. We cannot know them or understand them and they dislike us thoroughly. Kipling was absolutely right when he wrote "the East is East and the West is West, and never the twain shall meet."[29]

25. Diary entry, 24 July 1903, Straight Papers, Olin Library, Cornell University. Helen Dodson Kahn, "The Great Game of Empire: Willard Straight and American Far Eastern Policy" (Ph.D. diss., Cornell University, 1968), chaps. 1–4, deals in detail with Straight's childhood youth, and early years in the Far East.
26. Diary entry, 28 July 1903, Straight Papers.
27. Straight to Haenie [Charles Shongood], 27 March 1905, diary letters, Straight Papers. See also Straight to his sister Hazel, 4 April 1905, diary letters, Straight Papers.
28. Diary entry, 19 April 1903, Straight Papers.
29. Straight to Luther Mott, 18 December 1904, diary letters, Straight Papers.

To his sister he wrote in a similar vein:

> They certainly seem very much less human than the others. They are a great mass and not an aggregate. One cannot feel the individuality of the men themselves. . . . [The Russians] are white, and that means much. . . . The Japanese will have to change a good deal before thay [*sic*] cease to cause one to look for the tail.[30]

However, Straight was prepared to write sympathetically of Japan's marvelous progress and even to acknowledge that she too was entitled to a sense of mission. From the Seoul consulate in 1905 he watched in open admiration as Japan tightened her grip on Korea.[31]

In 1906 Straight received a consular appointment to Mukden at the request of E. H. Harriman, who had use for his services there. Straight reached his post in October, and as he ceased to be the detached observer his attitude hardened into an uncompromising hostility toward the Japanese in Manchuria and a newfound sympathy for the oppressed Chinese, whose fate he feared would be that of the Koreans. From the outset in 1906 through 1908, his reports to Washington reflected his suspicions.[32] "I do not wish to be an alarmist; but I really cannot see any evidence that the Japanese in this part of the world are willing to play the game fairly."[33] He indicted Japan for wishing to exclude the United States from Manchuria and for depriving American trade of equal opportunity in that market.

The indictment is a curious one. Straight knew that his charge of trade discrimination ran contrary to other information on the postwar economic situation in Manchuria and moreover lacked specific evidence. He even frankly confessed that the indifference of American businessmen did more to damage his country's commercial future in Manchuria than Japanese discrimination itself.

> A great deal has been said about the Japanese control of the Manchurian market. Certain privileges certainly were acquired during the war, but I believe that should they ultimately secure a control as has been described, it will be not because they have benefited by prefer-

---

30. Straight to Hazel, 18 May 1905, diary letters, Straight Papers. He repeats these views on the Chinese and Japanese in a dispatch to Reuters, 15 May [1905], and in an article submitted to *The Nation* on 28 July [1905], Straight Papers.

31. Straight to Bragdon, 1 November 1905, and Straight to Whitey, 30 November 1905, both in diary letters, Straight Papers.

32. Straight, report to the State Department, 18 November 1906, NF 914/9.

33. Straight to Rockhill, 8 May 1907 (quoted in Rockhill to Root, 17 May 1907, NF 551/46–47).

ential rates but because foreign firms have not been willing to adopt the aggressive tactics which alone will secure success in this field.[34]

Why then did Straight maintain his view of Japan's sinister intentions? The likely explanation lies in his conception of the role he wished to play in Manchuria. He required the challenge of an adversary relationship to prove his worth. The Japanese offered the perfect opponent, the necessary foil. By painting a picture of a Japanese demon, drawn from racial stereotypes and past resentments, Straight created the preconditions for the great game he wished to play in Manchuria. His behavior reflected his conception of his role. In Mukden he displayed an extreme sensitivity to slights, real and imagined, by which, he was convinced, Japan meant to demean his person, his office, and his country's prestige. In his reports he denounced the corrupting influence of the Japanese civilians in Manchuria, chiefly such "undesirable elements" as prostitutes and gamblers, thus adding the appropriate warts to the Japanese image.[35]

While Straight prepared to push the activist viewpoint from Manchuria, Huntington Wilson promoted it within the State Department. He had been born in Chicago in 1875. His indulgent and well-to-do parents had given him a good education, acquainted him with Europe, and left him with an egoistic and abrasive personality. Before graduating from Yale (class of 1897) Wilson had decided on a career in diplomacy and had traded on his father's political connections to secure the post of second secretary in the Tokyo legation. He served in Japan between 1897 and 1905, and after going through another round of sustained political lobbying in 1906, Wilson moved up to the post of third assistant secretary of state.[36]

Wilson brought back a low opinion of the Japanese. "I tried to see their good points; but they were always impressing me with their bad ones."[37] His policy recommendations, consistent in their hostility to Japan and the Japanese, reflected these early unfavorable impressions.[38] He also acquired in Japan a fascination with the exotic sexual temptations of the East, which

34. Straight to Edward N. Vose (editor, *Dun's Review*), 13 February 1907, Post Records, Mukden, To, Misc. (Records of the Foreign Service Posts of the Department of State, National Archives). See also Straight's "Report on Commerce in Manchuria," enclosed in a report to the State Department, 4 May 1907, NF Minor File; and record of an interview with Straight at the Foreign Office by G. J. Kidston, 9 September 1908, FO 371/433.

35. Straight, report to the State Department, 22 May 1907, NF 7611/-, and Straight to William Howard Taft, memo [late November 1907], NF 2413/99.

36. Wilson recalls his early years up to 1906 in chaps. 1–20 of his *Memoirs of an Ex-Diplomat* (Boston, 1945).

37. Ibid., p. 72.

38. See Neu, *An Uncertain Friendship*, p. 126, for an example of Wilson's views during the immigration controversy with Japan.

at once attracted and repelled him. Even after forty years, he could still recall "voluptuous" Japanese architecture and that austere bareness of Japanese rooms which brought "pleasant sin" to his mind.[39] After his return to the United States Wilson struck out at the troubling temptations which had in Japan excited his fancy. In 1906 he personally led a campaign for morality and decency on the China coast, where, he had discovered, the term "American girl," a euphemism for a prostitute, discredited his country in the eyes of Chinese as well as other foreigners.[40] On another occasion he warned that any American posted to the Manchurian interior, inhabited by what he considered immoral Japanese, would need "enough strength of character not to be demoralized by exotic conditions."[41] The close association of sin and the Orient in Wilson's mind is evidence of his superficial knowledge of Japan and the psychological tensions created by his exposure to that mysterious land.

Once in Washington, Wilson devoted himself to advancing his career. Through part-time study in a crash course, he set off to earn his law degree, a prerequisite for full membership in the club of State Department lawyers. On the job he pinned his star to the issues of reorganization of the State Department and a tough policy toward Japan. Like other young activists, Wilson hoped to prove by his anti-Japanese campaign that he was vigilant in defense of national prestige and interests in Asia. Although Root found Wilson personally obnoxious, he accepted part of Wilson's reform package by creating the Division of Far Eastern Affairs and assigned Wilson to oversee its work. Wilson thus acquired his own small bureaucratic bailiwick to staff with like-minded associates and to use as a platform for his views on Japan.

Wilson had hardly settled into his new job when he began offering advice on the situation in Manchuria. He recommended in July 1906 that the United States peremptorily demand that Japan restore equality of opportunity in Manchuria. The need of the moment, Wilson felt, was "to see Japan's hand."[42] If Japan genuinely cooperated in opening the door in southern Manchuria, all would be for the good. If she refused, the reaction of American as well as British official and public opinion would be an irresistible force compelling her to acquiesce. At the same time China's cooperation was needed. But, he observed, offering a pearl of

39. Wilson, *Memoirs of an Ex-Diplomatist,* p. 59.
40. Wilson to Straight, 14 December 1906, NF Minor File; and Thomas F. Millard, *America and the Far Eastern Question* (New York, 1909), pp. 391–96.
41. Wilson to Galloway, 7 February 1908, NF 10868/7A.
42. Wilson, "Memorandum on policy regarding Manchuria. . . ," July 1906, MCD. See also his *Memoirs of an Ex-Diplomatist,* p. 116.

wisdom treasured by old China hands, "China yields only to force."[43]
Therefore, the best means to move her, like Japan, in the right direction
were vigorous pressure and tough words. Through the remaining years of
the Roosevelt administration, Wilson bombarded Secretary Root with his
fears of Japanese political and commercial expansion in Manchuria.
Again and again he pushed forward the well-worn phrases of the open
door.

> Japan's present policy in Manchuria, if continued, must result in
> grave impairment to America's policy for the preservation of the ter-
> ritorial integrity of China, and in serious detriment to the accepted
> principle of the "open door" and equality of opportunity in Man-
> churia.[44]

Wilson found allies in the State Department. Charles Denby, Jr., the
chief clerk in the department and son of the former minister to China,
shared Wilson's concern over Japan's policy, particularly her "determined
effort to secure trade control in Manchuria."[45] After Denby was assigned
to Shanghai as consul general, Wilson found new support in William
Phillips. Phillips came from an independently wealthy and prestigious
Boston family. Born in 1878, he had received his undergraduate education
at Harvard, where, on the advice of John Hay, Phillips had also studied
law to prepare for a diplomatic career. He had subsequently served as
private secretary to Ambassador Choate in London and as second secretary
in Rockhill's legation in Peking.[46] In 1907 Phillips became Wilson's
subordinate in charge of the daily operations of the Division of Far Eastern
Affairs. Like other members of the circle of activists, Phillips could use
such phrases as "champion of China" and "vast opportunities for our
trade in the Far East" without embarrassment or self-consciousness.[47]
Like the others, he was alarmed by Japan's treatment of China and of
American trade.

> China is looking to us to help her out of her difficulties. . . .
> . . . The United States ought to decide whether it is going to carry
> out Mr. Hay's policy in regard to the Far East.

43. Wilson, memo, July 1906, MCD.
44. Wilson to Root, memo, 6 March 1908, NF 551/92. In the same vein, see the products of
his campaign in early 1908 to convince Root of his views: Wilson to Root, 9 March 1908, NF
551/102; and Wilson, printed draft circular titled "Notes on the policies of the 'Open Door' . . . ,"
early March 1908, especially pp. 16–20, NF 551/99.
45. Denby to Bacon, memo, 17 July 1906, MCD.
46. Phillips has recounted this period in his life in *Ventures in Diplomacy* (Portland, Me., 1952),
chaps. 1–3.
47. Phillips to Wilson, memo, 14 February 1908, NF 2321/19–20.

It is a subject of vast importance to our trade interests and one which ought not to be shelved to await further developments.

Shall the United States use its influence to preserve the integrity of China or shall we let Manchuria go to Russian and Japanese influences?[48]

However, Phillips, cautious and less opinionated than Wilson, hung back from the heat of battle over Far Eastern policy, preferring instead a good match in Roosevelt's tennis cabinet.

Wilson could also count on some of the consular personnel in Manchuria to support his views. He carefully culled from their reports damaging testimony of Japanese wrongdoing. Willard Straight kept a steady stream of observations of this sort going back to Wilson. Charles Arnell, a like-minded acquaintance whose appointment to the consulate in Antung Straight had secured, similarly tried to oblige Wilson. In 1907 and 1908 he combed the rumor mill of his consular district for charges of discrimination and of other Japanese misdeeds. But Arnell had to confess that he could find no proof for the charges which he relayed to Washington.[49]

In the spring of 1908 Wilson, backed by Phillips and Straight, made a major effort to bring the secretary around to their view. Wilson brought the drive to a climax when he submitted to Root a draft statement on the preservation of the open door in Manchuria. He included the information and accusations provided by Straight on Japanese misconduct. Replete with references to violations of the sacred principles of the open door—preservation of commercial opportunity and of China's integrity—Wilson's paper roundly condemned Japan and to a lesser degree Russia for their policies in Manchuria.[50] Here was a formal brief which he hoped would convince Root of the necessity of confronting Japan with the vigorous diplomatic campaign the activists so ardently desired.

The charges of the activists most likely to excite Root's concern were those of trade discrimination. However, reports from one of the consulates in Manchuria and from the Peking legation, contrary to those from Straight and Arnell, threw doubts on these charges. From mid-1907 through 1908 Roger S. Greene, the consul at Dairen, the site of many of the alleged Japanese violations of the open door, repeatedly poured cold water on the activists' fire. Free of anti-Japanese prejudice, he could make a more dispassionate assessment of the situation. Greene could not find any

48. Ibid.

49. Arnell (vice-consul in charge, Antung), "Preferential Rates on the South Manchurian Railway," 8 January 1907, NF 4360/6; Arnell to Straight, 18 July 1907, NF 143/74, and 23 January 1908, NF 788/153–55; and Arnell to Rockhill, 10 July 1908, NF 551/108.

50. Wilson, printed draft circular of early March 1908, NF 551/99.

evidence of discrimination against foreign trade, and for that matter he did not suspect that it was taking place to any degree that should concern the United States. The Japanese-run South Manchurian Railway was acting evenhandedly in its treatment of foreign firms and goods, and the Japanese authorities in the port were generally courteous and helpful to foreigners.[51] He suggested that one must look elsewhere to discover the reasons for the differing fortunes of American and Japanese trade in Manchuria.

> Japan enjoys such great natural advantages in dealing with Manchuria that it seems only reasonable to anticipate that she will come to have a larger and larger share of its foreign trade, just as American trade predominates in Canada and Mexico.[52]

To reinforce Greene's view, Root had available to him two reports on trade in Manchuria. One, prepared in the Bureau of Statistics of the Department of Commerce and Labor, dealt with the reasons for the decline of the American cotton trade in Manchuria since the end of the war and concluded that natural economic causes, not Japanese discrimination, were responsible for the drop.[53] A reply to this report was prepared within the State Department; it found nothing to quarrel with. Its authors, who felt that American exporters did not put enough energy into this trade, were plainly impatient with them for not seizing the advantages which the State Department struggled to maintain.

> Very little energy, enterprise, or systematic effort is given by the American manufacturer or merchant interested in Far Eastern trade relatively [*sic*] to the painstaking and organized efforts of private commercial enterprises of other countries.[54]

Rather than fault Japan for discrimination, this report recommended that the Department consider ways of assisting American enterprises to compete more effectively.

Root's reaction to the activists' views pushed forward during their spring offensive of 1908 indicated he was simply not interested. In the absence of evidence, it was safer for him to assume that the Japanese were not guilty

51. Greene to the State Department, 17 and 21 October 1907, and 24 October 1908, NF 221/ 34, 35, 85; 29 January 1908, NF 551/90; and 11 April 1908, NF 13896/1. See also Greene to Rockhill, 4 June 1908, NF 221/65.

52. Greene, report to the State Department, 29 January 1908, NF 551/90.

53. O. P. Austin to Oscar S. Straus (secretary of commerce and labor), 13 March 1908, NF 12471/-1.

54. Memo prepared jointly by the Division of Far Eastern Affairs and the Bureau of Trade Relations, early spring 1908, NF 12471/-1.

of trade discrimination. In early March, when he saw Japanese Minister Takahira, Root noted the advantages which Japanese enjoyed over Americans in Manchuria and admitted that "such a state of things is only natural to occur where one nation has special interest and influence. The condition of affairs in the Panama Canal Zone is another example."[55] Later Wilson got the bad news. Root sent back the draft statement on the open door policy stripped of Wilson's prize handiwork. Early in April the innocuous remainder of the statement went out to American diplomatic posts abroad.

55. Takahira to Hayashi, 28 February 1908, Telegram series, Archives of the Japanese Ministry of Foreign Affairs (microfilm), Library of Congress (quoted in Neu, *An Uncertain Friendship*, pp. 263–64).

9: CHINESE INITIATIVES

Chinese leaders operated from two centers of power in trying to draw the United States into Manchuria. In Peking Yüan Shih-k'ai worked to create a climate favorable to cooperation between the two countries. From Manchuria Hsü Shih-ch'ang and T'ang Shao-i, relying on Yüan's support and advice, brought forward two major projects by which they hoped to involve the United States more deeply in Manchurian affairs. They advanced one, the Hsinminfu–Fakumen railway project, through the American consul general in Mukden. To realize the other, the financing of a development bank for Manchuria, T'ang himself undertook a diplomatic mission to Washington.

T'ang Shao-i played the leading hand in the railway project, which become the first test of the possibilities of cooperation. Earlier, he had supported the campaign to limit foreign economic rights and interests in China. But now T'ang agreed with Hsü Shih-ch'ang that it was important to Manchuria's future to grant attractive concessions to friendly powers. In a memorial written soon after taking office, T'ang elaborated the idea that the Chinese could use the railway project as well as the bank loan to create a balance of power within Manchuria while at the same time strengthening their control there.[1]

T'ang looked to the United States for money and diplomatic support. He had long been aware that that country was free from the network of international agreements which hedged China in.

> The great powers of Europe, aside from Germany, openly give to Japan the advantage over us and conclude with her agreements to our detriment; but the United States continues to have in the Far East a national policy independent of all foreign alliances.[2]

The conclusion by the powers of the new round of Far Eastern agreements in 1907 made the independent policy of the United States all the more

1. This line of reasoning is pursued in a memorial of June 1907, contained in TKTCS, 1:480–87, which internal evidence indicates was written by T'ang Shao-i.
2. Bapst to Pichon, 5 March 1905, Min. Aff. Et., Chine, NS 178.

attractive. But could the United States be made to lend China her support? T'ang knew that the United States government jealously guarded the contracts secured by its nationals in China. By giving Americans contracts in Manchuria, could not China thus enlist American diplomacy against the interference of other powers there? To discover the answer, T'ang tried to find American investors for the Hsin–Fa railway.[3]

Shortly after settling in Mukden, T'ang learned through the Revenue Council of E. H. Harriman's interest in Manchurian railways.[4] Harriman, the American railway magnate, had already built an unequaled railway empire at home and had then acquired control of a Pacific steamship company.[5] Upon these components he hoped to build a global transportation network to include Japan's newly won Manchurian railways, an additional line across Russia, and an Atlantic steamship service.[6]

In Tokyo in 1905 Harriman had made his first unsuccessful attempt to purchase the Manchurian link in his round-the-world transportation system. Assisted by the American minister, he conducted a whirlwind campaign, culminating in a tentative arrangement giving him partial control of what was to become the South Manchurian Railway. However, the opposition of Foreign Minister Komura, recently returned from Portsmouth, and the likelihood of protest by the public, already angered by the terms of the peace treaty with Russia, forced the government to cancel the agreement with Harriman.[7] In the spring of 1906 Jacob Schiff, a prominent financier associated with Kuhn, Loeb and Company, made another attempt to get the Japanese government to reconsider Harriman's proposal. When this too failed Harriman was forced to conclude that he had reached a dead end in Tokyo.[8]

Meanwhile, Harriman received reports from two experts whom he had sent to survey commercial and industrial possibilities in Manchuria; they

---

3. For evidence of T'ang's views, see J. O. P. Bland, *Recent Events and Present Policies in China* (Philadelphia, 1912), p. 218. Bland was an acquaintance.

4. The letter from the Revenue Council is mentioned in Ching-min (pseud.), *Hsü Shih-ch'ang* [Biography of Hsü Shih-ch'ang] (Canton and Hong Kong, 1922), pp. 9–11.

5. A sketch of Harriman by Frank H. Dixon appears in *The Dictionary of American Biography*, 8: 296–300.

6. George Kennan, *E. H. Harriman's Far Eastern Plans* (New York, 1917), pp. 1–8.

7. Ibid., pp. 9–37. Kennan reproduces the final draft agreement of 12 October 1905 on pp. 23–25 and the letter canceling the agreement of 30 October 1905 on pp. 29–31. These documents and others on the Harriman negotiations in Tokyo appear in NF 221/120–21. Komura's statement of opposition is in Kamikawa Hikomatso, ed., *Japan–American Relations in the Meiji–Taisho Era*, trans. Kimura Michiko (Tokyo, 1958), p. 279. Richard T. Chang, "The Failure of the Katsura–Harriman Agreement," *Journal of Asian Studies* 21 (November 1961): 65–76, finds the old explanations for the cancellation of the Harriman project unconvincing but does not offer a satisfactory substitute.

8. Kennan, *E. H. Harriman's Far Eastern Plans*, pp. 37–38.

indicated he should try the Chinese.[9] While switching his focus to China, Harriman remembered the impressive young man he had encountered in Seoul in 1905 who was interested in a consular post in Manchuria and who might be of use. Soon Willard Straight found himself appointed to the post in Mukden. A weekend at Harriman's country estate poring over Manchurian railway folders served as his informal induction as Harriman's agent.[10]

Straight, after consulting Harriman, also saw Roosevelt at Sagamore Hill.[11] He then proceeded to his post, buoyed by his brush with powerful men. He reached Mukden in October 1906. From his makeshift consulate he watched with sympathy Chao Erh-sun's struggle with the Japanese and then with interest the arrival of Hsü Shih-ch'ang and T'ang Shao-i in the spring of 1907. Although at first he surmised that the new officials were japanophiles and unlikely to offer serious resistance to Japan, he soon was giving them high marks for their firm but diplomatic handling of the Japanese. He also reported appreciatively on the new administration's internal reforms.[12]

From his side, T'ang watched the American consul with equal interest. In frequent conversations through the summer of 1907 he told Straight that Japan's recently strengthened diplomatic ties with Britain, France, and Russia as well as the American acquiescence in Japan's seizure of Korea had troubled him. But the ripening immigration controversy—punctuated by rumors of impending war—between the United States and Japan now allayed somewhat his fears of diplomatic encirclement of China.[13] At the end of the summer T'ang, with Hsü's concurrence, invited Straight to use his official and personal contacts to encourage his government's support for China in Manchuria and to increase American trade and capital investment in that region.[14]

Straight was easily won by this clear invitation. In September 1907 he urged the State Department to consider supporting this admirable regime.

9. Ibid., p. 40.

10. Ibid., p. 41. Straight's relationship with Harriman was ethically questionable for a man in public pay and clearly contrary to newly promulgated consular rules. See no. 1699 of the consular reorganization act in FRUS, 1906, pt. 1, p. 10.

11. Straight to Root, 13 August 1906, Mukden Consular Reports (Records of the Department of State, National Archives).

12. Straight, report to the State Department, 3 May and 28 September 1907, NF 2321/5 and 13; and to Rockhill, 23 July 1907, Rockhill Papers, Houghton Library, Harvard University.

13. Straight, report to the State Department, 10 August 1907, NF 1166/249; and Straight to Rockhill, 2 September 1907, NF 143/80.

14. Straight, report to the State Department, 2 July 1907, NF 143/70; Straight to Rockhill, 16 July 1907, NF 788/96–97; and Straight, report to the State Department, 28 September 1907, NF 2321/13.

A concrete expression of our professed interest would be appreciated now as at no other time. By proving that we are ready not only to insist that the door be open, but also to enter in, we would convince the Chinese of our desire actively to cooperate with them, and might, I feel confident, be largely instrumental in furthering and in directing the development which is bound to take place within the next few years.[15]

Straight thought that promotion of American trade with Manchuria was important, but he stressed that investment was the means best calculated to aid the Chinese, increase American influence, and even promote trade.

It is to be regretted that, important though our Manchurian trade undoubtedly is, we have no more tangible and concrete interests, as banks, mines, or railways. By identifying us more closely with the development of the country the possession of such interests would greatly increase our business.[16]

Straight dreamed of the time when American influence would spread outward from its Manchurian sphere to all of China.

By entering the field now . . . and by allying ourselves, at the outset, with the officials who, now in control in Manchuria, represent the most progressive and, at the present time, most influential party in China, we would aid them in this trying time, and later from Manchuria as a starting point, still cooperating with these officials, whose power seems likely to increase rather than wane, might extend our influence and activity to other portions of the Empire.[17]

Straight now was ready to act as intermediary between T'ang and Harriman. While cultivating the Chinese, Straight had sent Harriman a steady stream of reports. He informed Harriman that the Chinese would gladly entertain a proposition to build a Manchurian railway. Straight promised—with the salesman's concessions to truth—that it would prosper at once and would also share in the region's bright commercial future.[18]

In September 1907 T'ang and Straight agreed on the desirability of American investment in a specific railway project. T'ang had already given to Lord ffrench of Pauling and Company a contract to survey the

15. Straight, memo for William Howard Taft, 2 December 1907, NF 2413/98–99.
16. Straight, report to the State Department, 28 September 1907, NF 2321/13.
17. Ibid. See also Straight, memo for Taft, 2 December 1907, NF 2413/98–99; and Straight to Harriman, 7 October 1907 and 16 February 1908, Straight Papers, Olin Library, Cornell University.
18. Straight to Harriman, 31 October 1906, Straight Papers. See also his letters to Harriman of 15 November 1906 as well as 7 December 1906, Straight Papers.

Hsin–Fa railway route and an option on the construction contract.[19]
Straight saw his opportunity to realize Harriman's scheme as well as to
associate the British with the Americans in Manchuria. He immediately
wired the American railway builder, urging him to join in the project.[20]
On 6 October Harriman's unexpected and terse reply reached Mukden:
"Unsettled money conditions make impracticable."[21] The financial
crash in the United States had dried up the money which Harriman
needed for his Manchurian railway. The new Manchurian administration's hastily contrived first effort at involving the Americans had failed.

The Chinese, eager to seize on any promising opportunity to obtain
American support, had been prepared to tie their project to an investor
whose intentions were unclear to them. Whether Harriman would have
maintained his interest in the forbiddingly complex global transportation
scheme and finally invested his money in Manchuria if the 1907 crash
had not intervened is a moot point. But, more important, the Chinese had
misread the motives that impelled him toward involvement in Manchuria.
They thought him eager to invest his money abroad for sound economic
reasons; however, their terms, bonds issued at ninety-three paying 5
percent, were not in fact a significant improvement on domestic offer-
ings.[22] They failed to recognize that Harriman was drawn to Manchuria
by something more compelling and complex than economic calculations.
He himself had written of his venture onto the world stage:

> It is important to save the commercial interests of the United States
> from being entirely wiped from the Pacific Ocean in the future, and
> the way to find out what is best to be done is to start something.[23]

Of another Manchurian scheme, he was to comment:

> We are continuing to carry [it] from patriotic motives rather than give
> up a drop of the old Stars and Stripes. This may seem queer from a
> business standpoint, but sentiment enters into [it] more than sometimes
> we think.[24]

But he came closest to the mark when, on the subject of the Hsin–Fa
project, he claimed he was

> interested only in doing the thing itself. . . . The simply making

19. Jordan to Grey, 2 October 1907, FO 371/229.
20. Kennan, *E. H. Harriman's Far Eastern Plans*, p. 42.
21. Harriman to Straight, 6 October 1907, Straight Papers.
22. The loan terms are mentioned in Straight to Harriman, 3 January 1908, Straight Papers.
23. Kennan, *E. H. Harriman's Far Eastern Plans*, p. 4.
24. Harriman to Knox, 5 February 1909, Straight Papers.

money out of such an enterprise does not appeal to me, and would only do so in connection with having an equal voice at least in the enterprise itself, and seeing that it was properly and intelligently carried out.[25]

Alice Roosevelt Longworth recalled of Harriman, whom she encountered in Japan in 1905. "There was little of the pomp and none of the splurge of great wealth about him. What he wanted was power; quietly, deliberately, thoroughly, he worked to get it."[26]

Indeed, if profit alone had preoccupied Harriman, he would not have gone off on international adventures. Money could be invested either in the United States or in Europe with greater security at reasonably high rates. Furthermore, it is difficult to believe that the remote prospect of a financial glut at home would have prompted this old man to apply virtually the last of his energy in cutting through international political tangles in order to stake his money on the uncertain fate of embryonic enterprises. Rather, Harriman acted because his talents and appetite for power were becoming too confined at home. Before the turn of the century there had been opportunity to struggle for financial dominance in one region or industry. Afterwards, growing public criticism of malefactors of great wealth, government antitrust suits, and federal and state investigations had abruptly narrowed the field of endeavor. Constricted at home, Harriman tried to find scope for his managerial talents in financially unorganized and industrially undeveloped parts of the world. He became captivated by a grandiose vision of himself presiding over the application of American technology and organizational skills on a global scale.

Harriman's inexperience in international affairs, however, blinded him to the fact that international economic empires were not built in the same way as domestic ones. For example, in Tokyo in 1905 Harriman, oblivious to the political implications of his projects, had indicated to Japan that he would allow no more than "an apparent Japanese control" of any joint enterprise and only "if it be deemed advisable." The Japanese government would not settle for "apparent" control.[27] But the episode indicates that Harriman had thought that he could move in and purchase controlling interest of "Manchuria, Inc." as if the railway were not a potent instrument of national policy and a focus of international rivalries.

25. Harriman to Straight, 5 June 1908, Straight Papers. See also Harriman to Straight, 8 January 1908, Straight Papers.
26. Alice Roosevelt Longworth, *Crowded Hours* (New York, 1933), p. 107.
27. A copy of Harriman's proposed agreement, "Memorandum of Agreement, October 12, 1905," is in NF 221/120–21; and the final agreement, which incorporated the changes specified by Japan, appears in NF 221/120–21 as well as in Kennan, *E. H. Harriman's Far Eastern Plans*, pp. 23–25.

The crash of 1907 left unanswered whether the Chinese and Harriman could work together harmoniously, reconciling particularly the question of control, which was of such fundamental importance to China's plans for the defense of Manchuria.

The Hsin–Fa project went ahead without American participation. In late November the Manchurian administration contracted with Pauling and Company and the British and Chinese Corporation to build and finance it.[28] But a diplomatic storm, which was to destroy the project, had already begun to brew. The Japanese legation, with its unexcelled knowledge of Chinese internal affairs and its contacts within officialdom, had gotten wind of the Chinese plans, and in August 1907 the Japanese chargé had lodged the first of many protests against the project. He based his objections on an agreement China had made in 1905 prohibiting the construction of railroads parallel or harmful to Japan's South Manchurian Railway.[29] When consulted by the Wai-wu Pu on a reply to the Japanese, Hsü and T'ang suggested taking a bold front, contending that the question was an internal one of no concern to Japan and denying that the rail line would in any case be near or harmful to the Japanese rail line. The Wai-wu Pu adopted this response after softening the language, but it failed to moderate Japan's objections.[30] The monotonous exchange of views between the Chinese foreign office and the Japanese legation went on through the remainder of the year and intermittently through the first half of the next.[31] By mid-December 1907 the Wai-wu Pu had concluded that Japan was not going to yield.[32] Although the Chinese refused to abandon the project, they feared to provoke Japan by going ahead with it.[33]

The Manchurian administration had given the contract to a British firm with the expectation that the British government would support the claims of its nationals and thereby clear away the Japanese obstruction.[34]

28. The draft agreement with Pauling and Co. is reproduced in CWS:KH, ch. 207.10–13.

29. Abe Moritaro (Japanese chargé) to the Wai-wu Pu, 12 August 1907, LNCYJ, 5:93.

30. Hsü and T'ang to the Wai-wu Pu, received 3 September 1907, WWP: Hsin-Fa t'ieh-lu an [Hsin–Fa railway file], *ts'e* 1; and the Wai-wu Pu to the Japanese chargé, 10 September 1907, CWS:KH, ch. 205.1. The rebuttal by the Board of Posts to the initial Japanese protest is in LNCYJ, 5:95.

31. Hsü and T'ang to the Wai-wu Pu, 20 and 30 November 1907 and 12 December 1907, CWS:KH, ch. 207.9–10, 19–20, and ch. 208.8–9; as well as Japanese chargé to the Wai-wu Pu, 12 October 1907 and 19 December 1907, and Minister Hayashi to the Wai-wu Pu, 22 January 1908, LNCYJ, 5:97, 104, and 106–07.

32. The Wai-wu Pu to Hsü and T'ang, 12 December 1907, LNCYJ, 5:104–05.

33. The Wai-wu Pu to Minister Hayashi, 7 May 1908, CWS:KH, ch. 214. 1–3.

34. The Wai-wu Pu, slow itself to solicit British support, was content to let British commercial interests argue its case. The first documented instructions from the Wai-wu Pu to the minister in

he expectation proved false. The British government refused either to ipport Pauling's claims or to involve itself in the Sino–Japanese dispute espite pressure from commercial interests in Parliament and from the ress.[35] Sir Edward Grey would not attempt in Japan's sphere in Man-iuria what he would object to her doing in Britain's Yangtze preserve. [e insisted only on commercial opportunity for British subjects.[36]

In June 1908 the Japanese made the first of several offers to compromise. ut the Chinese rejected them as contrary to the interests which the Hsin–a line was meant to further.[37] Later in the year, a long-simmering dispute ith Japan over a Korean–Manchurian border area known as Chientao Yenchi) boiled over into local military clashes and became the major sue in Sino–Japanese relations.[38] When a new stage of Manchurian egotiations began in December 1908 in Peking, the Wai-wu Pu decided) soft-pedal its demands on the Hsin–Fa railway the better to preserve :hina's claim to sovereignty over the disputed land. Even so, the Chinese nd Japanese positions remained irreconcilable. The Hsin–Fa and other :lated issues were still pending on China's diplomatic agenda when Hsü ft his Manchurian post in early 1909.[39]

The ultimate obstacle to the Hsin–Fa railway had been the secret pro-)col of 1905. The origins of this document go back to the Sino–Japanese onference convened in Peking in November 1905 to define Japan's title) Russia's holdings in southern Manchuria. By mutual agreement of the .elegates, signed minutes were kept for each of the twenty-two conference essions.[40] At the end, the formal conclusions of the conference were

,ondon to present China's side of the story to the Foreign Office is dated 7 May 1908. CWS:KH, h. 214.2–3.

35. E-tu Zen Sun, *Chinese Railways and British Interests, 1898–1911* (New York, 1954), pp. 143–8, touches on British involvement in the Hsin–Fa project. Records of the parliamentary debates nd press clippings critical of the government's failure to support the British contractor are in FO 71/410. See also the clippings in NF 5315/113–18 and the translated extracts critical of Japan .ken from British and French papers, enclosed in T'ang to the Wai-wu Pu, 25 July 1908, WWP: [sin-Fa t'ieh-lu an, *ts'e* 2.

36. See the minutes of 9 December 1907 (FO 371/229), in which Grey acknowledged the justice f Japan's position and refused to become involved in the dispute either on China's or on Japan's .de. See also the minutes, n.d., by Grey (between 18 and 23 January 1908), and 31 January 1908, oth in FO 371/410.

37. Abe Moritaro to the Wai-wu Pu, 27 June 1908, CWS:KH, ch. 214.20–22. See also T'ang to ie Wai-wu Pu, 11 November 1908, WWP:Hsin-Fa t'ieh-lu an, *ts'e* 2.

38. Documents on this controversy are to be found in the collections of documents listed in foot-ote 33 in chap. 7.

39. The course of these negotiations through the last months of the Hsü administration can be)llowed in CWS:KH, ch. 218.12–13, and in CWS:HT, ch. 1.5–6, 13–14, 21–24, 29–32, 35–37, 0–42; ch. 2.32–38, 46–47; and ch. 3.3. See also Hsü to the Wai-wu Pu, 6 January 1909, WWP: [sin-Fa t'ieh-lu an, *ts'e* 2; and Cloud (vice-consul in charge, Mukden), report to the State)epartment, 20 March 1909, NF 5315/198.

40. CWS:KH, ch. 193.1.

embodied in a treaty and a supplementary treaty. But the protocol was in fact none of these documents. Instead, it was a collection of seventeen points chosen by the Japanese from the conference minutes. The Japanese supplied copies of the protocol confidentially to the United States and Britain as "an act of friendship," explaining that China had requested it be kept a secret.[41] When the Japanese government got word of the Hsin-Fa project in 1907, it immediately invoked the third article of the protocol.

> The Chinese Government engage, for the purpose of protecting the interest of the South Manchurian Railway, not to construct, prior to the recovery by them of the said railway, any main line in the neighborhood of and parallel to that railway, or any branch line which might be prejudiced to the interest of the above-mentioned railway.[42]

What is surprising in retrospect is that the Wai-wu Pu did not seriously attempt to discredit the document and that the British and American foreign offices, with all their legal skills, never closely scrutinized it. The proposition on Manchurian railways was drawn from the minutes of the eleventh meeting, which, like the others, were signed by the chief participants on both sides. First of all, it was dubious to claim that the minutes of a meeting which were not subsequently ratified by the throne were binding on China. In addition, Prince Ch'ing, the chief Chinese delegate, had been absent from this particular meeting and had left Yüan Shih-k'ai and Ch'ü Hung-ch'i in joint charge. Later, Prince Ch'ing signed his name on the minutes in Manchu; Yüan did not sign his name at all and only wrote the character for "noted," *hsien*. The chief Japanese delegate jotted something described by one student of the proceedings as unrecognizable.[43]

To further vitiate the Japanese claim, T'ang Shao-i, who was part of the Chinese delegation, and Ts'ao Ju-lin, a witness to the conference discussions of the Manchurian railways, recalled that the substance of the talks differed from the record. T'ang repeatedly denied to a variety of Americans and British in 1907 and 1908 that China had bound herself during the conference.[44] T'ang's version, similar to Ts'ao's, was that the

41. Japanese officials so told both Sir John Jordan and Willard Straight. Fletcher to Root (on an interview with Jordan), 29 January 1909, NF 5767/16; and Straight, report to the State Department, 12 February 1908, NF 6625/41.

42. The entire protocol is reproduced in CWS:KH, ch. 194.34–37. The official Japanese translation, provided the United States in 1905, appears in Edward H. Zabriskie, *American Russian Rivalry in the Far East: A Study in Diplomacy and Power Politics, 1895–1914* (Philadelphia, 1946), p. 208.

43. Wang Yün-sheng offers an incisive critique of the Japanese claim that the protocol was binding on China. LNCYJ, 4:345–54.

44. Bland, *Recent Events and Present Policies in China*, pp. 219–20; Straight, report to the State

Chinese delegation during the eleventh meeting had asked the Japanese to define more precisely such terms in their proposition as "in the neighborhood," "parallel to," and "which might be prejudiced to the interest of." When the Japanese refused clarification and the Chinese refused to accpet ambiguous wording, the discussion was dropped, but the proposition submitted by the Japanese remained in the minutes of this session. T'ang also denied the Japanese claim that China had wanted the minutes kept secret.[45]

The Chinese delegates' failure to have the minutes adjusted either to reflect the difference of views or to omit mention of the issue was a major diplomatic error. Nonetheless, it is doubtful that by initialing the minutes they signaled their acceptance of the Japanese proposition or that in any case their acceptance formally bound China. Japan's handling of the issue revealed a smoothness and sophistication which the Chinese could not match. It was also a candid admission of Japan's intention to control Manchuria's development and contain Chinese influence.

The impatient Manchurian administration decided to set aside the Hsin–Fa railway project and to press ahead with the more comprehensive scheme for a Manchurian development bank, originally conceived early in 1907. The bank was meant to further the same ends as the ill-fated railway—internal development and defense against Japan and Russia. The bank plan still included the building of a railway as one of its goals. When the Hsin–Fa project seemed hopelessly mired in controversy, the administration formulated a substitute, a railway from Chinchow to Aigun. The proposal for the new route appears to have originated within the Bureau of Mongol Affairs, which Hsü Shih-ch'ang had created to stem Mongol disaffection and to forestall Japanese or Russian attempts at exploiting it. Chu Ch'i-ch'ien, head of the bureau, suggested that a railway running through Mongol territory would facilitate colonization and speed sinicization among the Mongols, thereby strengthening China's control.[46] This new approach called for shifting the route westward,

department, 4 January 1908 and 12 February 1908, NF 6625/40–41; and Fletcher to Root reporting the views of Sir John Jordan), 29 January 1909, NF 5767/16.

45. T'ang related this version to Thomas F. Millard and to Straight. Millard, *America and the Far Eastern Question* (New York, 1909), pp. 250–51; and Straight, report to the State Department, 2 February 1908, NF 6625/41. See also Ts'ao Ju-lin's version in "I-sheng chih hui-i" [Recollections of a life], *Ch'un-ch'iu tsa-chih* [Spring and autumn magazine], no. 157 (1964): 16–17.

46. See Chu Ch'i-ch'ien's memo on the railway in TSSCL, pp. 1935–37, and Hsü Shih-ch'ang's memorial of 6 August 1908 in SL:KH, ch. 594.7. Chu's report on Mongol affairs is in TSSCL, p. 1803–27. For a sympathetic view of the plight of the Mongols under the kind of policy which Hsü pursued and which was continued under the Republic, see Owen Lattimore, *The Mongols of Manchuria* (New York, 1934), pp. 99–125. See also Hsü Shuhsi, *China and Her Political Entity* New York, 1926), pp. 290–92.

away from the South Manchurian Railway. The line was to be connected
with the Peking–Mukden railway at Chinchow. From there, it was to
be built northward section by section, like the Hsin–Fa railway, to Aigun
in northern Heilungkiang. Aside from a railway, the bank was also to
finance the construction of a related project, the ice-free port at Hulutao
earlier proposed by Chao Erh-sun. It was to restore a measure of Chinese
control to trade by checking Dairen's growing influence and by handling
the goods which were to be carried by the Chin–Ai railway.[47]

From October 1907 through the first half of 1908, the Manchurian
administration kept the bank scheme alive and before the attention of the
central government. In mid-October Hsü set off for Peking to resurrect
the imperial edict of the previous July approving the bank plan,[48] and
in January 1908 he memorialized on the matter.[49] Finally, in mid-March
Hsü convened in Mukden a secret conference of the Manchurian governors. They determined that a bank loan, to total at least 20 million tael
(equivalent in 1908 to $13 million), should be floated in the United
States and be repaid from Manchurian revenue and the uncollected part
of the American Boxer indemnity.[50] With these decisions made, T'ang
carried the plan to Peking for further discussions with the central government.[51]

The Hsü administration had to mark time while it waited for Washington to conclude the painfully slow deliberations on the indemnity remission. However, late in 1907 Hsü and T'ang had encouraged American
Consul General Straight to begin sounding out the opinions of his influential countrymen on the bank scheme. The American was quick to take
up the Manchurian administration's new plan as a workable alternative
to the Hsin–Fa scheme.

Straight's first opportunity to lobby for the bank came with the visit to
China of Secretary of War William Howard Taft in the late fall of 1907.
Taft enjoyed the president's confidence and would make a convert of
importance. As his party, which Straight had joined in Vladivostok, sped
along the Russian railway, Straight briefed the secretary on Manchurian
affairs and on the bank proposal. He played with apparent success on the
theme that the United States should return the excess indemnity without

47. TSSCL, pp. 1925–33, 6700.
48. TKTCS, 1:550–57, for the memorial of 21 October 1907; SL:KH, ch. 579.17, for the edict
confirming approval for the bank; and Straight, report to the State Department, 9 November
1907, NF 2321/16.
49. TKTCS, 2:661–63, for the memorial of 3 January 1908.
50. Straight to Fletcher, 11 and 12 March 1908, Fletcher Papers, Manuscript Division, Library
of Congress, and NF 2413/129 respectively.
51. Rockhill to Root, 28 April 1908, NF 2112/27.

strings and that the Chinese proposal for its use put within the grasp of the United States a rare opportunity to further its own and China's interests in Manchuria. When Straight got off the train in Harbin, he carried Taft's approval of the plan and his assurances that Root and Roosevelt would give it "favorable consideration."[52]

Straight hoped to use Taft's approval as a lever to nudge the State Department toward consideration of the bank-indemnity proposal.

> The Secretary of War, while wishing it clearly understood that the American Government could not presume to dictate the purpose for which the released portion of the Indemnity should be employed, nevertheless thought that the suggestion . . . , should it emanate from from China herself, might be favorably received.[53]

However, Taft, instead of promoting Straight's proposal, retreated from his brief foray into the world of foreign policy-making back to the safety of administering the War Department and to the pressing obligations of his quest for the presidential nomination. Straight was left stranded. The chief of the consular bureau curtly informed him he was not to meddle further: "If Congress shall authorize some remission of the indemnity all arrangements will be exclusively in the hands of the Minister at Peking."[54]

T'ang Shao-i, with whom Straight was to remain in contact, now took up the task of actively promoting the bank scheme on the American side. While in Peking during the spring of 1908 consulting with the central government on Manchurian affairs, T'ang paid a visit to Rockhill to explain his plan. He hoped to neutralize the well-known objections of the American minister with the reassurance that the bank would promote education, an activity dear to Rockhill's heart. But, Rockhill, already familiar with the plan from Straight, was not to be won to it and told his visitor so.[55]

At the same time, T'ang attempted to interest Harriman in a loan for the Manchurian bank. He worked through Straight to break down the American financier's insistence on investing only in railways. T'ang tantalized him with the suggestion that participation in the Manchurian bank would not only get Harriman his Manchurian railway but also win for him a major role in national railway enterprise. "The prospect of

52. Straight, memo, 23 November 1907, NF 2413/93. See also his memo which he presented to Taft during the interview and his progress report to Taft, both dated 2 December 1907, NF 2413/98–99.

53. Straight, report to the State Department, 9 December 1907, NF 2413/91. See also Straight to Fletcher, 12 March 1908, NF 2413/129.

54. Wilbur J. Carr to Straight, 10 February 1908, NF 2413/92–94.

55. Rockhill to Root, 28 April 1908, NF 2112/27.

directing the railways of a nation," which T'ang offered, was powerful bait.[56] Although T'ang could not have seriously meant what he said, his proposition won Harriman. He replied that he would begin discussions as soon as the Chinese had "an immediate, clear offer" to make on the railway, even if it were tied to the bank.[57]

Hsü and T'ang thereupon decided that the next logical step was to confront the State Department in Washington with China's wishes on the disposal of the excess indemnity and to negotiate a loan agreement with Harriman in New York, using the indemnity as security. They could bypass Rockhill by sending a special representative. Yüan Shih-k'ai supported the idea and accordingly slipped into a Wai-wu Pu memorial on the remission of the Boxer indemnity a seemingly innocuous request that a special minister travel to the United States to offer thanks for the generous deed. Several days later the requested imperial edict came down, naming T'ang for the job.[58]

Throughout the remainder of the summer, Hsü and T'ang laid the groundwork for their development plans. The support of the central government, Harriman's favorable response, and the American decision to remit the indemnity had cleared the way for them to act. Surveys for Hulutao had already begun. In August T'ang and Straight negotiated a draft memo on the bank and related matters to present to Harriman as a basis for talks in New York.[59] The following month T'ang signed a contract with Lord ffrench for the construction of the Chinchow–Taonan section of the bank-financed railway. Thus, before his departure for the United States, T'ang had with admirable smoothness brought together the partners—Chinese, British, and American—who a year before had considered building the Hsin–Fa railway.

Yüan Shih-k'ai did his best to support the program of his Manchurian colleagues in the councils of the central government. Although initially he had been preoccupied with his new duties and with meeting the attacks of his enemies, by the fall of 1907 he could afford to throw his full

56. The quote is from Straight to Harriman, 16 February 1908, Straight Papers. Straight to Fletcher, 17 March 1908, Fletcher Papers, describes T'ang's views on the role Harriman might play.

57. Alex Millar (Harriman's secretary) to Straight, 12 June 1908, Straight Papers. See also Harriman to Straight, 5 June 1908, Straight Papers.

58. Wai-wu Pu, memorial, misfiled under 23 July 1908, WWP: Mei-kuo mieh-shou p'ei-k'uan [The United States remits the (Boxer) indemnity]. The imperial edict of 18 July 1908 appears in CWS:KH, ch. 215.14. See also Rockhill to Root, 30 July 1908, NF 2413/157.

59. Memo drafted by Straight, enclosed in Straight to T'ang, 11 August 1908, Straight Papers. A copy of the final version, incorporating T'ang's revisions, also dated 11 August 1908, is enclosed in Straight to J. P. Morgan and Co., 13 December 1908, NF 2112/98.

weight behind the drive to involve the United States in Manchuria. He supported the bank proposal during the discussions in Peking in October 1907 and April 1908. Simultaneously, Yüan made contributions, uniquely his own, toward realizing the "American policy." He worked to create the climate of goodwill necessary for cooperation.

Yüan's first step was the appointment in September 1907 of Wu T'ing-fang as minister to the United States to replace Liang Ch'eng, who had served in the post since 1903. Wu's interest in the possibility of coopera-tion with the United States dated back to the previous decade and fitted with Yüan's policy. And since Wu had reportedly been a celebrated success during his first tenure in the legation, the United States would no doubt welcome his return.[60]

Yüan next decided to try to conclude a treaty of arbitration with the United States. That country had suggested the idea in 1904, but when Congress had refused to approve similar treaties with Britain and France, Minister Liang had temporarily shelved the United States–Chinese draft. Later, however, Elihu Root's efforts at the Second Hague Con-ference of 1907 had set the stage for the approval of revised bilateral treaties with Britain and France. The time seemed ripe to revive the Sino–American treaty as well, and Yüan took the initiative. Wu, to whom Yüan entrusted the details of negotiations, opened them late in the spring of 1908. In September, just as T'ang was preparing to leave China, Yüan secured imperial approval to conclude the treaty, and in October Wu and Root signed the agreement, which was finally ratified the following year.[61] Yüan could reasonably conclude that this success would set relations on a good pitch for T'ang's arrival the following month.

Another opportunity, which Yüan was quick to exploit, came with the visit of the U. S. Navy's battle fleet to the Pacific in the fall. A well-pub-licized visit in strength to such a major Chinese port as Shanghai would underline—with steel and powder—American concern for China. A sump-tuous greeting for the visitors, including an audience for the commanding officers, would make clear Chinese appreciation for the American show of force.[62] Yüan hoped to turn the visit into an expression of tightening

60. Imperial edict, 23 September 1907, THL: KH, p. 5720; and Bland, *Recent Events and Present Policies in China,* pp. 212–13.

61. The communications, mostly routine, between Wu and the Wai-wu Pu as well as memori-als and imperial rescripts on the treaty are in WWP: Chung-Mei kung-tuan chuan-yüeh an [File on the special treaty of arbitration between the United States and China]; CWS: KH, ch. 216.10–12; and CWS: HT, ch. 1.21 and ch. 3.4.

62. Shen Tsu-hsien and Wu Kan-sheng, comps., *Jung-an ti-tzu chi* [A record by the disciples of Yüan Shih-k'ai] (Taipei reprint, 1968), p. 212; and Millard, *America and the Far Eastern Ques-tion,* pp. 378–83.

relations between the two countries and thereby improve T'ang's chances for success in the United States.

As a fillip to Yüan efforts, the press in China made a Sino–American alliance a major topic of speculation in September and October. In part, Yüan inspired such talk through the English-language *Peking Daily News,* the semiofficial organ of the Wai-wu Pu. But the remission of the indemnity, the success of the negotiations in Washington over the arbitration treaty, and the prospect of the American fleet visiting China also fueled discussion about the real purpose of T'ang's mission.[63] Excitement over the prospect of a Sino–American alliance, reported in the European and American presses, infected the columns of the *New York Herald,* an ardent friend of China and sponsor of the China trade.

One English-language paper, *The Chinese Public Opinion,* in a remarkable series of editorials developed the idea of an alliance with great and perhaps inspired care. For the moment, it wrote, China needed freedom from outside interference while she set her house in order. The United States was the only country in a position to provide such protection, which China would requite with commercial and investment opportunities and possibly acquiescence in the American position on immigration. What was needed, then, was "some fast agreement which would guarantee China against the ambitious projects of Japan, and at the same time safeguard American commercial interests." Britain's vast stake in China and her friendship with the United States would help to keep Japan in check. The paper logically capped its argument with the observation that the T'ang mission to the United States would provide the "propitious occasion to draw closer, and if possible, seal by a mutual agreement, the bonds of friendship between the two countries."[64] The Chinese had high hopes for T'ang's mission. Whether they would be realized or prove an irrelevant diplomatic fantasy depended on the American response to this series of Chinese initiatives.

63. Press summaries in Min. Aff. Et., Chine, NS 178, dated 30 September, 29 October, and 11 November 1908. See also Sun Pao-ch'i to the Wai-wu Pu, received 21 September 1908, WWP: Sa-ssu-nien Sun Pao-ch'i shih-Te [Minister Sun Pao-ch'i in Germany in 1908].

64. This series of articles is found in FO 371/434. The quotes are taken from the issues of *The Chinese Public Opinion* of 15 October 1908 and 24 September 1908 respectively. See also the issues dated 22 and 26 September 1908.

By early 1908 Root had rejected suggestions by his subordinates which would have surely led to an American policy antagonistic to Japan's interests in Manchuria. Further, he had decided on a moderate response to Russia's initiative in Harbin. Together these decisions indicated that the Roosevelt administration did not want to become too deeply involved in Manchurian affairs. Consequently, Yüan's campaign of cultivating Sino–American friendship made little headway.

Yüan's first effort toward rapprochement with the United States, the appointment of Wu T'ing-fang as minister, was intended to increase amity. Instead, it created resentment in Washington. The State Department objected to the new appointee for a number of reasons. John Foster, a lawyer and former secretary of state who had been employed by Wu during the negotiations over the Hankow–Canton railway contract, charged that Wu was "a blackmailer and corrupt."[1] Further, there was a feeling in the Department of State that Wu was too minor a personage to fill the Washington post. The rumored appointment of Liang Tun-yen had earlier delighted the department because it considered him friendly to the United States and influential in Peking. Later, the department interpreted the withdrawal of Liang's name and the appointment of Wu as a slight. Finally, the State Department was influenced by reports from the Peking legation, which had taken a jaundiced view of Wu's activities in the Wai-wu Pu. These reports left the department with the lingering conviction that, during the cancellation of the American China Development Company contract, Wu had revealed himself as an extreme advocate of the rights recovery policy and that, during the immigration negotiations of 1904 and the boycott of 1905, he had fomented anti-foreign sentiment. The legation advised that Wu was "not to be trusted."[2]

Huntington Wilson led the fight within the State Department to reject Wu.

1. White House to the State Department, 27 September 1907, NF 5971/10–14.
2. The quote comes from Coolidge (chargé, Peking) to Hay, 20 January 1905, MCD. See also Conger to Hay, 1 March 1904 and 20 April 1904, MCD.

Since the Chinese have not a high regard for Wu and since Chinese officials must know and know that we know the objections to him, our blandly accepting him can, I think, only tend to bring us into contempt.

I consider it very important for the prestige of the United States in China that Wu Ting Fang be not allowed to return to Washington.

After negotiating with the Chinese, Lord Elgin once wrote of the disagreeableness of dealing with a people "who yield nothing to reason and everything to fear." The germ of this truth lingers modified in the Chinese character of to-day, and it is not good policy to be too easy-going with the Chinese, as I think we certainly should be if we accepted Wu as Minister.[3]

Wilson supplemented his hostile memo by inspiring some unfavorable press comments in Washington papers.[4] At the same time, his arguments against Wu were supported by new reports from China. Rockhill judged Wu of no political account either in the capital or with the clique of young officials from Kwangtung and concluded that the government unable to find anything useful for him to do at home, was sending him abroad.[5] One of the young activists, Charles Denby, Jr., sent from Shanghai a more vivid explanation for the change of ministers: T'ang Shao-had become jealous of Liang Ch'eng's successes in Washington and had had Yüan recall him. Liang Tun-yen had not been able to take the post because Yüan needed him in the Wai-wu Pu. Thus, the aged and eccentric Wu, the only man available, had obtained the appointment.[6]

The president, who had initiated the discussion in the first place by asking Root to investigate Foster's charges, finally recommended accepting Wu's appointment.

He is a bad old Chink and if he had his way he would put us all to the heavy death or do something equally unpleasant with us; but we cannot expect to get a Minister like the one that has just gone, and the loss is far more China's than ours; while I do not object to any Chinaman showing a feeling that he would like to retaliate now and then for our insolence to the Chinese.[7]

When delicate inquiries at the Wai-wu Pu revealed that the appointment was settled, Root let the matter drop.[8]

3. Wilson to Root, memo, 30 October 1907, NF 5971/10–14.
4. Press clippings, ibid.
5. Rockhill to Root, telegram, 2 November 1907, NF 5971/9.
6. Denby to the assistant secretary of state, 18 November 1907, NF 5971/18.
7. Roosevelt to Root, 26 September 1907, Morison, 5: 809.
8. Fletcher (chargé, Peking) to Root, 5 November 1907, NF 5971/15.

The episode is revealing for the way misinformation and prejudice influenced discussions of Chinese affairs in the State Department. Wu's political weight compared favorably with that of either of his juniors, Liang Tun-yen or Liang Ch'eng, whom Americans preferred to see occupy the Washington legation. Only earlier in 1907 had Liang Tun-yen occupied his first post of national importance, a vice presidency in the Wai-wu Pu. Wu T'ing-fang had already held that post in 1904 and 1905. As for Liang Ch'eng, the most prominent position he was to hold under the Ch'ing was that of minister to the United States, a post in which Wu had preceded him. In addition, Wu had in recent years seen service as vice-president of the Board of Commerce and as commissioner to negotiate the commercial treaties of 1903, and he had just completed a thorough and widely hailed revision of the legal codes. Rockhill overlooked this accomplishment when he intimated that Wu was being sent abroad because he was of no use to Chinese reformers. Rather, Wu's age, his lengthy experience in diplomacy, and his reform efforts tended to increase his prestige and authority at home. Rockhill thoughtlessly misread the record, and Wilson, blinded by his prejudices, simply could not see it. Both entirely misjudged Wu's stature.

Two other charges weighed against Wu: his "antiforeign tendencies" and Foster's accusations. As for the first, if Wu's nationalism were to be held against him, it should also have been held against both Liangs, who were no less patriotic than Wu. Wu's views were better known simply because he had been more prominent and outspoken than the others. Foster's charges of blackmail and corruption are more difficult to judge. They were, however, the kind of charges constantly brought against Chinese officials by foreigners like Foster who lacked an understanding of the Chinese bureaucracy. Perhaps Foster, a former employee of Wu's, may have had an ax to grind. That the president, who was not inclined to back away from a battle over principle, eventually called a halt to talk in the State Department of rejecting Wu suggests that the charges were either baseless, beyond proof, or an exaggeration.

The department's reaction to Wu's appointment put a cloud over Yüan's project to secure American support. At the same time, Yüan himself should not escape censure for acting on incomplete information. Wu had indeed achieved a popular success during his first stay in the United States. This popularity, together with his knowledge of the country and his diplomatic experience, qualified him, so Yüan thought, for reassignment to Washington. But Yüan did not understand that Wu's stiff and persistent protests against the mistreatment of Chinese and his role in repurchasing the Hankow–Canton railway had alienated official sympathy, particularly in the State Department. Yüan had at hand his American-trained lieutenants, who might have anticipated this antipathy, but it was not for them to speak out against a man who was their senior in age and rank and who was also a fellow provincial.

Yüan suffered a second check to his personal efforts in the fall of 1908. He had supposed that the visit of the American fleet would create an atmosphere of cordiality in which T'ang Shao-i could work. But Denby and Rockhill undercut him.[9] Rockhill did not want China to reach the unwarranted conclusion that the United States would stand behind her if she adopted a more aggressive policy against Japan in Manchuria. Therefore, he advised canceling or at least minimizing the event. Accordingly, only a squadron was dispatched to Amoy, a lesser port than Shanghai, while the bulk of the fleet called in Japan. Further, to cool enthusiasm for the event, Rockhill went out of his way to impress his opinion on other Americans in China and pointedly stayed away from Amoy in late October when the ships came in.[10] Finally, Rockhill tried to obscure Chinese disappointment over these developments by disingenuously reporting that Yüan was "quite pleased to learn that the Second Squadron would only visit Amoy."[11]

Ironically, the fleet visit also served as the occasion for the revival of the old coaling station proposal—a reminder of how out of tune were American goals and attitudes with those of the Chinese. As the squadron lay at anchor in the Amoy harbor, the minister to Tokyo, Thomas J. O'Brien, telegraphed a proposal to Washington that the United States secure a naval base nearby. Root judged the suggestion reasonable enough to consult immediately with the Navy's General Board. Now, unlike in 1900, the board was uninterested.[12] The visit, which stirred thoughts among Americans of acquiring Chinese territory rather than of helping to protect it, provided further evidence that Yüan would not succeed.

Rockhill, nurturing his own ideas on how the Chinese should use the remitted Boxer funds, led the opposition to the Chinese proposal for

9. Denby to Root, 18 April 1908, and Rockhill to Root, 21 April 1908, NF 8258/386 and 400. The edict of 27 September 1908 sending a delegation of officials to meet the fleet is in THL: KH, p. 5976. A recent study of this American naval adventure is Robert A. Hart, *The Great White Fleet: Its Voyage Around the World, 1907–1909* (Boston, 1965). Hart's account of the visit to Amoy (29 October–5 November), pp. 157–58, 232–58, and 205–07, relies too heavily and indiscriminately on the American press and historical stereotypes to be of use on the Chinese role in the visit.

10. Thomas F. Millard, *America and the Far Eastern Question* (New York, 1909), pp. 378–83.

11. Rockhill to Root, 4 May 1908, NF 8258/414.

12. NF 2413/160 contains O'Brien's telegram from Tokyo and the General Board's decision.

iverting the funds to a Manchurian bank. Rockhill's counterproposal, onsistently maintained, was that the remitted funds be used for education, with the money tied to the project by a formal commitment by the Chinese government, lest the Chinese quietly put his project aside and nd other uses for the money.

Rockhill felt that his program would benefit both China and the United States. In his view China needed nothing less than reform from op to bottom if she were to survive as an independent state. In education, "on modern lines" of course, he thought he saw the instrument suited o the task. The United States stood to gain too. Education would promote olitical stability and commercial progress, thus making China a sounder nd richer trading partner. At the same time the rise of American-educated leaders in Peking would give the United States unprecedented influence. Convinced that much hinged on the success of his proposal, Rockhill promoted it with tenacity in both capitals.[13]

Rockhill's views on how the indemnity should be used put him in a familiar, adversary relationship with the consul general in Mukden. traight—younger, less experienced, but more ambitious—had tried to onvert Manchuria into his private domain by bringing the consulates in ntung, Newchuang, and Harbin under his jurisdiction and by having ke-minded acquaintances appointed to these posts. From the start Rockhill had fought Straight's attempt at empire building and self-aggrandizement. The two had also differed over policy toward Japan and China. Rockhill was not perturbed by Japan's hold on Manchuria, whereas traight was strongly anti-Japanese. Conversely, Straight was inclined o help China (for reasons of both personal and national interest); Rockhill would go no farther toward a cooperative relationship than offering dvice. Straight, for example, arranged with T'ang Shao-i a publicity job or his vice-consul, George Marvin, focusing world opinion on Japanese ransgressions in Manchuria. Rockhill quickly secured Root's support a putting a stop to this partisan project.[14]

Washington was receptive to Rockhill's hopes for the education plan nd shared his suspicions about China's ability to otherwise use the idemnity constructively. Third Assistant Secretary of State Huntington Vilson agreed with Rockhill and informed Secretary of State Root that

13. Rockhill elaborated his program in letters to Roosevelt, 12 July 1905, Rockhill Papers, oughton Library, Harvard University, and to Root, 6 August 1907, NF 2413/79.
14. On the Marvin episode, see the documents in NF 12972. See also Straight's excited tele-ams on the Chientao dispute between China and Japan and Rockhill's laconic response. elegrams to Root from Straight, 6 July 1908, and from Rockhill, 10 July 1908, NF 9881/12 and

"the return of the indemnity should be used to make China do some o
the things we want. Otherwise I fear her gratitude will be quite empty."[1]
William Phillips, who under Wilson's supervision kept an eye on Chin;
for the department, and Root himself also supported Rockhill.[16] It wa
presumably on Rockhill's initiative and with Root's concurrence that th
consular bureau ordered Straight to leave the details of the remissior
question to the minister.

Even the president seemed won by the education proposition promotec
by Rockhill. In 1907, in his annual address to Congress, Roosevelt sug
gested the importance of having Chinese students come to the Unitec
States to study as a means of helping China adapt to modern conditions
His suggestion followed in the text of his address his recommendation i
favor of indemnity remission. The enthusiasts of education had managec
to link the two issues together in his mind.[17]

As early as 1905 Rockhill had let the Chinese know that the America
government favored using the excess indemnity for education. He genuine
ly believed that he had secured Yüan Shih-k'ai's and Prince Ch'ing'
tentative assent to the education project. Rockhill preferred to discoun
whatever reservations the Chinese might have expressed, and they ha
had every reason to treat the minister's pet project agreeably if doing s
would speed up the indemnity remission.[18] When T'ang in the sprin
of 1908 revealed the details of his project to use the indemnity for ;
Manchurian bank, Rockhill wrote back to Root, "I do not anticipate th
T'ang memorial [on the bank loan] will be acted upon; it seems to m
perfectly impracticable. I am only astonished that such an able man a
T'ang could have evolved it."[19]

Rockhill, however, wisely did not take the failure of T'ang's ban
project for granted. With past Chinese assurances in mind and with Root'
support guaranteed, he pressed for formal Chinese approval of his ow
education scheme. He bluntly informed representatives of the Wai-w
Pu that "any action on the part of China which might indicate a disposi
tion to ignore the assurances heretofore given us . . . might indefinitel

15. Wilson, memo, 22 November 1907, NF 2413/79.
16. Root to Rockhill, 27 May 1908, NF 2413/138A.
17. The address is in FRUS, 1907, p. lxvii.
18. Rockhill mentioned these informal assurances in his dispatch of 28 April 1908 to Roo
NF 2112/27, and in his letter to Roosevelt of 12 July 1905, Rockhill Papers. Rockhill informe
the Chinese minister in Washington of his views in an interview in 1905. See Liang Ch'eng
the Wai-wu Pu, received 13 May 1905, WWP: Mei-kuo mieh-shou p'ei-k'uan [The Unite
States remits the (Boxer) indemnity].
19. Rockhill to Root, 28 April 1908, NF 2112/27.

lelay final action in the matter."[20] Nonetheless, Rockhill was finally orced in July 1908 to accept an offer from the Wai-wu Pu to send students o the United States but without acknowledging any connection between he remission and this educational project. Rockhill's discovery later in he month that T'ang was to go to the United States revealed to him that he Chinese had not yet given up on the bank plan.

Rockhill immediately set to work to bolster his position in Washington. Ie warned William Phillips that the Chinese, hard pressed for funds, vere sending T'ang in search of relief and that the State Department nust not allow Chinese needs to upset a plan designed for their own ;ood.

> The carrying out of the educational mission is, in the long run, an infinitely more valuable return for the money than the wildcat schemes it would be employed in by the "Manchurian Bank."[21]

'hillips prepared the defenses in Washington against marauding Chinese. Ie alerted his superiors to the danger and suggested that they deter ['ang by publicizing the indemnity compromise which Rockhill had just eached in Peking.

> This having been done, T'ang will hesitate to request us to let China make use of the money for Manchurian purposes, which he really has a right to do, strictly speaking. . . . [22]

Rockhill also took the precaution of warning Root to be on his guard. Rockhill cautioned that T'ang, despite his deficiencies ("densely ignorant n all financial questions, and of political economy I doubt if he . . . .now[s] even the name"), was nevertheless "extremely ambitious and o long as his patron, Yüan Shih-k'ai, remains in power, T'ang will have o be counted with."[23] Duly warned, Root joined in the preparations for ['ang's arrival by approving the publicity plan. Phillips confidentially .ssured Rockhill that "every one here [is] absolutely in sympathy with 'our idea."[24]

The T'ang mission was the last act in Yüan Shih-k'ai's attempt to win American support for the bank. T'ang left China publicly commanded

20. Rockhill thus summarized his comments to T'ang Shao-i in his dispatch to Root of 28 April 1908, NF 2112/27.
21. Rockhill to Phillips, 1 August 1908, NF 2413/148.
22. Phillips to Adee, memo, 9 September 1908, NF 2413/148.
23. Rockhill to Root, 30 July 1908, NF 2413/157.
24. Phillips to Rockhill, 19 September 1908, Rockhill Papers.

to give thanks for the return of the indemnity and secretly authorized to negotiate a loan. Tang's American allies prepared for his arrival. E. H Harriman wished Willard Straight at hand during discussions with T'ang and Root recalled him. This was as far as Root, sympathetic to oversea investment, would go in giving official support to Harriman's plans Straight himself reached Washington in September, unintentionally adding an element of mock drama to the situation by carrying in a pouch attached to a string around his neck the memo which he had concluded with T'ang. In the ensuing discussions, which carried over into Novem ber, Kuhn, Loeb and Company agreed to take the loan for Harriman i T'ang provided satisfactorily detailed terms.[25] While Straight helped to pave the way for the loan, George Marvin, still in the employ of the Chinese government, attended to publicity and routine preparations fo T'ang's arrival. He prevailed on William Phillips to give him a hand locat ing a house in Washington for T'ang and his suite of twenty persons, and Phillips finally found a landlord with a satisfactory property who was will ing to rent to a Chinese. Phillips, who had just helped prepare the de fenses against T'ang, now excitedly observed, "It really looks as if Ameri can interests in the Far East [are] going to assume a pretty definit shape."[26]

T'ang reached Washington on 30 November 1908. He quickly go through the required formalities—the president's welcome and T'ang' presentation to him of a striking collection of porcelains from the palace storehouse in Mukden.[27] But T'ang made no progress with the unfriendly State Department. He even found it difficult to get to see the secretary o state to discuss the proposal to use the indemnity remission as security for a loan.[28] Frustrated, T'ang left for Europe in January 1909.

The Roosevelt administration was not interested in creating complica tions in the Far East. Root had already demonstrated considerable cautiousness during the Harbin dispute and in handling charges of trade discrimination against Japan. He certainly would not support China in

25. Phillips to Rockhill, 30 September 1908, Rockhill Papers; Root to Straight, 11 December 1908, NF 2413/213A; J. O. P. Bland, *Recent Events and Present Policies in China* (Philadelphia 1912), p. 313; George Kennan, *E. H. Harriman's Far Eastern Plans* (New York, 1917), p. 43–44 and Huntington Wilson, *Memoirs of an Ex-Diplomatist* (Boston, 1945), p. 168.

26. Phillips to Rockhill, 19 September 1908, Rockhill Papers; and Marvin, articles in *The Outlook*, 14 and 28 November 1908.

27. Morison, 6:1405–07; and Elizia R. Scidmore, "Mukden, the Manchu Home and I Great Art Museum," *National Geographic Magazine* 21 (1910): 311.

28. Huntington Wilson to Root, memo, 5 December 1908, and undated Straight memo, both in NF 2413/220. The record of T'ang's unproductive interview with Root on 9 December 190 is in NF 2413/218.

Manchuria to the point of provoking either Russia or Japan. Phillips told Rockhill as much:

> I do not think the Department intends to have trouble in Manchuria, either with Russia or Japan. The Secretary is especially anxious not to become embroiled in little incidents with either of those two powers. . . . [29]

T'ang, who was playing for high stakes in Manchuria, had come to the United States looking for a backer but found the American government suspicious of him and unwilling to accept risks even at second hand.

The most recent concrete expression of this American cautiousness was the Root–Takahira agreement, which guaranteed the status quo in the Pacific and smoothed relations between the United States and Japan. Only after concluding negotiations with Takahira and just before making the agreement public did Root finally reveal its contents to his own subordinates and to T'ang. Despite their objections,[30] Root cabled Rockhill to give the Chinese government "the good news" concerning the accord and added that he hoped it would be pleased by the way the agreement incorporated American concern for China's welfare and her traditional China policy.[31]

Yüan had gotten news of the agreement on 23 November, when Rockhill revealed the contents to the Wai-wu Pu.[32] A report from one of the young foreign affairs specialists, Hu Wei-te, then serving as minister to Japan, attributed the timing of the agreement to Japan's wish to confound the rumors of a Sino–American accord. Hu criticized the United States as well as Japan for carrying on the negotiations with such haste and secrecy. Japan was creating a place of diplomatic primacy for herself in the Far East through a series of international agreements, of which the one with the United States was the latest.[33] For Yüan, whose thoughts took a similar path, the agreement was another serious blow to his long-nurtured plans for Sino–American cooperation. He evinced "considerable disappointment and some irritation," so Rockhill reported with surprise and perhaps understatement. Yüan quizzed the American minister on the

29. Phillips to Rockhill, 19 September 1908, Rockhill Papers.

30. T'ang to the Wai-wu Pu, telegram, 25 November 1908, CWS: KH, ch. 218.1; Straight, two memos dated 11 November 1908, NF 16533/6 and 8; and Wilson, *Memoirs of an Ex-Diplomatist*, p. 170.

31. Root to Rockhill, telegram, 21 November 1908, NF 16533.

32. Liu Yü-lin, report, 24 November 1908, WWP: Jih-Mei hsieh-yüeh an [File on the Root–Takahira agreement]. See also Thomas A. Bailey, "The Root-Takahira Agreement of 1908," *Pacific Historical Review* 9 (1940): 28–30.

33. Hu to the Wai-wu Pu, 22 December 1908, WWP: Jih-Mei hsieh-yüeh an.

reasons for the sudden exchange of views between the United States and Japan and for informing China only immediately before T'ang's arrival in the United States. Rockhill could only repeat Root's cheery view that China should be pleased and blandly added that he thought the agreement would not hinder T'ang, whose only purpose, after all, was to give thanks for the indemnity remission.[34]

The Japanese did not, like Root and Rockhill, try to minimize the significance of the exchange of views for China. A memo sent by the Japanese minister in Peking to the Wai-wu Pu stressed that this agreement with the United States fit into the line of diplomatic developments initiated by Japanese understandings with Britain, France, and Russia over Manchuria and that they were all made of the same cloth.[35] The agreement was a sign not of American solicitude, as Root would have it, but of disaffection from China's cause, as the Japanese hinted. China was isolated and ignored in East Asian affairs. The bitter plaint of one Chinese paper commenting on this development could easily have come from Yüan's mouth: "It is truly as if our country were a guest whose affairs were to be managed by these nations which make arrangements together."[36]

Yet another obstacle to the success of T'ang's mission was the death of the empress dowager and its unsettling effect on Peking politics. They rendered uncertain T'ang's own standing at home and that of Yüan Shih-k'ai, on whose support his mission depended. T'ang had to move cautiously on the Harriman loan.[37] At the same time, Washington's open opposition to T'ang's plan for use of the indemnity in support of China's position in Manchuria and the unexpected conclusion of the agreement with Japan mocked Yüan's hopes for a policy of limited cooperation with the United States. The double failure made Yüan vulnerable to attack by his political opponents. As the attacks, justified by his enemies on more grounds than one, made headway, T'ang grew even more cautious. Thus, the setbacks to T'ang's mission and to the misplaced hopes for American assistance provided a handy pretext for toppling Yüan, and so also did Yüan's fall further diminish the prospect of T'ang's salvaging anything for Manchuria.[38]

34. Rockhill to Root, 3 December 1908, NF 16533/46.

35. The Japanese minister to China to the Wai-wu Pu, memo, 3 December 1908, WWP: Jih-Mei hsieh-yüeh an.

36. *Chung-yang ta-t'ung jih-pao* [Central daily news], December 1908, trans. in NF 16533/59.

37. See for example Schiff to Straight, 3 December 1908, and Straight to Edward C. Parker, 30 January 1909, both in Straight Papers, Olin Library, Cornell University; and T'ang, telegraphic memorial, 17 November 1908, SL: HT, ch. 1.14.

38. On T'ang's loss of support in Peking, see Rockhill to Root, telegram, 8 January 1909, NF 1518/212. Reports on T'ang's progress through Europe noted his apparent loss of authority

The State Department and Rockhill had been determined to protect the indemnity's ties to education and had refused to give serious consideration to this opportunity to promote American interests in Manchuria by helping China to strengthen her position there. They had altogether ignored China's desperate need for funds to carry on her program of frontier defense and the clear preference of Chinese to "strengthen their country a bit before distributing dynamics and moral philosophy in prize packages."[39] The president himself observed that "the Chinese are so helpless to carry out any fixed policy, whether home or foreign, that it is difficult to have any but the most cautious dealings with them."[40]

The State Department also helped to seal the fate of Yüan and T'ang by its timing of the Root–Takahira agreement and by its refusal even to give T'ang's proposal for use of the excess indemnity careful consideration. But the activists within the State Department, following their natural reflexes, heaped blame on Japan for the reverses which had made the Harriman loan an immediate impossibility. Straight, primed by T'ang's version of recent events in Peking, indicted Japan for interference in Chinese politics. "Unless great care be exercised this [Japanese] influence will menace the natural and legitimate development of foreign interests in China."[41] William Phillips decided that a conspiracy was at the bottom of these untoward events. "Of course, it is almost unnecessary to say that there are suspicions here of Japanese activity in high quarters in Peking."[42]

Root too began to show some agitation over the turmoil in Peking. Rockhill belatedly reminded him that Yüan was the "chief influence for order, stability and progress" in the Chinese government and raised the specter of "Manchoo reaction."[43] Root now decided that Yüan deserved more encouragement and cast about for a means to help him. At first,

---

to deal for financial aid. See reports to the secretary of state to this effect from Henry White (Paris), telegram, 1 March 1909, and from David J. Hill (Berlin), 12 April 1909; as well as Whitelaw Reid to Bacon, 13 February 1909. They are to be found in NF 2413/343, 240, and 235 respectively. An interesting summary of contemporary Japanese reports on Yüan's fall, still a matter for speculation, is provided by Ernest P. Young in "Politics in the Early Republic: Liang Ch'i-ch'ao and the Yuan Shih-k'ai Presidency" (Ph.D. diss., Harvard University, 1964), p. 411, n. 16. See also Bland, *Recent Events and Present Policies in China*, p. 314.

39. Straight (paraphrasing T'ang) to Fletcher, 17 March 1908, Fletcher Papers, Manuscript Division, Library of Congress.

40. Roosevelt to Kaiser Wilhelm II, 2 January 1909, quoted in Joseph B. Bishop, *Theodore Roosevelt and His Time* (New York, 1920), 2: 287. See also a dispatch on Roosevelt's views sent by German Ambassador Bernstorff to the foreign office, 2 January 1909 (quoted in Luella J. Hall, "The Abortive German–American–Chinese Entente of 1907–08," *The Journal of Modern History* 1 [1929]: 234).

41. Straight, memo, 7 January 1909, NF 1518/271.

42. Phillips to Rockhill, 9 January 1909, Rockhill Papers. British diplomats uniformly dismissed the charge that the Japanese were implicated in Yüan's fall. FO 371/612.

43. Rockhill to Root, telegrams, 2 January 1909, NF 1518/194 and 195.

Root had the fantastic thought of attempting a reconciliation between Yüan and K'ang Yu-wei, who had just drawn attention to himself by cabling to Roosevelt an attack on Yüan. Rockhill swiftly countered that Peking would not understand Root's motives.[44] Root, undaunted, decided to lodge a vigorous protest against Yüan's political disgrace and the damage it would do to China at home and in world affairs, particularly in relations with the United States; however, T'ang Shao-i intervened and convinced Root of the foolishness of this blatant interference, which might do more to endanger Yüan that to save him.[45] Root finally had to settle for mildly worded representations presented by Rockhill in team with the British minister.[46] Root moved too late, never realizing that he was a part of Yüan's problems.

44. K'ang to Roosevelt, telegrams, 14 and 30 November 1908, NF 1518/178 and 190; Root to Rockhill, 20 November 1908, NF 1518/181A; and Rockhill to Root, 24 November 1908, NF 1518/183.

45. Root to Rockhill, telegram, 2 January 1909, NF 1518/195. Root's canceled draft telegram is also in this file.

46. Rockhill to Root and Root to Rockhill, telegrams, 9 January 1909, NF 1518/221. See also Rockhill to Root, 15 January 1909, NF 1518/225.

11: NEW ADMINISTRATIONS AND NEW PLANS

Power routinely changed hands in Washington in March 1909 as President Theodore Roosevelt gave way to his chosen successor, William Howard Taft. The president-elect had difficulty finding a suitable secretary of state. Elihu Root declined, for personal reasons, to continue at the State Department. Senator Henry Cabot Lodge also declined. Finally, on the advice of Root, Taft offered the job to Senator Philander C. Knox, a fifty-five-year-old corporation lawyer and former attorney general.[1] Knox was diminutive and assertive, a contrast to Taft's corpulence and mildness. But the two were brought together by ties of political allegiance and profession. Both were able lawyer–administrators. The British ambassador in Washington, James Bryce, quickly and accurately sized up the new appointee as " 'first, last, and all the time' a lawyer, with the characteristic habits of mind which belong to that profession, and disposed to look at the questions primarily from the legal side."[2]

Knox entered the State Department altogether unfamiliar both with diplomatic practice and with any place beyond the continental bounds of the United States. Taft stood by to supplement these deficiencies as best he could. His three years of service as American proconsul in the Philippines and his experience as Roosevelt's emissary to the Far East in 1905 and again in 1907 seemed to suit him to play an active, intelligent role in shaping policy for that part of the world.

The match of Knox's administrative ability and Taft's diplomatic experience proved illusory. First, Knox wanted a large measure of independence, which the lethargic Taft granted him early in the administration. Second, Taft's vaunted experience in the Far East was limited. As governor of the Philippines, his job had been to crush and conciliate restless natives

---

1. Knox's background is sketched in two sympathetic accounts: Paige E. Mulhollan, "Philander C. Knox and Dollar Diplomacy, 1909–1913" (Ph.D. diss., University of Texas, 1966), pp. 1–20; and Herbert F. Wright, "Philander C. Knox," in Samuel Flagg Bemis, ed., *The American Secretaries of State and Their Diplomacy*, 9: 301–57. The most perceptive study is by Walter and Marie Scholes, *The Foreign Policy of the Taft Administration* (Columbia, Mo., 1970).

2. Bryce to Grey, 5 January 1909, FO 371/786. Bryce's final judgment on Knox was harsh. See Herbert A. L. Fisher, *James Bryce* (London, 1927), 2: 37.

with the aid of superior military force, but his work had not sensitized him to diplomacy or to the foremost international questions in East Asia. His two trips to the Far East as the president's emissary and observer also contributed little to his education in foreign affairs. He had come back from the first trip with a low opinion of the Japanese. "A Jap is first of all a Jap and would be glad to aggrandize himself at the expense of anybody."[3] The second tour of the Far East in 1907, timed to promote Taft's presidential aspirations, did nothing to change this opinion. He was fearful that Japan might some day threaten the Philippines, but he was also hopeful that Korea and Manchuria would keep the Japanese fully diverted. His only contact with China was several days spent in Hong Kong, Canton, and Shanghai. Taft filled his visit to Shanghai in 1907 with social amenities and speech-making, dutifully repeating the current platitudes on Sino–American friendship. What really roused his enthusiasm, however, was the controversial effort of the American court in Shanghai to purify the city's morals. China and the Chinese were to him considerably less absorbing than the comfortably familiar questions of reform and the law.[4] Taft, who had traveled more widely in the Far East than Roosevelt, sadly lacked the broad and sensitive feel for international relations or the curiosity and energy of his chief.

Knox asserted his control over foreign policy from the start, beginning with appointments within the State Department and for posts abroad.[5] Of these the most fateful was his decision to promote Huntington Wilson, Root's third assistant secretary, to the post of first assistant secretary. Wilson had been slated for assignment as minister to Argentina, but before his departure he had convinced Knox that he possessed the diplomatic experience which the new secretary might find valuable in his number-two man. The president, who had his own candidate for the post, gave way but developed a strong antipathy for Wilson. "I would just like to sit on Wilson once and mash him flat. What Knox sees in him I do not see."[6]

3. Taft to Martin Egan, 25 March 1905, Taft Papers, Manuscript Division, Library of Congress. Ralph E. Minger, "Taft's Missions to Japan: A Study in Personal Diplomacy," *Pacific Historical Review* 30 (1961): 279–94, deals with these two trips to the Far East. Some of Taft's reports (e.g., to McIntyre for Root or Roosevelt, 4 October 1907; to Root, 10 October 1907; and to Roosevelt, 6 August 1907) are in the Taft Papers.

4. Taft to Roosevelt, 5 October 1907, and to Root, 10 October 1907, both in Taft Papers. A reprint of Taft's Shanghai speech of 8 October 1907 is in the Knox Papers, Manuscript Division, Library of Congress.

5. On Knox's State Department, see Huntington Wilson, *Memoirs of an Ex-Diplomatist* (Boston, 1945), chaps. 24–30; and Mulhollan, "Philander C. Knox and Dollar Diplomacy, 1909–1913," pp. 21–29 and 34–40.

6. Taft quoted in Archie Butt to Clara, 8 June 1910, in Archie Butt, *Taft and Roosevelt: The Intimate Letters of Archie Butt, Military Aide* (Garden City, New York, 1930), 1: 371.

Alvey A. Adee, the experienced but uninspired workhorse, was kept on as second asisstant secretary. William Phillips got Wilson's old job as third assistant secretary, but before the end of the years Knox was to send him off to London as chargé. Willard Straight continued to serve in the Division of Far Eastern Affairs, where he had been since his return from Mukden. In June, however, he left to join a newly formed financial combine and was replaced by Ransford S. Miller, who as chief of the division was assisted by E. T. Williams. The only newcomer of note was Henry Hoyt, a lawyer and formerly close adviser to Knox in the Justice Department. Hoyt was appointed to the newly created post of counsellor where, much to Wilson's annoyance, he enjoyed considerable independence and direct access to Knox.

These appointments closed one era and introduced another. John Hay had brought the open door as a formal concept into American China policy. Those familiar with Hay's intentions and with the events of his tenure had one by one disappeared from the department. Now only Adee could recall from personal experience the details surrounding the writing of the open door notes, hardly ten years earlier. The new members of the department, for the most part young and inexperienced, were free to rewrite the open door to suit their own very different perceptions and preoccupations.

Secretary Knox quickly settled into routine—a couple of hours late in the morning in his office and a working lunch with Wilson three times a week. Wilson handled daily affairs and consulted with Knox solely on major questions of policy. Knox's own thinking on foreign policy was essentially a process of deduction from what he regarded as general principles of international affairs as well as from the digests of information prepared by his staff. Once he had decided on the outline of a policy, he depended on Wilson and his other subordinates to flesh it out and to execute it with only an occasional personal intervention. Knox's admirers argued that he was wise to avoid the tiring humdrum of routine, thereby saving time for quiet deliberation. His detractors countered that Knox was simply too indolent to master and keep up with the details of his job.

Taft generally respected Knox's wish to oversee departmental affairs without interference. The only exception in an otherwise harmonious relationship during the first year of the administration occurred over the choice of a new minister for China. Taft thought Rockhill too apathetic a servant of national interests in China and was eager to get him out.

Rockhill has outlived his usefulness in China, if he ever had any there.

He is a dilettante. . . . China is very friendly to us, and they are anxious to encourage American trade and the American investment of capital, because she does not distrust our motives. The opportunities it seems to me, therefore, for the development of the Oriental trade are great if we can only have a man on the ground who realizes the necessity and has the force and pluck and experience to take advantage of the opportunity.[7]

Taft considered and rejected a number of names before hitting upon that of Charles R. Crane, a Chicago Democrat who seemed to have the requisite energy and business experience.[8]

Crane accepted the post in July after getting from Taft the impression that he would occupy an influential and independent place in the administration. He decided that consultations with the State Department before his departure were not important. Instead, he gathered about himself his own advisers, George Marvin and Thomas F. Millard. The latter was a prolific journalist whose opinions on the identity of interests between the United States and China and on America's destiny in the Far East set him in a line of direct descent from Brooks Adams and Albert Beveridge.[9] Both advisers were antagonistic toward Japan. Crane began in September to speak his mind in public, criticizing Japan's foreign policy and revealing that the State Department was preparing a protest against a Japanese mining claim in Manchuria.

Knox was not happy taking a back seat to Taft in selecting a man for the China post,[10] nor did he like Crane's airs of independence and self-importance. Knox asked Taft to repudiate the minister-designate's indiscreet comments to the press. Taft reluctantly agreed and obliquely apologized for his role in the affair by reassuring Knox of his independence in foreign affairs.[11] Crane resigned, indignant with the administration both for Knox's uncivil treatment and for Taft's failure to support him. The affair created a major controversy in the press and left a residue of resentment among Crane's political associates, including members of Taft's cabinet.[12] After this contretemps, both Taft and Knox were con-

7. Taft to Rollo Ogden, 21 April 1909, Taft Papers. See also Taft to Bishop C. H. Brent, 10 July 1909, Taft Papers.

8. Taft to Nellie (Mrs. W. H. Taft), 14 July 1909, Taft Papers.

9. Thomas F. Millard, *The New Far East* (New York, 1906) and *America and the Far Eastern Question* (New York, 1909); and Millard to Taft, 23 July 1909, Taft Papers.

10. His pique shows through in a letter to Taft, 26 August 1909, Knox Papers.

11. Taft to Knox, 19 and 24 October 1909, Knox Papers.

12. On the Crane controversy, see Wilson, *Memoirs of an Ex-Diplomatist,* pp. 204–07; Mulhollan, "Philander C. Knox and Dollar Diplomacy, 1909–1913," pp. 30–34; and NF 20602 12E, 15, 20.

tent with simply transferring Rockhill to St. Petersburg and leaving Henry Fletcher in charge in Peking.

Knox formulated and Taft approved a radical shift away from Roosevelt's Far Eastern policy. This change was in large measure the result of anxieties over a somnolent China trade and of the anti-Japanese strictures of Knox's activist subordinates.

Knox along with Taft tended to refract the elements of the Far Eastern situation through the prism of commercial advantage. American exports to China in general and to Manchuria in particular had fallen sharply after the Russo–Japanese War. American cotton exports, always strongest in Manchuria and north China, were still markedly down. They had risen from .6 million pieces in 1907 to 1.5 million pieces in 1908 but were still far from the previous high of 12.6 million pieces in 1905. The United States carrying trade had also dropped, from second behind Great Britain to third behind Japan. American residents and firms in Manchuria, a useful index of the briskness of trade, were no more appreciably in evidence in 1909 than earlier. The only bright spot was the steady rise in kerosene exports by the Standard Oil Company of New York. Figures for 1909 were already pointing to an overall decline in American trade with China of about $2 million to $6 million (i.e., a 10 to 30 percent decline from 1908). American exports had since 1900 accounted for about 10 percent of China's total foreign trade, but there was no indication that the dreams of the China market were nearing realization. To the contrary, American exports to China (including Hong Kong leased territories), which had in recent years made up as much as 4 percent of total American exports, were to drop by 1910 to 1 percent. And Americans were falling behind their foreign competition in China. For example, Japan's trade with China had nearly doubled between 1901 and 1908, surpassing American exports by $16 million and garnering in particular a larger share of the Manchurian market.[13]

Knox's subordinates, both in the department and overseas, added to the gloom by expressing anxieties about Japan's policy and China's inability to withstand pressure from that quarter.

13. On the trade situation in 1908 and 1909, see Charles F. Remer, *The Foreign Trade of China* (Shanghai, 1926), p. 154; *Daily Consular and Trade Reports*, 8 October 1910; *The Journal of Commerce*, 12 November 1910; Max Müller to Grey, 28 October 1910, FO 371/874; J. B. Osborne (Bureau of Trade Relations), "Memorandum Relative to American Trade Possibilities in the Far East," 15 September 1910, Knox Papers; Division of Far Eastern Affairs, report on trade [late January 1910], Knox Papers; A. A. Williamson (vice-consul in charge, Dairen), report to the State Department, 13 May 1910, NF 7611/8; Fred Fisher (consul, Newchuang), report to the State Department, 17 September 1909, NF 19370/16; and Pan Shü-lun, *The Trade of the United States with China* (New York, 1924), pp. 48–49.

Japan is actively pursuing her policy of penetration and encroachment, not only in Manchuria, but in South China as well, while Russian designs constitute an ever present menace to Chinese sovereignty in the north.

The Peking Government at present requires encouragement, suggestion and support on the path of progress.[14]

Even Rockhill, before his departure for St. Petersburg, betrayed a new uneasiness that Japanese colonization in southern Manchuria might threaten China's integrity and sovereignty.[15]

Knox responded by becoming the champion of dollar diplomacy,[16] a program first advocated nearly a decade before by a small band of publicists and subsequently endorsed by the young activists in the consulates of Manchuria and in the State Department. Dollar diplomacy in Manchuria was essentially a commercial and financial policy in line with the broadly defined doctrine of the open door. Under Knox it would become part of a larger attempt to protect American markets in Latin America and in the rest of China by invigorating the government's foreign and commercial service, building up the merchant marine, encouraging business interests overseas, appointing financial advisers to foreign governments, and organizing financial instruments of national policy.

Within the department Huntington Wilson expressed the most coherent view of dollar diplomacy. He shared the fear, dating back to the previous decade, of overproduction glutting the domestic market. "It would be suicidal not to be provident enough to make the effort to build for the future and now to gain a foothold in what must be our future markets. This task falls to our diplomacy."[17] Knox agreed with Wilson. "Today diplomacy works for trade, and the Foreign Offices of the world are powerful engines for the promotion of the commerce of each country."[18] He was determined to help American trade hold its current share of the China

14. Straight (Division of Far Eastern Affairs), memo, 23 April 1909, NF 788/224. See also Straight to Knox, memo, 13 April 1909, NF 5767/39; and Fletcher to Knox, 28 August 1908, NF 1518/321.

15. Rockhill to the secretary of state, 3 March 1909, NF 5767/39.

16. "Dollar diplomacy" was intended as a term of opprobrium by critics of Knox's foreign policy, but Knox and others in the administration proudly adopted it in defense of their proceedings. The term came into general use only after the Manchurian phase of Knox's China policy had passed. See the speeches given by Knox, Taft, Wilson, and Straight from 1911 through early 1913 (in Knox Papers; the annual addresses of the president for 1911 and 1912; and Straight, "China's Loan Negotiations," in George H. Blakeslee, ed., *Recent Developments in China* [New York, 1913], pp. 119–61).

17. Wilson to Taft, 22 February 1910, Wilson Papers, Myrin Library, Ursinus College. See also Wilson to Knox, 1 September 1910, Wilson Papers.

18. "Summary of State Dept Policy and Actions" [fall 1909], Knox Papers.

arket. The department began to evince an unprecendented sensitivity to apanese pretensions in Manchuria and their possible effect on American aterests. During his first six months in office Knox on three separate ccasions seriously considered diplomatic protests against Japanese actions the region.[19]

Protests against interference were only a palliative. In the long run, merican trade would prosper only as the American investment stake in hina grew. Knox agreed with his advisers that investments were the atering wedge for a successful commercial policy. If the United States ung back while the other powers obtained major investment contracts, merican trade would eventually be shut out of China. Knox wished to e the State Department stimulate the flow of American capital to China order to neutralize the deleterious influence of Japan and the other owers and to invigorate the China trade.

> The Department has in view the general extension of American influence in China so that when the commercial interests and exporters of the United States turn their attention more vigorously toward securing the markets of the Orient, they will find those of China open to their products and the Chinese public favorably disposed toward American enterprise.[20]

nvestment in railway development, the prospects for which Knox thought articularly bright, seemed to be the most promising way of increasing merican trade and influence.

> The testimony of those familiar with conditions in China is unanimous as to the almost boundless commercial possibilities offered in the Empire. . . . Once railway development in that country is finally under way its progress may be comparable to that in America during the last twenty-five years. There is no doubt that the construction of railways to any considerable extent will be attended by enormous internal development, and that the further introduction into the Far East of the methods and improvements of western civilization will present countless commercial opportunities to American manufacturers and capitalists.[21]

19. See, e.g., Straight to Phillips, memo, 18 March 1909, NF 18321/10; Fletcher to Knox, 14 ugust 1909, NF 5767/79; and Wilson (acting secretary of state) to Fletcher, 24 August 1909, F 9146/30–31.
20. Phillips, memo, 10 May 1909, Knox Papers.
21. Knox quoted in J. B. Osborne, memo, 15 September 1909, Knox Papers. See Knox's ews reported in detail by Bryce (to Grey, 10 July 1909, FO 371/640).

The first concrete demonstration of how the administration planne to pursue its policy of financial penetration came in May and June of 190 with the United States involvement in the Hukuang loan. The Chines lacking sufficient funds themselves, had sought foreign financing for tł Hankow–Canton railway route—earlier repurchased with British mon from the American China Development Company—and for a long r line from Hankow westward to Chengtu in Szechwan. In January 190 the Germans underbid the British and won a part of the route runnir through the British sphere of influence in the Yangtze val!ey. In May 190 the British, who wished to neutralize the German advantage, and tł French, who had laid claim to the portion of the Hukuang line runnir through their Szechwan sphere, agreed to join the Germans in financir and building the entire line from Canton to Chengtu.[22]

Knox, alarmed that the United States was about to be shut out of major railway loan, lodged his first protest in mid-May. When tł European financiers and the Chinese government concluded a prelim nary agreement early in June, Knox on Wilson's suggestion precipitous demanded a quarter share in the loan. Knox at first maintained that tł Wai-wu Pu had promised in 1904 to give the United States the fir option if China should look abroad for help with the Hankow–Szechwa line.[23] When Knox discovered his claim was faulty, he hastily grasped other rationalizations for his settled purpose of securing a full share Chinese loans for his countrymen. He applied pressure on the weake link, China, rather than on the obdurate foreign offices of Europe. Back by a message from Taft to the Chinese head of state, Knox warned th formal ratification of the loan agreement with the Europeans would co China America's friendship as well as the excess Boxer money which w to be returned.[24]

In early June, anticipating the approval of his demands, Knox, secon ed by Taft, brought together some of the foremost firms on Wall Street take the American portion of the loan.[25] The creation of this financi instrument, in explicit imitation of the European model, was a bas

22. On general British and Chinese policy during this railway loan dispute, see E-tu Zen Su *Chinese Railways and British Interests, 1898–1911* (New York, 1954), chaps. 3–4. State Departme documents on the Hukuang dispute are assembled in NF 5315.

23. Fletcher to Knox, telegram, 7 July 1909, NF 5315/338.

24. Wilson to Peking legation, telegram, 19 June 1909 and 9 July 1909; Wilson, memo (on conversation with Taft), 19 June 1909; Knox to Fletcher, telegram, 14 and 20 July 1909; a Taft to Prince Ch'un, 15 July 1909. These documents are in NF 5315/259, 338, 296, 348, 3 351.

25. Bryce to Grey (repeating Charles R. Crane's account of a conversation with Taft), August 1909, FO 371/640.

novation in a China policy which consistently over the years had refused
go beyond assuring businessmen and financiers an equal opportunity
d freedom from unjust interference. The financial combination, known
the American Group, consisted of J. P. Morgan and Company; Kuhn,
oeb and Company; the National City Bank; and the First National
ink. Harriman, represented by Kuhn, Loeb and Company, was initially
e leading spirit in the group's operations. To express his appreciation
r Straight's earlier efforts, Harriman had urged Knox to appoint him
inister to China. When this effort failed, Harriman secured for Straight
job as the American Group's chief overseas negotiator, thereby maintain-
g their mutually advantageous working relationship.[26]
After Harriman's death in September 1909, J. P. Morgan succeeded
his place as *primus inter pares*. Morgan was a more conservative financier
an Harriman but no less self-assured and perhaps more self-righteous.
e joined the group at Knox's request both from *noblesse oblige* and as a
eans of preserving his firm's strategic position as banker to the govern-
ent. He could not afford to abandon to others his firm's prestigious,
ominant, and lucrative position at the crossroads of American finance.
Morgan did not expect profits to be immediately forthcoming, he at
ast counted on getting at a later date more preferred and profitable
isiness either in China or elsewhere.[27]
Of the other members of the group, Frank Vanderlip, president of the
ational City Bank, and Jacob Schiff, head of Kuhn, Loeb and Company,
d a wide range of interests and a developed sense of public service, which
t them apart from the individualistic and restless Harriman and the
incely, aloof Morgan. Schiff was a man of social conscience whose
sentment over Russian treatment of Jews had first drawn him into Far
astern finance in 1905, when his firm supported Japan in her war with
ussia. In 1909 he brought to the American Group the strength of his
uropean financial contacts—equaled only by that of J. P. Morgan and
ompany—and his long association with Harriman.[28] Vanderlip, younger
an the others, had entered finance through journalism. He had just
come the head of the National City Bank the year it joined the govern-
ent-sponsored financial venture in China. After 1909 Vanderlip would
ecialize in international finance, make his bank the largest in the nation,

26. Harriman to Knox, 5 February 1909; Schiff to Straight, 19, 26, and 29 March 1909;
raight to Schiff, 27 March 1909; and Straight to the assistant secretary of state, 9 June 1909.
l are in the Straight Papers, Olin Library, Cornell University.
27. Sketch of Morgan by Albert W. Atwood in *The Dictionary of American Biography*, 13: 175–80.
28. Cyrus Adler's portrait of Schiff, ibid., 16: 430–32.

and acquire for it a further stake in China by taking over the Internationa
Banking Corporation there.[29]

In late June Peking finally acceded to the vigorously stated threats from
Washington and agreed to delay final approval of the Hukuang loa
agreement. In July the first contentious meetings between representative
of the European financial groups and those of the American Group wer
held in London. Knox's abrupt, roughshod methods had created cor
sternation among the Chinese and cost him the goodwill of his prospectiv
partners.[30] But Taft, disregarding the cost, pronounced the outcom
"quite a diplomatic victory."[31] Knox had found a *modus operandi* for h
policy of railway and dollar diplomacy in China. With the Hukuan
loan on the road to a successful conclusion, Knox refocused his attentio
on Manchuria in the fall.

Several months before the inauguration of President Taft in Washingto
a new regime had taken control in Peking. On the nearly simultaneou
deaths of the empress dowager and the Kuang-hsü Emperor in Novembe
1908, the previously selected heir, still a young child, ascended the thron
as the Hsüan-t'ung Emperor. His father, Prince Ch'un, then age twenty
six, became regent and effective head of the government. He sought at th
very outset of his rule to get a grip on power by promoting friends, kin, an
trusted subordinates. Conversely, he purged his regime of enemies. Yüa
Shih-k'ai was the chief among these. Prince Ch'un had long carried
grudge against Yüan for his part in the 1898 coup, which had reduce
Prince Ch'un's brother, the late emperor, to a silent and pale puppet c
the empress dowager. The regent's first impulse was to have Yüan ex
ecuted, but Prince Ch'ing and Chang Chih-tung dissuaded him. Thus
instead of the ominous silken cord, Yüan in January 1909 received th
regent's gracious permission to retire from the burdens of office to h
ancestral home in Honan to nurse an "ailing" ankle.[32]

Other changes in personnel in turn affected Manchurian policy. Hs
Shih-ch'ang now felt vulnerable to his critics and requested a transfe
from Mukden. The regent assented after a decent interval. He shifted Hs
to the presidency of the Board of Posts and made Hsi-liang, a Mong

29. On Vanderlip, see Eugene E. Agger's account, ibid., 22: 677–79.
30. The reaction of the Chinese is conveyed in Fletcher to Knox, 19 June 1909, 14 July 190
18 August 1909, and 5 September 1909, NF 5315/412, 348, 530, and 550. The bitterness of th
European financiers is revealed in Straight to J. P. Morgan and Co., 8 July 1909, NF 5315/35
The department's position in the negotiations among the financiers of the United States an
Europe is explained in Wilson to the London embassy, telegram, 9 July 1909, NF 5315/338.
31. Taft quoted in Archie Butt to Clara, 18 July 1909, in Butt, *Taft and Roosevelt,* 1: 145.
32. Ts'ao Ju-lin, "I-sheng chih hui-i" [Recollections of a life], *Ch'un-ch'iu tsa-chih* [Spring an
autumn magazine], no. 161(1964): 19.

)annerman, the new governor general.[33] T'ang Shao-i had already retired
o his home in Tientsin. The new governor of Fengtien was Ch'eng Te-
:h'üan, who only a short time before had left Heilungkiang and who
was not linked to Yüan. The governors of Heilungkiang and Kirin, Chou
ihu-mo and Ch'en Chao-ch'ang, kept their posts.

In the Grand Council in Peking, Na-t'ung, an influential Manchu,
illed the seat vacated by Yüan. He retained his post as concurrent manager of the Wai-wu Pu while in fact superceding Yüan as the guiding spirit
within that ministry. The young diplomatists introduced into the middle
:chelon of that body by Yüan had proven their worth, were found amen-
able to new leadership, and were kept on. Liang Tun-yen, the most
enior of them, was promoted to Yüan's old post as president, but he did
not have the authority Yüan had enjoyed. Prince Ch'ing continued as
uperintendent, the highest post in the Wai-wu Pu, but age and other
'esponsibilities, as before, kept him away.[34] The series of changes in
)fficialdom was completed in April with the decision to assign Chang
Yin-t'ang as minister to the United States to replace Wu T'ing-fang.
Chang was an experienced diplomat who had previously served in the
Jnited States and who satisfied the unwritten rule that the minister be
rom Kwangtung.[35]

The regent, despite his success in ousting Yüan and reshuffling the
)ureaucracy to his satisfaction, was plagued by a variety of problems,
vhich in retrospect mark his accession as the beginning of the end for a
trong Manchurian policy as well as for the Ch'ing dynasty itself. The
oremost of these were his personal shortcomings, which prevented him
rom commanding the respect of his ministers. Chang Chih-tung, already
;ripped by pessimism over the fate of the dynasty, thought the new head
)f government lacked judgment.[36] Ts'ao Ju-lin, a young Japanese-
:ducated official, sized the regent up as a man whose ability and bearing
vere not those of a true ruler. This kind of estimate was common.[37] And
after several months of service under him, officials began to do the unheard
)f—openly to complain to foreigners of his inabilities.[38] The obvious com-

33. Ts'en Hsüeh-lü, *San-shui Liang Yen-sun hsien-sheng nien-p'u* [A chronological biography of
Mr. Liang Yen-sun (Shih-i) of San-shui] (Taipei reprint, 1962), pp. 73–74; and HTCC, ch.
.1; 4.21–22; 6.11; and 7.6,7,14.
34. On changes in the Wai-wu Pu: Rockhill to Root, 11 January 1909, NF 1518/265.
35. On the appointment of Chang Yin-t'ang see documents in NF 5971/4, 9, 61, 63, 70.
This time the State Department was content with the appointee.
36. Hsü T'ung-hsin, *Chang Wen-hsiang-kung nien-p'u* [A chronological biography of Chang
Chih-tung] (Taipei reprint, 1969), pp. 207, 220, and 223.
37. Ts'ao, "I-sheng chih hui-i," no. 160 (1964): 14; no. 161 (1964): 19; and no. 162(1964):
7.
38. Tenney, memo, enclosed in Fletcher to Knox, 2 July 1909, NF 1518/309–10; Jordan to

parison between Prince Ch'un and Tz'u-hsi was for him particularly unflattering. "The Old Buddha" had overcome the unfavorable associations
attached to rule by a woman, for which there was no precedent in Ch'ing
statutes, and had shown in the last decade before her death a political
sagacity, a strength of character, and a dignity of bearing that had won
the loyalty of her ministers and impressed foreigners.[39]

Other problems made Prince Ch'un's role as regent difficult. He
downgraded the Grand Council and depended instead on the advice of a
circle of Manchu kinsmen. This informal "inner Grand Council"—
composed of the regent's two younger brothers, his cousin Tsai-tse (fourteen years the regent's senior), and a more distant relative, T'ieh-liang—
introduced court politics more than ever into governmental affairs. However, even if the regent had chosen to rely on the Grand Council, he would
have found the strength of its members fading; four out of five were over
seventy.[40] In addition, the regent had come to power at a time when the
nine-year program of political reform launched by Tz'u-hsi was gathering
momentum, and popular participation and expectations were growing.
In this context the growing Manchu political role and feebleness in the
central government stirred antidynastic feelings among Chinese and
opened the way for provincial assertiveness.

The new incumbent in the governor general's yamen in Mukden was
Hsi-liang. His perceptions of the situation in Manchuria in early 1909 and
his prescriptions for the management of that frontier were substantially
like those of his predecessor, Hsü Shih-ch'ang. Hsi-liang was above all
concerned with the behavior of the two powers flanking Manchuria.

> We are so pressed on both sides that we will soon lack room for maneu-
> ver. Thus what we urgently need is a plan for conducting defense. We
> must first build up our real strength. This "real strength" consists of
> such principal policies as establishing a bank, building railroads, open-
> ing ports, developing industry, extending settlement, managing the
> border, and superintending the Mongols. All of these are urgent ad-
> ministrative matters which cannot be delayed.[41]

Grey, 28 June 1909, FO 800/44, and 31 January 1910, FO 371/866; and Reginald F. Johnston
Twilight in the Forbidden City (New York, 1934), pp. 60–61.

39. J. O. P. Bland and Edmund Backhouse, *China under the Empress Dowager* (London, 1911)
pp. 52, 417–35; Ts'ao, "I-sheng chih hui-i," no.159(1964): 17; and Yang Lien-sheng, "Female
Rulers in Imperial China," *Harvard Journal of Asiatic Studies* 23 (1960/1961): 56.

40. Ts'ao, "I-sheng chih hui-i," no.162(1964): 18; Jordan to Grey, 16 March 1909, FO 371/
636; and Esther Morrison, "The Modernization of the Confucian Bureaucracy: An Historical
Study of Public Administration" (Ph.D. thesis, Radcliffe, 1959), p. 1105.

41. Hsi-liang, memorial, 9 May 1909, CWS: HT, ch. 3.17–18.

Hsi-liang asked the regent to line up the money and support within the Peking bureaucracy essential to success. The regent gratified Hsi-liang with an immediate and favorable reply.[42]

While Hsi-liang's recommendations on Manchurian policy generally resembled those of Hsü Shih-ch'ang and T'ang Shao-i, there was a marked difference in personal and administrative styles. One wit captured it when he described Hsi-liang as frugal with his own and public money; Hsü careful with his own but lavish with public funds; and T'ang liberal in his spending from both sources.[43] This characterization provides a hint of Hsi-liang's austere life style and his moral rectitude, for which he was well known in officialdom. In his private life he eschewed things Western, from medicine to architecture. Although his attitudes caused some foreigners mistakenly to label him reactionary, one who watched him at firsthand wrote appreciatively that he was "a fine example of the best of the old fashioned Chinese official."[44]

A brilliant youth, Hsi-liang had gotten his *chin-shih* at twenty-one. In his maturity his stern, allusive, and often impassioned memorials reflected the lasting effects of this training on his personality. When he became governor general of Manchuria near the end of his fifth decade, he was at the apogee of his career. In his early years he had served under Li Ping-heng and Chang Chih-tung and thereafter had occupied high posts in the interior provinces and on the frontier. Along the way he had established himself as an able generalist and had become acquainted with the methods of frontier defense. He had proved himself loyal to the dynasty and a determined foe of foreign penetration.[45]

Hsi-liang arrived in Mukden in late May after consultations in Peking en route from his former post as governor general of Yunnan–Kweichow. At his new post he immediately demanded financial retrenchment and implied in reports to Peking that Hsü Shih-ch'ang had been guilty of waste. It was a charge that others had previously leveled against the former governor general. The financial reforms and investigations, which started from the premise that Chao Erh-sun had left Manchuria with a

42. Imperial edict, 9 May 1909, WWP: Yen-chi pien-wu an [File on Yen-chi border affairs], *ts'e* 3.
43. Ching-min [pseud.], *Hsü Shih-ch'ang* [Biography of Hsü Shih-ch'ang] (Canton and Hong Kong, 1922), p. 44.
44. Hsi-liang is described as "reactionary" in a variety of Western sources (e.g., Cloud, report to the State Department, 27 August 1909, NF 551/122–23). The quote is from Dugald Christie, *Thirty Years in Moukden 1883–1913* (New York, 1914), p. 235.
45. Biographical sketches in Chao Erh-sun, comp., *Ch'ing-shih kao* [Draft history of the Ch'ing] (preface, 1927), ch. 455.1–3 (reputedly written by Chao himself), and in HLIK, 1 : 1–3. Roger V. DesForges, "Hsi-liang: A Portrait of a Late Ch'ing Patriot" (Ph.D. diss., Yale University, 1971), is an illuminating political biography. Chaps. 11 and 12 deal with Manchuria.

full treasury and Hsü had left it empty, proceeded with the encouragement of Tsai-tse, president of the Board of Finance, but at length the investigations were called off by the regent himself. Hsi-liang supplemented his efforts at retrenchment with a purge of officials appointed during Hsü's tenure and with an administrative reorganization which eliminated what Hsi-liang regarded as superfluous offices. Hsi-liang carried his shake-up from Mukden to all of Manchuria.[46]

The new governor general wanted a lean, economical administration staffed by loyal officials, but his brusque methods left some of his subordinates dissatisfied and demoralized. His actions, moreover, were a calculated insult to Hsü, now president of the Board of Posts. However, Hsi-liang was aware that he was moving into territory formerly part of Yüan Shih-k'ai's fief and was prepared to pay the price of bad feelings to secure his own control. Hsi-liang purged those associated with Yüan's clique who were thought to be unsympathetic to the new regime in Peking and Mukden. They included two of Hsü's foreign-educated assistants who might have proven useful to Hsi-liang in his diplomacy. Their loss further weakened his administration's capacity to cope with a problem, which, as Hsi-liang himself had already observed, was basically a foreign one.[47]

Hsi-liang began to flesh out his comprehensive program for attacking that problem almost as soon as he reached Mukden. In early June he presented his first formal proposal, a plan for the organization of a bank to underwrite the multifaceted program of internal development and defense. The premier bank enterprise was to be the railway between Chinchow and Aigun, sponsored previously by Hsü Shih-ch'ang. Hsi-liang had already concluded that Manchuria was too improverished to generate by itself the funds necessary for this kind of project. Consequently, the Board of Finance would have to find the money for the Manchurian development bank either in its own coffers or through a foreign loan. Hsi-liang directed his request to the regent with the hope that he would instruct his cousin, Tsai-tse, to provide the needed subsidy. Hsi-liang also appealed to

46. HTCC, ch. 11.7, and ch. 12.20; and Ching-min (pseud.), *Hsü Shih-ch'ang,* pp. 13 and 46–47; as well as Hsü Shuhsi, *China and Her Political Entity* (New York, 1926), p. 319; Ts'ao ,"I-sheng chih hui-i," no.161(1964): 19; reports from acting British consul general Willis (Mukden), enclosed in Jordan to Grey, 20 July and 6 September 1909, FO 371/640; and Cloud to the State Department, 4 February 1909 and 5 June 1909 (in NF 1518/280 and 301) and 17 August 1909 (in NF 5767/87).

47. Many of the consuls in Mukden came to regard this failing as a basic flaw in Hsi-liang's management of Manchuria. See the views summarized in Fisher, report to the State Department, 27 May 1910, DF 893.00/(NF 1518/412).

Hsü Shih-ch'ang to continue to use his influence to further the Chin–Ai project.[48]

The regent did not reply until August, when he approved in principle the borrowing of money overseas both to finance Manchuria's development and to create a balance of foreign influence there. However, rather than specifically sanctioning Hsi-liang's development bank and a loan for as Hsi-liang had asked, the regent delayed a decision by referring the entire matter back to Mukden for further detailed consideration.[49] The regent moved more swiftly but no more decisively on the Chin–Ai railway, which he referred to the Board of Posts for further study.[50]

Hsi-liang was troubled by divided counsels in Peking on implementing the Chin–Ai proposal. He had hoped that Hsü, the president of the Board of Posts, would support him. Just before leaving Manchuria earlier in the year, Hsü had endorsed the Chin–Ai railway,[51] and the Board of Posts had already made provisional plans to survey the route.[52] Now, Hsü responded cautiously.[53] He was perhaps stung by the rough treatment Hsi-liang had given his former subordinates, his financial management, and some of his reforms. Furthermore, Hsü was now unsure of his political footing and consequently hesitated to take a strong stand on Manchurian policy. To make matters worse for Hsi-liang, the Wai-wu Pu and the Board of Finance favored delay. Na-t'ung, the effective head of the former body, who was to gain a reputation among foreigners for his sensitivity to Japanese views, foresaw that the Chin–Ai project would provoke Japanese opposition and complicate negotiations with Japan over the Hsin–Fa, Chientao, and other Manchuria issues. "It would be most appropriate to postpone this undertaking and avoid face to face difficulties."[54] Tsai-tse also withheld his support with the excuse that the government could not

48. Hsi-liang, memorial and supplementary memorial, 8 June 1909, HLIK, 2:893–94. See also his supplementary memorial, 20 May 1909, HLIK, 2:884.
49. Imperial edict, 19 August 1909, WWP: Yen-chi pien-wu an, *ts'e* 3.
50. Rescript of 12 June 1909, in Board of Posts to the Wai-wu Pu, 12 June 1909, WWP: Ni-hsiang Mei-kuo chieh-k'uan hsiu-chu Chin-Ai t'ieh-lu an [File on the Chin–Ai railway loan], *e* 1.
51. Hsü to the Wai-wu Pu, 30 January 1909, CWS: HT, ch. 1.5–6.
52. Board of Posts, memorial, 8 April 1909, *Yu-ch'uan Pu tsou-i fen-lei hsü-pien* [Supplement to the classified collection of memorials by the Board of Posts] (Taipei reprint, 1967), comp. by the Board of Posts and the Ministry of Communications, 4:15–26.
53. Board of Posts to the Wai-wu Pu, 12 July 1909, WWP: Ni-hsiang Mei-kuo chieh-k'uan hsiu-chu Chin-Ai t'ieh-lu an, *ts'e* 1; Board of Posts, memorial, 27 July 1909, *Yu-ch'uan Pu tsou-i fen-lei hsü-pien*, comp. by the Board of Posts and the Ministry of Communications, 4:91–92; rescript quoted in Board of Posts to the Wai-wu Pu, 29 July 1909, WWP: Ni-hsiang Mei-kuo chieh-k'uan hsiu-chu Chin-Ai t'ieh-lu an, *ts'e* 1; and Hsi-liang and Ch'eng Te-ch'üan to Hsü and reply, n.d., copies enclosed in Board of Posts to the Wai-wu Pu, 21 August 1909, ibid.
54. Wai-wu Pu to the Board of Posts, 25 August 1909, CWS: HT, ch. 7.47–48.

afford a loan to pay for either the railway or the bank.[55] The regent, b
failing to resolve the differences of opinion among his officials, left th
issue deadlocked, to the satisfaction of the opponents of Hsi-liang's plan.

By July Hsi-liang was also becoming disturbed by his government
handling of yet another railway controversy with Japan. Japan had cor
structed a narrow gauge line between Antung and Fengtien during he
war with Russia and now wished to reroute, improve, and connect :
with a Korean line. The Chinese, who were convinced that the line wa
too strategic for them to allow Japan to make any improvements on i
objected to these proposed changes. Neither Hsi-liang nor Liang Tun-yer
who successively carried on the negotiations with Japan, would yield, bt
the Japanese forced the issue by starting work on the railway withou
China's approval. The regent feared to take countermeasures and agree
to let Na-t'ung settle this and other Manchurian issues the best he could.

Hsi-liang, who was not privy to the last stages of the negotiations, pt
himself firmly on record against the Japanese demands. The governor (
Kirin, Ch'en Chao-ch'ang, was even more insistent that Peking resi:
them.[56] However, the Wai-wu Pu, in an agreement of 9 September 190!
made sweeping concessions on the An–Feng railway issue in order to hav
its way on the Chientao territorial question.[57] After this diplomati
defeat the only advice the Wai-wu Pu could offer on Manchurian polic
was that

> there must first be daily increasing achievements in domestic goverr
> ment and afterwards it will be easy to conduct foreign relations. Mar
> churia is decidedly a place under the pressure of strong powers. Natura
> ly, when the provincial officials are able to straighten things up, th
> place will gradually increase its real power with which to conten
> against the foreigners. Then, we can conclude treaties which safeguar
> sovereignty *in toto* and without loss.[58]

In effect Na-t'ung was advising that he would not accept Hsi-liang

55. Hsi-liang so indicts Tsai-tse in a memorial of 6 September 1909, HLIK, 2:950–51.

56. Hsi-liang's memorial on the An–Feng railway, 8 June 1909 (CWS: HT, ch. 4.6–9), and (
the agreement with Japan, 3 September 1909 (CWS: HT, ch. 8.33–34), as well as the undat(
cables exchanged between Hsi-liang, Na-t'ung, and Ch'en Chao-ch'ang (reprinted in the Pekir
Kuo-pao [National news] of 14 September 1909).

57. On the An–Feng railway and the related disputes during the latter phases of the negoti.
tions, see CWS: HT, ch. 3.27, 36–37; 4.44; 5.16, 39–40; 7.8–11. The agreement of 4 Septemb
1909 is in CWS: HT, ch. 8.37–39. See also the reports from the Mukden consulate and tl
Peking legation in NF 5767/39, 58, 79 and in NF 5315/214.

58. Wai-wu Pu, memorial, 5 September 1909, CWS: HT, ch. 8.40–43. The Wai-wu Pu al:
defended its handling of the Manchurian negotiations in a letter to Hsi-liang and the governo
of Manchuria, 12 September 1909, CWS: HT, ch. 9.7–11.

urried program, which set China and Japan on a collision course. The egent fully endorsed Na-t'ung's views.[59]

Through the summer, nationalists in Manchuria and elsewhere within he empire had been troubled by news of the negotiations with Japan. purred on by rumors of imminent partition by the powers and of cowrdice in Peking, they organized demonstrations as well as boycotts against apanese goods all along the China coast and petitioned government offiials.[60] Hsi-liang realized that the popular outcry, which reached an nparalleled intensity in Manchuria, was a dangerous phenomenon. He rged the central government to heed "the present upright clamor of ublic sentiment" and accurately predicted that "the announcement of his [September] agreement will again give rise to clamorous disorder."[61] "he subsequent appearance in the press of his official correspondence on he railway issue underlined his strong opposition to Peking's concessions.[62] 'or Hsi-liang, who had faith in the instincts of the people, this growing opular dissatisfaction was as deeply troubling as its cause, the weakness f the central government.

Hsi-liang had come away from an inspection tour of Manchuria in July nore than ever convinced of the desperate need to pursue an ambitious olicy of frontier defense.[63] But Japan's aggressiveness, continuing indeciion in Peking, and popular outrage now buffeted his plans and temorarily shattered his confidence and resolve.[64] What course, Hsi-liang ould well ask in despair, was left open to him? Two days after the conlusion of the agreement with Japan, he once more reiterated his plans for Manchuria and at the same time tendered his resignation. The regent

59. Edict of 5 September 1909, CWS: HT, ch. 8.42–43.

60. Documents on the national protest and the government's response are in CWS: HT, eh. .51; 7.4, 31–32; 8.19; 9.12. On the Manchurian protest movement: Manchurian students in apan to the Wai-wu Pu, 7 July 1909, CWS: HT, ch. 4.33; members of the Fengtien assembly and he Fengtien General Association for Commerce and Education to the Wai-wu Pu, 26 August)09, WWP: Chung-Jih An-Feng t'ieh-lu an [File on the Sino–Japanese Antung–Fengtien ilway], *ts'e* 2; and the gentry and people of Kirin to the Wai-wu Pu, 6 September 1909, CWS: T, ch. 8.47–48.

61. Hsi-liang and the governors of Manchuria to the Grand Council, 3 September 1909, WS: HT, ch. 8.33–34. See also Hsi-liang and Ch'eng to the Wai-wu Pu, 1 September 1909, WS:HT, ch. 8.29.

62. Wai-wu Pu, memorial, 15 September 1909, requesting an investigation into the publicaon by the Peking *Kuo-pao* and the *Chung-yang ta-t'ung jih-pao* [Central daily news] of these ispatches. The author of the memorial implied that the investigation should focus on Kirin. s a result of the memorial the two papers were closed. WWP: Yen-chi pien-wu an, *ts'e* 3; and TCC, ch. 19.7–8.

63. Hsi-liang, memorial, 7 August 1909, HLIK, 2:928–30.

64. See the testimony of the British consul in Mukden. Willis to Jordan, 18 August 1909, iclosed in Jordan to Grey, 6 September 1909, FO 371/640. See also Ts'ao, "I-sheng chih ui-i," no.161 (1964): 19.

would have to either help Hsi-liang defend the Manchurian frontier o
release him from an otherwise impossible situation. The regent, bestowing
perfunctory praise on his discontented official, rejected the resignation
and asked him to resubmit his policy views in detail for reconsideration.[6]

Hsi-liang determined to test the worth of these words of encouragement
from Peking. He temporarily set aside his comprehensive, long-range
bank plan in favor of a more immediately realizable railway, just as Hsü
Shih-ch'ang had done in 1907. Hsi-liang sent word to the American
consul in Mukden and to the chargé in Peking of his interest in making a
deal for the building and financing of the Chin–Ai railway.[66] Willard
Straight, who was in Peking as the representative of E. H. Harriman and
his financial associates, was duly informed of these hints and in short
order was on a train to Mukden, carrying with him an outline of possible
terms drawn up in previous days of fruitless consultation in Peking.[6]
Hsi-liang began discussions with Straight on 29 September, concluded a
draft agreement the following day, and pressured him into signing on the
evening of 2 October.[68] He himself also signed, even though he lacked
authorization to do so. Hsi-liang would present the regent with a *fait
accompli.*

Hsi-liang, anticipating Straight's acceptance of the terms, had boldly
wired Peking on 1 October:

> The representative of the American banks, Straight, has come to
> Fengtien. Your officials have had interviews with him and have dis
> cussed the proposal to borrow about three or four million pounds in orde
> to build the Chinchow–Taonan–Aigun railway. Straight has already
> approved and signed the draft agreement[!]. After I receive the
> Imperial edict [of approval] I will memorialize on the actual figure
> and all other details.[69]

Hsi-liang described the situation in Manchuria as "unmanageable" and
warned those in Peking whose approval he needed,

65. Memorial of 6 September 1909 and edict of 14 September 1909 in HLIK, 2:950–51.
66. Cloud (Mukden), report to the State Department, 20 August 1909, and Fletcher to Knox
23 August 1909, NF 5767/88 and 89.
67. Fletcher to Knox, 7 October 1909, NF 5315/578.
68. Details of the negotiations contained in Straight to Lord ffrench and to "Prather
[Fletcher], both dated 2 October 1909, diary letters, Straight Papers; and Straight to J. P.
Morgan and Co., 3 October 1909, NF 5315/587–90.
69. Hsi-liang and Ch'eng Te-ch'üan to the Grand Council, telegram, 1 October 1909, HLIK
2:959–60. The telegram was received by the Wai-wu Pu on 2 October. On the dating of the
memorial, see Grand Council to the Wai-wu Pu, 4 October 1909, WWP: Ni-hsiang Mei-ku
chieh-k'uan hsiu-chu Chin-Ai t'ieh-lu an, *ts'e* 1. The enclosed railway agreement was predated
2 October. It is reproduced in LNCYJ, 5:293–96.

If we do not build another railway apart from the railways of the two countries [Russia and Japan], we will not be able to save ourselves from disaster. It is as with man's body—when the vessels are cut, the members and trunk exist in vain and there is no way to make them live.[70]

70. Hsi-liang and Ch'eng to the Grand Council, telegram, 1 October 1909, HLIK, 2:959–60.

Hsi-liang intended by his unauthorized signature of the Chin–Ai railway agreement to break the deadlock in Peking over Manchurian policy. However, the regent continued to temporize. The day after receiving Hsi-liang's memorial requesting approval of the Chin–Ai railway agreement, the regent gave instructions to the Wai-wu Pu, the Board of Posts, and the Board of Finance to consult with Hsi-liang on the matter and memorialize on their conclusions.[1]

The ministries deliberated leisurely. Na-t'ung of the Wai-wu Pu and Tsai-tse of the Board of Finance, both cool to the railway project, politely insisted that the other draft the memorial requested by the regent. Both were careful not to offer the task to Hsü Shih-ch'ang, who would have dealt more gently with Hsi-liang's efforts.[2] Finally, on 20 November, seven weeks after it had received the edict, the Wai-wu Pu completed a draft response and circulated it for comments.[3] Four days later the formal memorial was presented to the regent in the name of the three boards.[4]

The main recommendation of the memorial was that the preliminary Chin–Ai agreement be abrogated. The memorialists had reached this recommendation through subtle maneuvering rather than head-on confrontation. The Wai-wu Pu in its first draft of the memorial had suggested voiding the agreement but continuing the talks with the representatives of the British and American interests.[5] Hsü considered the Wai-wu Pu's suggestion the best to be had and gave the Board of Posts' approval for the first draft.[6] Tsai-tse, however, was not prepared to accept the moderate position of the Wai-wu Pu and urged that the memorial make no reference

---

1. Edict, 3 October 1909, HTCC, ch. 20.4.
2. Wai-wu Pu to the Board of Posts and the Board of Finance, 8 October 1909; and the Board of Finance to the Wai-wu Pu, 11 October 1909. Both are in WWP: Ni-hsiang Mei-kuo chieh-k'uan hsiu-chu Chin-Ai t'ieh-lu an [File on the Chin–Ai railway loan], ts'e 2.
3. Wai-wu Pu to the Board of Finance and the Board of Posts, 20 November 1909, ibid.
4. Wai-wu Pu, Board of Finance, and Board of Posts, memorial, 24 November 1909, CWS:HT, ch. 10.42–44.
5. Wai-wu Pu, draft memorial, n.d., WWP: Ni-hsiang Mei-kuo chieh-k'uan hsiu-chu Chin-Ai t'ieh-lu an, ts'e 2.
6. Board of Posts to the Wai-wu Pu, 22 November 1909, ibid.

o a resumption of talks while, of course, retaining the recommendation hat the agreement be annulled. In place of the suggested deletion he substituted the much vaguer phrase, "if there is definitely a way of borrowing he requisite funds, then [let Hsi-liang] at all times communicate with the officials of the Boards on satisfactory procedures."[7] Tsai-tse's obvious intent was to force Hsi-liang to break off contact with the foreign representatives and to assert the control of the Peking ministries, his own included, over any future plans for Manchuria. The Wai-wu Pu incorporated Tsai-tse's suggestions in a second draft memorial, which it promptly dispatched to the Board of Posts for approval.

Hsü had assented to the terms of the first draft memorial as a concession o the views of his colleagues. But now he found these belated changes unacceptable. In his view, Tsai-tse's recommendations would further undercut Hsi-liang's authority and make the construction of the Chin–Ai railway an even more remote prospect.[8] It must have appeared to Hsü that Na-t'ung and Tsai-tse had surreptitiously come to an agreement on both how to frustrate the plans for the Chin–Ai railway and how to maneuver Hsü into joining their recommendation against it. Now he would have o frankly express his true opinion: that the preliminary agreement was in act a good basis for securing the Manchurian railway loan which he himself had earlier sought. Accordingly, Hsü in his reply to the Wai-wu Pu smoothly suggested that the memorialists simply omit any reference to voiding the agreement, which he argued might hinder further negotiations n the Chin–Ai railway.

The Wai-wu Pu declined to incorporate Hsü's suggestion in this second draft with the lame excuse that it could not secure the approval of Tsai-tse, conveniently absent from his office, before the appointed date for ormally submitting the memorial.[9] However, it tried to conciliate Hsü by promising to suggest to Hsi-liang that he go about voiding the preliminary agreement in a manner calculated to insure the continuation of negotiations with the foreign railway interests. This suggestion implicitly gave he Wai-wu Pu's sanction to further talks between Hsi-liang and Straight even though the memorial itself made no mention to this effect. Na-t'ung entrusted the task of writing the promised letter to a junior ministry official, Ts'ao Ju-lin, who had already handled the details of drafting the memorial.[10]

7. Board of Finance to the Wai-wu Pu, 21 November 1909; and text of the proposed amendments, 24 November 1909. Both are in ibid. The quote comes from the latter document.
8. Board of Posts to the Wai-wu Pu, 22 November 1909, ibid.
9. Wai-wu Pu to the Board of Posts, 24 November 1909, ibid.
10. Ts'ao to Hsi-liang, 21 [?] November 1909, ibid., *ts'e* 1.

The final recommendation which emerged from this muted bureaucratic battle reflected the still unresolved contradictions over Manchurian policy. The memorialists endorsed the idea of a foreign loan for Manchuria yet expressed the doubt, harbored by Tsai-tse, that sufficient funds were available to repay it. They acknowledged the desperation of the situation in Manchuria but all the same criticized Hsi-liang for acting too hurriedly The upshot of the memorial was that Hsi-liang cancel his railway agreement, a recommendation that was justified on the grounds that he had failed to draw up a financial balance sheet, that the terms were detrimenta to China's interests, and that the railroad should be combined and proceed parallel with other programs of development in Manchuria. Tsai-tse and Na-t'ung dressed their opposition to a strong Manchurian policy in the guise of mature, detailed consideration and of the fashionable argument of protecting China's rights. The regent acquiesced in these views of his ministers and appended to the memorial the formulaic words of approval, "Let it be as proposed."[11]

Hsi-liang had not—contrary to the regent's initial instructions—been consulted by the Peking ministries, and now he questioned their unfavorable conclusions.[12] In his formal riposte Hsi-liang repeated his contention that the Chin–Ai railroad was a means of creating a balance of power as well as of strengthening Manchuria's defenses and of laying out its internal communications.

If Manchuria is to be saved from the kind of danger which it faced both after the Sino–Japanese War and after the Russo–Japanese War, it must be done through involving the strength of the powers in [Manchuria's] difficulties. . . .

. . . The Americans have recently suffered injury to trade under Japanese domination of Manchuria, and they have become extremely indignant. They want investments to equalize opportunity. We have taken this chance to propose the building of the Chin–Ai railway, and the businessmen of that country have approved a great loan to us. Further, because England is allied with Japan, we must also involve Englishmen in the scheme in order to prevent her from being drawn into an attack on it. Therefore, we must allow an American–English

11. Rescript follows the memorial in CWS: HT, ch. 10.44.
12. Hsi-liang, memorial and supplementary memorial, 12 December 1909, HLIK, 2:1006–09 His commissioner of finance, Hsiung Hsi-ling, stressed in a letter to the president of the Board of Finance the broad strategic questions at stake on the railway in hopes of blunting the president' preoccupation with narrowly financial considerations. Hsiung to Tsai-tse, n.d., LNCYJ, 5:304–06.

group to handle this project. Although we call this a commercial railway, it is in fact part of a diplomatic and political policy.[13]

Indeed, Hsi-liang thought his critics were mistaken in finding fault with the proposed railway agreement as though it were for an ordinary commercial line. They had singled out for attack the provisions which put the operation of the railway during the life of the loan in the hands of a railway company (including American and British representatives). But they had conveniently ignored the provisions which gave China majority interest in the company and specified that the central government would appoint its head.[14] Additional safeguards included a Chinese veto over the selection of the chief engineer (a foreigner under the joint control of the Board of Posts and the railway company) and over the inclusion of new members in the company. The Peking memorialists had also charged that Hsi-liang had conceded to the company 10 percent of the net profit, an excessive amount in their opinion. However, the article of the railway agreement dealing with this issue was vaguely written, and the ministers in Peking had been unfair to interpret it so definitively. The critics had finally recommended that the agreement be abrogated, but they had chosen to overlook the provision for revision of terms unacceptable to China. In considering these points made by his critics, Hsi-liang could well have wondered how he was to involve the Americans in Manchuria, specifically to gain their necessary support in constructing and insuring the successful operation of the line, if he were not to give them a stake in it.

Na-t'ung and Tsai-tse had employed a second line of argument against the railway agreement. They had insisted that the railway by itself would do nothing to develop the region it traversed unless Hsi-liang first prepared a total plan of development to encompass colonization, promotion of business, and exploitation of natural resources. Their advice, essentially intended to obstruct Hsi-liang's proposal, was to organize a bank to oversee these projects as well as the railway and to insure a balanced program of development. Hsi-liang cogently replied that the railway was the chief means of internal development. Only it could introduce settlers speedily and carry goods cheaply. However, he also seized the favorable views of the Wai-wu Pu and the Board of Finance on the idea of the development bank as an opportunity to resurrect his months-old proposal for just such

13. Hsi-liang, supplementary memorial, 12 December 1909, HLIK, 2:1008–09.
14. A copy of the preliminary agreement is in John V. A. MacMurray, ed., *Treaties and Agreements with and Concerning China, 1894–1919*, vol. 1: *Manchu Period (1894–1911)* (New York, 1921), pp. 800–02.

a project.[15] Now, however, he purposely divorced the railway project from the bank to avoid sacrificing the railway as an independent enterprise.

In sum, Hsi-liang requested that the discussions with the Americans and British on the railway agreement continue, either in Peking or in Mukden, and that the bank loan be given separate consideration. The regent, characteristically indecisive, referred the first part of the governor general's request on the railway back to the same ministers who had just dealt with it.[16] He graced the supplementary memorial on the development bank with the equally noncommital notation, "Seen."[17]

While Peking was juggling the fate of the Chin–Ai railway, Knox in Washington was groping for a way to guarantee the American commercial future in Manchuria against Japanese encroachment. The method on which he ultimately decided was the neutralization of the foreign railways in Manchuria. The scheme, broached first to the British secretary for foreign affairs on 9 November 1909, was to bring the South Manchurian Railway and the Chinese Eastern Railway

> under an economic and scientific and impartial administration by some plan vesting in China the ownership of the railroads through funds furnished for that purpose by the interested powers willing to participate.[18]

Knox included in his proposal to Britain a bid for Anglo–American support for the Chin–Ai project. He had prepared this alternative against the possible failure of the neutralization plan.

Although the specific genesis of Knox's neutralization proposal is clouded, related developments suggest its origin. In the fall of 1909 the State Department was still preoccupied with the effects of Japan's growing influence in Manchuria. It was particularly worried by the September agreement between Japan and China. Knox ordered his subordinates to examine it in detail.[19] Henry Hoyt, counsellor for the department and one of Knox's right-hand men, concluded that "Japan is now skillfully and covertly attempting to do in southern Manchuria exactly what they complained of Russia doing in northern Manchuria from 1902 to 1904."[20]

15. Hsi-liang, supplementary memorial, 12 December 1909, HLIK, 2:1009–10.

16. Rescript appended to memorial, HLIK, 2:1008.

17. Rescript appended to Hsi-liang's supplementary memorial of 12 December 1909, WWP: Ni-hsiang Mei-kuo chieh-k'uan hsiu-chu Chin-Ai t'ieh-lu an, *ts'e* 1.

18. Knox to Reid, 6 November 1909, NF 5315/559.

19. Knox to Hoyt, 15 October 1909, Knox Papers, Manuscript Division, Library of Congress; and Knox to the Tokyo embassy, telegram, 11 November 1909, NF 5767/65.

20. Hoyt to Knox, 21 October 1909, Knox Papers. See also Hoyt to Knox, 11 October 1909, Knox Papers.

The Division of Far Eastern Affairs advised Knox that a protest was necessary to protect the open door.

> Japan is gradually encroaching in Manchuria and is becoming bolder and more open in her violation of the open-door principle. She is evidently trying to see how far she can go without offending the other Powers. A protest on the part of the United States at this time would doubtless check Japan in her present policy of penetration and absorption in Manchuria.[21]

Although Knox finally publicly denied press speculation that he would lodge a protest, he was plainly concerned by the underlying issues raised by the agreement. Meanwhile, charges of commercial discrimination by the South Manchurian Railway continued to reach Knox's desk, particularly from Frederick D. Cloud, Straight's successor in Mukden, who fully maintained the tradition of consular chauvinism there.[22] Thus, it was an easy step for Knox to resolve to check Japan's influence by attacking her control of the South Manchurian Railway. Moreover, the long-standing issue of the Harbin city government, an irritant in relations with Russia, was intimately related to the administration of the Chinese Eastern Railway. With the neutralization proposal Knox could hope with one blow to consolidate American influence against the threats from both Japan and Russia.

Knox's decision to propose internationalization of the Manchurian railways was also guided by other important calculations. While he was not prepared to predict Japan's reaction, he had reason to believe that Russia would respond favorably. St. Petersburg had for some time been considering selling the Chinese Eastern Railway. In 1903 the minister of war, an opponent of an adventuresome policy in Manchuria and Korea, urged the czar to return to China the section of the Russian railway running through southern Manchuria.[23] The idea of selling what remained of Russia's Manchurian railways appealed to some Russians even more after the war with Japan, which left their shrunken Manchurian sphere of in-

21. E. C. Baker, memo, 7 October 1909, NF 5767/143½. More reassuring views came from the missions in Peking and Tokyo, NF 5767/110, 114, 116, 137.

22. See, e. g., Cloud to the State Department, 4 September 1909, NF 788/310–11. For a convincing critique of Cloud's charges, see A. A. Williamson (vice-consul in charge, Dairen) to Cloud, 8 October 1909, NF 788/323–24. Cloud's indictment, leaked to the press, provoked a furor in the Japanese press and worried inquiries from American cotton exporters. NF 788/343, 347, 338, 344, and DF 693.003/375–76.

23. Alexei N. Kuropatkin, *The Russian Army and the Japanese War,* trans. A. B. Lindsay and ed. E. D. Swinton (New York, 1909), 1:151–53, 188–93, and 198; and B. A. Romanov, *Russia in Manchuria (1892–1906),* trans. Susan W. Jones (Ann Arbor, Mich., 1952), pp. 27–31.

fluence weak and exposed. Between 1905 and November 1909 this issue was repeatedly raised within the Russian government, discussed informally with foreign interests, but never definitely settled.[24]

Whatever information Knox initially possessed on the Russian government's attitude toward its Manchurian railway he had gained directly or indirectly from E. H. Harriman. He had been rebuffed in Tokyo in 1905 and again in the spring of 1906 and had lost the Hsin–Fa railway in 1907. Thereafter Harriman had concentrated on securing this Manchurian railway through St. Petersburg. Willard Straight encouraged him—and later the State Department—to believe that the Russians were eager to sell.[25] In the summer of 1908 Harriman used Jacob Schiff to sound out the Russian government. Minister of Finance Kokovtsov and Minister of Foreign Affairs Izvolsky approved the sale on the condition that Japan simultaneously sell her railway in Manchuria. When Japan refused in February 1909 to let go of the South Manchurian Railway, the Russian government accordingly decided to continue to bide its time. In the summer of 1909 Harriman, again through an intermediary, once more put his repurchase proposal before the minister of finance. Although the latter was still favorably disposed, Harriman died on 9 September before anything concrete could come of his efforts to secure a Manchurian railway.[26]

Knox learned from his St. Petersburg embassy that Harriman's demise had not affected interest there, particularly in the Ministry of Finance, in selling the railway and that, in fact, the Russian foreign office was interested in an entente with the United States to check Japan.[27] These dispatches from the Russian capital were yet another assurance for Knox of the timeliness and ultimate success of his neutralization proposal.

Knox intended to use the Chin–Ai project as a pawn in support of the larger neutralization scheme. To that end, he successfully backed the efforts of Willard Straight and Jacob Schiff against the mild opposition of J. P. Morgan to have the newly formed American Group add the Chin–Ai

24. Romanov, *Russia in Manchuria*, pp. 379–86; and Edward H. Zabriskie, *American–Russian Rivalry in the Far East: A Study in Diplomacy and Power Politics, 1895–1914* (Philadelphia, 1946), pp. 148–49.

25. See for example Straight to Harriman, 30 April 1908, Straight Papers, Olin Library, Cornell University; and Straight, report to the State Department, 9 December 1907, NF 2413/94. Straight in a letter to the Department, written shortly after Harriman's death, explained the relation between Harriman's repurchase proposal and his interest in securing an agreement with China to build the Chin–Ai railway. Straight to Wilson, 25 September 1909, Straight Papers.

26. Jacob H. Schiff to Baron Korekiyo Takashi, 24 February 1910, DF 893.77/809½; Romanov, *Russia in Manchuria*, pp. 383–85; J. O. P. Bland, *Recent Events and Present Policies in China* (Philadelphia, 1912), p. 315; George Kennan, *E. H. Harriman's Far Eastern Plans* (Garden City, New York, 1917), pp. 45–46.

27. Schuyler (St. Petersburg) to Knox, telegrams, 25 October 1909 and 19 November 1909, NF 2157/2, 5; and Zabriskie, *American–Russian Rivalry in the Far East*, p. 152.

railway loan to its current interest in the Hukuang railway loan.[28] The preliminary railway agreement would be useful to Knox, however, only after it received the formal sanction of China's central government. The agreement's fate was at first uncertain, the legation reported, because the regent, although leaning toward approval, was "a weak and vacilating [*sic*] man."[29] Finally, in late October Knox learned from Straight that the regent had sanctioned the agreement in a secret unpublished edict.[30] The alleged edict provided implicit assurance that if the neutralization proposal were to stumble on Russian or Japanese objections, Knox could turn with confidence to this alternative plan, knowing that China would support it.

The State Department hoped "for cordial cooperation with the British Government" in the Chin–Ai project, in which both British and American nationals had an interest.[31] The activists, now so numerous in the department, all shared the assumption that the United States and Britain had a common interest in protecting the open door in the Far East, including Manchuria. They viewed the Anglo–Japanese alliance as an aberration of British policy which would soon be rectified by experience in dealing with Japan and by the outcry in Britain against the sacrifice of the Hsin–Fa contract to the interest of her alliance partner. In October Knox tentatively inquired about the Foreign Office's attitude toward the Chin–Ai project. Grey's response was vague and circumstantial, but Whitelaw Reid reported it in such a way as to encourage Knox to believe that Britain would feel free to join the Americans if Japan's interests in her Manchurian railway were cared for.[32] Knox, allowing wishful thinking to take the place of specific assurances from Whitehall, later prepared his neutralization proposal, including what he thought were adequate concessions to Japan on the related Chin–Ai project.[33] He was confident that Britain would now follow him.

Despite all the favorable signs, Knox's breathtaking plan was ill-fated. At first the reaction from London indicated that Whitehall would accept his two related schemes, albeit conditionally. Grey told Ambassador Reid

28. Straight to J. P. Morgan and Co., 4 September 1909 and 3 and 4 October 1909, NF 5315/586, 587–90; Straight to "Prather" [Fletcher] and to Lord ffrench, 2 October 1909, both in diary letters, Straight Papers; J. P. Morgan and Co. to Straight, 8 September 1909, NF 5315/493; and Straight, memos on the Chin–Ai railway, n.d., NF 5315/555 and NF 5767/111.

29. Fletcher to Knox, 7 October 1909, NF 5315/578.

30. Straight to J. P. Morgan and Co., n.d., NF 2112/99$\frac{1}{2}$.

31. Wilson to the London embassy, telegram, 17 October 1909, NF 5315/551A; and Hoyt to Adee, 10 September 1909, Knox Papers.

32. Reid to Knox, 20 October 1909, NF 5315/559; and Grey to Bryce, 26 October 1909, FO 371/636.

33. See introductory paragraph of the telegram from Knox to Reid, 6 November 1909, NF 5315/559.

he approved the neutralization proposal in principle even though he preferred to defer it until the Hukuang loan issue had been disposed of Further, he was prepared to cooperate with the United States on the Chin–Ai line provided Japan be admitted to the project.[34] However, later consultations with his Japanese ally forced Grey to modify his attitude. He was soon admitting in private that he would not be able to support Knox but that he hoped to shift from himself the onus for torpedoing the American proposal. "We shall have sooner or later to tell the Americans that we cannot proceed with this in [the] face of Japanese opposition; but we can wait to let the Russians and Japanese come into line."[35] As a step in that direction, Grey informed Reid that the final decision on the practicality of the Chin–Ai project lay with St. Petersburg and Tokyo.[36]

Russia and Japan, once formally informed of Knox's plan, did exactly what Grey suspected they would do—"come into line." By mid-December leaks to the press and the resulting public speculation had forced Knox to present his plan to the Russian and Japanese governments although he had not yet secured Britain's full assent. In early January he made it public.[37] Knox was already too late in setting his proposals on the table for them to be news. As early as August the Japanese had warned the Chinese government against construction of a railway northward from Chinchow, which Tokyo regarded as disturbingly similar to the disputed Hsin–Fa railway.[38] Agents of Russia and Japan had penetrated the veil of secrecy dropped about the Chin–Ai agreement, and in the latter half of October their legations had begun making concerned inquiries at the Wai-wu Pu.[39] Russia and Japan viewed with even less favor the idea of handing over their Manchurian railways to international management.

Knox tried to persuade Russia by a show of diplomatic cordiality not to join with Japan. However, early in January his diplomats in Tokyo and St. Petersburg joined the British Foreign Office in signaling that his diplomatic maneuver was in trouble.[40] Finally, Russia and Japan announced on the same day, 21 January 1910, and in similar terms their

34. Reid to Knox, telegram, 26 November 1909, NF 5315/601.

35. Grey, minutes, 13 January 1910, FO 371/842.

36. Reid to Knox, telegram, 29 December 1909, NF 5315/657.

37. Knox to the London embassy, telegram, 14 December 1909, and circular telegram, 7 January 1910, NF 5315/628A, 672A.

38. Wai-wu Pu to the Board of Posts, 25 August 1909, CWS:HT, ch. 7.47–48.

39. Russian Minister Korostovetz to the Wai-wu Pu, 19 and 22 October 1909, WWP:Ni-hsiang Mei-kuo chieh-k'uan hsiu-chu Chin-Ai t'ieh-lu an, *ts'e* 1; and Fletcher to Knox, 26 October 1909, NF 5315/562.

40. Documents in NF 5315/574A, 584, 657A, 658, 669, 675, 690, 731; in NF 4002/270; and

veto of the neutralization proposal.[41] Ambassador Thomas O'Brien reported from Japan "that the Government, press and people are practically unanimous in opposition to our proposal."[42] Rockhill informed Knox that Izvolsky was waxing apoplectic over United States policy in Manchuria in general and over the Chin–Ai railway proposal in particular.[43] Britain, France, and even Germany were cautiously deferring to Japan and Russia and leaving Knox isolated and chagrined.[44] The second blow fell in early February when Russia and Japan warned the United States as well as China not to proceed on the Chin–Ai project without consulting them.[45]

Knox responded to these setbacks by continuing his exchange of views with St. Petersburg, only now his goal was to undo the damage his Manchurian initiative had done in driving Japan and Russia together. He looked forward to some understanding which might yet insure the success of his proposal; frustrate the prospect, already widely discussed, of a general Russo–Japanese understanding on Manchuria; and leave Japan in lonely opposition. However, this exchange of views in February and March 1910 also proved fruitless.[46] In May Knox made a final effort to conciliate the Russian government by giving way on the Harbin dispute, which he had inherited from Elihu Root. Neither Rockhill nor Knox had been satisfied with the preliminary Harbin agreement concluded between China and Russia in May 1909, and so the dispute between the United States and Russia had simmered along through the rest of the year with neither side giving way.[47] Knox had justified his neutralization proposal as a contribution to the solution of the Harbin problem, but Russian

Rockhill to Izvolsky, memo, 16 December 1909, Rockhill Papers, Houghton Library, Harvard University.

41. Kamikawa Hikomatso, ed., *Japan–American Relations in the Meiji–Taisho Era,* trans. Kimura Michiko (Tokyo, 1958), p. 289; telegrams by Rockhill and O'Brien to Knox, 21 January 1910, NF 5315/669, 703.

42. O'Brien to Knox, 22 January 1910, NF 5315/702.

43. Rockhill to Knox, 31 December 1909, NF 4002/270; and Rockhill, memo of conversation with Izvolsky, 19 January 1910, NF 5315/731.

44. Bacon (France) to Knox, telegrams, 7 January 1910 and 4 February 1910, NF 5315/674, 739; and David J. Hill (Germany) to Knox, 31 January 1910, DF 893.77/785.

45. Fletcher to Knox, 4 and 5 February 1910, NF 5315/783, 746.

46. Rockhill to Knox, 24 January 1910, NF 5315/744; Knox, memo to the Russian government, 8 February 1910, in Zabriskie, *American–Russian Rivalry in the Far East,* Appendix 3, pp. 211–13; Rockhill to Knox, in DF 893.77/852, 796, 864, 825, 1006½; and Knox, memo to the Russian ambassador, 18 April 1910, DF 893.77/901A.

47. Documents in NF 4002/167, 171, 180, 188, 195–98, 249B, 574A; Rockhill to the Wai-wu Pu, 23 June 1909, WWP: Tung-Ch'ing t'ieh-lu chan-ti chi le-chüan teng-an [File on the Chinese Eastern Railway's extension of land, extortion of taxes and other issues], *ts'e* 2; and Knox to the St. Petersburg embassy, telegram, 13 November 1909, Rockhill Papers. The Harbin agreement of 10 May 1909 is reproduced in MacMurray, *Treaties and Agreements with and Concerning China,* 2:1185–87.

Minister of Foreign Affairs Izvolsky, looking at the other side of the coin, had informed Knox that his "uncompromising stand" on Harbin only helped prejudice Russia's response on the Manchurian railways.[48] Now, in 1910, Knox belatedly agreed with the Russian's contention and abandoned his defense of principle in Harbin in hopes of saving the Chin–Ai railway or at least of offsetting Russia's inclination to reach an understanding with Japan.[49] But even this concession failed to provoke any grateful stirrings in the Russian government.

Through the first half of 1910, Knox also entertained hopes that the British might relent and give Pauling and Company, the British contractor working with the American bankers, a measure of diplomatic support.[50] Grey, however, refused to support Pauling against Japanese opposition. He was also held back by the growing fear in the Foreign Office of driving Russia and Japan together in Manchuria—a result, the Foreign Office ruefully discovered, already partially achieved by Knox's thoughtless proposal.[51] Knox stubbornly insisted that the British and American "positions obviously are not irreconsilable [*sic*],"[52] but his British counterpart maintained his benevolently neutral attitude toward the interests of Japan. Knox, who refused to go it alone on the Chin–Ai railway in the face of Russian and Japanese opposition, thus remained stymied.

For China, the timing of the Knox neutralization proposal may have been a surprise, but the idea itself was not novel. Since the Russo–Japanese War, China had been trying to achieve herself what Knox now proposed, even though she did not have the right to buy back the foreign owned and operated railways of Manchuria until 1932. The Wai-wu Pu as early as 1905 discussed the idea, which Minister Conger in turn warmly endorsed for Washington's attention.[53] Later in that year China's minister there put China's intentions more concretely. To sweeten the cancellation

---

48. On these opposing views, see Wilson to Rockhill, 3 January 1910, NF 4002/261; and Rockhill to Knox (on an interview with Izvolsky), 31 December 1910, NF 4002/270. The quoted phrase is Izvolsky's.

49. Knox to the Peking legation, telegram, 24 May 1910, DF 893.102H/281A. See also the documents in DF 893.102H/287 and DF 893.512/13.

50. Knox's view is expressed in DF 893.77/821, 988, 1011.

51. Whitelaw Reid explained the British hesitations in letters to Knox of 16 February 1910 (NF 5315/776) and of 18 February 1910 (Reid Papers, Manuscript Division, Library of Congress). See also Kamikawa, *Japan–American Relations in the Meiji–Taisho Era*, pp. 291–92; and Foreign Office minutes of 3 and 25 January 1910 (FO 371/621 and 845) expressing anxiety over a Russo–Japanese rapprochement.

52. Knox to Reid, 11 March 1910, Reid Papers.

53. Conger to Hay, 31 March 1905, MCD; and Hsieh Hsi-ch'üan (supervising censor), memorial, 18 May 1904, SL:KH, ch. 529.3–4.

of the Hankow–Canton railway contract, he offered American bankers first choice on any loan to repurchase from Japan the railway running between Port Arthur and Harbin.[54] However, for Washington, which was not yet interested, the proposal came prematurely.[55]

The repurchase idea lay dormant in China for several years but was revived by the Manchurian administration of Hsü Shih-ch'ang in the spring of 1908.[56] Hsü was hopeful that Russia might be willing to rid herself of the Chinese Eastern Railway in order to finally lay down the burdens she had carried in Manchuria. Such a sale, officials within the administration reasoned, would improve relations with Russia by altogether eliminating disputes associated with the administration of the railway, like the one then in progress over Harbin.[57] In December the separate efforts of E. H. Harriman and the Chinese to purchase the railroads came together briefly. While T'ang Shao-i was in the United States to negotiate the use of the Boxer indemnity remission, he discussed a railway repurchase loan with Harriman. Simultaneoulsy Hsü recommended the measure to the Wai-wu Pu.[58] Although T'ang was frustrated in his Manchurian bank loan, he received some encouragement in New York on redeeming the Chinese Eastern Railway. In January the Wai-wu Pu, acceding to Hsü's views, followed up on T'ang success by broaching the matter with the Russians, first informally through Sir Robert Bredon, the inspector of maritime customs, and then in a direct formal offer.[59] The Chinese proposal, discussed intermittently between the two governments, came to an inconclusive end in July 1909 when Russia agreed in principle to sell but only after the new, longer, strategically safer railway on Russian

54. Liang Ch'eng, memos, 28 August 1905, Notes from the Chinese Legation (microfilm records of the Department of State, National Archives).

55. The Chinese were unaware of Harriman's negotiations in Tokyo in the fall, and Japan made no effort to inform them, so T'ang Shao-i later claimed. Bland, *Recent Events and Present Policies in China,* p. 310.

56. A document in the archives of the British Foreign Office refers to ongoing negotiations in 1907 between Russia and China over the repurchase price of the railway, but I have seen no confirmation in other sources. Capt. J. Leader to Sir A. Nicolson, 4 May 1907, enclosed in Nicolson to Grey, 5 May 1907, FO 371/220.

57. Sao-ke Alfred Sze (Shih Chao-chi), *Reminiscences of His Early Years,* trans. Amy C. Wu (Washington, D.C., 1962), p. 50; Hsü to T'ang, 19 June 1908, WWP: Tung-san-sheng Chung-tung t'ieh-lu an [File on the Chinese Eastern Railway in Manchuria], *ts'e* 2. See also American consular reports from Mukden and Harbin in NF 5315/92, 93.

58. Bland, *Recent Events and Present Policies in China,* p. 315; and Hsü to the Wai-wu Pu, 27 and 29 December 1908, TSSCL, pp. 1989–94, 1995–2001.

59. Romanov, *Russia in Manchuria,* p. 383; Bredon, memo, 19 January 1909, WWP: Ha-pu ko-chan Chung-tung t'ieh-lu chieh-nei teng-an [File on the administration of Harbin and other miscellaneous issues concerning the Chinese Eastern Railway]; and Wai-wu Pu to Russian Minister Korostovetz, 1 February 1909, CWS:HT, ch. 1.8–9.

territory along the Amur River toward Vladivostok had been completed.[60]

Although Hsü and T'ang had left Manchuria by the time Russia replied to the Chinese railway proposal, the new governor general fully shared his predecessor's view on reclaiming the Chinese Eastern Railway. For example, in August 1909 Hsi-liang memorialized on the importance of buying back foreign concessions in Manchuria.[61] In the fall the Chinese government alerted by rumors of an impending meeting in Harbin between the Japanese resident general in Korea, Prince Itō, and the Russian minister of finance,[62] became alarmed almost to the point of panic by the thought that Japan might acquire the section of the Chinese Eastern Railway between Changchun and Harbin. Chinese officials frantically tried to uncover the real intent of the meeting.[63] However, these fears dissolved when a bullet, fired by a Korean assassin, struck Prince Itō down and disrupted the Russo–Japanese consultations.

Thus, by the time Knox presented his neutralization scheme in late 1909, the Chinese were still eager to acquire the foreign-held Manchurian railways. Chinese officials shared with Knox the assumption that these railways were the key to control of the region and that Russia at least might be willing to sell her holdings. Frontier defense no less than the broad open door could not be made effective until the status of these railways was altered. Nevertheless, the Chinese gave Knox's proposal a cautious reception. China, like Russia and Japan, had not been consulted before the proposal had been formally made to Britain and in fact had officially learned of it only a month and a half afterwards, on 20 December 1909.[64] When it arrived, the Wai-wu Pu found it disappointingly short on substance. Of the details, Knox's idea of giving the redeemed railways over to foreign supervision certainly roused no enthusiasm in Peking. The best reply the foreign office could muster was a perfunctory acknowledgement that Knox's proposal was "practically in agreement" with China's

60. Sa Yin-t'u (minister to Russia) to the Wai-wu Pu, 4 and 7 February 1909, CWS:HT, ch. 1.11–12, 18; Jordan to Grey, 3 March 1909, FO 371/621; Rockhill to Knox, 19 May 1909, NF 4002/198; and Romanov, *Russia in Manchuria*, p. 385.

61. Hsi-liang, memorial, 7 August 1909, HLIK, 2:928–30. The regent set the memorial aside.

62. Li Sheng-to (minister to Belgium) to the Wai-wu Pu, 7 July 1909; Wai-wu Pu to Hsi-liang, 10 October 1909; and Sa Yin-t'u to the Wai-wu Pu, 23 October 1909 (all in CWS:HT, ch. 4.34–35; 9.41; 10.3); as well as Sa Yin-t'u to the Wai-wu Pu, telegram, received 14 October 1909, WWP:O-Hu-Pu, Jih-I-teng tao-Ha chieh-hsia shou-lu an [File on the Russian minister of finance and Prince Itō meeting together at Harbin on the sale of the railway].

63. See the documents dated between 12 October and 8 November in WWP:O-Hu-Pu, Jih-I-teng tao-Ha chieh-hsia shou-lu an and in WWP:Ha-pu ko-chan Chung-tung t'ieh-lu chieh-nei teng-an, as well as in the collection of documents on Sino–Japanese relations taken from the Wai-wu Pu archives to be published by Li Yü-shu of the Institute of Modern History.

64. Fletcher to the Wai-wu Pu, memo, 20 December 1909, WWP: Ni-hsiang Mei-kuo chieh-k'uan hsiu-chu Chin-Ai t'ieh-lu an, *ts'e* 1.

ntentions.[65] The Wai-wu Pu decided that the success of the plan would depend chiefly on the United States and resolved to do nothing more than watch its progress.[66]

At this same time Knox made the unsettling discovery that the regent had not yet in fact approved the preliminary agreement for the Chin–Ai railway. Earlier, in November, the Grand Councillor Shih-hsü, a self-acknowledged proponent of the railway agreement, had assured Straight that a secret edict of approval had been issued. Now, in mid-December, the American chargé had to cable Knox that he could not verify its existence. Hsi-liang had just sent a message that no such edict had been issued, and the opinion of Liang Tun-yen, the new president of the Wai-wu Pu, and Fletcher's own investigations seemed to bear the governor general out.[67] Members of the Wai-wu Pu, reflecting the thinking of Na-t'ung and Tsai-tse, added to Knox's perplexity about Chinese intentions by dropping hints that they preferred to forget the Chin–Ai railway for the moment and to concentrate instead on the less controversial development bank.[68] Obviously, China's support was the indispensable precondition for making the railway a convincing alternative to the repurchase of the Manchurian railways. Knox, mindful of the tactical damage thus done to his neutralization proposal, was careful to withhold this information from Wall Street and to omit any reference to the fictitious edict in his neutralization proposal when he presented it to Russia and Japan.[69]

At this late date the only remedy for Knox was to conduct an intensive campaign through Fletcher to secure the Chinese government's acceptance of the Chin–Ai agreement as well as the neutralization scheme itself.[70] Although the Wai-wu Pu signified its acceptance of the neutralization plan in principle, the regent's government continued to move slowly on the former issue.

Finally, the pressure applied by Fletcher forced the ministries of the

65. Wai-wu Pu, draft reply to Fletcher, n.d., ibid. See also Fletcher to Knox, telegram, 23 December 1909, NF 5315/645.
66. Wai-wu Pu to the Board of Posts and the Board of Revenue, 12 January 1910, CWS:HT, ch. 12.20; Wai-wu Pu, telegram to diplomatic missions in Europe, 19 January 1910, WWP: Ni-hsiang Mei-kuo chieh-k'uan hsiu-chu Chin-Ai t'ieh-lu an, *ts'e* 1; and record of Fletcher's interview with Liang Tun-yen and Na-t'ung, 21 January 1910, ibid.
67. Reports from Straight and Fletcher in NF 5315/627, 630, 635, 706, and in NF 2112/98.
68. Fletcher to Knox, 7 and 9 December 1909, NF 5315/618, 724; and Jordan to Grey, 19 November 1909, FO 371/636.
69. J. P. Morgan and Co. to Knox, 10 January 1910, and Wilson, circular telegram, 15 December 1909, NF 5315/680 and 629A.
70. Fletcher to the Wai-wu Pu, 31 December 1909 (WWP: Ni-hsiang Mei-kuo chieh-k'uan hsiu-chu Chin-Ai t'ieh-lu an, *ts'e* 1) and 1 January 1910 (CWS:HT, ch. 11.40–41); and exchanges between Fletcher and Knox in the first half of January 1910 in NF 5315/670, 681, and in DF 893.77/800.

central government to reconsider the issues dividing them in order to pacify the Americans. Hsü Shih-ch'ang, as before, wanted the preliminary agreement approved, with terms unfavorable to China reserved for negotiations over the final agreement. He had also endorsed Hsi-liang's Manchurian bank plan.[71] Tsai-tse, by contrast, still was doubtful of the wisdom of a large foreign railway loan. He argued that the establishment of a new Manchurian bank had the disadvantage of requiring yet another foreign loan and of creating a financial competitor to the Ta-Ch'ing Bank under the control of his ministry. Tsai-tse, who had originally criticized Hsi-liang for not making a comprehensive railway-development bank plan, found that his delaying tactics had backfired. He had been surprised by Hsi-liang's quick-witted response in favor of both a bank and a railway loan. Now, the only way out for Tsai-tse was to minimize the advantages of the bank plan, which only a short while before he had favored.[72]

The Wai-wu Pu, which had initiated the exchange of views with the other two boards and which was again responsible for drafting the memorial on the Chin–Ai railway, was still inclined to a cautious Manchurian policy.[73] The memorial, presented on 20 January 1910 and immediately approved by the regent, once again reflected the loose accord between Na-t'ung and Tsai-tse.[74] It recommended delaying further discussion of the bank plan and giving the Ta-Ch'ing Bank interim responsibility for financing and supervising some of the Manchurian development projects. As for the Chin–Ai railway loan, the memorialists reiterated their concern for safeguarding China's economic rights in the agreement and for assuring financial solvency, but they did give Hsi-liang permission to negotiate an agreement with the American Group while maintaining close consultations with Peking. However, they did not specifically recommend approval of the preliminary agreement as Knox had been urging.

The significance of this most recent memorial on the Chin–Ai railway confused the head of the American mission in Peking. On the day the memorial was approved, Henry Fletcher, an inexperienced diplomat with

71. Board of Posts to the Wai-wu Pu, 16 January 1910, CWS:HT, ch. 12.24.
72. Board of Finance to the Wai-wu Pu, 14 January 1910, WWP: Ni-hsiang Mei-kuo chieh-k'uan hsiu-chu Chin-Ai t'ieh-lu an, *ts'e* 2; and comments on the bank loan [by the Board of Finance], n.d., ibid., *ts'e* 1.
73. Wai-wu Pu to the Board of Finance and the Board of Posts, 12 January 1910, CWS:HT, ch. 12.19–21.
74. Wai-wu Pu, Board of Finance, and Board of Posts, joint memorial, 20 January 1910, CWS:HT, ch. 12.35–37. Working papers, dated 17 to 19 January 1910, for this memorial are in WWP: Ni-hsiang Mei-kuo chieh-k'uan hsiu-chu Chin-Ai t'ieh-lu an, *ts'e* 2. The rescript is in HTCC, ch. 27.20.

so little understanding of Peking politics that he could not distinguish between an edict and a memorial, incorrectly wired the State Department that the preliminary agreement had been ratified.[75] The following day Liang Tun-yen told the American chargé in an ambiguous fashion that the memorial did not refer to the preliminary agreement of October 1909, and a formal note to Fletcher from the Wai-wu Pu confirmed in equally ambiguous terms what Liang had hinted at.[76] Nevertheless, Fletcher betrayed no uncertainty about the accuracy of his report to Washington. Finally Knox, who had developed doubts of his own, instructed Fletcher to take a second, more careful look at the memorial and the rescript.[77] Although the Wai-wu Pu remained evasive on the contents of the memorial and even refused him a copy of it, Fletcher still suspected nothing and did not understand that the memorial had been a charade, undertaken in part to satisfy the Americans, and that the railway project was no closer to approval than when Hsi-liang and Straight had signed the contract for it nearly four months earlier.[78] Fletcher's misunderstanding of the memorial in January, as with Straight's misinformation on the secret edict of the previous November, demonstrated that the subtleties of Peking politics tended at crucial moments to elude the grasp of Knox's agents.

By late January the Chinese government was chiefly preoccupied with the alarming prospect that the American Manchurian proposals might drive Russia and Japan together. The two powers, after hinting to China separately of their opposition to the Chin–Ai proposal, finally joined together against it.[79] Their common stand, endorsed by France and Britain in notes to the Wai-wu Pu,[80] caused officials in Peking and Mukden deep anxiety. Peking appealed to Washington for a show of support.

When the United States put the Manchurian proposal forward this time, it primarily wished to separate Russia and Japan. Now they have

75. Fletcher to Knox, 20 January 1910, NF 5315/697. For evidence of Fletcher's lack of even a rudimentary understanding of Chinese bureaucratic methods, see his dispatch to Knox of 16 January 1910, DF 893.77/800.

76. Interview between Fletcher and Liang Tun-yen, 21 January 1910, and Wai-wu Pu to Fletcher, same date, WWP: Ni-hsiang Mei-kuo chieh-k'uan hsiu-chu Chin-Ai t'ieh-lu an, *ts'e* 1.

77. Knox to Fletcher, telegram, 22 January 1910, NF 5315/704.

78. Fletcher to Knox, 24 January 1910, DF 893.77/840; Fletcher to the Wai-wu Pu, 24 January 1910, WWP: Ni-hsiang Mei-kuo chieh-k'uan hsiu-chu Chin-Ai t'ieh-lu an, *ts'e* 1; and Wai-wu Pu to Fletcher, 27 January 1910, CWS:HT, ch. 12.39.

79. Exchanges between the Wai-wu Pu and the Russian and Japanese ministers between October 1909 and March 1910 in CWS:HT, ch. 10.4 and 12.47–50, and in WWP: Ni-hsiang Mei-kuo chieh-k'uan hsiu-chu Chin-Ai t'ieh-lu an, *ts'e* 1 and 3.

80. Jordan, interview at the Wai-wu Pu, 7 January 1910, WWP: Ni-hsiang Mei-kuo chieh-k'uan hsiu-chu Chin-Ai t'ieh-lu an, *ts'e* 1; and French chargé to the Wai-wu Pu, 18 February 1910 (CWS:HT, ch. 12.49) and 4 and 18 March 1910, WWP: ibid., *ts'e* 3.

on the contrary joined together. If the United States has some remedy, what then is it?[81]

The State Department's reply—"China is still not in difficulty and must now maintain her resolve without wavering"[82]—was a familiar refrain, one which Americans in China, putting the best face on their discomfiture, had been playing since January. These abundant, encouraging, but none-theless meaningless assurances from the Americans did nothing to change the obvious fact that the neutralization proposal was dead beyond denial, the Chin–Ai railway contract still bogged down, and China dangerously isolated in Manchuria. Officials in Peking, abandoned by American policy-makers to their fate, awaited the worst: word of an agreement between their enemies in Manchuria.

In May and June warnings of an impending agreement between Russia and Japan became more frequent.[83] The crisis came to a climax on 4 July 1910 when the two governments signed their new accord. Altogether lacking in references to the open door or China's integrity, it was a worthy successor to their 1907 agreement. A telegram from Sa Yin-t'u, the minister to Russia, explained to the Wai-wu Pu that the first article, which provided for cooperation in railway affairs, meant that the two signatories intended to advance together in Manchuria. The second article, guaranteeing the status quo, was a warning that they would resist any attempt by China to lessen their influence in Manchuria. He reported that the third article was a commitment to joint consultations in case of a threat to the status quo and was generally interpreted in the Russian capital as a slap at the United States and its Manchurian propos-als.[84] To underline the seriousness of Russian and Japanese intentions, rumors began to circulate of a secret article of alliance.[85] Seven weeks after the signing of the agreement, Japan annexed Korea.

The Wai-wu Pu began to survey the diplomatic damage.[86] The minister

---

81. Wai-wu Pu to Minister to the United States Chang Yin-t'ang, telegram, 7 February 1910, WWP: Ni-hsiang Mei-kuo chieh-k'uan hsiu-chu Chin-Ai t'ieh-lu an, *ts'e* 1.

82. Chang Yin-t'ang to the Wai-wu Pu, telegram, 8 February 1910, ibid., *ts'e* 1. Other evidence of Chinese anxiety and American attempts to calm it is in Wai-wu Pu to the Board of Posts and the Board of Finance, 6 March 1910, ibid., *ts'e* 3; in NF 5315/691, 704; and in DF 893.77/840, 867, 873.

83. See for example the telegrams exchanged between the Wai-wu Pu and its ministers in Japan and Russia, 5 and 7 May 1910, CCS:HT, pp. 265–66.

84. Sa Yin-t'u to the Wai-wu Pu, telegram, 13 July 1910, CWS:HT, ch. 15.25.

85. See, e.g., Wu Chen-lin (chargé, Japan) to the Wai-wu Pu, telegram, 15 July 1910, CWS:HT, ch. 15.28; and Ch'en K'uei-lung (governor general of Chihli) to the Wai-wu Pu, 31 July 1910, CWS:HT, ch. 15.38–39.

86. Wai-wu Pu to its diplomatic missions in Germany, France, Belgium, Britain, Netherlands, and Japan, telegram, 12 July 1910, CWS:HT, ch. 15.23–24.

the United States reported that the feeling there was that China's sover-
ignty and with it American trade opportunity had suffered a fatal blow
nd that the United States, however much it disliked the agreement,
ould not undo the damage.[87] The American attitude, coupled with the
enerally nonchalant reaction among all the powers to the extinction of
orea, was a particularly ominous sign of the fate Manchuria might
uffer. In the major capitals attitudes toward the new agreement followed
ae lines of alliance; Chinese diplomats reported that Britain and France
ere pleased, while Germany and Austria along with the United States
ere quietly unhappy.[88] The Wai-wu Pu could be sure greater difficulties
ere in store for Manchuria. Although the former antagonism and distrust
etween Russia and Japan had not always worked to China's benefit,
aat relationship was far preferable to the new rapproachement, which
as to be surely inimical to China's interest in Manchuria. The best
eprise the Wai-wu Pu could manage under the new situation was to
eiterate that Russia and Japan had pledged themselves in the Portsmouth
reaty to respect China's sovereignty in Manchuria and the principle of
qual commercial opportunity as well as not to interfere in the commercial
nd industrial development of the area.[89] Manchuria suddenly seemed
erilously close to partition—much more so than it had been at any other
ime since the end of the Russo–Japanese War. No one knew better than
he Wai-wu Pu that appeals to old treaties would not avert it.

87. Chang Yin-t'ang to the Wai-wu Pu, telegram, received 7 August 1910, CWS:HT, ch.
5.2.
88. Telegraphic reports to the Wai-wu Pu from France (CWS:HT, ch. 15.26), from Britain
CWS:HT, ch. 15.27–28), from Japan (CWS:HT, ch. 15.28), and from Belgium (CCS:HT,
. 298).
89. Wai-wu Pu, circular telegram, 21 July 1910, CWS:HT, ch. 15.33, translated in MacMurray,
reaties and Agreements with and Concerning China, 1:802.

13: FAILURE

Knox did not immediately recognize that the Russo–Japanese agreement of 4 July 1901 proved that the calculations on which his Manchurian policy was based were erroneous. Huntington Wilson, who more than any other had led Knox on to the Manchurian diplomatic debacle, gave the secretary of state an inane and reassuring assessment, qualitatively on a par with his earlier advice. "I have just glanced it over but it seems fairly harmless," he wrote Knox. "One reaches the conclusion that the bark of moral effect is the main thing about this convention rather than its bite of legal force."[1] But at about the same time E. T. Williams, possessed of a greater knowledge of China and better professional judgment, gave Knox a different and painfully frank estimate.

> Our policy in Manchuria has won us the ill will of Russia, irritated Japan, and failed of support in France and Great Britain; should we now turn back, we shall have to count on the enmity of China also, and reckon with a decided loss of prestige throughout the Far East. The disgrace of the American China Development Company will be recalled and we shall be a target for ridicule and wrath.[2]

Knox also had critics outside the State Department. They faulted him for his alliance with the barons of Wall Street, for his interference in China's affairs, for his failure to get commercial results from his diplomacy and for straining relations with Japan. The press's unsympathetic reporting and commentary—like the acid observation on Knox, "he never meddles but he muddles"[3]—was doing the Taft administration public damage. Wilson, who handled relations with the press for the State Department, described its views for Knox as "put up or shut up" in Manchuria.[4] The

1. Wilson to Knox, 11 July 1910, Wilson Papers, Myrin Library, Ursinus College.
2. E. T. Williams (Division of Far Eastern Affairs), memo read to Knox, 28 August 1910, D 893.77/1058.
3. St. Louis *Post-Dispatch*, in *Literary Digest* 40(5 February 1910): 214.
4. Wilson to Knox, 27 July 1910, Knox Papers, Manuscript Division, Library of Congress.

secretary, however, wrote off the strictures of newspaper editors to ignorance.

> The reasons the newspapers attack our foreign policies so frequently and violently is because they make it a point to attack whatever they don't understand and the violence of the assault depends upon the depth of their ignorance.[5]

Even the financial and commercial community began to complain to Knox. One of its weightiest voices, *The Journal of Commerce and Commercial Bulletin*, looking over the situation in Manchuria, pronounced Knox's policy there "maladroit diplomacy" and professed to see no danger to the open door.[6] Cotton exporters looked at the declining trade figures and charged that Knox was not effectively protecting and promoting commerce.[7] Part of the financial community, whose interests Knox was also supposed to be serving, was even more restive. The exclusive character of the American Group, aside from provoking populist suspicions, excited jealousy among those who, in the words of one disgruntled financier, had to act as "jackals of the lions of Wall Street."[8] Their insistent complaints finally even stirred the lethargic Taft to trespass on Knox's foreign policy preserve. "I sincerely hope and believe that no effort has been made . . . to prefer Morgan's to any other American firm in promoting the extension of American credit to other countries."[9] Knox, of course, had been preferring Morgan and his associates in dealings with China and had no intention of dissolving his chosen financial instrument. From the time the American Group was organized, the State Department had had to stubbornly fend off on one pretext or another the persistent claims of of a number of investors to a share of the business secured by the American Group through government auspices.[10]

Even relations with the American Group, never easy, became increasingly strained. The department's insistence in 1909 on an equal share for Americans in the Hukuang loan, which had prolonged the negotiations,

---

5. Knox, jotting [October 1910], Knox Papers.

6. *The Journal of Commerce and Commercial Bulletin*, 9 March 1910. Paul A. Varg, *The Making of a Myth: The United States and China, 1897–1912* (East Lansing, Mich., 1968), pp. 62–67, 106–112, and 160–62, surveys this paper's editorial policy.

7. See, e.g., John H. Wisner (president, Cotton Goods Export Association) to Knox, 17 December 1909 (NF 788/338) and 8 December 1910 (DF 693.003/337).

8. J. Selwin Tait (manager of the International Banking Corporation) to Wilson, 22 September 1909, NF 5315/517.

9. Taft to Knox, 5 November 1910, Taft Papers, Manuscript Division, Library of Congress.

10. See correspondence interspersed in NF 5315/282ff, in DF 893.51, and in DF 893.77. Note Knox's defense of his association with the American Group in NF 5315/336, in DF 893.51/155, and in DF 893.77/871.

had already made the bankers impatient.[11] In 1910 the tribulations of American Manchurian policy and Knox's refusal either to reverse or to push to a conclusion American investments there caused "the lions of Wall Street," particularly the First National Bank and the National City Bank, to further question the value of their privileged relationship with the government. The bankers, who claimed to be more interested in "the maintenance of American prestige in the far East" than in "pecuniary gain,"[12] were discovering that patriotism was costly.

Knox did his best to ignore his critics in 1909 during the Hukuang loan controversy and the Crane affair, but in 1910 he found he could not do so indefinitely. When, for example, a writer for *The Outlook* indicated he thought Knox was guilty of undue interference in China, Knox had Wilson reply at length explaining his policy.

> As well leave the slum to manage its own sanitation and thus infest the whole city, as to allow an unenlightened government, unopposed, to create or maintain a financial plague spot to the injury of the general interest.[13]

This simile, meant to justify the department's proceedings, was an inadvertant admission of the very charges of interference Wilson was attempting to refute. His style as an advocate, heavy-handed and condescending, tended to be self-defeating, and Knox, perhaps realizing it, began to defend his China policy personally. In June 1910 he delivered a major address on the "altruism and unselfishness" of American diplomacy with the apparent hope of impressing the public with the benign influence of dollar diplomacy.[14] When a spirit of revolt began brewing in the ranks of the American Group later in the summer, Knox, urged on by Taft and assisted by Wilson, cajoled them into forgetting their qualms and continuing to carry the flag in China.[15]

11. See, e.g., George Marvin (now connected with J. P. Morgan and Co.) to Wilson, and Wilson to Marvin, 8 and 9 July 1909, and Wilson to the London embassy, telegram, 9 July 1909, all in NF 5315/344 and 338.

12. The quote is from Schiff to Knox, 30 October 1910, DF 893.51/205. In the same vein, see Schiff to Knox, 24 May 1910, DF 893.77/942; R. S. Miller (chief, Division of Far Eastern Affairs), memo, 22 July 1910, Knox Papers; and Wilson to Knox, 12 July 1910 and 8 August 1910, Wilson Papers.

13. Wilson to Elbert F. Baldwin, 19 January 1910, Reid Papers, Manuscript Division, Library of Congress; and Baldwin to Wilson, 21 January 1910, NF 5315/717.

14. Knox to Wilson, 20 May 1910, and "The Spirit and Purpose of American Diplomacy," commencement address at the University of Pennsylvania, 15 June 1910, both in Knox Papers.

15. Wilson to Knox, 23 July 1910, Knox Papers; E. T. Williams to Frank H. McKnight (of J. P. Morgan and Co.), 9 August 1910, DF 893.77/1068A; and corresponderce exchanged between Taft and Knox, 1 September 1910, Taft Papers.

Those who had formerly made China policy were equally restless. Elihu Root, now ensconced in the Senate, privately blamed Huntington Wilson for Knox's misadventures.[16] W. W. Rockhill, shuttled from Peking to St. Petersburg and finally to Constantinople by his new boss, knew that he was *persona non grata* with Taft, Knox, and Wilson. Consequently, he made only veiled criticism to the department, but to friends he was franker.[17]

Theodore Roosevelt was the critic whose barbs sank most deeply and drew from Knox his most considered, detailed, and personal defense. Roosevelt, on leaving office in February 1909, had prepared for Knox a summary of current policy. The outgoing president had stressed Japanese "touchiness," particularly on the immigration question, and the necessity of giving her leeway on other issues, including her policy toward China, if the United States were to have its way on immigration.[18] Knox had not heeded the warning, and by mid-1910 Roosevelt had become "seriously uneasy" about Manchurian policy.[19] In December 1910 he took it upon himself to remind Taft of the relation between the Japanese immigration question and China policy as it affected Japan, and in a meeting requested by Taft he told Knox the same thing.

> Our vital interest is to keep the Japanese out of our country, and at the same time to preserve the goodwill of Japan. The vital interest of the Japanese, on the other hand, is in Manchuria and Korea. It is therefore peculiarly our interest not to take any steps as regards Manchuria which will give Japanese cause to feel, with or without reason, that we are hostile to them, or a menace—in however slight a degree—to their interests. . . .
>
> . . . Our interests in Manchuria are really unimportant, and not such that the American people would be content to run the slightest risk of collision about them. . . .[20]

Wilson brushed Roosevelt's views aside as "queer" and "absurd."[21]

16. Philip C. Jessup, *Elihu Root* (New York, 1938), 1:53, 563, and 2:250–51.
17. Knox to Rockhill, 17 June 1911, Rockhill Papers, Houghton Library, Harvard University; Rockhill to Knox, 18 January 1910, NF 4002/272; and Rockhill to Hippisley, 9 July 1911, Rockhill Papers.
18. Roosevelt to Knox 8 February 1909, Morison, 6:1513–14.
19. Roosevelt to Henry Cabot Lodge, 24 May 1910, Morison, 7:86. See also Roosevelt to Henry White, 2 June 1913, Morison, 7: 730.
20. Roosevelt to Taft, 22 December 1910, Morison, 7:189–92. See also Theodore Roosevelt to Taft, 8 December 1910, and Theodore Roosevelt to Theodore Roosevelt, Jr., 5 December 1910, Morison, 7: 180–81 and 178. Roosevelt's advice to Knox is summarized in Roosevelt's letter of 22 December as well as in Knox to Taft, 19 December 1910, Knox Papers.
21. Wilson to Knox, 23 December 1910, Wilson Papers.

Knox prepared a lengthy and spirited refutation of them and submitted it
to Taft. In it Knox denied "any essential connection" between the Manchurian and immigration questions. On both issues he contended that the
United States acted from treaty rights and saw no reason why Japan
should feel offended. "We have no desire or intention to interfere with
any legitimate purpose of Japan in Manchuria. . . . Nor have we given
Japan at any time just cause to think that we wished to interfere."[22] Knox
argued that his Manchurian policy was nothing more than the defense of
the principles of the open door, which by themselves were so important
that "it would be much better for us to stand consistently by our principles
even though we fail in getting them generally adopted." Knox carefully
refused to rule out the possibility of a war with Japan over them.

> Whether the American people would ever go to war or not in defense of
> our interests in China . . . might depend on the nature of the provo-
> cation. But in any case it certainly is not for us to prejudice our case at
> the start by admitting to the world that we would *not*, under any
> circumstances, go to war.[23]

Taft characteristically did his best to minimize the differences between
Roosevelt and Knox. He set aside the draft reply to Roosevelt prepared by
Knox and wrote his own, expressing gratitude to Roosevelt for reaching a
"full understanding" with Knox during their interview and for the
"valuable contribution" in his letters.[24] Taft's decision to adopt a conciliatory tone was perhaps politically wise, but it left unexamined questions of policy weighty with long-term implications for the American role
in the Pacific.

Knox was everywhere confronted with evidence that his Manchurian
policy was a dismal failure. And by August 1910 he was beginning to
acknowledge it. The ominous understanding between Russia and Japan
now stood on the wreckage of his Manchurian railway plans. The State
Department was beset by self-doubts, attacked by the press, and pressed
by China for relief. The Hukuang loan negotiations were at a standstill,
and the American Group contracted a bad case of cold feet.

Knox and Wilson had ready explanations for what had gone wrong.
They were convinced that their Manchurian policy had thus far failed

22. Knox to Taft, draft letter in reply to Roosevelt's letter of 22 December 1910, dated 7
January 1911, Taft Papers. Another briefer version is in the Knox Papers.
23. Knox to Taft, draft letter, dated 7 January 1911, Taft Papers.
24. Taft to Roosevelt, 20 December 1910 and 17 January 1911, Taft Papers.

because it had been badly executed in St. Petersburg and because China and Great Britain had acted contrary to their real interests. They laid part of the blame on Rockhill because, following his common sense and his own interpretation of instructions from the department, he had entirely omitted reference to the Chin–Ai project when he presented the neutralization proposal to Izvolsky in December 1909.[25] Izvolsky, who later had learned of Rockhill's omission, had seized on the error to berate Washington for trying to keep him in ignorance. In fact, Izvolsky had already decided on an agreement with Japan and had used Rockhill's mistake to embarrass the United States.[26]

The failure of the British to support American policy was the bitterest medicine Knox and Wilson had to swallow. Wilson, "thoroughly disgusted" with their role, intemperately blamed their "chronic invertebracy," their "namby-pamby Russian friendship," and their "excessive infatuation" with the Japanese alliance.[27] Knox made crystal clear to British diplomats his resentment against British policy.[28] Both Knox and Wilson felt that the government in Peking had also failed them. Although in formulating their policy they had treated the Chinese as a mere cipher, they were nonetheless disturbed when they discovered American formulated plans were getting only halfhearted support in the Chinese capital. They had wrongly assumed China would meekly follow Washington's policy wherever it might lead.

The real problem in American Manchurian policy was, as Roosevelt had hinted, indeed Knox himself. He was from the beginning plagued by his inexperience in international affairs, his uneven judgment in selecting subordinates and making policy, and his haste in executing policy. He got no help from Taft because the secretary wanted none and because Taft too was deficient in experience and judgment.

Knox lacked a subtle mind and was not at all attuned to the crucial role of power and compromise in international relations. A professional

25. Rockhill to Knox, telegram, 26 December 1909, and Knox to Rockhill, telegram, 27 December 1909, both in Rockhill Papers; Rockhill to Knox, 31 December 1909, NF 4002/270; J. O. P. Bland, *Recent Events and Present Policies in China* (Philadelphia, 1912), pp. 318–19; and Wilson to Knox, 20 January 1910, Wilson Papers.

26. Edward H. Zabriskie, *American–Russian Rivalry in the Far East: A Study in Diplomacy and Power Politics, 1895–1914* (Philadelphia, 1946), p. 154; and David J. Dallin, *The Rise of Russia in Asia* (New Haven, Conn., 1949), p. 99.

27. Quotes from Wilson to Knox, 20 January 1910 (Wilson Papers) and 27 July 1910 (Knox Papers). See also P. Heintzleman (Division of Far Eastern Affairs) to Fletcher, 18 February 1910, Fletcher Papers, Manuscript Division, Library of Congress.

28. Interviews with Knox recounted in Mitchell Innes (chargé, Washington) to Grey, 11 November 1910, FO 371/875. See also Bryce to Grey, 24 August 1910, and Innes to Campbell, 2 November 1910, FO 371/920 and 248 respectively.

British diplomat saw Knox's problems as acutely as any of his contemp
raries.

> He is hopelessly ignorant of international politics and principles
> policy and is either too old or too lazy to apply his mind to the subje
> and try to learn. Nobody in his miserably organized department
> competent to instruct or guide him. No country but the U.S. could g
> on under such conditions.[29]

Henry Adams tartly observed that the new incumbent "did not kno
enough law to know that he was ineligible, and did not know enoug
diplomacy to organise his Department which he has thrown into confu
sion. He is not in the remotest degree fit for the post."[30]

Knox was a corporation lawyer who took business as the department'
chief client and in China assiduously cultivated its interests as he define
them. The work of his staff, more often examinations of treaties rathe
than of power relations,[31] reflected the secretary's legalistic bias. Britis
diplomatic representatives in Washington could not shake off the impres
sion that Knox was really a lawyer trying to pose as a diplomat: "To hir
a treaty is a contract, diplomacy is litigation, and the countries interested
parties to a suit."[32]

The new secretary of state had a confused conception of national
purpose in China. Together with Taft, he ignored the complexity of thei
self-imposed commercial and financial crusade and its relationship tc
broader considerations of policy. Examined from afar and in the abstract,
Knox's dollar diplomacy has an appealing clarity and consistency, but
when examined up close and specifically in its application to China, it
appears muddled. Through 1909 and 1910 the department carelessly
manufactured justifications for China policy to fit the occasion with
alarmingly little concession to internal consistency. The Hukuang loan in
1909 set the tone for this opportunism. American participation was defended at one time or other by a bewildering array of arguments: to prevent a breach of faith; to safeguard treaty rights; to preseve American

29. Bryce quoted in E. W. Edwards, "Great Britain and the Manchurian Railways Questions,"
English Historical Review 81(October 1966): 764. For the judgment visited on Knox by a profes-
sional American diplomat who had worked for him, see Lewis Einstein, *A Diplomat Looks Back*
(New Haven, Conn., 1968), pp. 84–85.

30. Henry Adams to Whitelaw Reid, 15 February 1909, in Harold D. Cater, ed., *Henry Adams
and His Friends: A Collection of His Unpublished Letters* (Boston, 1947), p. 637.

31. Typical is R. S. Miller, "Memo on Manchurian treaties," probably composed between
February and March 1910, Knox Papers; and Division of Far Eastern Affairs, memo on the
Chin–Ai railway [January 1911], DF 893.77/1107.

32. Innes to Grey, 11 November 1910, FO 371/875.

mmercial interests; to guarantee the United States a voice in the
uncils of the powers in future questions concerning China's finances;
d to fulfill the self-imposed role of protector of China.[33] The same debat-
g points were hauled out to bolster Knox's decisions as Manchurian
licy began to evolve later in the year. These arguments abounded in
tential contradictions which the department gave no sign of recognizing.
Knox's interpretation of the open door was similarly inconsistent. At
st, the open door was the rhetorical cloak which he threw over his policy
 dollar diplomacy in Manchuria. Knox had accepted the argument of
e young activists that the concept of the open door stood for equality
 investment as well as trade opportunity and thus could be used to
stify the commercial and financial goals of dollar diplomacy in Man-
uria. But by late 1910 Knox had confused his goals with his justification
r them, so that under attack from Roosevelt he defended his policy not
 one of commercial and financial necessity but as one of protection of
e principle of the open door.

Knox compounded his difficulties by choosing unsuitable subordinates.
untington Wilson and to a lesser extent Willard Straight and Henry
etcher exaggerated rather than minimized his errors and deficiencies.
ke Knox, they and the other activists in his service considered a sub-
antial American stake in China essential. In promoting this goal they
o demonstrated a lack of diplomatic experience, sound judgment,
tience, and caution. Knox gave over to Wilson the day-to-day operation
 the department, ostensibly to allow himself time to ponder the major
estions of policy, but he thereby deprived himself of the chance to be-
me familiar with the mechanics of his new profession and to gather at
sthand the information necessary to make independent decisions. His
liance on the information sent from China by Straight and Fletcher also
d him into error.

Knox's own personal failings and those of his staff caused him to make
ndamental strategic mistakes. In advocating the construction of the
hin–Ai railway and the neutralization of the foreign-owned railways
 Manchuria, Knox misjudged at one time or other between 1909 and
id-1910 the attitude of every government with an interest there. For
ample, from the outset Knox and his subordinates had counted on the

33. Some prime examples are: Wilson to the Peking legation, telegram, 19 June 1909, NF
15/259; Taft to Prince Ch'un, 15 July 1909, NF 5315/351; Taft to G. W. Painter, 6 September
9, Taft Papers; "The Chinese Loan," 30 September 1909, DF 893.51/368; "Summary of
te Dept Policy and Actions" [fall 1909], Knox Papers; "The Hukuang Loan" [February–
arch 1910?], DF 893.77/871; and annual addresses of the president for 1909 and 1910, FRUS,
09, p. xviii, and FRUS, 1910, p. xi.

support of the British Foreign Office and failed to anticipate or appreciat
the claims of Russia and Japan on British loyalties and the importance
tensions between Britain and Germany. Personnel in the State Departme
could not throw off the conviction, repeatedly refuted by events, th
racial and commercial interests would bring the United States and Brita
together in Manchuria.

British diplomats were dismayed by American policy. They we
troubled by the amateur tradition which pervaded the American forei
service and by the domination of the State Department by lawyers a
politicians; above all they detested the parochialism and bad manners
Huntington Wilson, described by one as "that pestilential beast."[34] S
Edward Grey, stung by Knox's criticisms of British policy, replied
kind:

> The only apparent result [of Knox's Manchurian policy] has been
> draw Russia and Japan closer together, and at the same time to ma
> the task of preserving the open door increasingly difficult.[35]

Knox also failed to find the support in China he had expected. H
agents seriously underestimated the division of opinion within Chine
officialdom over Manchurian policy and at crucial moments misled Kn
with misinformation. Symptomatic of the department's inability to ke
up with events in China was the plaint from the Division of Far Easte
Affairs that it could not locate Taonan, the terminal of the first stage
the Chin–Ai railway, on any of its maps.[36] The department, veheme
assertions of concern to the contrary, was just as unfamiliar with Ma
churia in 1910 as in 1903, when it had groped about for some suitab
treaty ports.

When Knox was not out of touch with Chinese aspirations, he was o
of sympathy with them. Even though he was conducting a self-interest
commercial policy which sometimes forced him to run contrary to China
wishes and to violate her integrity, he simply assumed that what serv
the United States also served China. Thus Knox repeatedly asked t
regent to commit his government to risky American projects in Ma
churia which, from the Chinese point of view, tended to take unfavorab
turns. For example, Knox had been prepared to admit Russia and Japa
to the Chin–Ai project, a development completely contrary to China
motives in proposing the railway in the first place. Similarly, when t

---

34. Innes to Campbell, 2 November 1910, and Bryce to Campbell, 24 September 1909, bc
in FO 800/248; and Bryce to Grey, 24 August 1910, FO 371/920.
35. Grey to Bryce, 22 September 1910, FO 371/920.
36. P. Heintzleman to Fletcher, 18 February 1910, Fletcher Papers.

Chinese later offered a Manchurian loan (concluded in October 1910) to improve relations with the United States, Knox ignored Chinese preferences and instead organized an international financial monopoly to control Chinese loans. Even Knox's neutralization proposal, on the surface similar to earlier Chinese efforts, carried a major drawback. Knox wished to create an international company, in which the powers would preponderate, to operate the railways of Manchuria. Somehow he had imagined that China, after contracting a large foreign loan to help repurchase them, would then be willing to hand them over in trust to this foreign consortium. "An economic and scientific and impartial administration" of these railways, as Knox had phrased it originally, was in the best spirit of progress and efficiency but totally out of tune with Chinese priorities. All in all, Knox and the Chinese had distinctly different ideas about the implications for American loans to China. On the one hand, Hsi-liang worked from the premise that "whoever borrows money also borrows the influence of the lender. Others use their influence to take over our interests. We then borrow their influence to consolidate our frontier."[37] Knox took the blatantly contradictory view that "the borrower is the servant of the lender."[38] It was thus understandably difficult to arrange a financial and political partnership. Knox, like Hay and Root, never understood the chief goal of China's frontier defense in Manchuria, which was to secure her own effective control, and so he continued to treat her as America's ward.

Knox fared no better in dealing with Russia. He had been convinced by unsubstantiated rumors and second-hand reports that she had tired of her Manchurian venture. Without preparing the groundwork, he abruptly invited her to leave the region. Knox was certain that even if officials in St. Petersburg hesitated to sell their railway, the arrangements for building the Chin–Ai line would force their hand. Both assumptions proved to be wishful thinking. Izvolsky, the minister of foreign affairs, whose views Knox had not bothered to sound out, reacted by effecting the rapprochement with Japan in order to sabotage American efforts.

Knox relegated Japan to an even less important position in the diplomatic scheme of things, as if her views carried no weight in London, St. Petersburg, or Peking. Consequently, the State Department dealt cavalierly with the Japanese, who had under Knox emerged as the primary villain in Manchuria. The activists, who had a simplistic and racist view of Japan's policy, were convinced that her leaders were fearful of unfavorable

37. Hsi-liang, supplementary memorial, 12 December 1909, HLIK, 2:1008–09.
38. Knox, jotting, 10 June 1909, NF 5315/251.

public opinion in the West and dependent on foreign loans and that with the first rumble of dissatisfaction from the Anglo-Saxon world they would tremble and repent of their wrongdoing.[39] Taft and Knox for their part were unimpressed when Japan's representatives tried to explain their country's interest in Manchuria.[40] Thus Knox fell in with the crusade to force Japan to show her true hand. The effort may have given him and his staff some psychologically satisfying moments, but diplomatically it was a failure.

The practitioners of dollar diplomacy measured their success by the coin of loan agreements, railway concessions, and export figures. By their own standards, which took little account of the fall of American stock on the diplomatic exchanges of Europe and the Far East, the policy which Knox and the activists had tried was bankrupt. American commerce stagnated. For example, in Manchuria Japanese cotton piece goods had by 1914 supplanted those from the United States, which had formerly been dominant there. Only the kerosene trade of Standard Oil of New York made any headway.[41] In fact, Knox's aggressive policy in Manchuria had actually backfired commercially because it had antagonized Japan, America's chief trading partner in East Asia. The administration of the South Manchurian Railway, which had generally favored American railway materials, suddenly decided in early 1910 that British goods and money were preferable to American. Knox protested in vain; the damage was already done.[42] In 1911 Knox experienced substantially the same disappointment when American manufacturers failed to win a share of the orders Japan placed for the Antung–Mukden railway.[43] Of all his initiatives in financial diplomacy in China, only the Hukuang loan had borne fruit. Even then, the American share was a mere $7 million.

Dispatches from Minister William J. Calhoun, who reached Peking in 1910, and the consuls in Manchuria and elsewhere were filled with indications that Americans were just not interested in the China market.[44]

39. Willard Straight was the most outspoken exponent of this pervasive attitude, which had taken hold during Root's tenure in the department. See, e.g., Straight, report to the State Department, 9 November 1907, NF 2321/16; Straight, memo to Taft, 2 December 1907, NF 2413/99; and Straight, memo for Bacon, 11 November 1908, NF 16533/8.

40. See, e.g., the record of their interviews with Count Komura and Marquis Katsura, 14 and 17 September 1909, Taft Papers.

41. Fisher (consul, Mukden) to Rockhill, 12 February 1914, Rockhill Papers; E. M. Gull, *British Economic Interests in the Far East* (London, 1943), pp. 55–58; and Charles F. Remer, *The Foreign Trade of China* (Shanghai, 1926), pp. 81–82.

42. On the shift in the purchasing policy of the South Manchurian Railway and the American reaction, see NF 221/13, 22, 63, 76, 130, 133, 136, 141, 146A, 151A, and NF 914/20.

43. DF 893.77/1118, 1127, 1135.

44. Reports in NF 7611/8, in DF 893.6172/39, in DF 893.77/1217, and in DF 693.003/383.

At home Knox saw at firsthand the indifference of the Wall Street financiers, who occasionally groaned under their patriotic burden. "What difference does it make whether the 'door' is open or shut," Calhoun asked Knox, "if we are not disposed to go in or out of it, even when it is open?"[45] But Knox stubbornly persisted, refusing to entertain the simple proposition that businessmen were interested in profit and not prophecy and that for the moment they could do better at home than in China.

Knox had sponsored in 1909 and 1910 a hothouse effort at creating a foothold in Manchuria but had ignored Japan's natural trade advantage, Russia and Japan's well-entrenched political position, and the attitude of the American business world. If he had given some thought to the resistance he could expect to encounter and the damage he might do to the United States diplomatically, Knox might have reached the same sound conclusion Roosevelt had come to some years earlier. "On the score of mere national self-interest [in Manchuria], we would not be justified in balancing the certainty of immediate damage against the possibility of future danger."[46]

45. Calhoun to Knox, 28 March 1912, DF 893.77/1217.
46. Roosevelt to Cecil Spring-Rice, 13 June 1904, Morison, 4:830–32.

14: THE FINAL ACT

While in 1910 Peking was immobilized by differences of opinion over Manchurian policy and by fear of Japan, Hsi-liang stoutly continued to advocate a vigorous policy of frontier defense. Russian and Japanese opposition to the Chin–Ai railway, of which the Wai-wu Pu had kept him informed,[1] had not daunted the governor general. On the contrary, the attempt by those two powers to impose their will on Manchuria had made the construction of this railway seem to him all the more important as a demonstration of Chinese independence and as a contribution to her strength. In February 1910 Hsi-liang resumed pleading its cause. He argued that China's railway agreement with Russia in 1896 had compromised China's sovereignty in Manchuria; the Chin–Ai railway would help restore it.

> Because China's power, as we ourselves have calculated it, is insufficient to hold back the advance of Japan and Russia, we must depend on the United States and Britain and on the policies of the open door and of the balance of power as a device to save ourselves from oblivion.[2]

A detailed, final railway agreement with the American financial group and the British contractor would be the most effective way of consolidating foreign support behind China's struggle for control.

Hsi-liang decided to push ahead on his own on this final agreement even though the preliminary agreement had not yet received specific sanction from the regent. In mid-February he asked Willard Straight to prepare for the next round of talks. Not until a month later did he reveal his intentions to the heads of the Peking ministries.[3] The Wai-wu Pu responded predictably by counseling delay, but Hsi-liang insisted and secured its reluctant consent.[4] In mid-March he dispatched his agents,

1. See, e. g., Wai-wu Pu to Hsi-liang and Ch'eng Te-ch'üan, 20 January and 13 February 1910, WWP: Ni-hsiang Mei-kuo chieh-k'uan hsiu-chu Chin-Ai t'ieh-lu an [File on the Chin–Ai railway loan], *ts'e* 1 and 3 respectively.
2. Hsi-liang and Ch'eng to the Wai-wu Pu, 19 February 1910, ibid., *ts'e* 3.
3. Straight to J. P. Morgan and Co., telegram, 15 February 1910, NF 5315/778; and Hsi-liang and Ch'eng to the Wai-wu Pu, Board of Posts, and Board of Agriculture, Commerce, and Industry, telegram, received 10 March 1910, CCS:HT, pp. 236–37.
4. Telegrams exchanged between the Wai-wu Pu and Hsi-liang, 12–15 March 1910, CCS:HT, pp. 238–39.

heng Hsiao-hsü, an entrepreneur and diplomat serving in the governor
:neral's secretariat, and Teng Pang-shu, a foreign affairs specialist em-
loyed in Kirin, to Tientsin for the talks; however, their labor was in
ain.[5] Any agreement on the railway would be meaningless as long as
:king feared to defy Japan and Russia. Although Hsi-liang pleaded for
:king's approval—"How can the ministers of state accommodate them-
:lves to the extinction of our dynasty's homeland; how can they bear not
⊃ rush out in defiance of death to plan a policy for its survival?"[6]—in
he end he could push policy no farther than Peking would allow.[7]

Hsi-liang, however, could not afford to remain inactive, and so in the
pring of 1910 he dusted off a pair of proposals he had made at the begin-
,ing of his incumbency. Both of them, like the Chin–Ai railway project,
vere meant to involve the United States in Manchuria and simultaneously
⊃ develop the region. Both were discussed with the American Group
luring the Tientsin talks. One of the projects was for completing the
:onstruction of a port at Hulutao at a cost of about 5 million taels (about
$3.3 million in 1910), to serve as a substitute for Newchuang. Chinese
)fficials in Manchuria had as far back as 1906 been considering the con-
servancy of the Liao River, necessary to maintain Newchuang as a viable
rival to Dairen; however, their discussions, continuing into 1911, were to
prove inconclusive.[8] Hsü Shih-ch'ang had previously decided to down-
grade the importance of Newchuang and instead to concentrate on building the new port at Hulutao.[9] Immediately on taking office Hsi-liang had
endorsed Hsü's decision and on his own initiative had continued the
preliminary work there already in progress. Then, in early May 1910,
Hsi-liang again pushed the project to the fore, presenting his plans to the
Wai-wu Pu.

In response the Board of Finance followed the already familiar pattern
of urging delay on a variety of pretexts.[10] When, later in the month, Hsi-
liang again appealed to the regent in a detailed memorial, the latter as

5. A sketch of Cheng Hsiao-hsü appears in Howard L. Boorman, ed., *Biographical Dictionary of
Republican China* (New York, 1967–71), 1:272. A copy of the draft final agreement is in LNCYJ,
5:332–45. Hsi-liang's detailed defense of the terms of the agreement, received by the Wai-wu Pu
on 22 May 1910, is in WWP: Ni-hsiang Mei-kuo chieh-k'uan hsiu-chu Chin-Ai t'ieh-lu an,
ts'e 3. See also Straight to J. P. Morgan and Co., 1 May 1910, DF 893.77/914.

6. Hsi-liang to the Wai-wu Pu, received 22 May 1910, WWP: Ni-hsiang Mei-kuo chieh-k'uan
hsiu-chu Chin-Ai t'ieh-lu an, *ts'e* 3.

7. Hsi-liang to the Grand Council, Wai-wu Pu, Board of Posts, and Board of Finance, 22 June
1910, CWS:HT, ch. 15.16–17; and Wai-wu Pu to Hsi-liang, 26 June 1910, CWS:HT, ch. 15.17.

8. TSSCL, pp. 1939–40, 6453–64; and documents in NF 17370 and in DF 893.811.

9. TSSCL, pp. 6469–71.

10. Hsi-liang and Ch'eng, received 1 May 1910; Wai-wu Pu to the Board of Finance, 5 May
1910; Board of Finance to the Wai-wu Pu, 12 May 1910; and Wai-wu Pu to Hsi-liang, 16 May
1910. All are in WWP: Hu-lu-tao k'ai-pu an [File on opening the port at Hulutao], *ts'e* 1.

usual referred the entire matter back to the Board of Finance, whic
confirmed its original position. The regent then agreed that it was best t
defer this project, like all the others that had issued from Manchuria.[11]

The other enterprise to which Hsi-liang gave new emphasis was th
development of Manchuria's mineral resources under the auspices c
Americans.

> Natural resources if not exploited for long will gradually rouse th
> interest of our powerful neighbors. The draft agreement which w
> previously discussed is in reality a plan to maintain [Manchuria] b
> opening it.[12]

In February 1910 he endorsed an application by an American–British–
Chinese joint stock company for rights to the Hailung gold mines. (Although the project was later approved, the company never began operations.[13]) In April Hsi-liang suggested to the bankers of the American
Group that they select two coal mines along the proposed Chin–Ai railway
route to operate jointly with the Chinese.[14] (However, this venture, linked
to the doomed railway project, also failed to bear fruit.)

The Russo–Japanese agreement in July, followed by the Japanese annexation of Korea in August, alarmed Hsi-liang. "What has happened to
Korea can happen to Manchuria."[15] The governor general feared that the
entente between Russia and Japan might force the United States to reach
an understanding, perhaps even an alliance, with Japan to save her
stake in Manchuria. Should this happen China would be without foreign
support on this frontier of the empire.[16] Hsi-liang thought immediate and
vigorous counteraction necessary.[17]

In August and September 1910, almost a year after Hsi-liang's threaten-

11. Hsi-liang, memorial and rescript, 20 May 1910, HLIK, 2:1139–40; as well as Board
of Finance and Wai-wu Pu, joint memorial, n.d., and Grand Council to the Wai-wu Pu, 22
June 1910, both in ibid.

12. Hsi-liang and Ch'eng to the Wai-wu Pu, received 3 April 1910, *K'uang-wu tang* [Records on
mining affairs] (Taipei, 1960), comp. by the Institute of Modern History, Academia Sinica,
6:3942. See also HTCC, ch. 29.14–16, for his memorial of 17 February 1910.

13. The Hailung mine negotiations are covered in *K'uang-wu tang*, 6:3927–47.

14. Translation of Hsi-liang and Ch'eng to the American Group, 30 April 1910, DF 893.63W
51/1.

15. Hsi-liang, memorial, 16 October 1910, HLIK, 2:1233–34.

16. Hsi-liang to the Wai-wu Pu, 17 September 1910, collection of documents on Sino–Japa-
nese relations to be published by Li Yü-shu of the Institute of Modern History; and Fisher to the
State Department (on an interview with Hsi-liang), 27 May 1910, DF 893.00/(NF 1518/412).
Hsi-liang had become suspicious of an American sellout in Manchuria the previous December.
See his supplementary memorial of 12 December 1909, HLIK, 2:1008–09.

17. Hsi-liang to the Grand Council and the Wai-wu Pu, telegram, received 20 June 1910,
CWS:HT, ch. 15.16.

ed resignation and the conclusion of the preliminary Chin–Ai agreement, a flurry of recommendations rained down on Peking from Mukden. Hsi-liang capped his efforts with a visit to the capital and an audience with the regent, whom he asked once again to sanction work on the proposed railway.[18] At the same time he pushed forward less controversial projects, for the construction of the port at Hulutao and for the opening up of coal mines in remote areas of Heilungkiang and Kirin by building rail lines to them. Above all, Hsi-liang gave new emphasis to colonization, the slowest but most certain way of filling up the frontier and ultimately of guaranteeing China's hold on Manchuria. Hsi-liang requested that the Board of Finance appropriate 20 million taels to carry out these and related programs, including a Manchurian bank of modest scope.[19]

The steadfastness of the heads of the Board of Finance and the Wai-wu Pu, tested for over a year by the tenacious governor general of Manchuria, finally weakened. The developing crisis in Manchuria, about which Hsi-liang had long warned them and to which, in their opinion, his precipitate launching of the Chin–Ai railway in October 1909 had contributed, no doubt weighed heavily on their minds. They no longer had to fret over the prospect of a Russo–Japanese rapprochement and trim policy to forestall it. The rapprochement was an accomplished fact which China could not alter. Although they continued to throw obstacles in the way of the related Chin–Ai railway and Hulutao projects,[20] the Peking ministries were ready to give Hsi-liang at least some of the financial support essential to a strong Manchurian policy.

In early September the Board of Finance together with the Wai-wu Pu

18. Hsi-liang to the Grand Council, telegram, 7 July 1910, CWS:HT, ch. 15.18; Hsi-liang, memorial, 16 August 1910, HLIK, 2:1184–86; and Hsi-liang to the Wai-wu Pu, 30 August 1910, WWP: Ni-hsiang Mei-kuo chieh-k'uan hsiu-chu Chin-Ai t'ieh-lu an, *ts'e* 3.

19. Hsi-liang, memorials, 16 and 26 August 1910, HLIK, 2:1184–86 and 1203–04; Hsi-liang and Heilungkiang Governor Chou Shu-mo, memorial, 5 September 1910, in *Chou chung-ch'eng fu-chiang tsou-kao* [Memorials of Governor Chou of Heilungkiang] (Taipei reprint, 1968), 1:567–73; and Hsi-liang, memorials, 9 September 1910, 16 October 1910, and 31 December 1910, HLIK, 2:1204–06, 1233–34, and 1259–60. Construction at Hulutao continued into 1911 when the Chinese approached the American Group to undertake the remaining work on the basis of the April 1910 agreement. The revolution of 1911 brought the talks to an inconclusive end and made further Chinese financing of the project impossible. See DF 893.156Hu. The development of the Heilungkiang coal mines was earlier dealt with in Chou Shu-mo to the Wai-wu Pu, 1 August 1909, CWS:HT, ch. 6.3–4; and Hsi-liang and Chou, memorial, 11 September 1909, in *Chou chung-ch'eng fu-chiang tsou-kao*, 1:279–81. Governor Ch'en Chao-ch'ang urged the use of foreign funds to develop the coal mines of Kirin in his memorial of 22 September 1910, HTCC, ch. 41.11–12. Colonization, particularly important in Heilungkiang, was earlier covered in a memorial of 17 August 1909 by Governor Chou of that province. *Chou chung-ch'eng fu-chiang tsou-kao*, 1:273–76.

20. Their unchanged attitude toward the Chin–Ai railway and Hulutao is summarized in Hsi-liang's memorial of 26 August 1910, HLIK, 2:1203–04. See also Wai-wu Pu, memo, 30 August 1910, WWP: Ni-hsiang Mei-kuo chieh-k'uan hsiu-chu Chin-Ai t'ieh-lu an, *ts'e* 3.

promptly approved Hsi-liang's proposal for a Manchurian development loan. The regent, who had asked for the boards' opinion in the first place, quickly accepted their recommendation that the governor general should negotiate the loan himself and then submit it for their approval.[21] Hsi-liang began negotiations with foreign financial agents with whom be had been in contact since early December 1909. He finally gave the new loan to Americans represented by the former American consul general in Mukden, Frederick Cloud. However, at the same time the Board of Finance, which had decided to float a loan for national currency reform, proposed combining the currency loan with the Manchurian loan. In early October the regent approved, took the Manchurian loan from Hsi-liang's jurisdiction, and blocked the deal between Hsi-liang and Cloud by refusing it an imperial guarantee. The Board of Finance, after making overtures to the American Group, first for one, then for both loans, finally in late October concluded a $50 million loan agreement and asked for imperial sanction. Tsai-tse, the president of the board, as usual had gotten his way.[22]

The decision to place a large loan in the United States was burdened with political expectations. During the summer after the Russo–Japanese agreement, the Chinese capital buzzed with rumors about the embarrassing diplomatic reverse the United States had suffered. As Peking looked for some sign of support, the American minister and his staff enjoyed the sea breezes at Peitaiho. Their negligent attitude seemed to confirm the rumor that they were washing their hands of Manchuria.[23] Even so, Chinese officials had only one place to turn in their distress, back to the United States again.[24] The Chinese government offered the combined Manchurian-currency loan specifically to maintain American involvement in Manchuria as well as to get a new commitment of support for China.

The regent himself advanced the effort to arrange American support by ordering Liang Tun-yen, the recently retired president of the Wai-wu Pu, to go to Washington. There as well as in Berlin he was to issue invitations to join Peking in reaffirming the open door. Such a reaffirmation might

21. Board of Finance and the Wai-wu Pu, joint memorial and rescript, 5 September 1910, CWS:HT, ch. 16.32–34.

22. The memorial by the Board of Finance, the rescript of approval of 29 October, and the agreement itself are in CWS:HT, ch. 17.41–43. The English version of the agreement, signed on 27 October 1910, also appears in John V. A. MacMurray, ed., *Treaties and Agreements with and Concerning China, 1894–1919*, vol. 1: *Manchu Period (1894–1911)* (New York, 1921), p. 851.

23. Correspondence from China in DF 893.77/1043, 1045, and in DF 711.93/15; and Max Müller (chargé, Peking) to Grey, 27 July 1909, FO 371/920.

24. See, e.g., Sheng Hsüan-huai's telegrams of 30 July 1910 and 1 August 1910, YCTK, ch. 53.6–7.

fset the Russo–Japanese agreement and dispel the appearance of Chinese olation.[25] In addition to Liang's mission, the central government preared lavish welcomes for American visitors in the fall of 1910. The A-.erican secretary of war, whom the Chinese hoped might be carrying some romise of support from President Taft, was the most distinguished of 1ese. But even a delegation of American businessmen was treated to a reeting so warm that it caused foreign diplomats in Peking to blink in onder. Moreover, the press, as in 1908, got into the act by again raising he prospect of a Sino–American alliance.[26]

Late 1910 and early 1911 was a transitional period for American China olicy. The emergence of a strong legation in Peking and of new experts n Chinese affairs together served to balance and neutralize some of the nsound judgments of Huntington Wilson and others on whom Knox had eaned in shaping his China policy through 1909 and the first half of 1910. In mid-1910 the legation regained the authoritative voice lacking during he interregnum following Rockhill's transfer to St.Petersburg a year before. During that period the youthful and inexperienced chargé Henry Fletcher had been working out of his depth. Knox finally selected William J. Calhoun to fill the post of minister. Calhoun, aged sixty-one, was a Chicago lawyer with a moderately impressive record of public service.[27] Although his knowledge of the "Orient" was nil and he had had only a brushing acquaintance with diplomacy, Calhoun was supported in his new post by able subordinates.

Lewis Einstein, a professional diplomat blessed with cool intelligence, served as secretary of legation.[28] Because the new minister was debilitated initially by several months of ill health (during which he later confessed that "he had seen nothing, heard nothing and understood nothing"[29]), he gladly availed himself of Einstein's experience and advice. Einstein thus began to exercise a disproportionate influence over the legation's reporting. Calhoun also had at hand an able Chinese secretary, Charles D. Tenney, a missionary educator who had lived in China almost steadily

25. State Department reports on Chinese intentions in DF 893.00/437, 468, and in DF 893.51/1405.

26. Müller to Grey, 28 October 1910, FO 371/874; Calhoun to Knox, 19 December 1910, DF 893.51/292; and Robert Dollar, *Memoirs of Robert Dollar* (San Francisco, 1917), 1:159–200.

27. Sketch of Calhoun by Stephen Bonsal in *The Dictionary of American Biography*, 3:420–21.

28. Lawrence Gelfand's account of Einstein in Lewis Einstein, *A Diplomat Looks Back* (New Haven, Conn., 1968), pp. xv–xxix.

29. Quoted in Margerie to Pichon, 27 November 1910, Min. Aff. Et., Chine, NS 378. See also Calhoun to Henry B. Favill, 31 August 1910, Taft Papers, Manuscript Division, Library of Congress.

since 1882.[30] His familiarity with the convoluted politics of the countr
supplemented Einstein's broad diplomatic perspective. During this perio
E. T. Williams, an equally able sinologist, was brought into the Stat
Department's Division of Far Eastern Affairs, where he too could con
tribute some of the substantial information on which Knox should hav
been making policy but in fact had not had available.

Einstein did the most to convince Knox of the virtues of a policy of rea
cooperation, particularly one less directly antagonistic to the interests o
Russia and Japan. Einstein wished to see the United States join Britain
France, and Germany in an international financial consortium in order to
preserve the status quo in China and to moderate the aggressive policies o
Russia and Japan. Feebleness and demoralization among the Manchu
rulers and the high diplomatic costs of Knox's independent forward policy
made such a change in course imperative. He stressed that the price of
safeguarding American interests and the open door was an accommodation
with the other consortium members on the divisive diplomatic questions
of the day. His experience in Istanbul, where he had witnessed the impending breakup of the Ottoman empire, had convinced him of the
advantages of great power cooperation. He subsequently elaborated and
disseminated his ideas in a book, several articles, private correspondence,
and official dispatches sent to Washington in Calhoun's name.[31]

The advice the Peking legation was offering Knox in 1910 substantially
resembled the path he had previously taken in the Hukuang loan in 1909.
At the outset of that controversy, the department had composed a ration-
ale for United States participation in that loan which seemed now more
appropriate than ever.

> Full and frank co-operation [is] . . . best calculated to maintain the
> open door and the integrity of China and . . . the formation of a
> powerful American, British, French and German financial group would
> further that end.[32]

With the neutralization and Chin–Ai proposals, however, the department
had moved ahead in Manchuria on an entirely different course, ignoring

30. Sketch by Esson M. Gale in *The Dictionary of American Biography*, 9:371–73.
?1. *American Foreign Policy by a Diplomatist* (Boston, 1909); "The New American Policy in China" (written in early fall 1911), Knox Papers, Manuscript Division, Library of Congress; Calhoun to Knox, 14 September 1910 and 1 October 1910, DF 893.51/118, 198; and Einstein to Knox, 17 October 1910, Knox Papers. See also Einstein, *A Diplomat Looks Back,* pp. 85–86. Having helped to reorient American China policy during his brief service under Calhoun, Einstein was awarded the post of minister to Costa Rica late in the fall of 1910 after only eight years in the foreign service.
32. Wilson to Phillips, draft telegram, 9 June 1909, NF 5315/251.

ritain's and France's ties with Russia and Japan and threatening the
nterests of those latter two powers. But in the fall of 1910, after several
nonths of troubled reflection, Knox finally saw the disadvantages of his
ndependent proceedings in Manchuria and the potential value of closer
onsultations with the other powers interested in China. Although Hun-
ington Wilson held out hopes for the success of his Manchurian policy
and tried to minimize the damage already done,[33] Knox began redirecting
his entire China policy along the line already taken in the Hukuang loan.

Knox signaled the tendency of his thinking by turning his back on
Chinese overtures for support in the latter half of 1910. In July and August,
as the Chinese waited uncomfortably for the American riposte to the
Russo–Japanese agreement, the State Department was content to polish
up the empty words of reassurance used earlier in the year to buck them
up.[34] Its advice for Hsi-liang, that "the chief questions in Manchuria are
such that their solution depends primarily upon China itself," made
particularly clear that Knox had nothing to offer now aside from "hearty
moral support."[35] Within the department comments on China's insecurity
were tarter and entirely unsympathetic. "I cannot see," Wilson told the
secretary with monumental disdain, "why China should get so very
panicky as this process is familiar enough to her!"[36] Later, Knox refused
to acknowledge that the acceptance of the attractive currency-development loan carried with it the obligation to back China diplomatically.
The visit of the American secretary of war to Peking in September was
kept routine, to the disappointment of his hosts. Minister Calhoun, who
did not want to arouse unjustified expectations among the Chinese,
persuaded the distinguished visitor to set aside a letter from the president
and settle for a few noncommital remarks to the regent and his court.[37]
Again, during Liang Tun-yen's visit to Washington during the winter,
Knox parried Liang's proposal that the United States join China and
Germany in a reaffirmation of the open door or assist China in some other
way.[38]

Knox gave the definitive signal that he would not entertain the diplo-

33. Wilson to Knox, 11 July 1910 and 1 September 1910, Wilson Papers, Myrin Library, Ursinus College.
34. Wilson to the Peking legation, telegram, 19 July 1910, DF 893.77/1016; Wilson to Calhoun, 17 August 1910, DF 711.93/15; and Chang Yin-t'ang to the Wai-wu Pu, telegram, 21 August 1910, CWS:HT, ch. 16.16.
35. Wilbur J. Carr to Fisher (consul, Mukden), 18 July 1910, NF 1518/418.
36. Wilson to Knox, 15 July 1910, Knox Papers.
37. Calhoun to Knox, 3 October 1910, DF 711.93/18; and Einstein, *A Diplomat Looks Back,* p. 102.
38. See HTCC, ch. 42.3, 11, for the edicts of 4 and 6 October 1910; and the documents in DF 893.51, particularly numbers 288, 1404, 1408–10.

matic approaches from the Chinese when he sought an understandin
with the other powers on the currency-development loan. The America
Group had previously laid dubious claim to Hsi-liang's Manchurian loa
on the basis of an unofficial agreement made in 1908 between T'an
Shao-i and Willard Straight.[39] Then, on Knox's advice, it had negotiate
for the currency loan and finally taken the combined loan. When th
European financiers laid claim to a portion of the loan and offered t
admit the American Group into the European financial consortium,[4]
Knox welcomed the offer and sanctioned the admission of his financia
instrument into the consortium.[41] The London agreement, signed on 1(
November 1910, in effect extended the Hukuang railway loan arrange
ment to encompass effectively all future major foreign loans to China. The
cooperative policy thus came into its own as the American Far Eastern
policy.

The negotiators for the currency-development loan—Tsai-tse, Sheng
Hsüan-huai and Calhoun—disagreed over the price of the loan, the au
thority of a foreign financial adviser, and the desirability of including the
European members of the international consortium. In the initial agreement, concluded on 27 October 1910, they compromised on the cost of
the loan. In the subsequent dealings, which carried over into 1911, the
Chinese successfully resisted efforts to give the adviser substantial authority but had to give way to the American demand that the European
bankers be given a direct stake in the loan. The final agreement for the
combined loan was signed on 15 April 1911.[42]

Knox had made his decision in favor of cooperation with the European
powers, but he only slowly realized the price he would have to pay.
Through the first half of 1911, the State Department maintained its
habitually vigilant watch over American commercial rights in Manchuria.[43] At the same time it betrayed no fear that the Manchurian loan

39. See the documents in DF 893.00/468; in DF 893.51/122, 127–29, 134, 138, 140, 142, 147;
in DF 893.77/1071, 1082; in FO 371/643; and in Min. Aff. Et., Chine, NS 378. On the disputed
loan agreement of 1908: Straight–T'ang memo, 11 August 1908, NF 2112/98; Straight to J. P.
Morgan and Co., 13 December 1909, ibid.; Calhoun to Prince Ch'ing, 2 September 1910, WWP:
Ni-hsiang Mei-kuo chieh-k'uan hsiu-chu Chin-Ai t'ieh-lu an, *ts'e* 2; and documents in DF
893.51/118, 129, 145, 149, and in DF 893.77/1052, 1061, 1063, 1086.
40. Paul M. Warburg to Kuhn, Loeb and Co., cable, 1 September 1910, DF 893.77/1063; and
C. S. Addis to S. Simon, 14 September 1910, FO 371/871.
41. Knox to the Peking legation, telegram, 6 October 1910, and to the British chargé in Washington, 17 November 1910, both in DF 893.51/138, 196.
42. Documents in HTCC, ch. 51.1–3; and in DF 893.51/122, 134, 136, 156, 162, 166ff. The
final agreement is in MacMurray, ed., *Treaties and Agreements with and Concerning China*, 1:841–49.
43. E.g., DF 693.003/383, 391; DF 893.00/534; and DF 693.001/143.

might run afoul of opposition. However, bit by bit, Knox discovered that to accommodate his new partners in finance and diplomacy he would have virtually to abandon Manchuria.

The biggest sacrifice required by his new policy was the withdrawal of active support from the Chin–Ai railway project. Through mid-1910 Knox had refused to abandon all hopes for this cornerstone of his policy to neutralize Manchuria.[44] But he also refused to implement it without the British behind him. When, for example, Hsi-liang, who wished to get the project moving, suggested building initially only the first section as far as Taonan, the State Department balked even though the American bankers were willing to accept.[45] Huntington Wilson together with R. S. Miller of the Division of Far Eastern Affairs feared that the abbreviated route "might result in an abortive and useless line which might even be ridiculous."[46] Wilson, finally alerted to the dangers of precipitate action in Manchuria, now advised Knox to consult with Germany and Britain before making a decision. Accordingly, Knox once again sounded out the attitude of the British Foreign Office. Sir Edward Grey refused to endorse even the revised, truncated version of the Chin–Ai project.[47]

As his cooperative policy took shape in the fall, Knox put the Chin–Ai project from his mind. Even so, in the minds of others it died a fitful death. Pauling and Company wished to build the shorter, compromise line to Taonan or find a suitable alternative. Hsi-liang, who favored Pauling's plan, knew that American financial participation and diplomatic support were essential. When in Peking for talks with the regent and the Grand Council, Hsi-liang pressed Washington to clarify its intentions. Knox put him off with a reply that Hsi-liang and Pauling should wait patiently for some unspecified resolution of the issue in the distant future. Knox's words had their intended effect in Peking and New York. Prince Ch'ing and Na-t'ung refused to go on without support from the government in Washington, and the American Group decided after all that it would neither cooperate on a shorter line nor withdraw from the project.[48]

Willard Straight, who had helped father the Chin–Ai project, also

44. Knox expressed this opinion in interviews with Mitchell Innes (to Grey, 11 November 1910, FO 371/875) and to Liang Tun-yen (E. T. Williams, memo, 4 February 1911, DF 893.51/1410).

45. Peking legation to Knox, telegram, 14 July 1910, extract in DF 893.77/1016.

46. Wilson to the Peking legation, telegram, 19 July 1910, DF 893.77/1016; and Wilson to Knox 15 and 27 July 1910, Knox Papers. The quote is from the letter of 27 July.

47. E. W. Edwards, "Great Britain and the Manchurian Railways Questions," *English Historical Review* 81 (October 1966): 765; and Reid to Knox, telegram, 2 August 1910, DF 893.77/1039.

48. Documents in DF 893.77/1046, 1050–51, 1059, 1063, 1082, 1116, 1136.

maintained his personal concern for it. Along with Pauling and Company's representative, Lord ffrench, he continued through 1910 and 1911 to look for ways to proceed. During the first half of 1910, while the State Department awaited new developments, he worked closely with the administration of Hsi-liang. He was confident that both the Chinese and Russian governments would eventually line up behind the railway project.[49] Later he embraced the vain hope that the new cooperative policy would work a change in British and Russian attitudes toward the Chin–Ai railway. Even in the midst of the 1911 revolution, the hyperactive Straight lobbied for it without in fact the remotest possibility of success. As his sense of the possible, never well developed, began to fail him, his diplomatic schemes became increasingly complex—indeed fantastic. Only with the fall of the Ch'ing and China's descent into further political confusion did Straight reluctantly surrender his dreams for Manchuria.[50]

The Chin–Ai railway project was only the first major casualty of Knox's decision to pursue a cooperative policy. A close second was the abandonment by the State Department of its insistence that China employ an American currency adviser if she were to take the American currency loan. When, early in 1910, the department received hints that China might undertake a reform of her finances, Huntington Wilson had suggested having an American adviser oversee the program and thereby ensure its efficiency and success. Accordingly, when the department announced the acceptance of the currency loan by the American Group, it had specified that China would have to appoint an American adviser and suggested Jeremiah Jenks, a Cornell University economist and perennial Republican favorite.[51] Tsai-tse and Liang Tun-yen curtly dismissed the suggestion and stoutly refused to grant any foreigner control over the reform as broad as the United States wished.[52] The other powers finally got wind of the secret and now deadlocked American proposal and began making their own similar demands of the Chinese.[53] In February 1911 Knox gave up

49. On Straight's activities and intellectual gyrations during this period see: letter to Wilson, 19 December 1909, NF 5315/706; reports to J. P. Morgan and Co., 16 February, 4 March 1910 and 28 June 1910, DF 893.77/856, 880, 1011; and letter to H. P. Davison, 12 March 1910, DF 893.51/106$\frac{1}{2}$.

50. Notable examples of Straight's views are in communications in DF 893.51/267, 465, 662, 729, 734; in DF 893.512/12; as well as in Straight to Rockhill, 11 December 1910, Rockhill Papers, Houghton Library, Harvard University. Straight's reports on the political situation in China in 1910, 1911, and 1912 are in DF 893.51/220, 683, 786.

51. Documents in DF 893.51/106, 111A, 122, 132, 138, 175A, and in DF 711.93/15.

52. Documents in DF 893.51/108, 134, 1404, 236, 246, 292, 288, 285.

53. Documents in DF 893.51/221, 222A; and Taft to Knox, telegram, 7 November 1910, Taft Papers.

●n the appointment of an American adviser after having done consider-
.ble—and ineffective—arm-twisting in Peking.[54]

Knox's Manchurian policy suffered the final and crowning blow when
ɪe had to agree to drop the Manchurian portion of the currency-
levelopment loan. From the start, the Russian foreign office, which viewed
●ts stake in northern Manchuria essentially in political terms, attributed
American support for the Manchurian loan to similarly political pre-
ɔccupations and worried about how the Chinese might use the funds.[55]
The Russians entered into consultations with the Japanese government
and, moreover, secured the support of the French minister of foreign
affairs, who shared the view that American intentions were "uniquely
political."[56] Through late 1910 and the first half of 1911 the Quai d'Orsay,
serving within the consortium as the watchman and defender of Russian
and Japanese interests, succeeded in blocking the Manchurian portion
of the loan.[57] Knox tried in June 1911 to reassure Russia, and Calhoun
even stopped off in Mukden on his way home to the United States to
caution Chao Erh-sun, the new governor general there, against giving
offense to Japan or Russia.[58] But Knox was finally constrained to bow to
the insistence of his French financial partners in China that the Manchurian loan be eliminated.[59] The eventual inclusion of Russia and
Japan in the financial consortium in 1912 was the ultimate admission by
Knox that he could do business in Manchuria only on terms set by the
two preponderant powers there. By March 1912 Calhoun had written
off Manchuria as lost to China, a conclusion the British had reached the
year before.[60]

The cooperative policy continued to develop under Knox's hand from
1911 through early 1913. The powers interested in the Hukuang loan had

54. Documents in DF 893.51/299, 305, 314, and in DF 893.77/1120.

55. On Russian Far Eastern policy from late 1910 through 1912, see Edward H. Zabriskie, *American–Russian Rivalry in the Far East: A Study in Diplomacy and Power Politics, 1895–1914* (Phila-delphia, 1946), pp. 174–89; and David J. Dallin, *The Rise of Russia in Asia* (New Haven, Conn., 1949), pp. 106–17.

56. Subdirectorate for Asia of the French Ministry of Foreign Affairs to S. Simon, 15 Novem-ber 1910; Ambassador A. Gerard (Tokyo) to Minister of Foreign Affairs Pichon, 24 November 1910; and Pichon to the Peking legation, telegram, 21 November 1910, all in Min. Aff. Et., Chine, NS 378; Gerard to Pichon, 10 December 1910, and Minister Margerie (Peking) to Pi-chon, 9 February 1911, ibid., NS 379; as well as Minister of Foreign Affairs Cruppi to Ambas-sador Paul Cambon (London), 27 May 1911, ibid., NS 380.

57. Documents in DF 893.51/329, 437, 446–48.

58. Knox to the St. Petersburg embassy, telegram, 6 June 1911, DF 711.93/24A; and Calhoun to Knox, 14 June 1911, DF 893.51/514.

59. Documents in DF 893.51/502, 508, 491, 596, 668, 679.

60. Calhoun to Knox, 15 March 1912, DF 893.00/1244; M. W. Lampson (Far Eastern Division of the British Foreign Office), memo, 29 April 1911, FO 371/1091; and Jordan to Campbell, 4 August 1911, FO 800/245.

resolved their differences in November 1910 and in May of the followin year signed the final agreement with the Chinese government. In th fall of 1911 the consortium began negotiations with the faltering imperi: government for another major loan and in 1912 continued the talks, no with the indigent Republican government of Yüan Shih-k'ai.[61] Througl out, Knox took a back seat as the consortium struggled to establish monopoly over Chinese loans and to secure a strong supervisory role ove China's financial administration. The cooperative policy limited Ameri can response to political changes in China. Despite the hue and cry withi the United States in favor of the new Republican government, Knox wa obliged to shape his policy to the requirements of his partners, who stoo firmly against *de jure* recognition.

After an eventful four years, dollar diplomacy in China, most recentl under the guise of the cooperative policy, was called to a halt by the ne Democratic administration in Washington. Woodrow Wilson, promptl after taking office in March 1913, repudiated Knox's financial instru ment,[62] and in May he recognized the Chinese Republic independentl of the other powers. The American Group, which had again become restive in 1911 and remained so subsequently, seemed relieved to be free at last of their thankless and profitless responsibilities in China.[63] Al though Woodrow Wilson had nothing to put in the place of dollar di plomacy except the rhetoric of the open door and of friendship, he had at least cut through the tangle in which Knox had gotten American China policy.

Late 1910 and early 1911 was also for the Chinese a transitional period in Manchurian policy, as frontier defense efforts ground to a halt. The regent's government had already revealed itself averse to showing a strong hand in Manchuria. As domestic opposition to its policies, parti cularly on the timing of political reform, grew in scope and intensity, the regent became even more cautious in Manchuria. Under these conditions, resistance to Russia and Japan became all but impossible.

During this period the inhabitants of Fengtien and Kirin put on an unprecedented display of that political consciousness which had been

---

61. The best balanced account is Ernest P. Young, "Politics in the Early Republic: Liang Ch'i-ch'ao and the Yuan Shih-k'ai Presidency" (Ph.D. diss., Harvard University, 1964), but also see Frederick V. Field, *American Participation in the China Consortiums* (Chicago, 1931), pp. 70–117, A. Whitney Griswold, *The Far Eastern Policy of the United States* (New York, 1938), pp. 170–73, and the documents in DF 893.51/610ff.

62. Wilson's press release, 18 March 1913, DF 893.51/1355$\frac{1}{2}$; and Arthur S. Link, *Wilson: The New Freedom* (Princeton, N. J., 1956), pp. 283–88.

63. On the group's attitude see documents in DF 893.51/620, 1307, 1341–42.

developing with rapidity since the end of the Russo–Japanese War. Local gentry, merchants, and students, the most vocal and influential groups within the community, took the lead in expressing dissatisfaction with the inability of the Ch'ing to resist foreign aggression and with the drawn-out program of political reform first announced in 1906. Open criticism of the regent reflected an unprecedented unrest among the general populace, which took the form of popular risings, student strikes, and a campaign to accelerate the pace of reform. Preparations for local self-government, part of the nationwide program of constitutional reform, had long been in progress. Provincial assemblies had been elected in Manchuria as elsewhere in 1909. At first, Hsü Shih-ch'ang and then Hsi-liang had had no difficulty keeping these activities within the bounds set by Peking. However, after 1909 the task was much more difficult.[64]

Popular disaffection presented Hsi-liang with a dilemma. The governor general agreed with the popular verdict that the regent had mismanaged Manchurian policy, but at the same time Hsi-liang was deeply loyal to the dynasty. As pressure mounted within the province to advance the date for calling a national assembly, the strain on Hsi-liang increased. He finally telegraphed the popular demands to Peking late in the fall of 1910. The regent, furious, rejected the plea. A second round of demonstrations in Mukden, more tumultuous than the first, culminated in a gathering of twenty thousand before the governor general's yamen. Again, after hesitation, Hsi-liang bowed to popular pressure and urged the regent to speed the pace of reform. The regent's reply, late in December, was a severe rebuke to Hsi-liang. But when Hsi-liang tried to resign, the regent ordered him to stay on.[65]

In his last months in office, Hsi-liang was saddled with the heavy responsibility of a domestic policy with which he did not fully agree and of a foreign policy which he lacked the authority to execute. The people were restless, and Russia and Japan were watching events closely. To add to his worries, Hsi-liang was now confronted with the unnerving spectacle of a plague sweeping across the region, attributed by some to the Japanese.[66] His health, never good in recent years, began to fail him. Ill and discouraged, he asked to be relieved. Finally, in May 1911 the regent

64. Robert H. G. Lee, *The Manchurian Frontier in Ch'ing History* (Cambridge, Mass., 1970), pp. 171–74; and Chang P'eng-yüan, "The Constitutionalists," in Mary C. Wright, ed., *China in Revolution: The First Phase 1900–1913* (New Haven, Conn., 1968), pp. 148, 150–52, 155–56.

65. HTCC, ch. 51.12, 13; and the reports from the Mukden consulate and the Peking legation in DF 893.00/480, 487, 490, 494, 496.

66. Carl F. Nathan, *Plague Prevention and Politics in Manchuria 1910–1931* (Cambridge, Mass., 1967), chap. 1; and Dugald Christie, *Thirty Years in Moukden 1883–1913* (New York, 1914), pp. 234–57.

replaced him with Chao Erh-sun, who had served as the last military governor of Fengtien.[67]

The civil turmoil in Manchuria worsened through 1911 and brought a definitive end to the hopes of conducting an effective policy of frontier defense. The light of public concern had in a striking degree shifted between 1905 and 1911 from the foreign threat to the feebleness of the Ch'ing. In Manchuria as elsewhere this disaffection with the dynasty fed revolutionary sentiment. Some revolutionaries had begun to think of Manchuria as a promising place from which to launch an anti-Ch'ing uprising. In 1907 Sung Chiao-jen had established a branch of the T'ung-meng Hui in Mukden. The sudden and unexpected revolt that erupted in Wuchang in October 1911 inspired his converts, including some young army officers, to improvise a Manchurian rising. However, Governor General Chao, a native of the region, used the troops of Chang Tso-lin, a former brigand, and the specter of foreign intervention to contain the challenge. Chang shattered the T'ung-meng Hui organization in a brief bloodbath. Throughout, Chao, who had his hands full maintaining control at home, kept aloof from the struggle going on to the south between imperial and Republican forces.[68]

In 1912 the political situation in Manchuria stabilized. But political disintegration within the new Chinese Republic put an effective frontier defense beyond hope. In the years after the revolution, Chinese authorities in Manchuria would have to accommodate themselves to an increasingly strong Japanese presence.

67. Reports from the Mukden consulate and from the Peking legation in DF 893.00/498, 525, 528.

68. Narrative accounts of the revolution in Manchuria: Li Kuang et al., *Chin-tai Tung-pei jen-min ko-ming yün-tung shih* [History of the people's revolutionary movement in modern Manchuria] (Changchun, 1960), chaps. 5–6; Ning Wu, "Tung-pei hsin-hai ko-ming chien-shu" [Brief account of the 1911 revolution in Manchuria], in *Hsin-hai ko-ming hui-i-lu* [Recollections of the 1911 revolution] (Peking, 1963), 5:536–59; Shang Ping-ho, *Hsin-jen ch'un-ch'iu* [Annals for 1911 and 1912] (Taipei reprint, 1962), ch. 23.2–4; Christie, *Thirty Years in Moukden*, pp. 258–69; and reports in DF 893.00/843, 867, 1111, 1147–48, 1166, 1265, 5409, 5420, 5427.

RETROSPECT

Manchuria was a number of things in the American imagination in the years after 1895. At the outset, Charles Denby and Edwin H. Conger dreamed of a great market traversed by railways. Brooks Adams and Albert Beveridge translated the dream into an imperative program of national action. Henry Miller occupied himself with strategems to open the Manchurian oyster to Americans and to keep it open. Manchuria was also a personal frontier that had attracted a long line of adventuresome consular' chauvinists running from Miller to Willard Straight and his associates and on to Frederick Cloud. But even those of the activists who never set foot there vicariously lived the excitement of playing for high stakes on that far frontier. The Manchuria that existed in the American imagination entered its last phase as Philander C. Knox and his State Department subordinates converted it in their own minds into a field of righteous battle where they struggled to protect the principle of the open door. However, by 1911 the battle was lost, thus ending the effort, begun in 1899 by John Hay in his simple statement of policy, to keep Manchuria open to Americans.

Americans, with the exception of a few skeptics, cast Manchuria (like the whole of China) in molds too rigid to contain the reality of the region and too dependent on American experience, preoccupations, and hopes. An ethnocentric disdain for the object of their interest caused Americans to idealize Manchuria and to overlook both difficulties and opportunities. By 1911, hopes began to give way, even among the most fervent activists, but there remained the illusion that the Chinese, not their own dreams, had failed them.

If Manchuria was lost, the rhetoric of the open door and of friendship with China associated with it survived to rise phoenix-like from the ashes of the structure built by Knox and the activists. After 1911, as before, this rhetoric nourished the assumption that the United States had a vital stake in China to protect and that the United States was committed by a compelling tradition to a sympathetic concern for the future of the Chinese and support for their country's independence. By 1913 dollar diplomacy was a burnt-out case, but the older idea of the open door still had years ahead in its evolution from a diplomatic tactic to its place as holy writ in the shrine of American foreign policy.

Throughout the late Ch'ing, colonization did the most to ensure that in the long run Manchuria would remain part of China. In 1897 the population of Manchuria was about 6 million. By the end of the dynasty the region had between 15 million and 17 million inhabitants, 90 percent of whom were Chinese.[1] For this success Chinese authorities could claim only marginal credit. After repealing the ineffective statutory prohibitions on settlement in Manchuria, they had encouraged it to the best of their limited resources. But in essence it was the natural phenomenon of populaton pressure in central and northern China which filled the uninhabited areas of Manchuria with Han Chinese.

Chinese officials in Manchuria had strained to introduce innovations in frontier defense. At the outset, in the 1890s, as the foreign threat to Manchuria grew, they had difficulty learning the lessons which the imperialist powers had to teach. Only with the arrival on the scene of imaginative leaders such as Ch'eng Te-ch'üan, Hsü Shih-ch'ang, T'ang Shao-i, and Hsi-liang was consideration given to turning foreign tricks against the foreigners. But even during the most promising period of frontier defense in 1907 and 1908, when Hsü and Yüan Shih-k'ai won the empress dowager and Prince Ch'ing to their comprehensive program, frontier defense projects made slow and scant headway. The Americans did not respond as hoped, and the emergence of factional conflicts after the dowager's death destroyed the all-important accord between leaders in Peking and Mukden on Manchurian policy. The resulting divergence in views after 1908 hobbled Hsi-liang throughout his entire tenure. The regent and his trusted ministers were frozen into inaction by financial and military weakness[2] and by the absence of American support. Thereafter, the centrifugal political trend, which became clearly evident in 1911, made futile any effort at frontier defense by Chao Erh-sun, as the Mongols in Manchuria and Inner Mongolia grew restive,[3] banditry increased,

---

1. Alexander Hosie, *Manchuria: Its People, Resources and Recent History* (London, 1904), pp. 155–56; Li Kuang et al., *Chin-tai Tung-pei jen-min ko-ming yün-tung shih* [History of the people's revolutionary movement in modern Manchuria] (Changchun, 1960), p. 158; and Ho Ping-ti, *Studies on the Population of China, 1368–1953* (Cambridge, Mass., 1959), p. 283.

2. On late Ch'ing military strength in Manchuria, see Wen Kung-chih, *Tsui-chin san-shih-nien Chung-kuo chün-shih shih* [A history of Chinese military affairs in the last thirty years] (Taipei reprint, 1962), vol. 1, pt. 2, pp. 3, 49; report by Fisher (consul, Mukden), 20 October 1911, DF 893.00/681; and report under minutes of 18 November 1907, FO 371/214.

3. Owen Lattimore, *The Mongols of Manchuria* (New York, 1934), pp. 115–16, 119–20, 124–25.

ussia and Japan grew bolder, and the other powers despaired of China's
lding Manchuria.

Despite the growing sophistication Chinese officials in Manchuria
d shown in analyzing the ills and suggesting cures for the region, they
d encountered difficulties in the capital. Policy-making there had usual-
not been preceded by any systematic planning, had often been carried
without benefit of close coordination between responsible authorities
of supervision from above, and had been slowly if at all translated into
tion. High officials in the capital were frequently unfamiliar with the
agnitude of the problem confronting the Manchurian administrations,
nappreciative of the taxing job involved in daily meeting the foreign
robings, and unsympathetic to some of the financially costly and diplo-
atically risky departures in the methods of frontier defense which these
dministrations wanted so badly to take.

The hesitations in the capital are in one sense understandable. The
atter years of the dynasty were frequently punctuated by expressions of
opular dissatisfaction with Ch'ing rule. Foreign exactions, chiefly the
Boxer indemnity, which alone ate up one-third of the central government's
uncommitted revenues, emptied China's treasury. Japan and Russia
ocked some of the bolder Chinese plans. Frontier defense was a com-
ination of domestic and foreign policies, and domestic and foreign
pressures all too often diverted the central government from a more
consistent and courageous course.

The performance in Manchuria was a disappointing contrast to Ch'ing
achievements elsewhere, for example in tearing down the German sphere
of influence in Shantung and in reclaiming China's mines and railways
from foreign control.[4] But the Chinese had to move more carefully in
Manchuria than elsewhere in China. Peking abandoned important projects like the Hsin–Fa and Chin–Ai railways and the Manchurian bank
loan out of fear of Russia's and Japan's military superiority. Forty years
would pass before the reemergence of a central government which would
be prepared to devote the nation's resources to defending Manchuria
in order to make good China's full claim to it.

During the first decade of the twentieth century, Chinese officials made

4. John E. Schrecker, *Imperialism and Chinese Nationalism: Germany in Shantung* (Cambridge,
Mass., 1971); Li En-han, "Chung-Mei shou-hui Yüeh-Han lu-ch'üan chiao-she" [Sino–American negotiations over the recovery of rights over the Hankow–Canton railroad], *Chi-k'an* [Bulletin
of the Institute of Modern History, Academia Sinica], no. 1 (1969), pp. 149–215; Arthur L. Rosenbaum, "China's First Railway, The Imperial Railways of North China, 1880–1911" (Ph.D.
diss., Yale University, 1971); and Stephen R. MacKinnon, "Liang Shih-i and the Communications Clique," *Journal of Asian Studies* 29 (May 1970): 581–602.

cooperation with the United States one of the important aspects of the
policy of frontier defense in Manchuria. They repeatedly tried to forg
diplomatic and financial links with the United States, but they wer
rebuffed every time. In 1903 Prince Ch'ing failed to interest Theodor
Roosevelt in confronting the Russians. In 1907 and 1908 Hsü Shih-ch'an
and T'ang Shao-i attempted unsuccessfully to get E. H. Harriman to inves
in China's anti-Japanese policy of development, first in the Hsin–F
railway and then in the Manchurian bank. Later, despite the professe
interest of Philander C. Knox and the American Group in similar rail
way and bank projects, Hsi-liang also failed to make any progress. In th
latter half of 1910, even the regent saw the possible benefits of closer tie
with the United States, but he likewise could not make his vision a reality
Still, after all these disappointments, Chinese officials continued througl
the crisis-filled months of 1911 to discuss and sporadically to propose ar
appeal for American support.[5]

The failure of cooperation was due in part to Chinese misunderstanding
of American policy. Chinese officials seemed to act on the premise that
the lure of profit dominated American calculations and ignored the diplomatic and other noncommercial considerations that might influence
individual and national behavior. Chinese officials concerned with Manchuria translated this bit of popular wisdom into a policy based on the
assumption that the foreigners were so eager to exploit Manchuria's
riches that China need only provide the opportunity and they would
flock to the region. When threatened first by Russia and later by Japan
as well, China attempted to take advantage of this foreign proclivity by
turning it against China's enemies. It was a specie of the old stratagem
of using barbarians to control barbarians.

Chang Chih-tung was the first to apply this formula to Manchuria.
He recognized the advantage to China of adopting the open door, a
term which he frequently used in literal translation from English. Chang
believed that if China opened up Manchuria, the increasing number and
influence of American and British merchants, supported by their governments, would quickly create a balance to the Russians. The conception
was appealing in its simplicity and economy, and, essentially unchanged,
it was taken over by Ch'eng Te-ch'üan and Chao Erh-sun.

However, China's first attempt to manipulate the commercial open door

5. See, e.g., memorial by Wu Lu-chen, 16 February 1911, WWP: Kuo-min ko-ming tang ch'i-i,
t'ing ko-sheng fang-wu an [File on the Kuomintang rising and the court's provincial defense
measures], *ts'e* 3; and memorial by Shen Jui-lin (minister to Austria), 10 July 1911, HTCC, ch.
55. 20–23.

to its own advantage did not produce the desired results. At first, it was Japan's army and navy, and not foreign trade, that broke Russia's hold on all of Manchuria. Even after the war, with Manchuria fully opened up, the open door strategy worked no better for China. By 1907 foreigners could reside and do business in no less than fifteen cities in the region and in addition had at hand a remarkably well-developed railway network on which to travel and to ship their goods. But the long-awaited commercial invasion never materialized. On the contrary, American commerce fell off, the old grouping of what Chang had considered the commercial powers fell apart, and worst of all Japan began to consolidate her influence in southern Manchuria while Russia maintained her grip in the north.

Hsü Shih-ch'ang, looking over this situation in 1907, concluded that China had not tried hard enough to draw American money and governmental influence into the region and that he would have to offer Americans attractive investment opportunities. By attempting to play on the financial as well as commercial avarice of Americans, Hsü thus substantially supplemented Chang Chih-tung's version of the open door strategy. Chinese officials acting on Hsü's new formulation proceeded to dangle the temptations of Manchuria before American eyes.

> Where will you then find a place for your surplus product and capital? Europe is not the place, for it has the same problem as you and perhaps even more serious. "New China" is the place. . . .
>
> . . . In the thousands of square miles of virgin soil in Manchuria, there is grand opportunity to employ your surplus capital, the ability of captains of the great farms in your Middle West and your good farming machines.[6]

This kind of rhetoric, no matter how effective the Chinese thought it, did not move Americans to action, and so the efforts of the Hsü administration, as those of the administrations before it, proved fruitless. His successor, Hsi-liang, acting on the same set of assumptions, maintained the open door to American financiers and merchants, but in the end he did not improve on Hsü's performance.

Hsi-liang offers the clearest example of one who made policy on the mistaken premise that the Americans were driven by greed. He knew nothing at first hand of the United States or of Americans and had had

---

6. Ch'en Chin-t'ao, address to the Republican Club of New York, May 1908, E. C. Gardner Collection, Sterling Library, Yale University.

little personal contact with foreigners. Hsi-liang's staff, moreover, could not or simply did not try to alert him to the flaws in his reasoning. Hsi-liang made matters even worse by coming to rely on Willard Straight for advice, particularly on American intentions in Manchuria. Straight's views in general confirmed Hsi-liang's mistaken assumption that Americans coveted the wealth of Manchuria and would seize any preferred opportunity to share in it. From Straight Hsi-liang learned that American merchants resented Japan's unfair competition and that the new Taft administration would help them resist it.[7] From Straight too came Hsi-liang's conviction that the United States was not only willing but also able to play a larger role in Manchuria. "The United States is financially the best situated country in the world today. Its rich businessmen are bedeviled by labor union restrictions and all think of investing in the Far East."[8] Moreover, in his exchanges with the governor general, Straight stressed the value to China of the experience of Americans in railway building, which had contributed so much to developing their frontier. "America's rise to eminence thus took no more than one hundred years," Hsi-liang observed, "and now it has no equal in wealth. It can serve as an example."[9] Finally, Straight tried to disarm any suspicions that Hsi-liang might harbor with assurances that his country had no wish to interfere in Chinese affairs. Hsi-liang thus reported confidently that each side had probed and understood the "hidden intentions" of the other and therefore they could work together with assurance.[10]

As late as November 1910 Hsi-liang was still faintly hopeful despite his lack of success in attracting Americans into Manchuria. In that month he endorsed for the last time all the assumptions which had become associated in Chinese minds with the open door.[11] Subsequently, the Wai-wu Pu, which under Na-t'ung had become skeptical of American assistance, made a sharply critical reply intended to demolish the belief that foreigners lured by greed into Manchuria might serve as a balance to Russia and Japan.

What advantage is there to opening up Manchuria since as before the only ones who will take advantage of the opportunities will be our

7. See, e.g., Hsi-liang, supplementary memorial, 12 December 1909, HLIK, 2:1008–09; and Hsiung Hsi-ling to Tsai-tse [late fall 1909], LNCYJ, 5:304–06.
8. Hsi-liang, memorial, 9 September 1910, HLIK, 2:1204–06.
9. Hsi-liang, memorial, 12 December 1909, HLIK, 2:1006–08.
10. The phrase is used in ibid.
11. Hsi-liang, memorial, 17 November 1910 (endorsing Hsiung Hsi-ling's memorial of 25 September 1910), HLIK, 2:1240–42.

neighbors and not the Americans and Europeans. . . . Thus, this proposal is not a good way of achieving a balance of power.[12]

early 1911 Peking was too disillusioned with American policy and
ukden too beset by internal unrest for either to give any more serious
ought to using the device of the open door in defending Manchuria.

China's attempt at enlisting the United States behind her banner in
anchuria ran up against American interference and insensitivity.
nese were the characteristics of the policy that the Roosevelt admini-
ration had inherited from the nineteenth century and passed on un-
ipaired to the Taft administration. Hay, Roosevelt, and Root repeatedly
monstrated a disregard for Chinese attitudes and for the impact of
eir decisions on China, as witnessed in the formulation of the open door;
e negotiations for the commercial treaty of 1903; the immigration and
ankow–Canton railway controversies of 1904–05; the period of peace-
aking after the Russo–Japanese War; the negotiations over foreign trade
nd residence in the Manchurian open ports in 1906; the Harbin dispute
f 1908; and the talks over remission of the excess Boxer indemnity. Roo-
velt and Root merit praise for their willingness to seek an accommoda-
on with Japan in the Pacific. They were correct in assuming that the
Jnited States had no important concrete interests to guard in Manchuria.
'et if Root and Roosevelt deserve praise for recognizing that Japan was
 power (and that China was not), they also deserve censure for their
ndifference to Chinese nationalism and for the legalism which, as practiced
y Root, was but a facet of ethnocentric American attitudes toward
'the lesser breeds." Sadly, few American statesmen have even matched
Theodore Roosevelt's uneven performance in East Asia.

Taft and Knox certainly did not. As insensitive to the Japanese as
o the Chinese, they replicated the flaws but not the virtues of their pre-
lecessors' Far Eastern policy. Knox and his subordinates were long
unaware of the division of opinion in the Chinese government over the
Chin–Ai project. When Knox drew up the neutralization plan, he gave no
thought to China's interests. And when he pushed his plan forward, his
only major accomplishment was to unite the powers threatening Manchuria. In the Hukuang issue, Knox proceeded full tilt against first
official and then popular opposition in China.

Chinese overtures also miscarried because of the condescension and
disdain which Americans felt for the "poor Chinks."[13] The American

12. Wai-wu Pu, Board of Finance, and Revenue Council, joint memorial, 15 January 1911,
CWS:HT, ch. 18.31–34.
13. Two essays which have stimulated my thought on this problem of American attitudes to-

response to Chinese overtures was burdened by racial stereotypes, ignorance, and misinformation; American leaders consistently eyed their Chinese opposites warily and, when approached, withdrew suspiciously.
Chinese—with the occasional exception of the Westernized ones—were
not considered by Americans their social equals. The stereotypes held
the Chinese—their fawning manners, their hesitation and delay, their
untruthfulness, and their blind devotion to traditional values—made
them contemptible to the out-and-out imperialist and caused their friends
to despair. Although Hay, Root, and Knox each professed an abstract
concern for China's welfare, their concern was always that of the superior
for the inferior. When inevitable and unforeseen differences developed,
American officials habitually resorted to intimidation as the best means
of dealing with a recalcitrant China. "Conciliation is the worst argument
to employ in dealing with her."[14]

Even Americans in China, who occasionally had to rub elbows with
the natives, were in general as suspicious and contemptuous as those in
Washington, an ocean and a continent away. Lacking geographical
barriers to hide behind, they created artificial ones. They preferred to
retreat into their closed foreign communities, which surrounded them with
the comfortably familiar aspects of home and thus served as a refuge in
which they could serve out their exile away from the strange and stubborn
natives. These Americans did not regard the distance they kept as any
particular disadvantage because they were essentially future oriented.
They had come to China not to understand it but to change it. And so
contemporary China and its great tradition were irrelevant. Change had
to come; progress, they knew, was inevitable. Inspired by contradictory
impulses—their self-appointed mission to save the Chinese and their self-
interested search for personal and national advantage—Americans thus
planned and worked with the blueprint of some imaginary China in
mind. For them China as it existed was disturbing and alien.

How much so is revealed by the contrasting American perceptions of
China and of Europe. Perceptions of Europe were generally various and
complex while those of China remained singularly uniform and shallow.
China, unlike Europe, was not a cultural world in which Americans could
easily participate and which, thereby, they could grow to appreciate or at

---

ward China are William E. Leuchtenberg, "Progressivism and Imperialism: The Progressive
Movement and American Foreign Policy, 1898–1916," *Mississippi Valley Historical Review* 39
(1952): 483–504; and Jonathan Spence, *To Change China: Western Advisers in China, 1620–1960*
(Boston, 1969).

14. P. Heintzleman (vice-consul in charge, Shanghai, thereafter assigned to the Division of
Far Eastern Affairs, and later named chargé in Peking), report of 14 August 1909, NF 5767/82.

ast understand. Many Americans were prepared by formal education
nd daily experience to move comfortably in the European milieu. There
as no comparable preparation for the traveler to China. So, even for
e few open to novel experience, the impact of the arrival was blunt and
ard.

Americans relied on rumors and speculation for their understanding of
e issues and personalities of Chinese politics. They settled for crude
bels such as "pro-Japanese" and "pro-Russian," "reactionary" and
progressive," as a substitute for detailed biographical information and
ersonal contact. Americans were sadly out of touch with the dreams of
e Chinese for the future. Cooperation between the two in the end proved
npossible because American attitudes and self-imposed isolation inhibited
n open and thoughtful response to Chinese overtures.

"A table of values hangs over every people" was the way one Westerner
escribed the human condition. He could not have otherwise more suc-
inctly or more precisely explained why China and the United States failed
o join hands in cooperation. On the face of it, there was good reason for
ach to cooperate with the other, but they had been shaped by different
istories and traditions. The inheritance of the past haunted their present,
nd, until they could in some measure exorcise it, neither could under-
tand the other. It is important, however, to note that understanding was
ot an impossible task and that some diplomats on each side did better
than others.

Such experts as W. W. Rockhill, Wu T'ing-fang, and T'ang Shao-i
did exist in the foreign services of the United States and China and were
to a degree able to explain one side to the other. But they had to operate
under a disabling occupational handicap. They had gained familiarity
with another culture by standing apart for a while from native soil and
suspending judgment. Consequently, they ran the risk of being misunder-
stood as well as maligned for having associated too much with foreigners.
Thus, on their return these experts found it difficult to communicate their
unique insights to their stay-at-home fellows, and particularly to the ultimate shapers of policy both in Peking and in Washington, who had only
a primitive knowledge of each other's country.

Strikingly, the new Chinese "barbarian tamers" appear to have done
better than their American counterparts; certainly they rose higher in
officialdom. A partial reason for the contrast is that the United States held
trump cards in dealing with China and that acting on misinformation
was not so dangerous for the United States as it was for China. In addi-

tion, American disdain for Chinese culture made that country an u
attractive object of study for Americans. Thus, whereas Chinese educat
abroad were given official preferment, American officials on the whc
wrote off familiarity with China as the marginally useful ornament of
dilettante.

But, all in all, the ideal in both the Wai-wu Pu and the State Departme
was not the foreign expert. It was, instead, the omnicompetent offici;
defined by his peculiarly narrow kind of education. In the late Ch'i
the model bureaucrat was one who had passed through the system of sta
examinations after lengthy preparation in the classics. Even though I
1905 the old examination system had collapsed altogether, those officia
who had been schooled primarily in the ancient and complex litera
tradition still dominated the upper reaches of the bureaucracy. The
were sadly lacking in sensitivity to and knowledge of foreign affairs, b
at the same time the prerequisites of a good Chinese bureaucrat and
well-bred, well-educated Chinese gentleman suited them to the tasks
diplomacy in other ways. Their sense of courtesy, attentiveness to inter
personal relations, circumspection, discretion, and ability to dissimulat
were all qualities useful to any good diplomat.

What education in the classics and a *chin-shih* were to the Chinese
a legal education and the LL. B. were to the Americans. Four lawyers–
Hay, Root, Taft, and Knox—oversaw American China policy betwee
1899 and 1911. They were assisted by other lawyers and followed by ye
a fifth and sixth, Bryan and Wilson. Their education in fact did little t
prepare them for their work and gave them no basis for understanding
alien cultures like China's. The lawyers who ran the State Departmen
tended to take a static view of diplomacy as the defense of treaties and the
writing of notes. It was no accident that policy during these years suffered
so consistently from an excess of legalism.

During the last fifteen years of the Ch'ing, Chinese attitudes toward the
United States emerged distinctly for the first time and then underwent
a remarkable evolution. In the beginning, some Chinese officials decided
that the United States was a friendly power. "Most respectful and submissive" was the antique mold in which Wu T'ing-fang cast his favorable
view of the United States. Sheng Hsüan-huai saw "that America's friendship is most genuine and that she has not the slightest aggressive intentions."[15] Chang Chih-tung, influenced by this sort of assessment, favored
an American company with the Hankow–Canton railway concession.

15. Sheng to the Wai-wu Pu, telegram, 5 July 1902, CWS:KH, ch. 159.2.

In turn, the elaborate and well-publicized attempt by the United States to reduce China's total Boxer indemnity and the open sympathy of Americans for China's difficulties during Russia's occupation of Manchuria tended to lend substance to these favorable impressions.

However, in 1904 and 1905 Chinese estimates of American intentions began to shift. In those years public opinion first awoke to the issues of discrimination and rights recovery and found itself at odds with the United States on both counts. Chinese became displeased with the influence the American government brought to bear to keep China out of the Russo–Japanese conflict and thought the United States guilty of both unwarranted interference and unwise advice. These new points of friction in Sino–American relations, when placed against the background of America's advance across the Pacific and participation in crushing the Boxers, led Chinese to paint a new picture of the United States as a growing threat to China.

> The United States in the last few years has shifted from Monroe-ism to imperialism and from agricultural operations to industrial operations. In the past several years goods for export have gradually increased. . . . Although formerly American influence in general flourished on the eastern shore of the Pacific, recently it has hastened from the eastern shore to the western shore. Thus Hawaii was occupied, the Philippines acquired, the axis of trade between the United States and Asia seized, and American influence extended to East Asia.[16]

An inherent part of this new view, bolstered by appropriate quotes from McKinley and Roosevelt, was that the dangers of overproduction were driving the Americans in search of new markets in China. Hay's enunciation of the open door, American opposition to Russian occupation of the Manchurian market, the construction of the Panama Canal, the buildup of the Pacific fleet, and interest in an American naval base on the coast of Fukien province were all specific instances which seemed to prove to Chinese that the United States had "malicious designs" in China.[17]

This new view of the United States was not influential enough at first to deter Chinese officials in Manchuria from pursuit of the obvious advan-

16. "Lun Mei-kuo tsai Chung-kuo chih chü-tung" [On the behavior of the United States in China], *Ching-chung pao* [The tocsin], 25 September 1904. See also in the same paper "Lun T'ai-p'ing-yang lieh-ch'iang chih shih-li" [On the influence of the powers in the Pacific], 19 August 1904; and "Lun Jih-O i-ho hou chih Chung-kuo wai-chiao" [On Chinese diplomacy after the Russo–Japanese peace negotiations], *Shih pao* [Times], 4 November 1905.

17. Hsü Nai-lin, *Chou-pien ch'u-yen* [Plain talk on managing the frontier] (Taipei reprint, 1969), ch. 4.29, written shortly after the Russo–Japanese War.

tages of cooperation, but the cool reception given T'ang Shao-i in Washington and the haggling over the terms of the remission of the excess American Boxer indemnity must have caused some to pause and ponder. Although Hsi-liang embraced the cooperative policy, ministers in Peking by 1909 were beginning to have doubts. Even those officials formerly in favor of cooperation, like Wu T'ing-fang and Hsü Shih-ch'ang, were growing wary of America's expansionist tendencies and search for new markets at China's expense.[18]

From the Chinese point of view, American policy became decidedly more wayward once Knox took office. The results in China were official disillusionment and popular resentment. Knox's intervention in the Hukuang loan dismayed proponents of the loan by forcing them to defy the European bankers and by keeping the issue in the public eye.[19] Opponents of the loan accused the United States of working hand in glove with the other major powers to extract concessions from China.[20] Throughout, the secretary of state discounted the importance of the tempest he had helped to stir up. "The plea of provincial opposition [is] worn threadbare and fails to carry conviction" was Knox's injudicious assessment on the eve of the revolution.[21] American consuls on the scene were no more disturbed than Knox, even as the agitation by "riff-raff," "a disgruntled few," and "a small minority" built up toward the October outbreak against the dynasty.[22]

The currency loan, on which negotiations were opened in 1910, also served to broaden the anti-American front and put the already unsteady central government under greater popular pressure. The press and even moderate reformers announced opposition to their government's signing the new loan, which, they charged, meant foreign interference in China's financial affairs.[23] The newly inaugurated Senate in Peking translated general discontent into the specific demand that Tsai-tse not concede any powers to a foreign financial adviser, as the United States wished. Officials in the capital were, moreover, alarmed by the prospect of the United

18. See, e.g., Wu T'ing-fang to the Wai-wu Pu, 18 September 1909, CWS:HT, ch. 9.18; and Hsü Shih-ch'ang, *Ou-chan hou chih Chung-kuo* [China after the European war] (Taipei reprint, 1966), pp. 103–104.

19. Notes to the Wai-wu Pu in CWS:HT, ch. 13.1–4; 15.46–47; 16.39–40; 17.38–40; 18.9–10.

20. See, e.g., *Chung-yang ta-t'ung jih-pao* [Central daily news], 24 and 27 July 1909; and *Kuo-pao*, [National news], 23 and 25 July 1909.

21. Knox to the Peking legation, telegram, 14 April 1911, DF 893.51/385A.

22. Consular reports from Chungking, July 1911, in DF 893.77/1152–53.

23. "Ts'ang-chiang" [Liang Ch'i-ch'ao], "Wu-hu hsin-wai-chai ching-ch'eng" [Alas, the new foreign loan is finally concluded!], *Kuo-feng pao* [National spirit], 19 April 1911, pp. 59–61; and press opinion summarized by the French legation in Peking (Margerie to Pichon, 23 November 1910, Min. Aff. Et., Chine, NS 378).

States's joining with the other powers in order to create a "bankers' ring" to monopolize China's foreign loans. The same Sheng Hsüan-huai who a few years before had praised the United States for its friendship was now troubled by doubts about American intentions, and Liang Tun-yen, an American-educated official, was equally upset by the new departures in American policy. Carrying the burden of protest, Liang at first indirectly and finally personally informed Knox, with unaccustomed bluntness for a Chinese official, of his government's concern.[24] Typically, Knox responded by professing puzzlement at "Chinese inconsistency in begging for co-operation between powers for her protection and protesting against the most effective means to insure such protection."[25]

Thus, by the close of the Ch'ing, the image of the Unitee States had changed. The Chinese began to fit the United States into their emerging picture of a Darwinian international environment in which the strong ground down the weak. In their view the United States had shown itself an expansionist power, bent on avoiding a glut in the home market by acquiring a commercial empire in the Pacific to absorb excess capital and production. American treatment of the "lesser breeds," Chinese as well as Filipino and Cuban, fed the Chinese anxiety over the specter of a "white peril" and even of ultimate racial extinction for the Han.

The issue of imperialism by 1911 brought to the fore the ultimately irreconcilable differences which had always separated Chinese and American policies and which accounted for the failure of cooperation between the two countries in Manchuria.

24. The views of Chinese officials were relayed in Fletcher to Knox, 19 June 1909, NF 5315/412; E. T. Williams, memos, 6 December 1910 and 4 February 1911, DF 893.51/1404 and 1410; Calhoun to Knox, 19 December 1910, DF 893.51/292; and Heintzleman (chargé, Peking) to Knox, telegram, 5 August 1911, DF 893.51/525.
25. Knox, jotting [October 1910], Knox Papers, Manuscript Division, Library of Congress.

"THE GREAT GAME" IN CHINA: WILLARD STRAIGHT AND THE HISTORIANS

It is strange that at a time when students of American China policy have stressed the themes of cultural incomprehension, diplomatic naïveté, and commercial miscalculation, they have allowed Willard Straight to escape unscathed.[1] Although he was clearly guilty of all these failings, historians have been reluctant to indict him, so taken have they been by the romance of his years in China. As a result, the Straight legend seems as safe today as when it sprung up shortly after his death in France at the end of World War I.

Herbert Croly in his study simply titled *Willard Straight* (New York, 1924) was the first to put the legend between book covers.[2] The young American who "played the game" in the Far East, often against impossible odds, and who later supported the progressive cause at home by financing *The New Republic* naturally appealed to Croly. As a student of international affairs, he shared Straight's aspirations and attitudes. Croly considered China second in importance only to the Western hemisphere as an arena for American activity and looked ahead confidently to that country's "industrial and political awakening."[3] He, like Straight, feared that Japan would play the spoiler and predicted that the United States might in response become long and deeply engaged in China's defense.[4] There was a second reason for the biography. At the end of World War I, Croly had become interested in personality development and in the

1. On these themes, see respectively: Stuart C. Miller, *The Unwelcome Immigrant: The American Image of the Chinese, 1785–1882* (Berkeley, Calif., 1969); Jonathan Spence, *To Change China: Western Advisers in China, 1620–1960* (Boston, 1969); Gunther Barth, *Bitter Strength: A History of the Chinese in the United States, 1850–1870* (Cambridge, Mass., 1964); Marilyn B. Young, *The Rhetoric of Empire: American China Policy 1895–1901* (Cambridge, Mass., 1968), and Tang Tsou, *America's Failure in China, 1941–50* (Chicago, 1963); and Paul A. Varg, *The Making of a Myth: The United States and China, 1897–1912* (East Lansing, Mich., 1968).

2. An account of Straight, "American in Asia," by Louis Graves did appear in serial in 1920 and 1921 in *Asia*, vols. 20 and 21. The series, consisting essentially of lengthy excerpts from Straight's dairy and correspondence, had no substantial historiographical impact.

3. *The Promise of American Life* (New York, 1909), p. 309.

4. Ibid., pp. 309–10.

relation between individual growth and society.[5] Straight's death in 1918 came at a fortuitous moment. Here was a full and finished life, documented by the colorful and carefully kept papers of a man whom Croly had known personally, through which he could trace the dual themes of self-development and of practical idealism in international affairs.

The vitality of the Straight legend owes much to Croly's skillfully told story, which has had either directly or indirectly an enormous historiographical influence. Students of American foreign policy have long used Croly's *Straight* as a reliable guide—all the more valued for its literary art—through the complexities of American and Chinese policy. The first to fall under his influence was A. Whitney Griswold, who wove Straight's story and Croly's judgments into the fabric of *The Far Eastern Policy of the United States* (New York, 1938). Griswold took at face value Croly's estimation that "Willard Straight had contributed more than any other single man" to financial diplomacy in China[6] and so made Straight over into the chief theoretician and practitioner of dollar diplomacy in China.

> Not only had Straight paved the way for an American challenge to Japanese financial supremacy in Manchuria; he had actually committed the United States to a contest over the European financial monopolies in China proper. . . . Taft and Knox remained to preside over the diplomatic program that he, more than any other single individual, had helped to inaugurate.[7]

Those who have followed in Croly's and Griswold's tracks have treated Straight generously. The most egregious examples of works based on the premise that Straight is the key to understanding American China policy are by Charles Vevier and Helen Dodson Kahn.[8] But other works by historians of the foreign policy of the Roosevelt and Taft administrations[9]

5. George Soule, "Herbert Croly's Liberalism 1920–1928," *The New Republic* 63 (16 July 1930): 253–57.

6. *Willard Straight*, pp. 452–53.

7. *The Far Eastern Policy of the United States*, p. 143.

8. Charles Vevier, *The United States and China, 1906–1913* (New Brunswick, N. J., 1955); and Helen Dodson Kahn, "The Great Game of Empire: Willard Straight and American Far Eastern Policy" (Ph.D. diss., Cornell University, 1968). See also in the same vein the less ambitious dissertations by Leon McKinley Bower, "Willard D. Straight and the American Policy in China" (Ph.D. diss., University of Colorado, 1954); and Gloria E. Blazsik, "Theodore Roosevelt's Far Eastern Policy and the T'ang Shao-i Mission" (Ph.D. diss., Georgetown University, 1969).

9. E.g., Raymond A. Esthus, *Theodore Roosevelt and Japan* (Seattle, Wash., 1966), chap. 14, and his "The Changing Concept of the Open Door 1899–1910," *Mississippi Valley Historical Review* 46 (1959): 435–36; William E. Leuchtenberg, "Progressivism and Imperialism: The Progressive Movement and American Foreign Policy, 1898–1916," ibid. 39 (1952): 490; Paul A. Varg, *The Making of a Myth* (East Lansing, Mich., 1968), pp. 52–53, 112, 129; Edward H. Zabriskie, *American–Russian Rivalry in the Far East: A Study in Diplomacy and Power Politics, 1895–*

and by biographers of Straight's contemporaries[10] have given Straight nearly as prominent a place. Even studies in English on Chinese relations with the United States[11] and on the Chinese side of the Manchurian problem[12] have incorporated this standard view of Straight and have as a matter of convenience refracted United States policy through him. The pervasiveness of the Straight legend reaches ludicrous proportions when it pops up in Chinese accounts. It has filtered down into studies from Taiwan and from the mainland on Chinese foreign policy and Sino–American relations[13] and even into one recent Chinese history of modern Manchuria.[14] In these latter cases, some authors have simply borrowed uncritically from American sources while others, of a Marxist–Leninist persuasion, have seized on Straight as an archetypal imperialist agent in the service of finance capital.

Why has Straight had such perennial and universal appeal as an historical character? To a great degree the explanation lies in the archival trap which Straight carefully put together during his lifetime. The ampleness of his papers—indeed voluminous for one whose life was so short—and the obvious pains which he took to make them a full and enduring record are testimony of their importance to him. During his years in East Asia he meticulously preserved his correspondence and industriously recorded his activities and views in his diary. The collection, which grew year by year, was an extension of his personality. Straight was deficient in self-esteem and inordinately sensitive to the impression he made on others. At the same time he was ambitious and wished to make his mark on his time. These related preoccupations drove Straight to strike those poses which he calculated would appeal to his audience, whether in the

---

1914 (Philadelphia, 1946), chaps. 6–7; and Jerry Israel, *Progressivism and the Open Door: America and China, 1905–1921* (Pittsburgh, 1971), chaps. 2–3.

10. E.g., Paul A. Varg, *Open Door Diplomat: The Life of W. W. Rockhill* (Urbana, Ill., 1952), pp. 99, 101; Paige E. Mulhollan, "Philander C. Knox and Dollar Diplomacy, 1909–1913" (Ph. D. diss., University of Texas, 1966), chap. 6; and Henry F. Pringle, *The Life and Times of William Howard Taft* (New York, 1939), pp. 681, 687.

11. E.g., Akira Iriye, *Across the Pacific: An Inner History of American–East Asian Relations* (New York, 1967), p. 122; and Thomas E. LaFargue, *China'e First Hundred* (Pullman, Wash., 1942), pp. 119–20.

12. E.g., Robert L. Irick, "The Chinchow–Aigun Railroad and the Knox Neutralization Plan in Ch'ing Diplomacy," *Papers on China* 13 (1959): 80–112; and E-tu Zen Sun, "Plans for the Northeastern Provinces," chap. 6 in her *Chinese Railways and British Interests, 1898–1911* (New York, 1954).

13. E.g., Huang Cheng-ming, *Chung-kuo wai-chiao shih* [History of China's foreign relations] (Taipei, 1959), pp. 238–44; and the essays in Sun Yü-t'ang et al., *Mei-ti-kuo chu-i ching-chi ch'in-Hua shih lun-ts'ung* [Collected articles on the history of American imperialist economic agression against China] (Peking, 1953).

14. Li Kuang et al., *Chin-tai Tung-pei jen-min ko-ming yün-tung shih* [History of the people's revolutionary movement in Manchuria] (Changchun, 1960), pp. 155–56.

present or in the future. His papers served him as a record of his personal progress and adventures in meeting the opportunities and trials of "the great game." He kept his papers both to bolster his self-esteem during his lifetime and to give him immortality in the minds of posterity after his death.

By happenstance, this archival trap has marvelously survived the tests of time, and unsuspecting historians, finding it as inviting as Croly did, have one after the other fallen in.[15] The Straight Papers owe much of their enduring attraction to the absence of other private collections which can match them for sheer volume of material on China policy. The personal papers for many of those with whom Straight was associated are either slim or not yet open to the public. Papers for E. H. Harriman and J. P. Morgan, for example, are not available, if they exist. Those for Elihu Root, Jacob Schiff, Huntington Wilson, Henry Fletcher, and William Phillips are disappointingly slim. Even the papers of Philander C. Knox, William Howard Taft, and Theodore Roosevelt cannot match Straight's in volume and vividness. Only the papers in the State Department archives are richer than Straight's on American China policy in these years. Use of the relevant primary Chinese source material has been beyond the ability of most. Historians as a result have continued to rely on Straight for an insight into many of the public events of his time.

The Straight Papers are undeniably an excellent source for the adventures of young Straight, particularly as he saw them with all their Horatio Alger overtones. But as a general historical source they have led scholars to some unfortunate judgments. Historians relying on these papers have unwittingly taken as their own Straight's ethnocentric attitudes toward the Chinese and his egocentric appraisal of his own importance in American foreign policy. They have treated Straight as a leading man rather than as what in fact he was, a personage of the second rank employed as the financial agent and middleman for the shapers of policy. Historians thus have tended to mistake the shadow for the substance, the effect for the cause. In particular, his contributions to the theory and practice of dollar diplomacy have been consistently overestimated. Straight did not invent dollar diplomacy. American publicists were already discussing its essential tenets about the time he reached China in 1902. Straight was not alone in urging the new directions in China policy. A number of figures of approximately equal stature both in the State Department and in the foreign service in China had worked either before him or side by

15. The Straight family gave the papers to Cornell University, his alma mater, in 1953. They are now housed in the John M. Olin Library there.

side with him for a forward policy. Above all others, Huntington Wilson contributed to its consummation under Knox and exercised an overall influence far surpassing Straight's.

The impact of the Straight legend on American interpretations of Chinese and Japanese policy has been deleterious. Most historians, Chinese as well as American, have shared Croly's impatience with those people who, in his words, were "incapable of efficient national organization"[16] and like Croly have given the Ch'ing dynasty short shrift. Straight's papers, which have conveniently seemed to offer answers to all the questions of who and why in Manchuria, have reinforced this tendency. As a consequence, Straight has overshadowed Chinese policy initiatives and obscured Chinese attitudes toward the United States. Historians have therefore incorporated the stereotype of passive and grateful Chinese and endorsed, at least implicitly, Straight's faith in energy and enthusiasm as substitutes for understanding. In relation to the Japanese, Straight has been pictured as a righteous crusader for the ideals of the open door against Tokyo's Machiavellian schemes. One would think it unnecessary to say, if historiographical facts did not offer such plain evidence to the contrary, that Straight's japanophobia has helped distort American views of Japan's intentions in Manchuria.

Historians impressed by Straight's purpose and flair for the dramatic have treated him too kindly. Much of the romance surrounding him, when examined closely, seems shoddy play-acting. Straight was an ambitious hustler, a consular chauvinist, and an opportunistic adventurer. His observations were generally not acute. He was self-deceived on such critical points as the Chinese attitude toward the United States, the American commercial and financial future in Manchuria, and the foreign policy of other interested powers. His grandiose hopes were never so near to success as he—and his historians-admirers—have dreamed. His greatest success, one he was never to enjoy personally, was in convincing them to put in his hands posthumously the power and influence that he never managed to hold in real life.

16. *The Promise of American Life,* p. 308.

Chang Chih-tung 張之洞
Chang Hsün 張勳
Chang Po-hsi 張百熙
Chang-shun 長順
Chang Tso-lin 張作霖
Chang Yin-huan 張蔭桓
Chang Yin-t'ang 張蔭棠
Chao Ch'i-lin 趙啓霖
Chao Erh-sun 趙爾巽
Ch'en Chao-ch'ang 陳昭常
Ch'en Chen-hsin 陳振先
Ch'en Chin-t'ao 陳錦濤
Ch'en K'uei-lung 陳夔龍
Cheng Hsiao-hsü 鄭孝胥
Ch'eng-hsün 誠勳
Ch'eng Te-ch'üan 程德全
Ch'ien Neng-hsün 錢能訓
Chin-ch'ang 晉昌
chin-fei 金匭
chin-shih 進士
Chou Ch'ang-ling 周長齡
Chou Shu-mo 周樹模
Chou Tzu-ch'i 周自齊
Chu Ch'i-ch'ien 朱啓鈐
Chu Pao-k'uei 朱寶奎
Chu Tzu-wen 朱子文
Ch'ü Hung-ch'i 瞿鴻禨
Empress Dowager Tz'u-hsi (Tz'u-hsi
　Huang t'ai-hou) 慈禧皇太后
Hsi-liang 錫良
Hsieh Hsi-ch'üan 謝希銓
hsien 閞
hsiu-ts'ai 秀才
Hsiung Hsi-ling 熊希齡
Hsü Chüeh 許珏
Hsü Nai-lin 徐鼐霖
Hsü Shih-ch'ang 徐世昌
Hsü Shih-ying 徐世英
Hü Wei-te 胡惟德
Huang K'ai-wen 黃開文
hunghutzu 紅鬍子

Jung Hung 容閎
Jung-lu 榮祿
K'ang Yu-wei 康有爲
Kao Erh-lien 高爾謙
Li Hung-chang 李鴻章
Li Ping-heng 李秉衡
Li Sheng-to 李盛鐸
Liang Ch'eng 梁誠
Liang Ch'i-ch'ao 梁啓超
Liang Ju-hao 梁如浩
Liang Tun-yen 梁敦彥
Lien-fang 聯芳
Lin Shao-nien 林紹年
Liu K'un-i 劉坤一
Liu Shu-t'ang 劉樹棠
Liu Yü-lin 劉玉麟
Lu Ch'uan-lin 鹿傳霖
Lu Pao-chung 陸寶忠
Lu Shu-fan 陸樹藩
Lu Tsung-hsing 陸宗輿
Lü Hai-huan 呂海寰
Ma Hsiang-po 馬相伯
Meng En-yüan 孟恩遠
Na-t'ung 那桐
Ni Ssu-chung 倪嗣冲
pai-lien chiao 白蓮敎
Prince Ch'ing I-k'uang (Ch'ing
　ch'in-wang I-k'uang) 慶親王奕劻
Prince Ch'un I-huan (Ch'un
　ch'in-wang I-huan) 醇親王奕譞
Prince Ch'un Tsai-feng (Ch'un
　ch'in-wang Tsai-feng) 醇親王載灃
Prince Kung I-hsin (Kung ch'in-wang
　I-hsin) 恭親王奕訢
Sa Pao 薩保
Sa Yin-t'u 薩蔭圖
Shen Jui-lin 沈瑞麟
Sheng Hsüan-huai 盛宣懷
Shih Chao-chi 施肇基
Shih-hsü 世續
Shou-shan 壽山

265

Sun Chia-nai 孫家鼐
Sun Pao-ch'i 孫寶琦
Sung Chiao-jen 宋教仁
Ta-kuei 達桂
T'ang Shao-i 唐紹儀 (怡)
tao-t'ai 道台
Teng Pang-shu 鄧邦述
T'ieh-liang 鐵良
Ting Chen-to 丁振鐸
Tsai-chen 載振
Tsai-t'ao 載濤
Tsai-tse 載澤
Ts'ang-chiang 滄江
Ts'ao Ju-lin 曹汝霖
Ts'ao K'un 曹錕
Ts'en Ch'un-hsüan 岑春煊

Tseng Chi-tse 曾紀澤
Tseng-ch'i 增祺
Tsou Chia-lai 鄒嘉來
Tuan Chih-kuei 段芝貴
tzu-k'ai 自開
Wang Chih-ch'un 王之春
Wei Ch'en-tsu 魏宸組
Wei Kuang-tao 魏光燾
Wu Chen-lin 吳振麟
Wu Lu-chen 吳祿貞
Wu T'ing-fang 伍廷芳
Yang Ju 楊儒
Yang Shu 楊樞
Yüan K'o-ting 袁克定
Yüan Shih-k'ai 袁世凱
yüeh-k'ai 約開

SELECTED BIBLIOGRAPHY

CHINESE LANGUAGE SOURCES

Manuscript and printed primary sources

A Ying 阿英 [Ch'ien Hsing-ts'un 錢杏邨], comp. *Fan-Mei Hua-kung chin-yüeh wen-hsüeh chi* 反美華工禁約文學集 [Collected literature on opposition to the American treaty excluding Chinese laborers]. Peking, 1960.

Board of Posts and Ministry of Communications, comps. *Yu-ch'uan Pu tsou-i* 郵傳部奏議 [Memorials by the Board of Posts]. Taipei reprint, 1967.

Chang Chih-tung. *Chang Wen-hsiang-kung ch'üan-chi* 張文襄公全集 [Collected works of Chang Chih-tung]. Compiled by Wang Shu-t'ung 王樹枏. Peking, 1928.

Ch'eng Te-ch'üan. *Ch'eng chiang-chun shou-chiang tsou-kao* 程將軍守江奏稿 [Memorials on Military Governor Ch'eng's defense of Heilungkiang]. Taipei reprint, 1968.

China. Records of the Wai-wu Pu. Diplomatic Archives, Institute of Modern History, Academia Sinica, Nankang, Taipei, Taiwan.

Chou Shu-mo. *Chou chung-ch'eng fu-chiang tsou-kao* 周中丞撫江奏稿 [Memorials of Governor Chou of Heilungkiang]. Taipei reprint, 1968.

Chu Shih-chia 朱士嘉, comp. *Mei-kuo p'o-hai Hua-kung shih-liao* 美國迫害華工史料 [Historical materials on American oppression of Chinese laborers]. Peking, 1959.

Chu Shou-p'eng 朱壽朋, comp. *Kuang-hsü ch'ao Tung-hua hsü-lu* 光緒朝東華續錄 [Supplement to the Tung-hua records for the Kuang-hsü reign]. Taipei reprint, 1963.

Hsi-liang. *Hsi-liang i-kao tsou-kao* 錫良遺稿奏稿 [Collected papers of Hsi-liang: memorials]. Compiled by the Third Institute of History, Chinese Academy of Sciences. Peking, 1959.

Hsü Shih-ch'ang. *T'ui-keng t'ang cheng-shu* 退耕棠政書 [Collected official papers of Hsü Shih-ch'ang]. Taipei reprint, 1968.

————. *Tung-san-sheng cheng-lüeh* 東三省政略 [Administration of the three eastern provinces]. Taipei reprint, 1965.

Institute of Modern History, Academia Sinica, comp. *K'uang-wu tang* 礦務檔 [Records on mining affairs]. Taipei, 1960.

National Palace Museum, comp. *Chung-Jih chiao-she shih-liao* 中日交涉史料 [Historical materials on Sino–Japanese negotiations]. Peking, 1932 and 1933.

Sheng Hsüan-huai. *Yü-chai ts'un-kao* 愚齋存稿 [Collected papers of Sheng Hsüan-huai]. Taipei reprint, 1968.

Ta-Ch'ing Hsüan-t'ung cheng-chi 大清宣統政紀 [Political records of the Hsüan-t'ung reign]. Manchuria, 1937.

Ta-Ch'ing li-ch'ao shih-lu 大清歷朝實錄 [Veritable records of successive reigns of the Ch'ing dynasty]. Manchuria, 1937.

Wang Liang 王亮, comp. *Hsi-hsün ta-shih chi* 西巡大事記 [Journal of the western inspection trip]. Published as a supplement to Wang Yen-wei and Wang Liang, *Ch'ing-chi wai-chiao shih-liao*. Peking, 1935.

Wang Yen-wei 王彦威 and Wang Liang, eds. *Ch'ing-chi wai-chiao shih-liao* 清季外交史料 [Historical materials on late Ch'ing diplomacy]. Peking, 1935.

Wang Yün-sheng 王芸生. *Liu-shih nien-lai Chung-kuo yü Jih-pen* 六十年來中國與日本 [China and Japan in the last sixty years]. Tientsin, 1932–34.

Yüan Shih-k'ai. *Yang-shou-yüan tsou-i chi-yao* 養壽園奏議輯要 [Selected memorials of Yüan Shih-k'ai]. Compiled by Shen Tsu-hsien 沈祖憲. Taipei reprint, 1966.

Memoirs and contemporary accounts

Ning Wu 宁武. "Tung-pei hsin-hai ko-ming chien-shu" 東北辛亥革命簡述 [Brief account of the 1911 revolution in Manchuria], in *Hsin-hai ko-ming hui-i-lu* 辛亥革命回憶錄 [Recollections of the 1911 revolution], vol. 5, pp. 536–59. Peking, 1963.

Shen Tsu-hsien 沈祖憲 and Wu Kan-sheng 吳闓生, comps. *Jung-an ti-tzu chi* 容庵弟子記 [A record by the disciples of Yüan shih-k'ai]. Taipei reprint, 1966.

Ts'ao Ju-lin. "I-sheng chih hui-i" 一生之回憶 [Recollections of a life]. *Ch'un-ch'iu tsa-chih* 春秋雜誌 [Spring and autumn magazine], nos. 156–62 (1964).

Ts'en Ch'un-hsüan. *Lo-chai man-pi* 樂齋漫筆 [Random notes from the studio of Lo]. Taipei reprint, 1962.

Secondary works

Chang Jo-ku 張若谷. *Ma Hsiang-po hsien-sheng nien-p'u* 馬相伯先生年譜 [A chronological biography of Mr. Ma Hsiang-po]. Changsha, 1939.

Chang Ts'un-wu 張存武. *Kuang-hsü sa-i-nien Chung-Mei kung-yüeh feng-ch'ao* 光緒卅一年中美工約風潮 [Public upheaval in 1905 over the Sino–American labor treaty]. Taipei, 1966.

Ching-min 警民 [pseud.]. *Hsü Shih-ch'ang* 徐世昌 [Biography of Hsü Shih-ch'ang]. Canton and Hong Kong, 1922.

Fei Hsing-chien 費行簡. *Chin-tai ming-jen hsiao-chuan* 近代名人小傳 [Sketches of famous men of modern times]. Taipei reprint, 1968.

Fu Ch'i-hsüeh 傅啓學. *Chung-kuo wai-chiao shih* 中國外交史 [History of China's foreign relations]. Taipei, 1966.

Hsü T'ung-hsin 許同莘. *Chang Wen-hsiang-kung nien-p'u* 張文襄公年譜 [A chronological biography of Chang Chih-tung]. Taipei reprint, 1969.

Huang Cheng-ming 黃正名. *Chung-kuo wai-chiao shih* 中國外交史 [History of China's foreign relations]. Taipei, 1959.

Huang Chia-mu 黃嘉謨. *Mei-kuo yü T'ai-wan* 美國與臺灣 [The United States and Taiwan]. Taipei, 1966.

Ko Kung-chen 戈公振. *Chung-kuo pao-hsüeh shih* 中國報學史 [A history of Chinese journalism]. Shanghai, 1927.

Kuo T'ing-yee 郭廷以. "Tung-pei ti k'ai-t'o" 東北的開拓 [The opening of the Northeast], in Ling Shun-sheng 凌純聲, ed. *Pien-chiang wen-hua lun-chi* 邊疆文化論集 [Collected essays on frontier culture], vol. 1, pp. 38–56. Taipei, 1953.

Li En-han 李恩涵. "Chung-Mei shou-hui Yüeh-Han lu-ch'üan chiao-she" 中美收回粵漢路權交涉 [Sino–American negotiations over the recovery of rights over the Hankow–Canton railroad]. *Chi-k'an* 集刊 [Bulletin of the Institute of Modern History, Academia Sinica], no. 1 (1969), pp. 149–215.

Li Kuang 黎光 et al. *Chin-tai Tung-pei jen-min ko-ming yün-tung shih* 近代東北人民革命運動史 [History of the people's revolutionary movement in modern Manchuria]. Changchun, 1960.

Li Kuo-ch'i 李國祁. *Chung-kuo tsao-ch'i ti t'ieh-lu ching-ying* 中國早期的鐵路經營 [Early railway enterprise in China]. Taipei, 1961.

Liu Ta-nien 劉大年. *Mei-kuo ch'in-Hua shih* 美國侵華史 [History of American aggression against China]. Peking, 1951.

Liu Yen 劉彥. *Chung-kuo wai-chiao shih* 中國外交史 [History of China's foreign relations]. Taipei, 1962.

Shen Yün-lung 沈雲龍. *Hsien-tai cheng-chih jen-wu shu-p'ing* 現代政治人物述評 [Collected articles on leading political figures of contemporary China]. Taipei, 1966.

_____. "Hsü Shih-ch'ang p'ing-chuan" 徐世昌評傳 [A critical biography of Hsü Shih-ch'ang]. *Chuan-chi wen-hsüeh* 傳記文學 [Biographical literature] 13, no. 1 (July 1968) through 14, no. 6 (June 1969).

Sun Yü-t'ang 孫毓棠 et al. *Mei-ti-kuo chu-i ching-chi ch'in-Hua shih lun-ts'ung* 美帝國主義經濟侵華史論叢 [Collected articles on the history of American imperialist economic aggression against China]. Peking, 1953.

T'ao Chü-yin 陶菊隱. *Mei-kuo ch'in-Hua shih-liao* 美國侵華史料 [Historical materials on American aggression against China]. Shanghai, 1951.

Ts'en Hsüeh-lü 岑學呂. *San-shui Liang Yen-sun hsien-sheng nien-p'u* 三水梁燕孫先生年譜 [A chronological biography of Mr. Liang Yen-sun (Shih-i) of San-shui]. Taipei reprint, 1962.

Wang I-nien 汪詒年. *Wang Jang-ch'ing hsien-sheng chuan-chi* 汪穰卿先生傳記 [A biography of Mr. Wang Jang-ch'ing (K'ang-nien)]. n.p., 1938.

Wang Shu-hwai 王樹槐. *Wai-jen yü wu-hsü pien-fa* 外人與戊戌變法 [Foreigners and the reform movement of 1898]. Taipei, 1965.

Wu T'ing-kuang 伍廷光. *Wu T'ing-fang li-shih* 伍廷芳歷史 [A history of Wu T'ing-fang]. Shanghai, 1922

WESTERN LANGUAGE SOURCES

Manuscript and printed primary sources

Butt, Archie. *Taft and Roosevelt: The Intimate Letters of Archie Butt, Military Aide.* Garden City, New York, 1930.

France. Archives of the French Ministry of Foreign Affairs. Paris.

Great Britain. Records of the British Foreign Office. Public Records Office, London. By permission of the Controller of H. M. Stationery Office.

Houghton Library, Harvard University, Cambridge, Mass. Papers of William Woodville Rockhill. By permission of Harvard College Library.

Lodge, Henry Cabot. *Selections from the Correspondence of Theodore Roosevelt and Henry Cabot Lodge, 1884–1918.* New York, 1925.

MacMurray, John V. A., ed. *Treaties and Agreements with and Concerning China, 1894–1919.* Vol. 1: *Manchu Period (1894–1911).* New York, 1921.

Morison, Elting E. et al., eds. *The Letters of Theodore Roosevelt.* Cambridge, Mass., 1951–54.

Myrin Library, Ursinus College, Collegeville, Pa. Papers of Francis M. Huntington Wilson.

Olin Library, Cornell University, Ithaca, New York. Papers of Willard Dickerman Straight.

Thayer, William R. *The Life and Letters of John Hay.* London, 1915.

U. S. Department of State. Record Groups 59 and 84 (records of the State Department and of its foreign service posts). National Archives, Washington, D. C.

U.S. Department of State. *Papers Relating to the Foreign Relations of the United States.* Yearly series (1895–1913). Washington, D.C.

U.S. Library of Congress, Manuscript Division, Washington, D.C. Papers of Henry D. Fletcher, John Hay, Philander C. Knox, Whitelaw Reid, Theodore Roosevelt, Elihu Root, and William Howard Taft.

Memoirs and contemporary accounts

Adams, Brooks. *America's Economic Supremacy.* New York, 1900.

Beveridge, Albert J. *The Russian Advance.* New York, 1904.

Bland, J. O. P. *Recent Events and Present Policies in China.* Philadelphia, 1912.

Bland, J. O. P. and Edmund Backhouse. *China under the Empress Dowager.* London, 1911.

Christie, Dugald. *Thirty Years in Moukden 1883–1913.* New York, 1914.

Conant, Charles A. *The United States in the Orient: The Nature of the Economic Problem.* New York, 1900.

Denby, Charles. *China and Her People.* Boston, 1906.

Einstein, Lewis. *A Diplomat Looks Back.* New Haven, Conn., 1968.

Hosie, Alexander. *Manchuria; Its People, Resources and Recent History.* London, 1904.

Inglis, J. W. "Moukden in 1911." *Chinese Recorder and Missionary Journal* 42 (July 1911): 393–98.

Kuropatkin, Alexei N. *The Russian Army and the Japanese War.* Translated by A. B. Lindsay and edited by E. D. Swinton. New York, 1909.

Mahan, Alfred Thayer. "Effects of Asiatic Conditions upon International Policies." *North American Review* 171 (November 1900): 609–26.

Martin, W. A. P. "A Trip to Manchuria." *Chinese Recorder and Missionary Journal* 39 (January 1908): 55–56.

Millard, Thomas F. *America and the Far Eastern Question.* New York, 1909.

———. *The New Far East.* New York, 1906.

Miller, Henry B. "Notes on Manchuria." *National Geographic Magazine* 15 (1904): 261–62.

———. "Russian Development of Manchuria." *National Geographic Magazine* 15 (1904): 113–27.

Parsons, William B. *An American Engineer in China.* New York, 1900.

Phillips, William. *Ventures in Diplomacy.* Portland, Maine, 1952.

Robertson, Daniel T. *The Story of Our Mission in Manchuria.* Edinburgh, Scotland, 1913.

Rockhill, William W. "The United States and the Future of China." *The Forum* 29 (May 1900): 324–31.

Rosen, Roman. *Forty Years of Diplomacy.* London, 1922.

Ross, John. *Mission Methods in Manchuria.* London, 1908.

Smith, Arthur H. *China and America To-day: A Study of Conditions and Relations.* New York, 1907.

———. *Chinese Characteristics.* Shanghai, 1890.

Strong, Josiah. *Expansion under New World Conditions.* New York, 1900.

Sze, Sao-ke Alfred [Shih Chao-chi]. *Reminiscences of His Early Years.* Translated by Amy C. Wu. Washington, D. C., 1962.

Whigham, Henry J. *Manchuria and Korea.* New York, 1904.

Wilson, Francis M. Huntington. *Memoirs of an Ex-Diplomatist.* Boston, 1945.

Witte, Sergei. *The Memoirs of Count Witte.* Translated and edited by Abraham Yarmolinsky. Garden City, New York, 1921.

Wu T'ing-fang. *America Through the Spectacles of an Oriental Diplomat.* New York, 1914.

Secondary works

Bailey, Thomas A. "The Root–Takahira Agreement of 1908." *Pacific Historical Review* 9 (1940): 19–35.

———. "The World Cruise of the American Battleship Fleet, 1907–1909." *Pacific Historical Review* 1 (1932): 389–423.

Beale, Howard K. *Theodore Roosevelt and the Rise of America to World Power.* Baltimore, 1956.

Blum, John M. *The Republican Roosevelt*. Cambridge, Mass. 1954.

Boorman, Howard L., ed. *Biographical Dictionary of Republican China*. New York, 1967–71.

Braisted, William R. "The United States and the American China Development Company." *Far Eastern Quarterly* 11 (February 1952): 147–65.

_____. *The United States Navy in the Pacific, 1897–1909*. Austin, Texas, 1958.

Burton, David H. *Theodore Roosevelt: Confident Imperialist*. Philadelphia., Pa., 1968.

Cameron, Meribeth E. "American Recognition Policy toward the Republic of China, 1912–1913." *Pacific Historical Review* 2 (1933): 214–30.

_____. *The Reform Movement in China, 1898–1912*. New York reprint, 1963.

Campbell, Charles S., Jr. *Anglo–American Understanding, 1898–1903*. Baltimore, Md., 1957.

_____. *Special Business Interests and the Open Door*. New Haven, Conn. 1951.

Chang, Richard T. "The Failure of the Katsura–Harriman Agreement." *Journal of Asian Studies* 21 (November 1961): 65–76.

Ch'en, Jerome. *Yuan Shih-k'ai, 1859–1916: Brutus Assumes the Purple*. London, 1961.

Chu, Charles C. H. "The China Policy of the Taft–Knox Administration, 1909–1913." Ph.D. dissertation, University of Chicago, 1956.

Clyde, Paul H. *International Rivalries in Manchuria, 1689–1922*. Columbus, Ohio, 1926.

Coolidge, Mary R. *Chinese Immigration*. New York, 1909.

Crane, Katherine. *Mr. Carr of State: Forty-Seven Years in the State Department*. New York, 1960.

Croly, Herbert. *Willard Straight*. New York, 1924.

Dallin, David J. *The Rise of Russia in Asia*. New Haven, Conn., 1949.

Dennett, Tyler. *Americans in Eastern Asia*. New York, 1922.

_____. *John Hay: From Poetry to Politics*. New York, 1933.

_____. *Roosevelt and the Russo–Japanese War*. New York, 1925.

Dennis, A. L. P. *Adventures in American Diplomacy, 1896–1906*. New York, 1928.

DesForges, Roger V. "Hsi-liang: A Portrait of a Late Ch'ing Patriot." Ph. D. dissertation, Yale University, 1971.

Edwards, E. W. "The Far Eastern Agreements of 1907." *Journal of Modern History* 26 (1954): 340–55.

_____. "Great Britain and the Manchurian Railways Questions." *English Historical Review* 81 (October 1966): 740–69.

Esthus, Raymond A. "The Changing Concept of the Open Door 1899–1910." *Mississippi Valley Historical Review* 46 (1959): 435–54.

_____. "The Taft–Katsura Agreement—Reality or Myth?" *Journal of Modern History* 31 (1959): 46–51.

_____. *Theodore Roosevelt and Japan*. Seattle, Wash., 1966.

Fairbank, John K. "'American China Policy' to 1898: A Misconception." *Pacific Historical Review* 39 (1970): 409–20.

Fairbank, John K., ed. *The Chinese World Order: Traditional China's Foreign Relations*. Cambridge, Mass., 1968.

Feuerwerker, Albert. *China's Early Industrialization: Sheng Hsüan-huai (1844–1916) and Mandarin Enterprise*. Cambridge, Mass., 1958.

Field, Frederick V. *American Participation in the China Consortiums*. Chicago, Ill., 1931.

Forsythe, Sidney A. *An American Missionary Community in China, 1895–1905*. East Asian Research Center, Harvard University, Cambridge, Mass., 1971.

Gale, Esson M. "Edward Thomas Williams, 1854–1944." *Far Eastern Quarterly* 3 (1943–44): 381–83.

Griswold, A. Whitney. *The Far Eastern Policy of the United States*. New York, 1938.

Gull, E. M. *British Economic Interests in the Far East*. London, 1943.

Hall, Luella J. "The Abortive German–American–Chinese Entente of 1907–08." *Journal of Modern History* 1 (1929): 219–35.

Hart, Robert A. *The Great White Fleet: Its Voyage Around the World, 1907–1909.* Boston, 1965.

Ho Ping-ti. *Studies on the Population of China, 1368–1953.* Cambridge Mass., 1959.

Hofstadter, Richard. *Social Darwinism in American Thought.* Boston, 1955.

Hsü Shuhsi. *China and Her Political Entity.* London, 1926.

Hu Sheng. *Imperialism and Chinese Politics.* Peking, 1955.

Hummel, Arthur W., ed. *Eminent Chinese of the Ch'ing Period.* Washington, D.C., 1943 and 1944.

Hunt, Michael H. "The American Remission of the Boxer Indemnity: A Reappraisal." *Journal of Asian Studies* 31 (May 1972): 539–59.

Irick, Robert L. "The Chinchow–Aigun Railroad and the Knox Neutralization Plan in Ch'ing Diplomacy." *Papers on China* 13 (1959): 80–112.

Iriye, Akira. "Public Opinion and Foreign Policy: The Case of Late Ch'ing China." *Approaches to Modern Chinese History,* edited by Albert Feuerwerker et al., pp. 216–38. Berkeley, Calif., 1967.

Isaacs, Harold. *Scratches on Our Minds: American Images of China and India.* New York, 1958.

Israel, Jerry. *Progressivism and the Open Door: America and China, 1905–1921.* Pittsburgh, Pa., 1971.

Jessup, Philip C. *Elihu Root.* New York, 1938.

Johnson, Allen and Dumas Malone, eds. *The Dictionary of American Biography.* 23 vols. New York, 1927–58.

Kahn, Helen D. "The Great Game of Empire: Willard Straight and American Far Eastern Policy." Ph.D. dissertation, Cornell University, 1968.

Kamikawa Hikomatso, ed. *Japan–American Relations in the Meiji–Taisho Era.* Translated by Kimura Michiko. Tokyo, 1958.

Kennan, George. *E. H. Harriman's Far Eastern Plans.* Garden City, New York, 1917.

Kent, Percy H. *Railway Enterprise in China: An Account of Its Origin and Development.* London, 1907.

Kosaka, Masataka. "Ch'ing Policy over Manchuria (1900–1903)." *Papers on China* 16 (1962): 126–53.

LaFargue, Thomas E. *China's First Hundred.* Pullman, Wash., 1942.

Lattimore, Owen. *Inner Asian Frontiers of China.* New York, 1951.

_____. *Manchuria, Cradle of Conflict.* New York, 1932.

_____. *The Mongols of Manchuria.* New York, 1934.

Lee, Robert H. G. *The Manchurian Frontier in Ch'ing History.* Cambridge, Mass., 1970.

Lensen, George A., ed. *Korea and Manchuria between Russia and Japan, 1895–1904.* Tallahassee, Fla., 1966.

Leopold, Richard W. *Elihu Root and the Conservative Tradition.* Boston, 1954.

Leuchtenberg, William E. "Progressivism and Imperialism: The Progressive Movement and American Foreign Policy, 1898–1916." *Mississippi Valley Historical Review* 39 (1952): 483–504.

Liu Kwang-ching. *Americans and Chinese: A Historical Essay and a Bibliography.* Cambridge, Mass., 1963.

Livermore, Seward W. "American Naval-Base Policy in the Far East, 1850–1914." *Pacific Historical Review* 13 (June 1944): 113–35.

MacKinnon, Stephen R. "Liang Shih-i and the Communications Clique." *Journal of Asian Studies* 29 (May 1970): 581–602.

McClellan, Robert. *Heathen Chinee: A Study of American Attitudes Toward China, 1890–1905.* Columbus, Ohio, 1970.

McCormick, Thomas J. *China Market: America's Quest for Informal Empire, 1893–1901.* Chicago, Ill., 1967.

Minger, Ralph. "Taft's Mission to Japan: A Study in Personal Diplomacy." *Pacific Historical Review* 30 (August 1961): 279–94.

Morrison, Esther. "The Modernization of the Confucian Bureaucracy: An Historical Study of Public Administration." Ph.D. thesis, Radcliffe, 1959.

Morse, Hosea B. *The International Relations of the Chinese Empire.* Vol. 3: *The Period of Subjection, 1844–1911.* New York, 1918.

Mowry, George E. *The Era of Theodore Roosevelt, 1900–1912.* New York, 1958.

Mulhollan, Paige E. "Philander C. Knox and Dollar Diplomacy, 1909–1913." Ph.D. dissertation, University of Texas, 1966.

Nathan, Carl F. *Plague Prevention and Politics in Manchuria 1910–1931.* East Asian Research Center, Harvard University, Cambridge, Mass., 1967.

Neu, Charles E. *An Uncertain Friendship: Theodore Roosevelt and Japan, 1906–1909.* Cambridge, Mass., 1967.

Nish, Ian H. *The Anglo–Japanese Alliance: The Diplomacy of Two Island Empires, 1894–1907.* London, 1966.

Overlach, T. W. *Foreign Financial Control in China.* New York, 1919.

Pan Shü-lun. *The Trade of the United States with China.* New York, 1924.

Pearl, Cyril. *Morrison of Peking.* Sydney, Australia, 1967.

Pelcovits, Nathan A. *Old China Hands and the Foreign Office.* New York, 1948.

Perkins, Bradford. *The Great Rapprochement: England and the United States, 1895–1914.* New York, 1968.

Powell, Ralph L. *The Rise of Chinese Military Power, 1895–1912.* Princeton, N. J., 1955.

Pressman, Harvey. "Hay, Rockhill, and China's Integrity: A Reappraisal." *Papers on China* 13 (1959): 61–79.

Pringle, Henry F. *The Life and Times of William Howard Taft.* New York, 1939.

Reid, John Gilbert. *The Manchu Abdication and the Powers, 1908–1912.* Berkeley, Calif., 1935.

Remer, Charles F. *The Foreign Trade of China.* Shanghai, 1926.

Rhoads, Edward J. M. "Nationalism and Xenophobia in Kwangtung (1905–1906): The Canton Anti-American Boycott and the Lienchow Anti-Missionary Uprising." *Papers on China* 16 (1962): 154–97.

Romanov, B. A. *Russia in Manchuria (1892–1906).* Translated by Susan W. Jones. Ann Arbor, Mich., 1952.

Rosenbaum, Arthur L. "China's First Railway: The Imperial Railways of North China, 1880–1911." Ph.D. dissertation, Yale University, 1971.

Scholes, Walter V. and Marie V. Scholes. *The Foreign Policy of the Taft Administration.* Columbia, Mo., 1970.

Schrecker, John E. *Imperialism and Chinese Nationalism: Germany in Shantung.* Cambridge, Mass., 1971.

————. "The Reform Movement, Nationalism, and China's Foreign Policy." *Journal of Asian Studies* 29 (November 1969): 43–53.

Schulman, Irwin J. "China's Response to Imperialism: 1895–1900." Ph.D. dissertation, Columbia University, 1967.

Shin, Linda P. "China in Transition: The Role of Wu T'ing-fang (1842–1922)." Ph.D. dissertation, University of California at Los Angles, 1970.

Smith, Henry Nash. *Virgin Land: The American West as Symbol and Myth.* Cambridge, Mass., 1950.

Spence, Jonathan. *To Change China: Western Advisers in China 1620–1960.* Boston, 1969.

Sun, E-tu Zen. *Chinese Railways and British Interests, 1898–1911.* New York, 1954.

Tan, Chester C. *The Boxer Catastrophe.* New York, 1955.

Varg, Paul A. *The Making of a Myth: The United States and China, 1897–1912.* East Lansing, Mich., 1968.

_____. *Open Door Diplomat: The Life of W. W. Rockhill.* Urbana, Ill., 1952.

Vevier, Charles. *The United States and China, 1906–1913.* New Brunswick, N. J., 1955.

White, John A. *The Diplomacy of the Russo–Japanese War.* Princeton, N. J., 1964.

Williams, William Appleman. "The Frontier Thesis and American Foreign Policy." *Pacific Historical Review* 24 (1955): 379–95.

Wright, Mary C., ed. *China in Revolution: The First Phase, 1900–1913.* New Haven, Conn., 1968.

Yang Lien-sheng. "Female Rulers in Imperial China." *Harvard Journal of Asiatic Studies* 23 (1960/61): 47–61.

Young, Ernest P. "Politics in the Early Republic: Liang Ch'i-ch'ao and the Yuan Shih-k'ai Presidency." Ph.D. dissertation, Harvard University, 1964.

Young, Marilyn Blatt. *The Rhetoric of Empire: American China Policy 1895–1901.* Cambridge Mass., 1968.

Young, Walter. "Chinese Immigration and Colonization in Manchuria." *Pioneer Settlement: Cooperative Studies,* pp. 330–59. New York, 1932.

Zabriskie, Edward H. *American–Russian Rivalry in the Far East: A Study in Diplomacy and Power Politics, 1895–1914.* Philadelphia, Pa., 1946.

INDEX

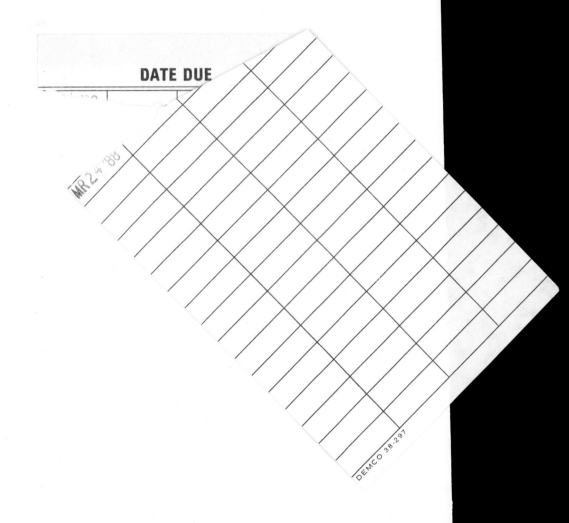

DATE DUE

MR 2 4 '88

DEMCO 38-297